THE KLEINIAN
DEVELOPMENT

THE KLEINIAN DEVELOPMENT

Donald Meltzer

Published for
The Harris Meltzer Trust
by

KARNAC

First published in this edition in 1998 by
H. Karnac (Books) Ltd
58 Gloucester Road
London SW7 4QY

Freud's Clinical Development originally published in 1978 by The Roland Harris
Educational Trust

Richard Week-by-Week originally published in 1978 by The Roland Harris
Educational Trust

The Clinical Significance of the Work of Bion originally published in 1978 by The
Roland Harris Educational Trust

This edition published in 2008 by
Karnac Books Ltd
118 Finchley Road
London NW3 5HT

British Library Cataloguing in Publication Data

A.C.I.P. for this book is available from the British Library

ISBN-13: 978-1-85575-678-6

Printed and bound in Great Britain by Biddles Ltd., King's Lynn, Norfolk

www.harris-meltzer-trust.org.uk

CONTENTS

CONTENTS

Part Two
RICHARD WEEK-BY-WEEK
(A Critique of the 'Narrative of a Child Analysis'
and a Review of Melanie Klein's Work)

CONTENTS

Part Three
THE CLINICAL SIGNIFICANCE
OF THE WORK OF BION

Introduction

If we take the beginning of Anna O's treatment with Breuer as the start of the Psycho-analytical Era, 1980 would be its centenary. There can be little doubt of the influence that this science has had upon Western thought and culture, both acknowledged and denied. It is certainly the premier method of clinical research into the deeper sources of personality development and functioning. It nourishes with its methodology and its discoveries a host of related disciplines. But it is not a unified discipline itself. It has developed in many different directions, in method, phenomenology, theory. The difficulty in describing the ineffable events of the consulting room has widened the manifest gap between various lines of development, in a way that probably generates political groupings, where genuine disagreements, as against differing points of view, may very well be minimal. It is no tribute to the efficacy of psychoanalytical therapy, and its slight variant the training analysis, that analysts eagerly attach themselves to these political groupings and play out in their societies dramas hardly distinguishable from the internal affairs of emergent nations.

This volume is certainly not intended to enhance these polarizations. On the contrary, it seems reasonable to hope that a clarification of the particular line of development in psychoanalytical method and theory associated with the name of Melanie Klein might diminish the tensions, enabling people either to take an intelligent interest or an equally intelligent disinterest in this particular strand of scientific history. In order to do this it is necessary to review the development of Freud's work so as to identify the jumping-off place of Mrs Klein's thinking, and then to do the same with Bion *vis-à-vis* Freud and Klein.

This all sounds, of course, like an undertaking in scholarship but these three sets of lectures will be found to be most unscholarly. Although they are bound tightly to the literature of these three workers (only in one instance do I introduce any clinical experience of my own), the approach is far too personal to pass academic muster. To explain this it is necessary to trace a little the history of the undertaking of these lectures. In the hope of following Milton's dictum of 'teaching others . . . himself may learn', yet being an unwilling student of the literature, I engaged myself in various commitments to force an indolent spirit. Six years of work and teaching to develop a new curriculum at the Institute of Psycho-analysis (subsequently abandoned because the students were dissatisfied with so historical and rigid a procedure) were followed by six years of teaching at the Tavistock Clinic, primarily to various classes in the training of child psychotherapists. These lectures therefore are the outcome of some twelve years of study and teaching aimed, in the secret egocentricity, at answering the questions in my own mind concerning the problems of continuity and discontinuity in my own development as a psychoanalyst.

From the age of sixteen, when I first read Freud under the influence of my elder sister's friend Nathaniel Apter, to the age of twenty-two when Loretta Bender (strangely) introduced me to the work of Melanie Klein, and on to the age of forty, when Bion's personality and thought began to impinge upon me, my development has been dominated by transference to, and identification with, these three extraordinary people. But two events, Mrs Klein's death and Bion's subsequent departure for California, both of which served to disrupt a phantasy of family happiness amongst the followers of Mrs Klein, also served to make me aware that these three figures were not in a happy relation to one another in my mind and somehow also in my work.

I do not, of course, mean that I was concerned in any way with the history of their personal or professional relations, Freud to Klein or Klein to Bion. This was purely personal and internal to me, related to my own analysis obviously, my oedipal conflicts at various levels, etc., etc. But the infantile levels are not the central point for giving lectures although they may be for analysing dreams. The study and lecturing (and now the *public*-ation) were intended to discover and define the continuity or discontinuity in my psycho-analytical development in terms of success or failure to develop a combined psychoanalytical object 'under whose aegis' I might hope to work creatively and courageously some day.

Consequently the three sets of lectures that follow are a very personal integration of the work of these three people. My Freud, my Klein, my Bion may not correspond precisely with anyone else's. I would be distressed if they were not at least congruent with these figures in quite a few of my colleagues' minds. This somewhat tedious protest is not, however, without its point: namely to stress the absence of authority in what follows: either my authority or theirs, for not only are the lectures personal and therefore idiosyncratic, but they are also critical; a critique, non-reverential. This means also that they cannot stand alone but are meaningless except as an adjunct to serious study, a vademecum. For those who think they know the works of Freud, Klein and Bion well, the lectures should, if they succeed in their intention, come as a surprise that drives them back to the texts. For the beginning student they should serve as companion and guide. They are meant to assist in the organization of reading seminars and to help people in finding their way back to the literature for reference in writing papers. Above all they are meant to give one possible longitudinal view of this one line of development in psychoanalysis in a way that rectifies the conceptual confusions wrought by the overlapping of linguistic usage.

The overall burden of my song is that an unfolding can be seen in the work of these three masters when the language has been rectified, an unfolding of method, leading to discovery of new realms of phenomena, generating in turn new models of the mind, which then modify method, etc. The explicit (or implicit in the case of Mrs Klein), models of the mind I have called neurophysiological, mythological (or theological) and philosophical. That they are not mutually exclusive but relate as root, trunk and branch to what flowers and fruits in the consulting room is my theme, my contention, probably my faith.

PART ONE

Freud's Clinical Development

(METHOD—DATA—THEORY)

Acknowledgements

I wish to thank Mrs Martha Harris, Mrs Margaret Williams, Mrs Catherine Mack Smith and Mr Eric Rhode for their help in the preparation and proofing of the text.

Introduction

These lectures were delivered in 1972 and 1973 to the students and guests of the Child Psychotherapy Course at the Tavistock Clinic, London. The students were largely in the first pre-clinical year of the course, so that the lectures served as background for acquaintance with Freud's work from reading seminars in this and in the following year. The aim of the lectures was to prepare the students for systematic study of the work of Melanie Klein by giving a firm foundation in Freud's writing on method, data and clinical formulation, somewhat at the expense of any systematic concern with his theory of the mind. Its emphasis was therefore heavily weighted on the clinical papers and on those aspects of his thought which can be seen to have had a development in Mrs Klein's work, It was also the intention to lecture in a critical way, searching out the order, meaning and significance of Freud's work rather than in any way to summarize it.

For this reason it is essential to the understanding of these lectures that the reader, like the student, should at least have refreshed his knowledge of the papers and books discussed, particularly the following 'required' reading:

Chapter

I   *Studies on Hysteria*, SE II, 1–18, 21–47

II *Studies on Hysteria*, SE II, 135–182
    Further Remarks on the Neuropsychoses of Defense, SE III, 159–187
    The Interpretation of Dreams—a Specimen Dream, SE IV, 106–121

2

Chapter I   Why History?

The recommendation that people who are interested in learning to practise psycho-analytic therapy should apply themselves diligently to the study of Freud seems at first glance to
scent of the cult of the personality, to ring of the gospel, and to
suggest that nothing else is worthy of study. While it is certain
that the recommendation has been used in all these ways, to
the detriment of students and psycho-analysis alike, there is
another rationale for the advice. There is a cogent justification
which has to do with the essential nature of science: namely
that it is truly rational in its history. This is formed around a
thread of logical necessity. To borrow an image from Freud's
early writing, in the history of psycho-analysis revelations
or discoveries – whichever they be – adhere to a chain of
logically necessary propositions as garlands of flowers wind
about a wire.
   It may be objected that this does not justify its discoveries
being taught as the personal history of a particular worker,
even if he can reasonably be called 'the father of psycho-
analysis', or the greatest figure in its development, or the fore-
most authority, etc. It will be said, as it has been said, that
Lavoisier was the father of chemistry, but we do not teach
chemistry by starting with Lavoisier's life, not even his laboratory life, to say nothing of his intimate personal life. It is true
that chemistry's history is not the history of people; its logical
necessity lies in the relation of particles to one another under
varying conditions. However, when you look at the curriculum
for the training of chemistry scientists you will find that it
adheres absolutely, of necessity, to a sequence which corresponds to the historical development of the science.
   Furthermore, it may be objected that not even artists, who
are positively addicted to history, study the intimate lives of
their great forbears; only their works and methods. In short,
only scholars and busybodies nose about in the personal
biographies of great men. Perhaps. My concern here is not to
give a scholarly exposition, nor is it to be a busybody; it is not
with Freud's personal, intimate life, but with his works. I hope
in fourteen chapters to construct *an*, not *the*, historical Freud:

4

Freud the monument of literature, not really Freud the man; and above all, the Freud of this particular writer's – D.M.'s – imagination. This, of course, immediately presents itself as the most futile purpose of all, since D.M. never knew Freud. Would it not be better for him to present his personal Melanie Klein, or himself? Well, the latter would not do because no case could be made out for his being a key figure in psychoanalytic history. Why not Melanie Klein then? Well, for a perfectly good reason: relative lack of documentation. Consider, for instance, what you would do if you wanted to write the history of 13th Century manorial life; you would not necessarily determine which was the biggest, most powerful, most successful, most beautiful or most anything-else manor, to study its manorial rolls. You would first determine which manorial rolls were the most completely preserved and select your manor accordingly. If this turned out to be the biggest, richest, etc., it would be only slightly wide of coincidental. Similarly, the documentation of Freud's scientific development is certainly not a function of his having been in e ery way superlative, but of his having been a compulsive writer. You must consider: twenty-three volumes of some four hundred pages each; say about nine thousand pages in forty-odd years. That comes to a book of over two hundred pages every year; twenty papers of ten pages each! In addition, by his hand, we have the letters to Fliess, the Project for a Scientific Psychology, letters to Abraham, and probably many more unpublished papers, case reports, etc., all guarded in the archives by the jealous dragon called Kurt Eissler. No, the most cogent reason for studying Freud is that he has left us a documentation of his thought and experience that is unparalleled.

Can we not, then, just forget that we are studying a man's life and works and concentrate on the material, the data, the method, the ideas? Suppose it were Newton; we would not, in studying the evolution of his work in mathematics, optics, etc., concern ourselves with his rather mad theological ramblings any more than we would with his sexual life. Indeed, we could ignore that aspect of Newton because his writings in theology are quite separate from his works in mathematics and physics. With Freud, however, as with the 13th Century manorial rolls, fact and fancy, truth and distortion, new experiences

5

and preconception, revelation and vituperation are all mixed together. We cannot say that we will study volumes III, V and VIII but not bother with IV, VI and VII. Nonetheless, a certain mode of concentration of effort is possible and is rewarding; namely, to stick very closely to the works that are clear in their clinical reference. And this is what we shall study: the case histories, dream interpretation, technical papers; and draw on the major theoretical works only for the light they throw on the more clinical ones. There is another sorting device we can also use, though more cautiously. We can use the 1895 'Project' as a template for identifying preconceptions in Freud's thinking about his data.

This is a somewhat delicate process which requires some explanation and an historic setting to make it understandable. Looking back through the agency of the 'Autobiography', Jones's biography, the Fliess letters, the 'Project' and others, one is surely struck by the incongruity of the young Freud vis-à-vis the great Freud, the revolutionary. Of course, we tend to be blasé about the psycho-analytical revolution today, in consequence of which the embattled Freud of the 1890s tends to be as unreal to us as the barricades of 1848. But he was a revolutionary of the methodical-constructive rather than the rebellious-destructive sort and his early scientific career gives no hint of the future. He seems to have been one of the innumerable young men whom medical science, in its historical heyday, gathered to it for many reasons – of adventure, glamour, status, economic possibilities. For a young Jew these attractions were all potentiated. And how wide were his interests: the cocaine experiment, histology, neuro-pathology, clinical neurology, and only latterly psychiatry. Many letters suggest the impatience of the parvenu, the opportunist, seeking alliances with promising contemporaries, currying favour with the great tyrants who ruled the laboratories and wards like oriental potentates, offering his services as translator, taking the burden of routine lectures. Of course it is tempting to weave an Ariadne-like thread from the staining of motor neurones through the paralyses of children to the motor manifestations of hysteria: and in a way the 'Project' offers itself as such a 'web': but it is not really true. If it were, a very different concept of growth and development of the mind would be required from that which psycho-analysis offers – one which would see the mind like a blossom unfolding in all its beauty and perfection, given a suitable environment. Gone would be the ideas of conflict and decision; realization of error, remorse, reparation.

The greatness of Freud did not unfold like a blossom and its environment was far from congenial. The clinical method of description and isolation of syndromes and the investigation of predisposing, specific and contributory aetiological factors was establishing a nosology which was lifting medicine out of a welter of confusion, quackery and noxious meddling. Great names were beginning to take their place in history through therapeutic and prophylactic achievements, particularly in bacteriology.

In this golden tradition, not more than a century old, psychiatry was taking shape through classification, generally now associated with the name of Kraepelin. This carried the implication that in due course, aetiologies would be discovered, cures and preventions would be evolved. It was an optimistic era in every way! The great mental hospitals were the laboratories of the descriptive science, and access to them was as prized then as access to a cyclotron or a huge computer is now by physicists. It seemed that nothing could be done without access to these great pools of clinical material. One must also remember what a bourgeois world it was and the Jewish and commercial tradition that lay behind Freud. The aim was clearly to make a name for oneself as expert and authority in a small segment of the whole and gradually to expand one's kudos, territory and hegemony. Today, over a century since his birth, is the climate so different for the medical student and young scientist, despite the apparent advance of social consciousness and responsibility?

Freud was a child of his time, a 'normal' and 'well-adjusted' person (if we must use these banal descriptive and normative concepts) and he tried to make his mark in the bourgeois world: with cocaine, neuro-pathology, paralyses of children, aphasia and finally hysteria. The dependent aspects of his character demanded support and encouragement. The list which starts with Meynert and Breuer and grows so tenuous with Fliess does not really stop for another decade until the

7

defection of Jung, when Freud is about fifty-five years old. The methodology and social order were set about him in solid phalanx against the development of the psycho-analytical method. Nor was there yet really a 'mind' to be studied. It would be erroneous today to think of depth psychology as a well-established field of scientific enquiry, with psycho-analysis as its premier method. Perhaps even more today than at the time of Freud's death, the concept of 'the mind is the brain' holds the field against that of 'mind as phenomenon'. In Freud's youth the 'phenomenon' was still the realm of theologians, metaphysicians and cosmologists. The practical bourgeois world had turned its back and closed its laboratory doors to such thinking. How ironic, in this context, to think that the most appreciative review that the 'Studies on Hysteria' received was from a professor of the History of Literature, entitled 'Surgery of the Soul'. One wonders if this did not cause a shudder of anxiety rather than a tingle of pleasure in Freud.

Nor is it surprising that an historian should be the prophet, for psycho-analysis teaches us that the acknowledgement of the past as the foundation of the present is the only means of making the concept of 'future' obedient to reason. Lacking this obedience to continuity, the idea of 'future' loses its meaning and simply becomes equated with 'wish' or 'intention'. In the same way every student of psycho-analysis must traverse in his ontogeny the history of this peculiar scientific species of ours. Each of us has been brought up in a milieu from whose values, methods and aspirations we need, gradually, to free ourselves in order to learn, utilise and make discoveries by – the psycho-analytical method. In a sense we also need to abandon, in Freud's words, 'the expectation of lasting fame, the certainty of wealth and complete independence': as he did when the 'seduction theory', the 'specific aetiology' of hysteria crumbled at the revelation that infantile sexual phantasies had been confused with memories by both patients and investigator.

Here too, in the realm of social and personal attitudes toward sexuality, we must avoid smugness. A century has produced a great swing of the pendulum, not a little of which has been rightly attributed to the impact of Freud's work on Western culture. But the pendulum has swung from the hypocrisy of the Victorian double standard to the hypocrisy of decadence. The milieu which favoured the formation of symptoms in the realm of sexual conflict now favours the hardening of perversion into character. As Freud had to face the suspicion of being an 'amoralist', today's believer in psychic reality will need to face, internally and externally, the even more sanctimonious charge of 'moralist'. No use for us to smile indulgently at the trepidation with which he put forward to his colleagues the need to investigate the sexual life of the psycho-neurotic. The icy epithet of 'fairy-tale' he faced is unchanged today, only directed against the investigation of the immediate reality of the mind rather than the past reality of traumatic experiences.

There can be no doubt that Freud paid heavily for his arrogance in placing his evidence first before public values. He could have written as freely as he wished about sexuality had he, like Krafft-Ebing and others, dealt with the pathological behaviour as symptoms of underlying disease rather than as aetiological factors in themselves; had he confined himself to the perverse activities of adults and the masturbation of children. But by assaulting the mores with an insistence on the significance of *lack* of satisfaction, of sexual *needs* in adults and the reality of sexual *capacity* in childhood, he opposed the 'scientific' and 'progressive' spirit of the age. The Fliess letters tell the story: from the elation which culminated in the 'Project' (1895), soon followed by the catastrophe of the collapse of the 'seduction' theory (1897), to the self-analysis, whose brain child was 'The Interpretation of Dreams'; and the resolution of the ambivalent relation to Fliess, whose fruit is the 'Letters' itself. The mounting clinical evidence in favour of the 'seduction' theory had begun to invade Freud's own relationships past and present, as it began to seem statistically likely that all parents committed incestuous assaults on their children. The incongruity – and the anxiety coming closer to home, along with the upheaval of his father's death – must have been powerful factors in the inception of the systematic self-analysis. But while the anxiety drove Freud, in his step toward greatness, to apply the method to himself, it could only be expected, as a source of social anxiety, to generate hostility. After the 'seduction' theory, which could be coldly rejected as a 'fairy tale',

9

came the great steps toward recognition of the universality of the unconscious: the 'Traumdeutung' (1900), 'Psychopathology of Everyday Life' (1901), 'Wit and its Relation to the Unconscious' (1905), and 'Three Essays on Sexuality' (1905). What a manifesto! And how he paid for it with isolation, abuse, contempt, the threat of poverty.

But, of course, every crank and crackpot pays this price for insisting on the validity of his intuitions, any of which may in fact turn out to be correct. Freud, like other creative geniuses, paid the price of devotion to a method, the findings of which inevitably turned out to be wrong! For instance, all that Freud says about hysteria can now be considered 'wrong' because there is no such thing as 'hysteria' in the sense in which it was discussed by Charcot in Paris, Bernheim in Zurich or Breuer in Vienna, at the turn of the century. You may recall that the paucity of interest in Freud's work among his Viennese colleagues was partly an expression of apathy about hysteria itself. They could not take it seriously as a 'disease' but considered it to be some elaborate form of malingering, until the experiments with hypnosis reproduced its clinical phenomenology: or rather, until it was proved that hypnosis was not an elaborate form of suggestion – which it is!

Similarly, it might be cogently argued that the whole idea of psycho-pathology is 'wrong' and that we should leave it out of the curriculum as the theory of 'humours' is left out of a modern course in patho-physiology. Has not psycho-analysis abandoned the concepts of 'disease' and 'cure' and become the field of 'depth psychology' that it is so often called? So here again, the swing of the pendulum presents today's student with the same problems within his culture that Freud faced, only upside down, you might say. His evidence could be thrown out of court by the Establishment because it was gained from study of 'diseased' minds and could therefore bear no relation to 'normality'. Today the evidence of psycho-analysis regarding psychic reality, the primacy of internal experience over external, the relation of 'health' and the values connected with the 'good' are similarly ignored on the grounds that there is no good; all is relative, semantic, unmeasurable; therefore unreal.

Freud grasped slowly (and we must allow for the possibility that we will grasp even more slowly) that the study of psycho-pathology was the entrée to the mind, if only a method could be found which passed beyond mere external description. Perhaps this realization was more available to a neurologist than it would have been to a surgeon, physician or pathologist, for whom the most imposing situations were those analogous to an invasion of a closed system by alien chemicals, objects, bacteria, protozoa, etc. Embryology of the individual appeared to be complete long before birth, except for increasing size and maturation of the sexual organs. Even neuro-embryology seemed to reach completion shortly after birth. But in the methods of examination and the near-mathematical localizing diagnosis of the neurologist alone amongst clinical fields, the interruption of normal functioning took pride of place over the questions of abnormal function and specific aetiology. Furthermore, studies in neuro-pathology of childhood showed how different could be the clinical phenomena of a lesion, depending on the age of the patient: whether it was interfering with the development of new functions, or destroying functions already established and thus allowing more primitive ones to reappear.

These principles of neurological localization and their reference to a developmental process came gradually to impose themselves on Freud and to wrest from his mind the neuro-physiological preconceptions of the 'Project'. In this departure from the concrete, and in his extraordinarily open-minded and non-moralistic approach to sexuality, he broke with the community and became an outcast, propounding a theory of the mind as a developmental phenomenon whose units were thoughts, not neurones, whose energies were impulses with aims seeking objects, whose dislocations produced anxieties, whose traumas could not be apprehended descriptively but only in relation to the momentary state of mind.

Again we must turn to the present community to recognize that this developmental conception of psycho-pathology is as intensely resisted now as it was then; again the pendulum has swung. As with the false dichotomy of the mind-body problem, so are we confronted with the false dichotomy of the nature-nurture problem. It is difficult to avoid being embroiled in it, in the treacle of sanctimony, placing the blame (as if psycho-analysis had anything to do with placing blame) on the parents or on the child, on the community, the times, fate, sunspots, or God! With the realization in 1897 of the falsity of the 'seduction' theory of hysteria, Freud leapt forward to the realization of developmental conflict, resistance and the transference. The conflicts – and resistances – are no less today and no less in us than in the Viennese of seventy years ago. Only the form of the resistance is altered.

An instructive way of recognizing how Freud was bound by the modes of thought of his milieu and had to struggle to free himself lies in a study of the imagery, models and analogies that he employs in his writing. I will give a series of these chronologically, to demonstrate the trend.

I. *Studies on Hysteria* – 1893–95 (SE II, p. 264)
'The point at which a symptom' (of hysteria) 'has already broken through once forms a weak spot at which it will break through again the next time. A psychical group that has once been split off plays the part of a "provoking" crystal from which a crystallisation which would otherwise not have occurred will start with the greatest facility.'

II. *The Neuropsychoses of Defence* – 1894 (SE III, p. 60)
'In mental functions something is to be distinguished – a quota of affect or sum of excitation – which possesses all the characteristics of a quantity (though we have no means of measuring it), which is capable of increase, diminution, displacement and discharge, and which is spread over the memory-traces of ideas somewhat as an electric charge is spread over the surface of a body.'

III. *The Aetiology of Hysteria* – 1896 (SE III, p. 192)
'In hysteria too there exists a similar possibility of penetrating from the symptoms to a knowledge of their causes. But in order to explain the relationship between the method which we have to employ for this purpose and the older method of anamnestic inquiry, I should like to bring before you an analogy taken from an advance that has in fact been made in another field of work.

'Imagine that an explorer arrives at a little-known region where his interest is aroused by an expanse of ruins, with remains of walls, fragments of columns, and tablets with half-effaced and unreadable inscriptions. He may content himself with inspecting what lies exposed to view, with questioning the inhabitants – perhaps semi-barbaric people – who live in the vicinity, about what tradition tells them of the history and meaning of these archaeological remains, and with noting down what they tell him – and he may then proceed on his journey. But he may act differently. He may have brought picks, shovels and spades with him, and he may set the inhabitants to work with these implements. Together with them he may start upon the ruins, clear away the rubbish, and, beginning from the visible remains, uncover what is buried. If his work is crowned with success, the discoveries are self-explanatory . . .'

– the optimist!

These are three examples from the pre-self-analysis period, of analogies regarding symptom formation, psychic energy and methodology. Compare:

IV. *Fragment of an Analysis of a Case of Hysteria* – 1905, written 1901 – (SE VII)
a. (p. 55) 'Contrary thoughts are always closely connected with each other and are often paired off in such a way that the one thought is *excessively intensely conscious while its counterpart is repressed and unconscious.* This relation between the two thoughts is an effect of the process of repression. For repression is often achieved by means of an excessive reinforcement of the thought contrary to the one which is to be repressed. This process I call *reactive* reinforcement, and the thought which assets itself with excessive intensity in consciousness and (in the same way as a prejudice) cannot be removed I call a *reactive thought*. The two thoughts then act toward each other much like the two needles of an astatic galvanometer. The reactive thought keeps the objectionable one under repression by means of a certain surplus of intensity; but for that reason it itself is "damped" and proof against conscious efforts of thought.'

b. (p. 87) 'The *motive force* which the dream required had to be provided by a wish; it was the business of the worry to get hold of a wish to act as the motive force of a dream.
'The position may be explained by an analogy. A daytime thought may very well play the part of an entrepreneur for a dream; but the entrepreneur, who, as people say, has the idea and the initiative to carry it out, can do nothing without capital; he needs a *capitalist* who can afford the outlay, and the

13

capitalist who provides the psychical outlay for the dream is invariably and indisputably, whatever may be the thoughts of the previous day, a wish from the unconscious'.

c. (p. 116) 'What are transferences? They are new editions or facsimiles of the impulses and phantasies which are aroused and made conscious during the progress of the analysis; but they have this peculiarity, which is characteristic of their species, that they replace some earlier person by the person of the physician. To put it another way: a whole series of psychological experiences are reviewed, not as belonging to the past, but as applying to the person of the physician at the present moment. Some of these transferences have a content which differs from that of their model in no respect whatever except for substitution. These then – to keep to the same metaphor – are merely new impressions or reprints. Others are more ingeniously constructed; their content has been subjected to a moderating influence – to *sublimation*, as I call it – and they may even become conscious, by cleverly taking advantage of some real peculiarity in the physician's person or circumstances and attaching themselves to that. These, then, will no longer be new editions, but revised editions.'

Well, we need go no further. The change is clear, I am sure. The literal and mechanical quality of the earlier models has given way to imaginative, near poetic, and vital images and models in the later writing. For instance, examine the rather dramatic 'archaeological' model from the 'Studies'. What Freud is describing is the reconstruction of the environment of the ancient culture, its houses, temples, markets, tools, organization of services, technology. These are 'self-explanatory'. But the life of the people is not, and can only be found in the written record. You may remember that Sir Arthur Evans had recently – 1898 or so – excavated Knossos and Mycaenae, uncovering great treasure, and Linear B. But no Napoleon presented him with a Rosetta Stone with which to translate this script. It had to wait sixty years until the techniques of cryptography and etymology could be brought together in a wonderfully creative way by Michael Ventris (see 'The Decipherment of Linear B', John Chadwick, Cambridge 1958) for the life of the people to be revealed. Freud seems to have had the idea that dreams were the Rosetta Stone of the

unconscious and he their translator. We can see more clearly
how he underestimated the difficulty. Perhaps they are the
Linear B of the unconscious!

In the first chapter I am discussing the period of Freud's
work as a psychotherapist, which is fundamentally prior to the
development of the basic psycho-analytical method. You will
recall that Freud was a neurologist and research worker in
clinical neurology by training and experience: take for example
the work on aphasia and the paralyses of children, and neuro-
anatomy, particularly the central pathways which he was
investigating by special silver staining techniques. He did not
easily become a psychologist, and it was not until 1910 that he
gave himself that name. His interest in the work of Charcot in
Paris, Liebault in Nancy and Bernheim in Zürich was not
primarily directed toward an understanding of the mind, but
of the brain. The phenomenology of divided consciousness,
fugue states, hypnosis, suggestion and dreams attracted his
interest not as vicissitudes of people's emotional and intellectual
experiences of life, but as evidences of the complex working of
the brain and of its malfunction. The possibility of brain
damage, inherited tendencies, degenerative disease (and of
course the universal suspicion of central nervous system
syphilis) hung constantly in the periphery of his mind. His
initial approach to what was to become his life's work, his
collaboration with Breuer and the publication of the 'Studies
on Hysteria' (1895), was a purely medical one, which sought the
relief of symptoms. In a sense it stood in the same relation to his
great love, neurophysiology, as had the experiment with
cocaine. It was a bid for status and it almost wrecked him, as
we shall see. When we study in some detail the famous 'Dream
of Irma's Injection' from the 'Traumdeutung', it will become
clearer how the ambition-which-impairs-judgment haunted
Freud, and how he struggled against it by constructing a
method by which he could impose some basic discipline on
himself. He was by this time a young man no longer – married,
with children – aged nearly forty years. He had tried many
ways of advancing himself in the Austrian medical establishment by working in the university hospital, doing research,
translating the works of Charcot, lecturing. But of course the
opportunities were relatively poor for a Jew. The record

sounds fairly opportunistic, and there can be little doubt that he was a highly ambitious man who felt his prime slipping away from him with very little to show for it. The mishaps with cocaine weighed heavily on him and failure to receive recognition for pioneering its legitimate use embittered him.

Accordingly, Freud's sections of the 'Studies' have a tone that contrasts sharply with the humble one of Breuer who was awed by the phenomena, somewhat enamoured of his intelligent patient, Anna O., and basically unwilling to reveal to the world a relationship which had ended in the shock of Anna's erotic attachment to him and in near tragedy owing to his wife's intense jealousy over the matter. It is clear in the joint 'Preliminary Communication' (1893) that Breuer was a fairly unwilling participant in the publication, and that an undercurrent of disagreement swamped the relationship. Freud of course was relatively young, unestablished, and in that sense riding on Breuer's high reputation, probably more dependent on the older man than he realized. As the relationship cooled after the publication of the 'Studies' it seems to have been replaced by the intimacy with Fliess, but here Freud recognized his dependence, and in a sense his ambivalence and exploitation, insincerity and high-handedness toward the other man. In the 'Studies' we meet a fairly unexceptional man in Freud and a rather impressive one in Breuer. Ten years later, in the 'Fragment' on Dora we will meet a great man. How did the change come about and what were the scientific experiences and accomplishments that accompanied or moved this transformation? Let us start by taking stock of Freud as he reveals himself in the 'Studies' side by side with Breuer – and with his patients.

The Spiral of Method and Data
Chapter II (Studies on Hysteria)

In the first chapter I suggested that the fate of the creative scientist, as compared with the intuitive crank, is to be 'wrong' in all his conclusions. Freud knew this very well and for this reason never hesitated to publish his current ideas nor to abandon them for later approximations. If we try to take the measure of the history of psycho-analysis from the theoretical point of view, we would be in the maelström of swirling ideas, models, imagery, from which we would only escape by an arbitrary grasping at what Freud said – in the 'Introductory Lectures' for instance but not in the 'Ego and the Id' – or, worse still, to establish our own reading of Freud as *the* correct one: i.e. an orthodoxy.

But science (and art, for that matter) is not carried forward by theories but by advances in method, in technique. Jokingly one may say that the inventor of psycho-analysis was Anna O. with her 'talking cure' and 'chimney sweeping', and I would think that Freud was sincere when in the 1910 lectures at Clark University he gave credit for the origin to Breuer.

Although this famous case is so badly presented, compared with the flow and lucidity of Freud's writing, one is struck with the immense time, interest, concern, ingenuity, patience – and modesty – with which the clinical work and collection of data were carried out. This is perhaps the best evidence we can obtain in order to understand why Breuer stood so high in the younger Freud's esteem and to give him his rightful place in psycho-analytic history. Remember that the therapeutic methodology of the day was utterly different: sedation, warm baths, faradic current stimulation for the paralyses, massage for the contractures – anything but attention to the mind of the patient. One might say that the phenomenology of hysteria was dealt with as mental by the hypnotists, but only in the sense of 'trauma' impinging on a defective apparatus, not as experience affecting a sensitive person. Breuer's admiration for Anna O.'s character and intellect, his respect for her as a person and his therapeutic intent seem to have been leading his scientific curiosity and perhaps left him too vulnerable to the anxiety

17

which her erotic transference aroused. But it was an attitude strongly in contrast to the contempt of his times for the 'neuropathic' and the 'degenerate'. By comparison with the older man, we tend to find the younger Freud of the 'Studies' harder, more ambitious, his therapeutic drive more egocentric. Only the touching fragment of 'Katarina', the girl of the Alpine village, reveals the depth of warmth and tender concern which can later be seen in relation to 'Dora' or 'Little Hans'. Is it not interesting that the tenderness then was similarly accompanied by vulnerability, for Dora hurt Freud as Anna O. frightened Breuer? But while the latter was driven by the pain away from further investigation, the great man grasped the nettle and comprehended for the first time the crucial significance of the transference in the psychoanalytical method.

Let us return for a moment, then, to the 'joke' that Anna O. was the originator of the psycho-analytical method. Personally I take it quite seriously that the history of our science is one of collaborative investigation by patient and analyst and would not have the slightest hesitation in saying that the essence of the method is one in which the 'patient' is always the 'investigator' and that self-analysis is the key to the process. Clearly the greatest of the 'patients' would be the fellow whom Freud analysed in his self-analysis. Taken from this point of view, the whole of our literature may be read as self-revelation by its various authors. Does this perhaps give some clue to the great difficulty in analytic writing, the amount of anxiety it engenders, the courage it requires? Reading the case of Anna O. supplies ample evidence of the creativity of this young woman, and Breuer is surely telling the truth when he says that '. . . it took me completely by surprise, and not until symptoms had been got rid of in this way' (i.e. the 'talking cure') 'in a whole series of instances did I develop a therapeutic technique of it' (i.e. the 'Cathartic Method').

What was Anna O.'s method, then? First of all it consisted of states of 'autohypnosis' in which she 'talked out' all the hallucinatory and anxiety phantasy experience of the day. Then she evolved an anamnestic period in which she talked out the internal events of the corresponding day of the previous year (1880–81). Thirdly she set a time period of one year to the process, declaring that she would stop on the anniversary of her being moved into the country after her father's death. (When it happened ten years later that the illness of the young Mathilde H. self-terminated on the anniversary of the breaking of her engagement, Freud recognized the link to mourning processes and that the credit received for the cure by his hypnosis was spurious – p. 163). Fourthly, Anna O. traced back in association current symptoms to their initial appearance. Fifthly, she found the link between symptoms and dreams, especially the moving dream of the snake. In the end she investigated the problem of the reality of 'the unconscious' and its relation to the splitting in herself with regard to the problem of the 'will', convincing Breuer, perhaps more than herself, that her pathological states of 'naughtiness' had been beyond her control, even if only in the sense that the 'will' to control their outward manifestation was lacking.

So impressive is Anna O.'s performance that today one would question the diagnosis of hysteria and tend to consider her illness one of neurotic depressive reaction connected with impeded mourning, the prognosis of which was probably good and self-terminating – for is not the mourning process a self-analytical one of its very nature? In discussing the part played by nursing the dying in the aetiology of his cases, Freud suggests as much (p. 162). Recall that Anna O.'s illness, or at least the aspects of it treated by Breuer, ended in June 1882 and the 'Studies' were published in 1895, two years after the Preliminary Communication. Compare this thirteen years of 'incubation' of the method with the next ten years, which saw the realisation of the great seminal works of psycho-analysis – the 'Interpretation of Dreams', 'Psychopathology of Everyday Life', 'Wit and its Relation to the Unconscious', 'Fragment of Analysis of a Case of Hysteria', and 'Three Essays on Sexuality'. Remember the crucial year 1897, the collapse of the 'traumatic' theory and the beginning of Freud's self-analysis. To follow the development set in train by Anna O. and Breuer, let us examine the evolution as revealed in the cases themselves: Emmy von N. 1889, Lucy R. 1892, Dora 1900. These of course are treatment and not publication dates.

Emmy von N.'s physician is a stranger to us and not a very likeable one, I fear. As Freud says, he was completely under the sway of Bernheim's method of suggestion and appears also not

19

to have liked his patient very much. We may not find this surprising, as it is doubtful that she would be considered an hysteric today, but rather a severe obsessional character with marked paranoid trends, diffuse hypochondria, and somatic delusions as well as hysterical symptoms. The treatment consisted of two brief periods, seven and perhaps nine weeks long, separated by a year, with a brief follow-up visit one year later and a note three years later indicating a relapse. The tone of the description is unpleasantly assertive, shallow and arrogant, in keeping with the methods – and the data is rather boring. The method was as follows: warm and cool baths, massaging 'her body all over' each day and then hypnosis each evening, during which a description of her fears and symptoms was elicited along with their chronology – reported in reverse order, as with Anna O. The disappearance of these symptoms would then be ordered by the so-called 'suggestion'. Freud seems to have told her 'white lies', cautionary tales, played hypnotic and post-hypnotic tricks and finally tyrannised over her with an ultimatum (about drinking alkaline waters). Her attempts to induce him to listen more to her recollections found at best irritable compliance, in contrast with the friendly response of Breuer to Anna O.'s similar request. It is however very interesting to see, from a footnote, that Freud was systematically analyzing his own dreams at this time, though not consciously for the purpose of self-analysis: rather as part of the work on the 'Interpretation of Dreams', studying the day-residue, false connections, compulsion to associate, etc. But Freud's own sad footnote of 1924 reminds us to save the 'smile of pity' for our own poor efforts.

In the brief treatment of Lucy R. (only nine weeks) we find a different man, using a different method. He has found himself an indifferent hypnotist and is now relying upon 'forcing' associations by pressure of his hand on the forehead. Obviously delighted to have been able to dispense with the hocus-pocus of the hypnotic situation, he is more able to think, speak and feel with his patient. Note, for instance, how in the discussion of the splitting of consciousness and forgetting, he refers his understanding of the process in his patient's mind to similar events in his own (p. 117). His intuition is alive and his approach, as when he suggests to Lucy that she is in love with

20

her employer, is both bold and tender. The case is hardly a 'case' at all, but rather a transient hysterical symptom, accompanying a period of mild depression in an unmarried woman secretly in love, attached to the children and husband of her deceased mistress. But the patient's fundamental mental health also misled Freud into underestimating the inaccessibility of the repressed, for in his discussion of this case he almost begs the question of the unconsciousness of the 'traumatic' event. This is extremely important in relation to the development of the method, which was still excessively directed toward the resolution of symptoms and therefore bound to therapeutic success as the test of theoretical formulaion. Neither Emmy von N., Lucy R. nor Katarina led Freud back to dreams nor to early childhood with the same creative relentlessness that was exerted on Breuer by Anna O. What Freud had said about the 'Studies' is so true. The clinical material read like 'short stories', all about human relations, feelings, hopes, phantasies – and the discussions read like accounts of the physiology laboratory. The cleavage between the clinician and the theoretician in Freud is so apparent, for he had not yet begun to struggle against the hope, expressed in the 'Project' of 1895, of reducing psychology to neurophysiological, quantifiable items, with Greek letters as a notation.

The 'first full length analysis', as Freud called it, also reads like a short story, but important advances in technique already had declared themselves in relation to Elizabeth von R. and new data was impinging on Freud's mind. Again the pressure technique was used in lieu of hypnosis generally and the 'excavation' of the material 'layer by layer' was meticulously pursued – by which he meant tracing the so-called 'causal chain' of memories (not association, notice) back to the original trauma, which was then to be fully 'abreacted'. Freud found this attractive, 'cheeky' and 'cock-sure' girl of 24 far less docile when confronted with secret longings for her deceased sister's husband, than had been the governess Lucy R. from Glasgow. But he faced this storm (which he calls 'resistance' for the first time) manfully, and 'consoled' the distressed young woman in two ways: that she was not responsible for her feelings, and that her illness was testimony to her good character. Amusing

21

Victorian consolation, but it brings into focus an important aspect of this 'full length analysis': namely that Freud became deeply identified with the girl, one suspects, and went far beyond relieving her symptoms. He sought actively to bring about Elizabeth's marriage to her brother-in-law by way of a discussion with the mother, for which the patient probably never forgave him. He says ruefully about her not returning to see him in follow-up that 'it is characteristic of the personal relationship which arises in treatment of this kind': a harbinger of the concept of the 'transference', and an indication of the pain of the counter-transference.

These phenomena we must link with Freud's evasiveness about the entire problem of infantile sexuality and incestuous desires, as evidenced in the distortion of the clinical material with both Katarina and Rosalie H., where he altered the references to sexual conflict from the father to an 'uncle'. By leading his patients in the enquiry, rather than following, as Breuer had done with Anna O., he could only find confirmation for his theories of retention, multiple trauma, symbolization etc., while preventing the patient's tendency (mentioned in almost every case) to follow associations back into early childhood.

No, one must recognize that Anna O. herself is the heroine of the 'Studies' and Freud's future greatness only peeps through in his discussion of the psycho-therapeutic method, where we can see that the experiences were impinging on him and making him re-think his preconceptions. These elements stand out: first, the growing sensitivity to the mental pain in the patient which manifests itself as resistance to the investigations when the crucial memories were approached; secondly, the resistance due to the transference, for it is here that the concept is erected for the first time into an essential component of the method.

When we turn to the case of Dora, five years after the publication of the 'Studies', we are astonished at the change in the man and can hardly find evidence in the published writings of the intervening period to trace the metamorphosis in method and in mastery. The Fliess letters tell us only the drama of the evolution of the theoretician, not of the clinician, in whom we are more interested. We can see from the evidence cited in the various papers of 1894–97 that the methods we have already discussed were leading him to the discovery of the important role of sexuality – abstinence, lack of satisfaction, infidelity, masturbation and perversion – in the adult lives of his patients and, with increasing frequency, the recollection of passive traumatic sexual experiences in childhood at the hands of adults, followed by active experiences with other children in the case of the obsessional patients. By 1897 the 'seduction' theory had collapsed, and the self-analysis had begun wherein Freud was to discover the oedipus complex and the universality of infantile sexuality. But of course, the clinical method and data are not available to us, except for a peep under the tent in the papers on forgetfulness, screen memories, and in the books of this period – the 'Traumdeutung', 'Wit' and 'Everyday Life'.

In the next chapter we will turn to the great Freud in his clinical work with Dora and see again how the new methods were bringing new data which enriched the psycho-pathology of hysteria. To review briefly: in this second chapter I have traced the evolution of the method by its various contributors – Anna O., Breuer and Freud – in a way which was intended to show how the changing data thrown into relief constitutes the real substance of the concepts of psycho-pathology. The theories I have merely alluded to, as they are less important than the phenomenology, since we are dealing mainly with Freud's views on psycho-pathology and not with the evolution of the psycho-analytical theory of the mind.

The Crystallization of the
Chapter III   Method Dream Analysis – (Dora)

The great Freud and the psycho-analytical revolution really begin at the inception of the self-analysis in 1897, after the collapse of the 'seduction' theory of hysteria, the 'specific aetiology'. We may safely assume that the writing of the 'Traumdeutung' (1900), 'Wit' and 'Everyday Life', belong to the epoch of the 'Cathartic method' in which Freud's interest in the working of the mind was beginning to separate itself from the neurophysiologist's interest in the brain. He was working with new ideas: splitting of consciousness, retention of affects, mental pain due to unacceptable ideas, psychic trauma, etc., applied essentially to old data available to psychiatrists. In his isolation, he still hoped for a fair hearing and scientific interest in his findings. Even in the introduction to 'Dora', where he both pleads for a hearing and defends himself against foreseen criticism, he is of the opinion that the data is available to any psychiatrist who will take the trouble to collect it. It seems naive and amusing for Freud to suggest that anyone who follows the directions in the recipe book, the 'Traumdeutung', can analyse dreams. And we know in fact that as late as 1910 he said that anyone who would analyse his own dreams could practise the new science.

We must conclude that the clinical work revealed in the case of 'Dora', done in 1900, shows a development of technical virtuosity in Freud which he did not recognize himself. How it should have arisen in the five short years since the publication of the 'Studies', or rather in the three short years since the collapse of the 'seduction' theory (for this is when the method changed), we can hardly imagine. We must simply take as given, that Freud's genius was in full spate for the first time and the outpouring between 1900 and 1905 is incredible. More incredible still is the fact that, as you will see later on, this spate was repeated in the period 1920–26 – from 'Beyond the Pleasure Principle' to 'Inhibition, Symptom and Anxiety'. An early flowering, age circa 45 – and a late flowering, age circa 65.

But only with the writing of 'Dora', which he viewed mainly as a 'supplement' (p. 114) to the 'Traumdeutung' rather than as a continuation of the 'Studies', does the truth seem to come through to Freud, that he has invented a way of penetrating the depths of the mind through its pathology and that its data cannot be available except to those who can – and do – faithfully follow the method. You will recall that he writes in the Postscript, 'I have in this paper left entirely out of account the technique, which does not at all follow as a matter of course, but by whose means alone the pure metal of valuable unconscious thoughts can be extracted from the raw material of the patient's associations. This brings with it the disadvantage of the reader being given no opportunity of testing the correctness of my procedure . . .'. Not until the technical papers of the 1910–14 period did he describe the technique, but from 'Dora' we can derive it. Because we keep in mind that 'Dora' is a landmark in the development of the psycho-analytical method since in it Freud recognized the methodological importance of the transference for the first time, we will look for evidence particularly of transference interpretations – but in vain. Only in the postscript, where Freud acknowledges that his failure to analyse the transference led to the premature interruption of the treatment after three months, will we find an example of what he wished he had said (p. 118) to elicit evidence of the transference.

So from the point of view of the methodological importance of the transference, 'Dora' is a negative landmark. But in other respects we can see the technical advances in action. The clinical data of the marvellously written study shows, as the introduction proclaims, that Freud had abandoned the 'pressure' method of 'forcing' associations for a new one of free association (so-called) or, really, that he had ceased to lead and was now content to follow the patient. In consequence the inevitable references to early childhood *development*, and not merely traumatic incidents, stand forth. The humanity with which Freud traces Dora's development is very different from the romanticism with which he investigated the love life of Lucy R. or Elizabeth von R. The coolness and suspension of moral judgment with which he traces her normal and perverse sexual interests is very changed from the icy detachment with which he guarded himself from recognizing his identification with Elizabeth, for instance. We can believe, in reading this case, that the 'Three Essays on Sexuality' derived from his clinical experience in the treatment of neuroses and that it cannot be taken as preconception which he imposed upon the material. See the way in which he has elicited the information from the eighteen-year-old Dora of her knowledge about fellatio, linking it to her childhood habit of thumb-sucking and ear-pulling; how he assumes that the symptoms of pressure sensation on her thorax after the 'kiss' at age fourteen by Herr K. was a displacement of the sensation of pressure from Herr K.'s erect penis; how he joins her childhood symptoms of aphonia to her being a poor eater; how the heterosexual and homosexual aspects of her relation to the K's is connected with the easy shift from nipple to penis as object of oral cravings in childhood.

In all of these evidences of facility of thought and virtuosity of linking we see unmistakeable evidence of a different man from the psychotherapist of the 'Studies'. Note also that when Freud mentions the care with which he sought evidence of Dora's existing knowledge of sexuality, he boldly declares that he did so, not to avoid the charge of corrupting an innocent girl but to avoid contaminating the reliability of his data. Really, one must be a little aghast at the courage of this lonely man at the turn of the century. The method had seized him and he was pressing on with the excitement – nay, recklessness – which only the thrill of the pursuit of knowledge can explain. The traits of ambition and the urgency of the parvenu are gone. And with them is banished the therapeutic test of theoretical validity – as for instance when he hesitates to claim a success in eliminating Dora's nervous cough. How bold indeed to publish such a 'fragment' of unsuccessful treatment altogether. Clearly the internal validity of the data about the human being in question has become the testing ground. Correspondingly, we see that Freud's thinking has abandoned final causes and has embraced 'overdetermination' as the principle for the comprehension of the symptoms. Even a formula such as the one that 'neurosis is the negative of perversions' is not put forward in a mechanistic sense but rather with a view to considering the neurosis as the sexual life *per se* of the neurotic person. But we will return to this in a little while when we come to take stock of the change in the nature of the whole concept of psycho-pathology which inheres in the psycho-analytical revolution that took place in those few years. Before turning to that stock-taking, we must pay some attention to the two dreams and the method of dream analysis they reveal, in order to see that the tripartite core of the analytical method – dream analysis, transference analysis, resistance analysis – was already shaped, and that the 'Fragment' is its methodological manifesto.

In the work of analysis of the two dreams we see the virtuoso at work, more in the skill with which he elicits his associations (such as the brilliant recognition that Dora had given him two weeks notice – secretly – like a servant) than in the imagination with which he sorts and collates the material that is produced. He is already a master at recognizing equivocation, evasiveness, gaps in the material, 'switch words', allusions to childhood (cf. an 'accident in the night' = bedwetting), verbal linkages, puns, visual imagery (the brilliant realisation that the reference to the painting of nymphs in a wood symbolizes the female genitals, the labia minora or nymphae among the pubic hair).

But, as with Breuer and Anna O., we must give some of the credit to Dora, for she seems to have been a superb patient, another analyst manquée, so that we are prone to join with Freud in regretting that his as yet inadequate technique for dealing with the transference did not enable her to curb the impulse to *act out* (the first reference to what was later conceptualised in the paper on transference) what Freud called the 'new edition' or 'revised edition' of her infantile relation to her father. If he had been both identified with and a little in love with Elisabeth von R., Freud was surely now finally in love with the method that was carrying him forward. We see the poet, rather than the neurophysiologist, formulating images of symptoms woven around an incident, as a pearl is formed around a grain of sand, or thoughts weaving themselves around an event like garlands of flowers around a wire.

It cannot have escaped notice, and may have caused some irritation, that in these chapters I have spoken little about the various stages of Freud's thought on the nature of hysteria, his psycho-pathological theories. I have not done so because, first of all, they are laid out beautifully in the papers and annotated splendidly by Strachey, and secondly, I do not regard them as

27

greatly important in themselves. But I do wish to spend a little time reviewing the evolution of Freud's thought about psycho-pathology in general, and hysteria in particular, in a way that is somewhat different from that of the discussion in Chapter One concerning his modes of thinking, preconceptions, and model building.

The field which Freud entered with Breuer's help was one dominated by concepts which set psycho-pathology apart from normality on an underlying assumption of damage to the brain. This engendered terms such as 'degeneracy', assumptions of 'hereditary taint', suspicion of congenital or acquired syphilis, or dismissal as malingering. The Freud of the 'Project' could take no other view despite his work, already six years old, with Breuer. These ideas of 'brain' had in that publication already yielded their place as 'specific aetiology' to one of 'predisposition'. Although Freud never fully embraced Breuer's idea of the 'hypnoid state' as the precondition for the formation of hysterical symptoms, and finally abandoned it openly in the 'Fragment', it is clear from his letters to Fliess, as late as the writing of the 'Dora' case record, that he had not yet given up the idea of 'organic factors'. These however had become attached to the biochemical processes he assumed lay behind bisexuality (one must remember, hormones had not yet been discovered). When he wrote in 1896 of the 'specific aetiology' of hysteria as a traumatic seduction in childhood, he still meant this to be imposed upon some organic sexual pre-disposition in order for hysteria to appear in later life. It is probably correct to say that Freud never fully freed himself from the neuro-physiological nor the biological view of pre-disposition, but he clearly abandoned the concept of brain for one of mind in committing himself as a 'psychologist'. The term 'metapsychology' with its four-part structure, only appeared in 1915 with the publication of 'The Unconscious' (SE 14), but if we examine these earlier writings on psycho-pathology in the light of topography, dynamics, economics, and genetics, we can see – albeit in a sort of swirling confusion – that Freud's theoretical views were already sorting themselves out under these four categories.

I have tried to indicate that the split between the clinician and the theoretician which Freud himself noted and referred to as the 'short story' quality of his clinical reports, was dissolving by the time the 'Fragment' was published. He was clearly thinking of Dora's personality, character, temperament, interests, phantasies, longings, as well as her conflicts. She comes out to us as a person in a manner which makes human such theoretical terms as 'splitting-of-consciousness', 'defense', 'inadmissable ideas'. The topography of levels of consciousness had already been put forward as universal in the three volumes 'Traumdeutung', 'Wit', and 'Everyday Life'. Furthermore, the *'unconscious'* (for Freud had already abandoned on the one hand the alternative term 'subconscious' to differentiate his views from the hypnotists, and the term 'the repressed' as too narrow) is presented as a realm of mental activity and not as a sub-cellar of rejected ideas and forgotten experience. Even hints of the structural ideas of the Twenties are adumbrated in reference to multiple personality organizations, as Breuer also noted with Anna O., (or rather as she noted to him). *'Stratification'* of memories in 'at least three different ways', *'files of memories'* and other ideas of a structural order in the mind are sprinkled through the theoretical sections.

Dynamic concepts include *defence,* the *relation of mind and body* through *'symbol formation'* and *'somatic compliance'*, the use of *one relationship to ward off another,* the *projection of ideas,* the function of *dreams to link the past and the present,* of *words to hold experience in consciousness,* and many others. The idea of *trauma* was broadening into one of *cumulative experience* and *over-determination.* The economics of the mind still held a quantitative hydrostatic, *energetic mode* of exposition through the idea of 'cathexis'; but the attempt to distinguish between *motives, reasons, tendencies, impulses, aims, object choice, choice of neurosis,* the *balance between progression and regression* and other ways of formulating the problems of quality were pushing the more physical and neurophysiological models into the background.

The genetic category was firmly entrenched in the 'Three Essays' and the 'Fragment'. Clearly the hope of a 'complete analysis' was being given up, as it depended heavily on the idea of trauma as the ultimate cause of a pathological chain of events. *'Proof'* was giving way to *'understanding'* and the thera-peutic power of analysis could no longer be attributed to the impingement of the analyst on the patient, but must wait for the patient to make use of the realizations that the analyst has made available. The humility of the first psycho-analyst was a far cry from the domineering and demanding psycho-therapist of the 'Studies'.

It will be recalled that in speaking of Freud's work, I emphasized the necessity for following the essential split in his functioning as a scientist: a split which can be fairly clearly defined as dividing the theoretician from the clinician. Here I wish to investigate with you the application of this conception of his mode of work to the evolution of dream interpretation. Throughout the length of Freud's fifty years of work as a psychologist, his attitude towards dreams, from the theoretical point of view, never really seems to have shifted from the early preconceptions expressed in the 'Project', and the theoretical ideas expressed in the famous seventh chapter of the 'Interpretation of Dreams'. The central idea of this conception was that dreams were a rather simple mental function with a very simple purpose: namely, to keep the dreamer asleep; and that whatever was of interest about dreams was of interest not because of their meaningfulness in mental life, but because of what they could inadvertently reveal to the psycho-analyst. This essentially trivial function of dreams was seen as being implemented by means of a process akin to hallucination; and its effectiveness in keeping the dreamer asleep was based on a process of wish-fulfilment through hallucination.

Freud describes that his interest in dreams was really aroused in the course of the early work with hysterical patients, when he was still following Breuer's technique of catharsis and tracing symptoms back to their origins. He discovered that in the place of events, or occurrences, or thoughts, the patients did occasionally tell him dreams that had occurred. From this he construed that it was technically legitimate for him to treat the dreams as if they were 'thoughts like any other thought', but not to treat the dreams theoretically as if they were arranged in a continuous chain of mental process. Instead he conceived of them as being essentially concocted by an elaborate process in which wishes were granted fulfilment in a hallucinatory form, with the proviso that they sufficiently disguised themselves either to meet the requirements of an internal censorship, or 'cleverly' to evade this censorship.

Freud therefore tended to consider the manifest content of the dream as being patent nonsense, while the latent content of the dream – or the dream-thought and its significance – had to be construed in a piecemeal fashion – what he called the 'jigsaw puzzle' method. Taking each part of the dream in sequence and eliciting its associations, which then had first to be translated by means of the analyst's recognition of the dream work that had taken place, the analyst could then translate the assembled parts back to its 'original form', as it were, prior to the dream work that was dedicated to the evasion of the censorship. They could then be fitted together to produce the 'dream thought' whose significance could then be construed. The dream interpretation, as he says in a later paper on the technique, can therefore be divided into two phases: the first a phase essentially of translation; the second a phase of interpretation; and he likens it to translating a passage of Livy into German. This is of course a commentary on the kind of schooling he himself had, assuming that translation should naturally fall into these two phases: firstly translating from the Latin word to the German literal word, and then construing the propositional meaning and expressing this in literary or colloquial German. The teaching of language today, even of ancient languages, is in rebellion against this cerebral method – and so I would think is the approach to the interpretation of dreams.

Therefore in summary one might say that Freud treated dreams as if they were intrinsically useless artefacts of mental functioning with only the trivial function of keeping the dreamer asleep; and that it was the fact that the psychoanalyst could make use of them which elevated them to a position of importance in mental life. This was his theoretical position; and of course one might say that the yield of scientific data that he reaped from dreams under the aegis of this theory was very considerable indeed. He did construe from what he felt were 'wishes' (which I think we can take to mean something like the primitive impulses combined with rather omnipotent means of effecting the desires) something of the mental mechanisms by which people deceive themselves; and this, you might say, was gradually evolving into the theory of the mechanisms of defence. Certainly he construed something of

31

the affects and passions that lay hidden in the depths of the mind and which were suggested or sometimes seen quite openly in the dreams. But on the other hand, the method in practice, and the yield from applying the method in practice, was vastly greater than the yield seen through the eyes of the theoretician.

In practice he treated the dreams as life events. For instance in the famous case of the Wolf Man, he has clearly implied that the most crucial event in this man's life occurred at the age of four when he had this particular dream of the wolves sitting in the tree. And probably most important of all, though something of which we know very little, Freud did utilize his own dreams to conduct his self-analysis following the deterioration of his relationship with Breuer and the collapse of the theory of the 'specific aetiology' of hysteria, which he had put forward in 1896. The collapse of his hopes of fame together with the death of his father at this time probably threatened him with the collapse of his mental health; and where others undoubtedly would have taken refuge in external flight, Freud turned inward, utilising his method to conduct his self-analysis, which seems to have been one of the most successful analyses in history.

We have many glimpses into this self-analysis in his 'Interpretation of Dreams', because Freud used many of his own dreams to illustrate his points there. But the clearest of all and the most revealing, owing to the wealth of associative material which he presents with it, is the famous 'dream of Irma's injection'. You will recall that this is essentially a dream in which he meets this patient, Irma, who complains to him that his treatment of her has not succeeded, and he replies that it is her own fault because she has not accepted his solution, and there follow various interactions between her and his friends Otto and Leopold, who examine her. It is of special interest that this dream is presented as an example of the method for interpreting dreams, and is preceded by a preamble in which Freud specifically abandons what he calls the 'popular' methods: that is the use either of inspiration or of decoding. Now it is true that by these two popular methods he means something like the extremes of a continuum, with inspiration at the one end and decoding at the other. 'Inspiration' would be a procedure by which the interpreter simply 'knows' the meaning of the dream without having to give any thought to it, without having to collect any information about the dreamer or the circumstances of the dream. Whereas the method of decoding would be a rigidly mechanical system of fixed-symbol translation of the 'Dream Book' variety. It would not involve any element of interpretation of the significance of the dream (and analogously, the method of inspiration would pay no attention at all to the individual details of the dream). In presenting his own method, Freud does not give the impression that he is offering a method which lies somewhere in between these two extremes, but rather claims that he is following an entirely different method. If anything, he seems to see his method as closer to the decoding, if only because he takes his material in detail and not 'en masse', as he says. But his claim is that in following the elements of the dream into their associative connections in the patient's mind through free association he is able to determine the individual meaning of the symbols, rather than by relying on some form of standard dream-book decoding. It is therefore the function of inspiration that he primarily eschews.

I wish now to turn to two examples of Freud's work with dreams in practice: the specimen dream of Irma's injection, and the first in the 'Fragment of a Case of Hysteria': Dora's dream of the jewel-case; in order to examine the question whether these three claims have any validity: the claim that he is examining a process whose only function is to keep the dreamer asleep; that he is avoiding the use of inspiration, but rather relying on a purely inductive method of collecting items of information from which he then draws out scientifically valid conclusions. I believe that Freud at that time was very concerned with scientific respectability, trying to establish not only his own but also that of psycho-analysis as a method. We are talking of a time when the concept of scientific procedure as inductive was in great force in Germany, probably mainly on the basis of Emmanuel Kant's conceptions of *a priori* thought as an extension of experience. It was only beginning to be questioned, or rather to cause serious disturbance in scientific circles, following the work of David Hume and Poincaré and others who took the view that the idea of induction was a kind of self-idealisation, with the scientist really denying the extent to which he was avoiding looking at those other phenomena which might not substantiate the conclusions that he had reached by the inductive method of generalising his limited experience. The difficulty in Freud's thought resides, as it still resides in psycho-analysis, in not recognising that the procedures that could be considered scientific when dealing with the inanimate world are not only somewhat delusional when it comes to dealing with animate matter, but quite beyond possibility where mental processes are concerned.

When we examine the analysis of the 'specimen dream', we find that Freud does as he promises: faithfully takes the dream bit by bit and gives his association for each part. This goes on for ten pages, and then suddenly we are confronted by the statement: 'I have now completed the interpretation of the dream'. We are astonished to read this, but he goes on to say: 'While I was carrying it out, I had some difficulty in keeping at bay all the thoughts that were bound to be provoked by comparison between the content of the dream and the concealed thoughts lying behind it. And in the meantime the meaning of the dream was borne in upon me'. We are to understand therefore that the interpretation of the dream is something different from the construing of its meaning; and Freud summarises the meaning of the dream as follows:

> 'The dream fulfilled certain wishes which were started in me by the events of the previous evening: the news given me by Otto and my writing out of the case history. The conclusion of the dream, that is to say, was that I was not responsible for Irma's pains, but that Otto was.'

He then goes on to expand on this, and within two pages comes to what seems to be a very different conclusion:

> 'The group of thoughts that played a part in the dream enabled me retrospectively to put this transient impression into words. It was as though he (Otto) had said to me: "You don't take your medical duties seriously; you are not conscientious, you don't carry out what you have undertaken." Thereupon this group of thoughts seemed to have put itself at my disposal, so that I could produce evidence of how highly conscientious I

was and how deeply I was concerned with the health of my relations, my friends and my patients.'

Let us turn away for a minute from Freud's theoretical conclusions and discuss what we ourselves seem to learn from reading this dream and the wealth of associated material that Freud produces for it. We learn that we are dealing with an ambitious young man who had already made some fairly reckless experiments with cocaine that had resulted in deaths; who is worried that he is now engaged on another reckless experiment, and that his friends are turning against him. We discern behind this that he is troubled by his sexual interest in his women patients, and by his dependence on some of his men friends and their good opinion of him: most importantly on Dr M. We are given many indications that he is restless and uneasy in his marriage and dissatisfied with his sexual relationship with his wife and feeling guilty about difficulties in her health. We also learn that he is rather hypochondriacal himself, and still suffering from the consequences of deaths close to him. We also get a very clear indication that in the nebulous field of psychology he finds himself longing for the greater precision of biochemistry and anatomy. Therefore we would say that the extensive view of the inner life of the person Freud here afforded to us by the wealth of association gives a very different impression from the rather cold medical-student competitive atmosphere of the manifest content of the dream. Now I think one must realise that this is a dream of Freud's self-analysis and it therefore does not contain the structure of condensed transference significance that one might reasonably expect to find in the dream of a patient undergoing psychoanalysis. Its content and its associations roam freely over Freud's mental life at the time; even its fairly precise reference to the annoyance over the remark that Otto had made to him is only a starting point and not a real focus of the dream, as a similar remark by an analyst in his consulting room might be the focus for a patient's dream of the following night.

I would therefore suggest that examination of the dream does not at all bear out the method that Freud claimed to be following. I would suggest that the method hew as following in practice was to use the dream as an entrée into lines of association

35

which revealed the person's unconscious mental life. What resulted from it has the structure of a short story (as Freud himself described his case histories), rather than of a mathematical or scientific solution.

It is of interest, in line with Freud's self-analytic experience of these dreams, that, when we turn to the first dream of 'Dora' in the 'Fragment of a Case of Hysteria' we note that Freud took particular interest in the dream because it was presented by the patient as a repetitive one. That is, he does not seem to have taken interest in it as something referring to immediate events taking place in the analysis, but as something which could contribute to the reconstruction of the genesis of the patient's symptoms. This was natural because, although at the time he had discovered the functioning of the transference, he was considering it only to be a nuisance or an impediment and was making no effort to analyse it, even as a resistance. In the case of the Rat Man, Freud analysed the transference and its evolution for its own sake, but never considered it the premier method of psychoanalysis as we do today. The dream is short; I would like to present it as a unit:

> "The house was on fire. My father was standing by my bed and woke me up. I dressed quickly. Mother wanted to stop and save her jewel-case, but Father said: "I refuse to let myself and my two children be burned for the sake of your jewel-case." We hurried downstairs, and as soon as I was outside I woke up.'

Dora's treatment occurred in the same year as the publication of the 'Interpretation of Dreams': 1900. The case history was written primarily as an addendum to the dream-book, rather than as a case to present Freud's views on the psychotherapy of hysteria. It seems to have been written very rapidly after the completion of Dora's brief treatment, and was at first called 'Dreams and Hysteria': but its publication was then delayed for about four years for reasons that are not quite clear. It is clear from the work with Dora, however, that by this time Freud had given up directing the patient to follow the manifest content of the dream so carefully, piece by piece in producing associations, but gave Dora quite some leeway to follow her own bent. The associations which she produced and the ways in which Freud helped her to investigate these associations produce a wealth of interesting material about her relationship with Herr K., to her father and mother, to jewellery, and the early problem of bedwetting. In fact Freud does some symbol-translating on a purely inspirational basis: he translates jewel-case as vagina; he translates tear-drop earrings as semen. At this point Freud is no longer referring to the interpretation of the dream and its meaning, for some reason; he seems to be referring to the analysis and the synthesis as the two phases of this process. But this synthesis takes some six pages to describe. The analysis had taken twenty-five. Strangely enough, at the eighth page of the analysis we come to the astonishing statement as in the 'Irma' dream:

> 'Well, the interpretation of the dream now seemed to me to be complete.'

And in a footnote he says:

> 'The essence of the dream might perhaps be stated in words such as these: "The temptation is so strong, father, protect me as you used to in my childhood and prevent my bed from being wetted.'

With this banal and trivial statement we must compare the wealth of information and revelation about the life events, the temperament, the longings, the anxieties (and the relationship to Freud) that are revealed in this dream.

Freud did recognise that the dream recurred at this point in the analysis because it represented the repetition of a dangerous situation, and that she was experiencing the danger of sexual excitement and a sexual relationship to Freud as she had experienced it with Herr K. He did indeed come to regret that he had not dealt with this transference. It therefore seems reasonable to suggest that we have in the analysis of Dora's first dream an example of Freud the clinician using the dream, which is at considerable variance with Freud the theoretician talking about the function of the dream. It seems quite clear that he is using the dream as an entrée into the private, historical and emotional depths of the patient's mind, and from this material is also construing the immediacy of the unconscious situation in the transference. In theory what he is doing is

37

tracing back Dora's hysterical symptoms to the kiss by the lake, and defining the nature of the mental mechanisms, denials, reversals, wishes and counter-wishes which underlie the formation of such hysterical symptoms.

In our tracing of the development of Freud's work we have now come to, say, 1904, just before the famous 'Three Essays on Sexuality' and the Little Hans case; we have covered the period of the 'Studies on Hysteria', the early elaboration of the theory of the defence neuro-psychoses, the period during which Freud's explorations of the unconscious also produced the book on jokes, 'The Psychopathology of Everyday Life', and the great Dream book. I have been trying, by emphasizing what the clinical evidence reveals of the way Freud actually *worked* with his patients, to show the considerable split between the clinician and the theoretician. I would remind you that the essential theme of this book consists really in tracing the way in which Freud, over the years, gradually metamorphosed from the determinist neuro-physiologist of the 'Project for a Scientific Psychology' into the phenomenological psychologist of 'Analysis Terminable and Interminable'.

Chapter IV   Freud's Theory of Sexuality

We must now try to investigate a subject that runs through all Freud's work, and is at the very heart of the psycho-analytic method and the psycho-analytic understanding of the mind: namely, the problem of sexuality. In approaching this, as in approaching other aspects of Freud's work, I want to try to differentiate between the method with its associated data, and the theories which are often strongly influenced by preconceptions; and to remind you that I have spoken of the way in which Freud was transformed from the determinist neurophysiologist into a phenomenological psychologist over the period of the forty years of his psycho-analytic work. Freud is probably best known for his revolutionary views on sexuality; but I think when we study them in practice we will be less inclined to consider them as revolutionary views and more inclined to see them as real discoveries. In order to make this differentiation it is necessary to read the 'Three Essays' as laid out in the standard edition with great care, because it has been presented with a certain disingenuousness. Its format runs counter to the general format of the edition, which is chronological with cross-referencing. The editors for some reason have followed a different policy with the 'Three Essays'. I wish to remind you, to begin with, of the way in which one must read it if one is to get a chronological idea in one's mind of Freud's development.

There were six editions of the 'Three Essays' brought out in Freud's lifetime, beginning in 1905 and ending in 1926, of which four contain significant changes in his views: mostly additions, but also some corrections. The editors of the Standard edition have for some reason chosen to present the last (1926) as the basic text and to annotate this with footnotes. The result is that one has the greatest difficulty in reading it chronologically, because it is very difficult to read something and then, on the basis of a footnote, to remove it from one's mind in order to gain an idea of what Freud thought in 1905. If they had wished to present a truly chronological picture for the student to grasp, they should have presented the first edition and footnoted it with the additions and subtractions of later editions. Therefore, to begin with, I want to outline the major alterations to the original 1905 edition (there are large sections which have as it were to be 'removed'); and then later go on to present a more integrated picture of Freud's views on sexuality in 1905. In Chapter V the ideas will be seen in action in the work with Little Hans. The main parts which have to be removed are the section on pregenital organization (which came only in 1915) and the section on the sexual researches of children, which came in the 1910 edition. This latter includes the description of the Libido Theory and various changes in his description of object choice and the basis of perversions. Finally the views about the physiological basis of sexuality (that is the hormonal theory) were merely a speculation in the 1905 edition and could not reasonably of course have been based on scientific research until about the 1920's.

With these additions and other minor changes, it seems to me that Freud's views on sexuality remain virtually the same throughout his career. This is perhaps particularly surprising when we consider that the Three Essays are presented as being based primarily on information available to any practitioner of medicine, modified and in a sense limited by the interests and findings of psycho-analysis as far as it had progressed by 1905. The later editions show the modifications and findings that psycho-analysis could subsequently introduce to it. In presenting an ordered picture of Freud's views on sexuality, I am going to use a format which is quite different from that which he follows in his own presentation, which was primarily organised around the psycho-analytic problem of the explanation or exploration of aberrations of sexuality. Therefore Freud naturally starts with these aberrations, and only then goes back to the description and investigation of infantile sexuality and the developmental transformations of puberty. I want to follow a more developmental sequence, starting with the infantile sexuality, and then describing Freud's views on the psycho-pathology of sex.

At first, Freud seemed to have a preconception in his mind which one might call a rudimentary field theory of sexual behaviour. It consisted of dividing the determinants of sexual behaviour into three categories: the source of the sexual impulse, the aim of the sexual impulse, and the object of the sexual impulse. The concept of 'source' was more or less co-extensive with the concept of 'instinct', taking the view that the bodily organs developed tensions which required release, and that these tensions clustered around what Freud was calling the 'erogenous zones'. A few years later, in 1910 or 1915, he was inclined to extend this, to view everything on the surface of the body as capable of erogenicity; but still his view was that the primary erogenous zones were the genitals, the anus and the mouth. To this he added certain other functions or tendencies which he called the 'component instincts'. These he placed in a position of dependence upon experience for their mobilisation. Thus, for instance, the component instincts essentially consisted of voyeurism, exhibitionism, sadism and masochism. His view was that these component instincts were not necessary or physiologically based tendencies, but were latent tendencies called into play by the events in the child's life, which seemed to mean fundamentally by seduction or by example. The sexual instinct was therefore viewed as a bodily function that was essentially meaningless, finding its meaning only through the later elaboration of its connection with objects. His view therefore was that the relief of these tensions was a meaningless and auto-erotic activity until a certain period when object-seeking began. In his earliest views, this period of object-seeking does not seem to have commenced until somewhere around the third year, when the genital zone imposed its primacy on the sexual life. This implies that the earlier periods—those occupied with oral cravings and anal tensions – were fundamentally auto-erotic, meaningless, and did not in themselves contribute memories. They were not subject to the inhibitions due to conflict, and were therefore not sources of anxiety. They were not subject to repression and did not give rise to symptom-formation. His view was that only with the rising of the genital primacy and the object-seeking of the genital tension did the oedipus complex evolve, which placed the child in conflict in relation to its genital yearnings; that this conflict produced inhibitions; that these inhibitions functioned as dams to the flow of the sexual libido; and that when this flow of sexual energy or libido was blocked, it filled up what he called the 'collateral channels' of the pregenital impulses connected with orality and anality and the component instincts.

Therefore, in this earliest time Freud considered that the

sexuality of children, of an oral and anal sort, was something that was hardly detached from the general reservoir of instincts serving self-preservation; and that they more or less detached themselves and assumed the status of a separate organisation of instincts, only when object-seeking and the oedipus complex and conflicts relating to it arose, somewhere around the third year. Now, of course one does not know whether to call this a theory, or a model, or a mode of thought. I think probably it is more useful to think of it as the model or mode of thought that was most natural to Freud, natural to his era. It has been called the 'hydrostatic' model of instincts and mental functioning; and is based on a conception of there being a homogeneous excitation, equivalent in the body to the pressure of water or the voltage in an electrical system. It flows, has direction, and operates in time. It is subject to various kinds of interferences in this flow and therefore resorts to various types of distribution. Only when object-seeking enters into the picture are the activities related to sexuality seen as being meaningful, and it is only when they become meaningful that they are subjected to elaboration and phantasy and can enter upon a developmental process which can be thought of as essentially mental. It is only in this latter development that emotions and affects can be seen to play a part. It is a great weakness in Freud's model that it gives no scope for affects as qualitative factors in mental life, but necessarily reduces them to the status of a variable quantity of excitation; apprehended *as if* there were qualitative differences.

On the basis of this model of the auto-erotic phase, Freud discerned (or perhaps it was inherent in his model that this should exist) a certain gradient or differentiation between active and passive aims. This differentiation between active and passive aims of the instinct was seen by him as a foundation for the later establishment of tendencies which could be clearly delineated as masculine and feminine. He seems to have quite unequivocally considered masculinity to be essentially active and femininity to be essentially passive. But it is important to realise that he is not talking about modes of activity for the realisation of these aims (for he knew very well that a passive aim could be actively implemented and an active one could be passively implemented), but nonetheless in the realm of aims of the sexual instinct, this distinction seemed certain to him: that masculinity had active aims and femininity passive ones. I think one has to take it as a cultural aberration, or a pre-conception that was so ingrained in his times as to be un-equivocally fixed in his mind. It is quite incompatible with his attitude towards orality, for instance; he did not see orality as essentially passive. It also had implications for his views about the little girl's relation to her body, for it would seem to have been (on some mysterious kind of negative evidence) that little girls knew nothing of their vaginas; they knew only of their clitoris and their rectum. His view was therefore that little girls suffered from a sense of weakness and helplessness and inferiority in the genital area, and perhaps an inbuilt sense of guilt as if the smallness of their clitoris-penis was tantamount to evidence of their having already been punished for some crime or sin. 'Penis envy', as he called it, seemed therefore to be the most natural phenomenon in the world, while a corresponding masculine envy of femininity could not be formulated since the existence of the female organ and the functions implied were not seen to play a role in the life of children. This seems to have remained virtually unchanged throughout his work, though Freud later recognised that sexual development in the girl has special difficulties connected with it, primarily those related to the strength of her primary attachment to the mother and the difficulty this posed in turning to the father in her oedipal conflict.

By 1915 the phenomenon of narcissism came within Freud's purview and was inserted between auto-eroticism and object-relatedness in his view of the development of the libido. But while this opened for view a new range of clinical phenomena, it had little impact on his basic ideas on sexuality, develop-mentally speaking; although his attitude towards sexual pathology was certainly altered from that either stated or implied in the 1905 edition. There the sexuality of the child was characterised as 'polymorphously perverse', by which he meant subject to dissemination throughout the erogenous zones and only poorly under the domination of the genital. On this basis he could say that neuroses were the negative of perversions, brought about by inhibiting forces which were seen to originate mainly in the milieu, especially in the attitudes of the parents.

The central anxiety situation, castration anxiety, was a puzzle, as it might have had its inception from a threat connected with masturbation (Little Hans, the Rat Man), or from the perception of the differences between the anatomy of the genitalia of the sexes. This latter was seen as certain to be perceived as a mutilation, in boys and girls alike. Only with the analysis of the Rat Man did a purely internal conflict (between love and hate) take its place as a source of castration anxiety, and again in the Wolf Man (between masculinity and femininity).

This simple view of the relation of perversions to neuroses characterised Freud's theory until the Wolf Man revealed to him something of the complexity of perversity; how it was compounded of ambivalence, sado-masochism, fetishistic trends and passivity, all generating regression of the libido to pregenital points of fixation. In 1905 his view of the perversions was that they were simple, uninhibited actings of infantile sexual impulses, including the component instincts, while homosexuality was seen as primarily a matter of object choice, based on developmental experiences. The advent of a concept of narcissism and beginning recognition of the complex role of identification processes in development brought a sweeping change.

But what perhaps never changed was Freud's instinct-bound attitude towards sexuality: that its essential function was the relief of sexual tension, upon which biological function and meaningful object relations might be superimposed. For this reason, since this biological drive was seen to exist mainly in the male in connection with his constant production of semen, women were considered relatively asexual. Their biological drive was for children and it was to their children that their sexual love was given. How all this was compatible with the immaturity of the genitals in children, while nonetheless their sexuality was being insisted upon, is a little mysterious. However, this is perhaps one more area in which a split may be discerned between the clinician and the theorist. The case of Little Hans does not seem to bear out these basic concepts, but rather shows a little boy struggling with his love and hate, desire for knowledge, sadistic trends, and certainly his feminine as well as his masculine oedipal conflict. Freud, the clinician, even suspected that exposure to the primal scene played some role in his illness, an idea he brought to the attention of his followers only some thirteen years after the publication of the case of Little Hans, in the famous Wolf Man dream from which Freud reconstructed an event of exposure to parental coitus at the age of eighteen months.

In this chapter therefore, as an introduction to the case of Little Hans, which was written as an addendum to the Three Essays (as was *Dora* to the Traumdeutung) I have tried to pull together Freud's views on sexuality as they existed in 1905, in order to rectify the confused chronology which a reading of the Standard Edition tends to impose upon one.

Chapter V — The Case History of Little Hans (The Infantile Neurosis)

The case of Little Hans was published in 1909 only a few months before the publication of the Rat Man case. The clinical work on both these patients had taken place one year before this and the case of the Rat Man had in fact commenced some months prior to Freud's starting work with Little Hans' father to resolve the child's phobia. This case history stands in relation to the 'Three Essays on Sexuality' much as the Dora case stands in relation to the 'Traumdeutung': namely, as a clinical addendum to the theoretical publication and intended to illustrate the theory in action in the process of psycho-analytic therapeutic work. However, the publication of the Little Hans material had more meaning for Freud than merely that of a clinical exemplification of the theory in action; for it also signified a certain vindication (and, in a sense, proof of the truth) of his theory about infantile sexuality and of the existence of the infantile neurosis. Freud seems to have looked upon the opportunity of supervising the father's treatment of his child as something extraordinary and something whose frequent repetition could be little hoped for, since he could not envisage this sort of work being carried on by anyone other than a child's parent. In retrospect, this may seem rather peculiar to those who have grown quite accustomed to the treatment of children. In fact, the absolute opposite may seem to be true today. I am always rather surprised, however, that children will tolerate psycho-analytic treatment by anybody but their parents and find the evident ease with which little Hans confided his phantasies, acted out his hostility, recounted his dreams, and included Freud as the professor who was supervising his father – indeed the ease with which the whole process was contained within family life – highly impressive, but reasonable.

To review the content of the case briefly: you will recall that some years previously, Freud had asked people whom he called 'close adherents' (among whom were the parents of Little Hans) to send him observations illustrating the sexual researches of children. While he was in fact unable to obtain any information from the parents as evidence of the impact upon children of witnessing the primal scene (which I think was his particular interest), he continued to suspect very strongly that this factor was operative. After all, Little Hans had spent the first four years of his life in his parents' bedroom, including six months following the birth of his baby sister Hannah; and the event of being moved out of the bedroom for the night in order to allow his mother to give birth to Hannah, of coming back into the room and seeing bowls that were still filled with bloody water and so on, seems to have made a great impression on him. In any case, during the summer after the birth of Hannah, when the family stayed at the Gmunden resort, Hans' sexual life seems to have blossomed and his association with other children took on the colouring of his calling them 'his children'.

Now Freud apparently viewed this, not as evidence of his femininity and identification with his mother, but rather as his way of compensating himself for the loss of his mother's attention; and it is this tendency on Freud's part, namely to diminish the significance of the boy's femininity in favour of the role of his masculine castration complex in the formation of his oedipus conflict, which seems to be the chief weakness in the interpretative work. It might be attributed to a theoretical preconception of Freud's, or perhaps to a lack of differentiation between homosexuality and femininity in a male child. For although he does briefly talk about the homosexual implications of Hans' attachment to his father, he seems reluctant to leave the impression that Hans' sexual tendencies were what at that time would have been considered 'degenerate'.

To return: the incidents at Gmunden, which included such things as a little girl being warned not to go near a horse for fear he might 'bite her finger', and a little boy falling down after kicking a rock and his foot bleeding, seem to have mobilised a certain amount of castration anxiety in Hans. This gradually overcame him in subsequent months and produced an inhibition (or what Freud calls a repression) of his sexual impulses. These impulses had expressed themselves firstly in masturbation (for he had by now been moved out of his parents' bedroom and seems to have masturbated in the mornings or during his afternoon naps) and secondly, in an inhibition of his previously enthusiastic voyeurism and exhibitionism, of his interest in urine and faeces – for which he now showed a revulsion. It is of special interest that the record includes observations on the child's sexual development that the father had sent to Freud prior to the outbreak of the neurosis, so that we have some fairly accurate information upon which to construct the genesis of the illness. Anyway, Hans fairly suddenly developed a fear of going out of the house which he formulated as a fear of being bitten by a horse; and it is for this reason that Freud considered it a phobia. However, it seems clear from the development of the treatment after its prompt start, that the fear of being bitten by a horse was superficial compared to the agoraphobic aspect of the illness: that is, the fear of going out lest he encounter horses, particularly horses drawing heavily-laden carts, who might fall down and make a row with their legs. This central fear was connected with his own behaviour when told to go and sit on the toilet to defaecate; with the incident of the child who hurt his foot; and almost certainly, Freud thought, with observations of the primal scene. It evolves quite clearly that the heavily-laden carts represent the pregnant mother in particular; and that underlying the agoraphobia and anxiety state is Hans' great curiosity about conception and birth, about which he had been given no accurate information, but had been fobbed off with the stork story.

The development of the father's treatment of Hans under the careful supervision of Freud is fascinating and laid out in what might be called a perfect exposition of clinical work. It is undoubtedly the most delightful piece of writing in the whole of psycho-analytic literature, and every reading of it is of interest, not only because one sees new things in it each time, but because it is, after all, the prelude to child analysis. In a certain way, one is always inclined to feel that Freud drew much less of interest from this rich material than it actually contained. But this was not entirely a matter of blindness to the significance of clinical phenomena; it was also owing to the fact that Freud was interested in a limited exposition with reference to infantile sexuality and the evidences in favour of the existence of an infantile period of neurosis that was subsequently repressed and forgotten, forming the basis for a reappearance in adult life of neurotic symptomatology. He is particularly interested in demonstrating, through Little Hans' material, the reality of bisexuality, the reality of the genital and pre-genital drives and interests of children; the reality of the castration complex, of the oedipus complex, the evidences in favour of traumatic factors in the institution of castration anxiety: such as, in this case, the mother's threat to cut off Little Hans' 'widdler' if he touched his penis. And perhaps most importantly, he demonstrates the evidence for the part played in the development of the child of the birth of the next sibling: that is, the way in which it aroused his sexual curiosity, burdened him with intense jealousy and envy; and, in this case of a baby of the opposite sex, confronted Little Hans with the evidences of genital differences.

Now you will remember that at this time and through most of his career until the paper on female sexuality in 1928, Freud maintained his own belief and his own interpretation of clinical evidence that the female genital was viewed by all children, male and female alike, as a mutilation. Freud interpreted the evidence of Little Hans' attitude towards Hannah's genital as confirmation of this, although I think it is fairly unconvincing. The area that is convincing, and that Freud somehow fails to put together well, is Hans' construing that the birth of the baby was a painful and dangerous thing, judging from the sight of the bloody water in his mother's bedroom after the delivery and from hearing his mother's moaning (which he called 'coughing') during the birth. This is borne out by two sections of the material in particular: by the dream about the plumber taking away the bath tub and putting a bore into Hans' stomach (which clearly seems to be a phantasy of impregnation that links with Hans' other phantasies about joining his father in going under the rope into a forbidden space, or breaking a window in the railway carriage). And secondly, it is seen in Hans' play with the doll that had the little squeaker missing from its navel, into which he put the mother's penknife and then tore the legs open to extract the knife. Thus he illustrated his phantasy that something both penetrated *into* his mother in a painful way and something came *out* of her in a painful way that produced the bleeding. Freud had a very clear recognition of the fact that this sadistic concept of the creation of the baby played some part in Hans' sexual feeling toward his mother; particularly as expressed in his acknowledged desire to beat his mother in the way the coachman beat the horse.

The aspect of the case that is so fascinating to us as we read it today (and in which Freud took no special interest because, as I suggested before, it was not in line with what he wished to demonstrate), is the development of the treatment of the child. This starts with the purely phobic element: the fear of being bitten by the horse; goes on suddenly from that to the material about defaecation, the 'lumph' material; then moves quickly, by way of the sadistic element, into the material about the stork box and the birth of Hannah. From there the development moves to the phantasies about Hans' relationship to Hannah before she was born and, by implication, before he was born, when they lived together in the stork box. It is perhaps disappointing to us to see Freud treat this material in a rather trivial way and to view it as a means that Hans had of pulling his father's leg and having revenge on him for the lies he had been told about the stork. Freud overlooks, not the fact that it represents a phantasy about the mother's womb, but the fact that it is a problem to Hans: a problem of, as it were, life before conception: the child's difficulty in coping with the painful realisation that there was a time before he existed at all. Children are of course inclined to deny this in favour of the phantasy that they always existed inside their mothers; and of course, she must have always existed inside her mother, and she inside her mother, Russian-doll fashion back to the beginnings of time; and therefore also extrapolating into the future. The child has inside him babies who contain babies, who contain yet more babies ad infinitum. This aspect of the child's interest in the inside, its own inside and the inside of the mother in particular, does not seem to have attracted Freud's interest at all at this point. And it is in a sense quite different from his lack of interest in Hans' femininity. For it seems to me that he noted the evidences of his femininity but was reluctant to discuss or emphasize them. He therefore speaks very little of the feminine component in Hans' illness, namely, the one that came from his rivalry and envy of his mother and her capacity to have children, her capacity to be the father's wife and to receive his penis (or whatever Hans imagined she did that was represented by the penknife being put into the doll or the plumber putting the bore into Hans' stomach).

To turn away slightly from the actual case material and its virtues and deficiencies, back to its link with the 'Three Essays on Sexuality', it is perhaps important to remember that the way in which this piece of work is presented in the Standard Edition is somewhat difficult to read.* Therefore one reads about narcissism, about the sexual researches of children, about masochism and perversions, in a way that only came to Freud much later in his work and thinking. In 1905, the formula that neurosis was the opposite of perversions was a very satisfactory one to him. It may seem somewhat odd that at the time when he was realising how complicated neuroses were, he was still willing to consider that perversions were very simple: the putting into action of the infantile 'polymorphously perverse disposition'. We must also remember that by 'polymorphously perverse', Freud was referring to the formulation of source, aim and object. His conception of perversity was exclusively joined to the concept of erogenous zones with the exception of what he called the 'component instincts' of scoptophilia, exhibitionism, sadism, and masochism. At that time he did not see these as *necessary* parts of sexual instinctual life, but as potential parts that could be aroused by stimulation or seduction from the outside. He also regarded homosexuality purely from the point of view of object choice. In the paper on Little Hans he comes very close to his later formulation of homosexuality as being related to a phase of narcissism. However, he does not call it narcissism here, but does say that it relates to something in the development that stands somewhere between auto-erotism and object relation.

With this simple formulation of the perversions in mind, Freud felt quite justified in defending them against what he considered to be public prejudice and in insisting that they were essentially benign; that the difficulties into which they ran were primarily social difficulties that forced repressions of the infantile impulse and that it was from these repressions (under the influence first of family pressures and later social

* See p. 39 above.

pressures) that the damming-up of the libido ensued, to be followed subsequently by the conversion of the dammed-up libido into symptoms and anxieties.

Although the section of the 'Three Essays on Sexuality' that deals with the sexual researches of children was not added until some years after the publication of 'Little Hans', it is fairly clearly indicated in this latter paper that Freud viewed these sexual researches as the prototype of children's curiosity about the world; and therefore, as the basis (when sublimated) of the thirst for knowledge. The implication at this point, then, is that the thirst for knowledge is driven by anxiety, and that knowledge will inevitably be used for defensive processes. It is perhaps worth noticing here that this is a very different view from the one Mrs Klein adopted – perhaps from her experience of listening to small children, rather than as a preconception. She found that there existed in them what she called the 'epistemophilic instinct': an instinctual thirst for knowledge and understanding; the first object of which was the child's mother, her body, and particularly (as the children told her) its inside. When we link this fact to Freud's experience with Little Hans, we can see that it was precisely this aspect of the child's phantasy that Freud was unable to recognize as significant and that the treatment ended before Hans could really investigate this area of his mental life with his father. The treatment ended because Hans seemed to have recovered from his symptomatology; and this, after all, was the therapeutic aim itself, and not as an adjunct to his character development. Therefore in looking forward to the significance of the Little Hans case for the development of child analysis, one is immediately struck with the difference in the work here with Little Hans and the work that Mrs Klein began in the 1920s. The work with Little Hans is essentially reconstructive and is aimed at an understanding of the pathology and therefore tends to look backwards on the child's life. Mrs Klein's work, on the other hand, is developmental from the very outset, and tends to look forward to the factors that are involved in the child's development. It is not psycho-pathological in its orientation.

In closing, it is perhaps important to mention that Freud goes to some lengths in his summing-up to plead the cause of the psycho-analytic method as not being dangerous to children:

that is, it is not dangerous to arouse their sexual curiosity, to give them information, to relieve their repressions and arouse their interest in sexual subjects. This is certainly the slant of the postscript to the case, in which he reports a visit he had from Little Hans (aged nineteen) some fourteen years later, when he found that the boy had no memory of the events of his neurosis and that he was now a fine, strapping lad. While it may strike us as a little sad, it was apparently very heartening to Freud and was clearly taken as evidence that the work undertaken with him had not only helped him at the time, but had done no harm to his development. This plea is perhaps one that not all of us would absolutely endorse today: partly because we carry on much longer treatment processes that are considerably more searching and go much deeper; and partly because we treat children that are *far* more ill than Little Hans. He was not, after all, a fundamentally ill child; on the contrary he seems to have been eminently healthy, but to have developed a transient phobia as almost any child does at some time in his early years. I think that most child analysts today would feel that the investigation of a child's mental life, the opening-up of the stream of unconscious phantasies, the intrusion of a stranger into the close intimacy of the family, has many dangers.

In summary: the case of Little Hans is a useful clinical addendum to that part of the 'Three Essays on Sexuality' that deals with infantile sexuality. It also illustrates very richly for us the quality of Freud's thought at this point and serves as an excellent prelude to the study of the work that he was writing almost simultaneously: namely, the Rat Man case, in which we will see that he makes some extremely important discoveries that are implicit in the Little Hans case but not explicitly stated. These are discoveries about the role of ambivalence, the interplay of love and hate in the formation of internal conflict. Up to this time, the concept of conflict in Freud's writing seems mainly to embrace the conflict between instinct and the outside world and the position of the ego as it tries to manage these conflicting interests under the sway of the pleasure principal.

Chapter VI

The Rat Man (Obsessional Neurosis)

The case of the Rat Man seems to have taken place in 1907, which means that it started before the treatment of Little Hans by his father under Freud's supervision. The Rat Man was in treatment for some eleven months before he himself broke it off, feeling well, able to face his exams, and to get on with his life. Freud reports in a footnote later that, like so many young men of promise, he died in the First World War. Not only is the paper itself of great interest, but we have also the extraordinary luck to have Freud's notes for the first four months, the notes that he made in the evening after he had finished his day's work. They are fascinating, and give us probably the most accurate picture that we have of Freud actually at work in his consulting room. Therefore we can attempt to draw some inferences from these notes with regard to Freud's technique, and to compare them with the technical papers that begin to appear some three or four years later.

We are perhaps struck by the way in which he starts the treatment, and in the first few sessions seems to give the patient a theoretical exposition of the method of psycho-analysis and its therapeutic rationale. Most striking perhaps is the contrast with the Dora case, for we see here that Freud was able to follow his patient almost to the exclusion of his seizing the initiative in pursuit of his own enquiries. This may be due partly to the fact that the material did tend to bubble forth from the Rat Man, and that the resistances fairly quickly turned into transference resistances, in which the patient described to Freud under great stress and distress, the phantasies he had of a sadistic and sexual nature toward him, toward his daughter, toward his mother, toward his family generally.

One notices the calmness with which Freud dealt with these transference manifestations; perhaps because of his theoretical orientation to them; viewing them, as he wrote about trans-ferences, as new editions or re-editions of past events and rela-tionships, which essentially had nothing to do with him personally. This is indeed an extremely useful attitude in dealing with the transference, but one may be inclined to think

Freud adopted an aloofness towards the material which, while protecting him from countertransference involvement, may perhaps also have screened from himself the degree of his own emotional reaction to the patient's material and behaviour. There are not many instances that one would like to pinpoint as countertransference; the meal of herring that he served him does not seem to have been a breach of technique, for one suspects that Freud may have done this with patients quite regularly at that time. We must remember that there was not as yet a concept of countertransference. That only comes later, when Freud reports, around 1915, that he has become aware of the limitations of analysts: that they are limited by their perception of their own complexes and by the consequent countertransference. He is on the other hand troubled when he notices things that he can identify as breaches of technique or lapses in function such as when he felt uncertain as to whether a certain piece of material that he recollected did in fact belong to the Rat Man or was derived from some other patient.

The use that Freud makes of the transference is a little unclear; nor can we derive from his actual handling of it any idea of his attitude other than, as already noted, its being a repetition of past experience. He certainly seems to have derived information from it: that is, information from the transference that confirmed or refuted the formulations he was already deriving from the ordinary material of the patient's associations and recollections. One feels also that he perhaps derived a very special feeling of confirmation about reconstruction, in the same sense that, say, Little Hans' illness gave him a special confirmation of the existence of the infantile neurosis, the theory of which had been derived from the reconstruction of the material of adult neurotic patients. He does not seem to have viewed the transference as following any particular process in itself, nor to have made any attempt to follow it in its own right. He was probably dealing with it mainly as transference resistance, and allowing it to spend itself, while at the same time connecting its content with previous material.

Similarly, one may be disappointed to see how little he seems to have done with the many dreams that the Rat Man brought him, both current and past. There is nothing like the almost obsessive interest that he took in the Wolf Man's dreams some years later. And the analytic attention he does give the dreams in no way resembles the systematic jigsaw puzzle method he himself described. The comments on the dream of Freud's daughter with the dung over her eyes or the dream of the Japanese swords do not strike us as being particularly imaginative or penetrating.

From the point of view of therapeutic method, Freud seems still to have been following mainly the line of unravelling the history of the symptoms and their unconscious meaning. He does claim with some pride to have cleared up the main obsessions about the rat punishment. From the point of view of Freud's functioning in the consulting room one is very struck by the amount of fragmented and incomprehensible material that he seems to have been able to hold in his mind. If one had read (which unfortunately one seldom has) the notes before reading the paper, one would undoubtedly have experienced an overwhelming confusion about the material and then been utterly amazed by the way Freud has drawn it all together in his exposition. I would venture to say that there is very little in the notes which is not covered in the exposition; if not in the descriptive part, then later in the theoretical part. This seems quite amazing when you consider that the notes in our possession run to nearly the length of the paper itself. One must consider this a special aspect of Freud's genius: that he could allow so much disparate information to enter his mind and allow it gradually, very gradually, to become organized there. It is perhaps quite different from the usual picture that we have of Freud; of someone who had things highly organized in his mind and was always searching for confirmation of his theories. Perhaps the great virtue of this case history is that it shows us a side of Freud that we are not able to see in most of his writings: that is, Freud the phenomenologist. I think that one cannot but be filled with admiration at the minuteness of the details of his observation of character and character structure. I would think that most readers are rather bored by the lengthy exposition of the incident with the spectacles at the manoeuvres; and yet Freud was able to take an interest and to get all the details straight so that he could draw a map and knew exactly what transpired in this extraordinary incident of the paying back of the 3.8 kroner.

We see that he is able not only to pay minute attention to historical events of this sort but also to the phenomena that appear in the consulting room: the use of language, the patient's behaviour. He is for instance able to recognize immediately his patient being in a state of identification with his mother; able to recognize changes in mood and the evidence of emotionality of which the Rat Man was oblivious. One is struck by his non-judgmental attitude to this young man's sexuality and sexual behaviour; not only his phantasies but his relationships with women. One is inclined to think that some of Freud's revulsion was perhaps split off, as for instance when he gives an example not from the patient's material but from that of some other patient. (He reports that this man used to take the children of friends out into the country and when it would be too late to return by train, he would stay at a hotel and masturbate the girls. He was very offended when Freud asked him whether he didn't think this was dangerous.) Well, quite clearly Freud was shocked by this man's behaviour and not sorry to see him go away and not come back. But one feels that similarly he might have been a little shocked by the Rat Man's behaviour with his dressmaker, or perhaps most of all by his lack of feeling about the suicide of the earlier dressmaker, with whom he had had a prospective liaison; but that he kept his feeling about this at bay through his clinical detachment.

On the whole, Freud seems to have liked the Rat Man very well (though he does not come over to me as a particularly likeable person). Perhaps Freud's use of a concept of splitting and seeing the man as composed of three different personalities helped him to like the one that was most present to the world, the one that he calls affable. It is of interest to note that while he uses a concept of splitting of personality here as a way of explaining the nature of the psycho-pathology, it takes him another twenty-five years, to the paper on the 'Splitting of the Ego in the Service of Defence', to take an interest in this process with regard to the question of mental health. It is an example of the extent to which Freud was a psycho-pathologist and how late in his career it was that he began to take an interest in the mysterious processes of mental health. Even in the Leonardo paper, which is perhaps the first paper in which Freud can be said to take an interest in a person as a whole, and a life as a whole integrated process, his interest in Leonardo's creativity is not taken as evidence of mental health of unusually fine quality, but as a manifestation of a particular kind of psycho-pathology that has been diverted through sublimation into useful social channels.

Freud's theoretical summing up of the Rat Man case is brilliant and beautifully organized. The most significant historical landmark is his establishment of the concept of ambivalence: a term that he says he borrowed from Bleuler. In the Rat Man he comes for the first time to a clear recognition of the conflict between love and hate as a possible basis for neurosis. This is very different from the notion of unacceptable ideas, for instance, which always implies a conflict with the outside world as the primary focus. Even castration anxiety, as expressed in Little Hans, is given an external world anchorage. If not in actual threats of mutilation by parents, it is anchored to the perception of the sexual difference in children: that is, to Hans' perception that his little sister did not have a 'widdler'. So this paper of the Rat Man presents a very great step forward in acknowledging internal conflict; conflict that is internal in its *origin* and not merely in its *development*.

The second landmark, which is perhaps more clearly discussed here than anywhere else in Freud's work, is the recognition of omnipotence. Freud describes it as omnipotence of wishes, and it gives us some clue as to why he felt that the wish was such an important factor in the dream. There is the brilliant description here of the elliptical use of language, and one can begin to grasp that he meant that a wish, particularly an omnipotent wish, was a desire that was operating elliptically to leap from its inception to its fulfilment. The use of the concept that he makes here is perhaps a little disappointing, in that he attributes importance to it only insofar as the patient appears to be frightened of his omnipotence. This would seem to imply that if he were not frightened of his omnipotence, it would not play any part in his psycho-pathology. On the other hand, he does link omnipotence to infantile development, and links it directly to what he calls the megalomania of childhood;

although I must say that it is not at all clear to me what difference he wishes to draw between omnipotence and megalomania. The great analysis of obsessional doubting is probably the finest thing ever written about obsessionality. Freud's realisation that the doubting had its root in primal ambivalence and the formula that he educes that a man who doubts his love must necessarily doubt every lesser thing, is not only brilliant but poetically expressed. He has not apparently in this paper as yet forsaken his earlier formulation that obsessional neurosis had its roots in an active rather than passive sexual experience in childhood, but one can see that this formulation is weakened considerably in favour of locating the erotism as anal erotism and connected with sadistic, voyeuristic and exhibitionistic impulses.

So one might say that Freud had come at this point to a more complicated view not only of obsessional neurosis but of mental life in general. It is in keeping with this that his examination of the Rat Man's character strikes us as such an important advance and as a prelude to the examination of character which follows in later papers, such as the famous paper on anal erotism, on character types met with in analysis, and his investigation of the character of the Wolf Man. He writes in a very interesting way here about the attitudes towards death, superstition, and religion, of the obsessional neurotic. It seems reasonable to say that one of the advances marked by this case history from the point of view of the development of Freud's clinical thought is the way in which the concept of a child is beginning to 'flesh out' rather than being the bare schematic skeleton indicated in the 'Three Essays on Sexuality'. The evidences of Freud's awareness of the importance of identification processes; the recognition of divisions in the personality; the awareness of conflicts of love and hate and the role of omnipotence in infantile phantasy; all mark an advance in the complexity and richness of thought with regard to the commands that the Rat Man received. Some of these were dangerously destructive or self-destructive, such as the command to cut his own throat, or the command to kill the old woman. My impression is (though Freud does not state it explicitly) that he thinks these commands come from a deeply unconscious and very brutal part of the Rat Man's personality, and are

59

directed to one of the two pre-conscious personalities: namely to the infantile polymorphously perverse part. I would think that in the development of his thinking in later years he would probably have viewed these commands as coming from a harsh super-ego, and this seems to be a problem of his later thought that has greatly exercised workers who have followed him. The confusion between narcissistic phenomena and sadism, or harshness, in the super-ego, is a problem that is far from resolved today.

Finally, let us note Freud's view of the role of masturbation in the genesis of the neuroses as expressed in this paper. One would say that it differs from that expressed in earlier papers on the defence neuro-psychoses, or the aetiology of hysteria. One has the impression that Freud took a relatively benign view of the role of masturbation in earlier times and was inclined to view the absence of masturbation as an important item in determining the stasis of the libido and its being diverted into symptoms and anxiety. Here it seems more clear that he views masturbation as having some noxious influence on the life processes of the Rat Man, although it is not at all clear just how it operates. The impression is that as a substitute for sexual intercourse it is felt to be inadequate and somehow unsatisfying; but there are also indications that it brings him into conflict with the memory of his father, say, as represented in that particular piece of material where the Rat Man feels that his father is outside, knocking on the door; after he opens the door for him, he goes back into the house and looks at his genitals in the mirror – which Freud takes as a substitute for masturbation. So there is the beginning of a view that masturbation brings a child into conflict with an internal authority (the father) and in this way it is a prelude to Freud's later view on the role of the super-ego in promoting castration anxiety and neurotic conflict.

In summary, then, the case of the Rat Man represents a great advance in Freud's work in many directions: in the technical direction we see that his work with patients had become very committed to following the material rather than pursuing his own interests for the purpose of solving particular riddles of reconstruction. He seems to be making some use of transference phenomena, although it is not quite clear whether he is dealing with them as resistances only or also gathering important information from them. My impression is that he views these transference experiences as playing some role in the therapeutic process. From the phenomenological point of view, one sees a great advance in Freud's attention to mental phenomena, relatively unhampered by preconceptions of the sort expressed in the 'Project for a Scientific Psychology'. Only at one point in the paper does he depart from phenomenological procedure and launch into a vast generalisation, and that is the part about the role of the sense of smell in the phylogeny of human beings, and the important role of sexuality in the genesis of neuroses. One is reminded that this way of theorising about a sense of smell has a link back to his former relation to Fleiss, which by this time (in 1909) was completely in abeyance. What are called the theoretical sections of the paper are indeed very phenomenological and trace with great clarity the meaning and the significance, from the unconscious point of view, of the patient's symptomology and character structure. The case of the Rat Man is therefore much more of a research paper than the other case histories, which are (on the contrary) more in the nature of expositions and demonstrations of existing theories.

Chapter VII   The Leonardo Paper (Narcissism)

We have now reached 1910 and I want to spend this chapter on the Leonardo case. It is a paper I always used to dislike, although I have come to think better of it after re-reading it several times. I think that the reason I balked at it originally was that it is the beginning of a very bad tradition in psychoanalysis: Freud calls it a 'psycho-pathography', an investigation into the 'psycho-pathology of great men', and if one looks at it in that light it is a somewhat unpleasant thing. Although I believe most of the things he says about Leonardo are probably quite correct, and in a sense enlightening, I do not think it requires psycho-analytic insight to reach them. The aspect that is peculiarly psycho-analytic concerns the part about the bird putting its tail in the baby Leonardo's mouth, the preoccupation with the flight of birds, his flying machines, the supposed hidden vulture in 'The Virgin and Saint Anne' and similar material. Yet the writing is not good and to my mind is not really even interesting. Therefore I want to put aside this pathography aspect of the paper, which is the only one of its sort that Freud wrote and, in many ways, is one he apologises for and dissociates himself from at the end. However, one must remember that it is an important paper historically; the beginning of that extremely bad tradition in psychoanalytic writing which consists in scrutinising the private lives of great men by supposedly psycho-analytic methods from outside the psycho-analytic setting of the transference. I think it is boring and has probably done quite a lot of harm in particular to the relationship of psycho-analysis to the arts, since it is mainly artists and writers (and to some extent politicians and historical figures) who have received such treatment.

I want to consider now the important connection between Freud and Leonardo and the way in which the paper is autobiographical. It is autobiography in that it relates to the split which I have been talking about from the very beginning of these chapters: namely, the split in Freud between the theoretician and the clinician. As I have stressed, the clinician in Freud is really an artist at work, and he does at many points in his life accuse himself of being artistic or poetic, of 'writing novels' and so on. Of this very paper he said that he was writing a psycho-analytic novel about Leonardo, and this is probably correct. However, I think that by this time in his life, the accusation of artistry, imagination and intuition did not worry him as much as it did at the beginning of his work. One can see that by this point there were really three Freuds fairly distinct from one another: Freud the artist-clinician, Freud the rather obsessional theoretician and builder of speculative systems that were supposed to be inductive theories; and thirdly, Freud the political leader, the Moses figure, concerned to start a psycho-analytic movement and keep it separate from medicine while at the same time appropriating much of the prestige and respectability from medicine: concerned also for it not to be a Jewish science while at the same time making terrific onslaughts on Christianity, as in this and in later papers (to an even fiercer degree). He was the kind of political leader who drove out deviants from the party line – such as Adler and Jung – whom he scourged over and over again in his writings, quite unnecessarily from the scientific point of view. Of these three quite distinct personalities of Freud, the really lovable one is to my mind the clinician: and it is he whom I wish to discuss.

It amuses me on reading the paper again to find that towards the end Freud described Leonardo as being at the 'summit' of his life when he was painting the Mona Lisa and having what Freud called 'renewed sexual drives': that is, when in his early fifties, which was Freud's age when he wrote the paper (54). For indeed it was in the Leonardo paper that the evolution of the concept of narcissism was first stated, the beginning of a new surge in Freud himself. Moreover, I believe the Leonardo paper is the beginning of a new attitude in Freud to psychoanalysis as something that investigates the whole person and his whole life. From that point of view, the pathography – the attempt to describe a whole person and his whole life – is really a very important effort on Freud's part. I am accordingly inclined to view it as amongst the case histories, although only derivatively in that it uses material from outside the analytic setting and is thus in the same class as, for instance, the Schreber case. It is not clinical work inside the consulting room, but it is clinical thinking, and the data is drawn from literary work (mainly from Leonardo's notebooks and his paintings). Freud investigates Leonardo's life taking into account what other people (as Vasari in his 'Life') have said about his paintings. It is an application of psycho-analytic thought to a certain type of data. And while one must naturally bear in mind that to try to draw out the life of a person from such shreds as these seems too ambitious when an analysis takes years and thousands of hours of careful listening, nevertheless the idea of trying to understand a whole person and his whole life – the idea of the psycho-analytic biography (as opposed to the idea of psycho-analytic pathography) is not in itself a bad one. It presents a new dimension for psycho-analytic thought. As I say, when it is applied to psycho-analytic scholarship, I do not like it; I think it is wrong and has initiated a bad tradition which includes that of psycho-analytic art criticism. This pays too much attention to the content in art and not enough attention to the more important formal aspects, which psycho-analysis is not really in a position to approach.

Therefore if we consider the paper as Freud's attempt to see psycho-analysis as a science which tries to understand the whole person and his whole life, and if we recognize that Freud, in his choice of Leonardo, is seeing something which is greatly troubling him about himself – namely the split between the investigator or what he called the 'Conquistador', and the artist – then we shall be going in a very important direction. We come up against the two most interesting aspects of the paper: the first being the discussion of the relation between the search for knowledge and emotionality; and this is a point of paramount importance with regard to the understanding of Mrs Klein's work. In preparation for this I will now spend some time investigating this last point about curiosity and the search for knowledge; its relationship to emotions, and particularly its relationships to love and hate. Towards the end of the chapter I will talk a little about the second interesting feature: namely, Freud's early and, in a sense, crude formulation of the concept of narcissism, which is also embodied in the paper.

Freud pays a lot of attention to something for which I think there is no evidence at all: namely, that Leonardo had a sexless life. All the evidence seems to suggest that he was a homosexual; he was even accused and tried on that account, although acquitted; and during his life was always surrounded by beautiful boys whom he obviously loved. If you read his diaries you will see that he not only loved them but was incredibly patient with them – a point on which Freud touches. There was one nasty little boy, only ten or eleven years old, who was constantly stealing everything he could lay his hands on in Leonardo's studio, yet Leonardo was always bailing him out of trouble, buying him shirts, materials, jackets and suchlike. I believe that Leonardo was probably assumed to be homosexual by his contemporaries, and although homosexuality was then a legal offence, it was not really a social offence to any great extent at all. For example, one of the subsequent famous painters was nicknamed Sodoma because he was a known sodomite.

The emphatic assumption which Freud makes in viewing Leonardo's emotionally impaired sexual life as being related to the scientist-investigator in him and linked to sexual curiosity and the sexual researches of children, is in my opinion unsound. He seems to assume that Leonardo's own statement about the necessity for love to be subsumed under knowledge (a point about which Dr Bion writes) actually means that love *ought* to be subsumed under knowledge, and that one should not love an object until one understands it thoroughly, so that one can then love it for its 'true' qualities. As far as one can see there is no evidence whatsoever to bear out the idea that Leonardo actually lived in this way, or that he was capable of living within the pinched confines of his theory. There is no reason to suppose that during his life as an artist his feuds and intimacies were not as passionate (even if not as noisy) as those of Michelangelo; and certainly the hatred which these two entertained for one another was never doubted by their contemporaries, although Michelangelo was noisy and Leonardo was icy and aloof about it.

Freud makes a very important move here, in that he tries to distinguish between the kind of love which can result from really knowing the true qualities of an object (and loving it for these true qualities), and those conflicting emotions which in fact accompany human relationships. In identifying these last he links them to instinct, by which one assumes he means the feelings that are linked with infantile sexuality: that is to say, love and hate. What he does not distinguish between at this point is curiosity and the thirst for knowledge (that is, the desire to know the truth). Therefore, to refer this to his study of Leonardo, Freud makes no distinction between Leonardo's endless curiosity about everything; which, as is quite clear from his notebooks, included alchemy, witchcraft, necromancy and all sorts of black magic (facts hardly mentioned by Freud); and his genuine thirst for knowledge. For it seems clear that Leonardo was someone whose thirst for knowledge and whose childish curiosity were not differentiated from one another, running hand in hand just as rampantly as his childish pre-occupation with toys, all sorts of practical jokes, and startling pyrotechnics ran hand in hand with his most serious scientific investigations and his art work.

The reason Freud felt no necessity for differentiating between Leonardo's childish curiosity and the greatness of his most mature accomplishments (which were always intermingled with one another) is that this differentiation did not exist in Freud's own mind. The result is that his attitude to children's curiosity about sexuality is not at all one that distinguishes a category of hostile intrusiveness on the one hand, from desiring to know and understand the truth on the other. It is at this time that the addendum was made to the 'Three Essays' about children's sexuality and the sexual researches of children. But the very fact that he called them 'sexual researches' infuses them with a dignity indicating that he did not make a differentiation between children's destructive and intrusive curiosity and their loving and awestruck desire to understand and know the nature of the world. This is partly due to the fact that Freud saw this curiosity as arising somewhere around the third year; and he therefore tended to link it to either the birth or the expectation of the next baby and thus to his theory that the little boy (the little girl is forgotten), seeing that his little sister does not have a penis, is mobilized into castration anxiety. This, Freud speculated, drives him first of all to try to find out about the internal world, and secondly, with the onset of latency and its impaired curiosity and desire for knowledge in this area, to abandon finding out. Now I do not think Freud has any evidence for this. He tends to go back to the case of Little Hans, but I think there the evidence is, if anything, that the researches of Little Hans had started long before his third year; and that everything Little Hans was saying about being with his sister in the carriage, and the stork box, contains phantasies that probably long antedate his sister's birth and which are to a certain extent retrospective phantasies. They try, on the basis of later experience, to account for things he observed earlier in his life.

We reach the paper on the Wolf Man; at which point one sees that Freud himself invokes this idea of retrospective curiosity; he construes from the evidence that the Wolf Man made observations at the age of one and a half which he only began to understand retrospectively at the age of four; and that the famous 'wolf' dream was an attempt to understand something that he had observed at the age of one and a half, possibly at the age of six months, or at the latest two and a half. Thus Freud acknowledges that children make observations at a very early age which continue to puzzle them; and later they make other observations with which they go back to resolve the puzzles that had arisen earlier. According to Freud's theory at this point (1910), we are still to assume that this curiosity is about where babies come from; that it is not in fact aroused until the mother's next pregnancy (or if no pregnancy occurs, the child is still assumed to expect one for some reason that is not given) and that the child is therefore driven primarily by jealousy. It is, according to Freud, the resentment of the birth of this next baby (the expulsion from possession of the mother), and the discoveries about the differences between the sexes (in the case of the little boy having a little sister whose genital he sees and the resultant castration anxiety with its resentment) that cause the curiosity; in other words, it is caused by anxiety and hostility, by jealousy, resentment and the anxiety of castration and of expulsion in favour of the new baby. Since Freud's idea seems to be that this curiosity is fundamentally driven by anxiety and hatred, it is very puzzling that he should think of it as something that should drive the child in the direction of wanting to discover the truth. For his whole theory of repression is based on the assumption that there is a certain necessity or desire to defend *against* knowing the truth (which is also true of his theory of dream formation). And his theory about defence against anxiety entails the defence being made by a distortion of the truth. The theory of repression is mainly a theory of serial distortion of the truth, so that memories are forgotten or else (if they break through the repression) they emerge in a distorted form. Accordingly, the transference is this: the return of the repressed in a distorted form that is not the truth, but is permissible because it has undergone a certain amount of distortion; and it is therefore also equivalent to a dream which is able to enter consciousness for the very reason that it is the truth distorted; and so on. It is very puzzling that children's curiosity should be called 'researches', in the service of the discovery of the truth, when at the same time he is suggesting that it is driven by anxiety and resentment, all the hatred of the oedipus complex and fear of the birth of a new baby.

When Mrs Klein wrote her first paper in 1921, which was not really an analytic paper but a child observation paper, for some reason, probably through an ignorance of philosophy and perhaps also of Freud's work, she started out without preconceptions about these matters, and observed that a child has a thirst for knowledge which is in the first instance the desire to know all about the mother's body. This thirst for knowledge she thought instinctual in origin but driven by other instincts, first of all by the child's sadism and later by its reparative desires. It is one of the major differences between the work of Mrs Klein and Freud: namely, that a great deal of her work stems from this observation that emotional and intellectual growth are driven by the conflict between love and hate of the mother's body and person. She does say that a certain level of anxiety is necessary for growth and development, but that it is moved by love, and this is the foundation of her concept of the depressive position. The love of the object, and the wish to spare, to serve, to emulate, to give pleasure, is the main driving force in psychic development beyond the more primitive levels.

I draw your attention to this at this point in order to compare it with what is in my opinion the clearest statement in the whole of Freud's writings of his theory of knowledge. His theory of knowledge is not based on a wide philosophical study; he does not write about curiosity or the desire for knowledge with any regard to epistemological theories of the past. It is a purely psycho-analytical theory, to my mind a bad one, which is inconsistent with many of the other facets of his thinking about mental functioning.

In this paper, Freud takes Leonardo to task for his theory of love: that love breaks forth after the full knowing and recognition of the object's true qualities, and is based on this knowledge; and claims that this is not what happens. On the contrary both love and hate are connected with impulses, he says. It is noteworthy that in Freud's work he never does come to a real theory of affects as a central phenomenon in mental functioning; they are seen merely as a by-product of impulse life. At this point he is talking about love and hate and dealing with them as he did in the Rat Man paper, as being at the core of mental conflict. But he does not really think of this conflict as being essentially the loving and the hating in conflict with one another; he is thinking essentially of the impulses, of which the affects are no more than the noise. It is the impulses which are in conflict with one another. So in this respect he has not really come a great distance from his earlier tendency to think of affects as merely manifestations of different levels of excitation in the mental apparatus and therefore fundamentally quantitative rather than qualitative. He has moved a slight distance in recognizing the qualitative distinction between the affects in so far as they relate to different impulses, and are as it were the banners carried by these impulses; each with their different colours, patterns and different kind of noises; but he is not giving them a status of their own nor thinking of the conflict as being essentially emotional conflict. It is still impulse conflict and conflict between the impulse life and the requirements of the outside world. I think it is always important to keep this aspect of Freud's work in mind: that he never came to view anxiety as an affect, but saw it at first as a transformation of impulse, and then later, as a signal and therefore a type of internal information. Even when he passed on to a broader consideration of mental pain, it was tied to the concept of cathexis and thus with excessive accretions of stimuli. This is all relevant to the small section of the first chapter of the Leonardo paper where Freud mentions Leonardo's repression of affects and connects it with his obsessionality and the cold-bloodedness of his investigations: as when he would go to watch men being hanged and tortured in order to study their facial expressions. Furthermore, when he later comes to talk about the expressions on the faces of the Mona Lisa or Saint Anne, Freud discusses them for the purpose of revealing the extent to which Leonardo's emotions were repressed or not available to him, and documents his thesis in a way that is most unconvincing. Take for example the way in which he uses Leonardo's reporting his father's death in his diary with the repetition of 'at seven o'clock' as evidence of emotional repression and of Leonardo not being in contact with his feelings about his father's death. To my mind that is very poor psychoanalytic evidence; and is probably more accurately to be taken as demonstrating the way in which the theoretician in Freud can interfere with his respect for the evidence and the data. This part of the paper is nonetheless worthwhile re-reading, because of its instructiveness concerning Freud's idea of love, and its connection with his persistent idea about sublimation. The theory of sublimation is enlarged upon in this paper probably more explicitly than anywhere else.

At this point, however, I wish to turn to the section of the paper dealing with the origin of Leonardo's homosexuality. Freud deals with it as *latent* homosexuality, as homosexual relationships but not homosexual activities. Freud means, as you remember, 'inverted object choice'; and as we see from the 'Three Essays', he does not make any distinction between the man's femininity and the man's homosexuality. Moreover, the concept he produces with regard to Leonardo is one of Leonardo's being narcissistically identified with an androgenous mother, or a rather hermaphrodite figure.

The theory he evokes runs something like this: that Leonardo, an illegitimate child, born to a poor peasant girl, spent the first five years of his life being cuddled and kissed by his mother. There is no evidence at all for this, which is a point to bear in mind although it is irrelevant here since we are talking about Freud's theory of the origins of a particular type of homosexuality. He chose, perhaps quite wrongly, to use Leonardo as if he were a suitable example of it and we should not consider its application to Leonardo himself as serious. What Freud is describing is a little boy without a father, or with a very weak father in his life, who is rather pushed out of the picture by his weakness on the one hand and the mother's androgenous strength and capability on the other; she devotes her entire attention to the little boy and is both gratifying to him and erotically exciting, evoking an intense mutual idealization. At a certain point this little boy begins to have sexual feelings toward his mother; but up to this point it had never occurred to him that she does not have a penis; he is assuming that she does have a penis, and this assumption somehow has the same effect upon him as does the oedipus complex of another child, and brings about castration anxiety and the repression of his sexuality. And the repression of his sexuality is implemented primarily by means of his identification with the mother, so that his sexuality takes the form of seeking for an object that will be for him the ideal little boy that he was for his mother. It seems to me a good theory; and I am sure that it plays an important part in the genesis of certain types of very motherly homosexuality in men.

I wish to point out that this is the first statement about narcissism: that is, that the person loves a little boy who represents himself, and is therefore loving himself in the boy that he chooses as his sexual object. But it is a theory of narcissism in which is inherent an assumption of an identification; therefore the first theory of narcissism is not just a theory of him loving himself; it is a theory of being identified with the mother and loving himself as does the mother. Later on when we come to the development of Freud's theory of narcissism we will see that it changes; but this is the first statement, and the first statement is of particular importance because it brings out an aspect of narcissism which he tended to neglect later. As we go through the Schreber case and the Wolf Man we will see that the theory of narcissism begins to be filled out phenomenologically, but this idea of identification, which is very central to it, is somewhat lost. However, it is worth noting that at this point, in the first statement of narcissism, 'narcissistic identification' plays a central role. And thirty-six years later this will develop into Mrs Klein's concept of projective identification as the first description of a mechanism for the accomplishment of a narcissistic identification.

I would like now to say a few words about the ending of the Leonardo paper. I find this very moving; where Freud talks about how he has written a psycho-analytic novel and steps back to take a look at what he has been doing; what he has accomplished and what he has failed to accomplish. What he has to say indicates a very important realization about the nature of psycho-analysis and one which seems to me to have come to him for the first time at this point. Freud undoubtedly had ·a very strong tendency to think of psycho-analysis as an explanatory science; and all through his work he talks as if it were so. An explanatory science would imply the possibility of prediction, and the idea that psycho-analytic reconstruction would be essentially a demonstration of the inevitability of the person's life-history. I think that this is the only point in Freud's writings where he specifically says that this is not true. There are one or two other places where he talks about chance and fate, but this is the most specific instance in which he states that fate and chance play an overwhelming role in life; and that what psycho-analysis describes is 'what happens'; it does not explain 'why it happens'; and it does not cite the causes of things. So that, had circumstances been different, had the person's constitution been different, had other decisions been made, had other factors entered, the whole life-history could have been different.

Chapter VIII   The Schreber Case (Inner World)

It is of course with a reservation in mind that one includes the Schreber case among Freud's clinical papers, since its content does not relate to experiences in the course of analytical treatment. Freud himself, in a somewhat disingenuous way justifies both its use and the intrusion upon the privacy of the subject, Dr Schreber; but one can see that he was quite enthralled by the 'Memoirs' with special reference to the problem which exercised him – perhaps excessively – all through his scientific life: namely that of 'choice of neurosis'. However, it is not from this point of view that I wish to examine the paper, but rather from a more phenomenological one. In a certain sense, Freud was so occupied with using the case as material for exposition that he does not fully explore its rich content. Or at least he does not follow through this exploration. As the prelude to the theory of narcissism it stands close to the Rat Man in approaching a concept of splitting processes, and it is unique among Freud's writings in approaching a concept of 'the world' as an aspect of mental life.

Schreber's illness, which first manifest itself as a severe hypochondria, metamorphosed during its second phase into a paranoid deterioration, the chief persecutor of which was his previous physician, and then slowly underwent an elaboration into a grandiose delusional system in which the figure of God played a highly ambiguous role: half persecutor, half lover. It is characteristic of Freud's boldness that he could take an interest in these highly bizarre phenomena on the basis of an assumption that they were, nonetheless, comprehensible derivatives of the common impulses of the human mind. But while it is a bold stand, it may also be accused of a certain pedestrian determination which emerges at times, even to Freud's embarrassment, as when he has to apologise to the reader for the interpretation that the sun, whose rays Schreber boasts of being able to look upon with his naked eyes, is in the last analysis a symbol for the father. This reductionism is, of course, typical of Freud and one may cite this case as the most cogent example of the way in which his theory of symbolism tends to take the life out of things. Thus the defence for examining the 'Memoirs' as 'derivative' of common human impulses neglects the opposite possibility, namely that just such complex constructions may always, in some less disordered way, underlie the phenomenology of mental health. For instance, Freud consistently refers to Schreber's delusion of being transformed into a woman as a process of 'emasculation', but it is quite clear that in Schreber's mind the removal of his masculine attributes was a simple process compared with the complexity of endowing him with femininity. This represents then the same limited view that infuses all of Freud's views on sexuality: castration complex, children's sexual researches, etc. It can be traced to the preconception that femininity is essentially passive and derivative, a view quite in keeping with the history of Hellenic, Judaic and Christian thought. For instance it is of interest to note how similar in many ways is Schreber's cosmology and anatomy to that of Plato, as described in the *Timaeus*, in which the congruence between man and God is described in detail. The chief difference is perhaps that in his ambivalence to God, Schreber attributes to him the defect that he does not understand living creatures but only dead ones. His assumption that the 'basic language of God' is an antiquated German is not different from the Judaeo-Christian one that Hebrew was the universal language before God punished the people of Babylon for their presumptuous tower by inflicting the confusion of tongues, which Jesus then rectified for his apostles by his 'gift of tongues'. Our modern counterpart is perhaps Chomsky's universal generative grammar.

Thus it is that Schreber's relations to God and the sun may be viewed not as a boring elaboration of a child's relation to its father but as indeed a fascinating description, marred by intense ambivalence, of an elaborate unconscious phantasy, with its multiple splitting, variety of qualities and attributes, and diversity of functions, which underlies the conscious, simplistic conception. One need only take into account the reversal, by which God becomes childish and Schreber emerges victorious from their struggle, to see the normal child's conflict. But this reversal, with its attendant confusions, is not quite correctly seen by Freud with respect to the question of voluptuousness, for it is quite clear that Schreber has equated the voluptuousness of defaecation with that of the feminine experience in coitus. Correspondingly his sexual relation to God is that of a concubine, not a wife, as Freud insists. Amusingly, the subject of confusion of zones and functions only emerges as a joke about futility of interpretation: 'holding a sieve under a he-goat while someone else milks it'. One must consider that Freud had no conceptual framework as yet for differentiating between feminine and homosexual in Schreber's case, although he could easily see that contempt for women (the miracle birds, emphasis on the buttocks as the genital area, attribution of preoccupation with voluptuousness) was essential. This lack of differentiation mars the value of the important conclusion Freud was so keen to put forward: namely the connection between paranoia and passive homosexuality. Consequently the 'simple formula' by which love is turned into hate takes on a rather gimmicky quality. The concept of 'homosexual libido' has to be linked to castration anxiety and Adler's 'masculine protest' in order to explain the anxiety and revulsion it arouses. Because of this Freud's investigation of the means by which the 'reconciliation' between the paranoid and the grandiose delusional illnesses was brought about, loses much of its force.

But this brings us to the most fascinating and brilliant part of the paper, the 'world destruction' phantasy and Freud's investigation of its nature and consequences. Having noted the similarity between the structure of Flechsig and God in the two periods of the illness, Freud concluded that the development of the paranoia was related to a process of 'decomposition' or, more precisely, that 'paranoia resolves once more into their elements the products of the condensations and identifications which are effected in the unconscious' (i.e. in the course of development, I take it). This 'decomposition' is first investigated from the point of view of regression of the libido to the stage of narcissism as a development midpoint between autoerotism and object-love – a view he had already put forward in the 1910 edition of the 'Three Essays on Sexuality'. The defensive process against this regression is seen as aimed at the renewed 'sexualisation of the social instincts'. The 'simple formula' for turning love into hate is produced here and elaborated later in the paper on 'Jealousy, Paranoia and Homosexuality' (1922). To this formula he needed only add the concept of projection as an externalisation of an internal perception, to derive a satisfy-ing explanation of paranoia. And here we find his most detailed account of the relation of fixation, repression and eruption; or the 'return of the repressed'. It is in relation to this last that Freud discusses the 'world destruction' phantasy. (Here I believe there is an important error in translation: p. 68 reads '. . . and during the last part of his stay in Flechsig's clinic he believed "that the catastrophe had already occurred and he was the only real man alive." ' It should read: 'and at the climax of his illness he believed that the catastrophe had occurred during the last part of his stay . . .'). Freud writes that 'the end of the world is the "projection of his internal catas-trophe" ' but hedges about its mechanism. In the text he attri-butes it to Schreber's 'withdrawal of his love' from his 'sub-jective world' but in a footnote, where he quotes a poem from Goethe's 'Faust', it is attributed to the work of a 'powerful fist'. It is the rebuilding of this shattered 'subjective world' that is the work of the delusion formation. 'The paranoiac builds it again, not more splendid, it is true, but at least so that he can once more live in it'.

This brilliant analysis of the mechanisms by which the transition from the early paranoid to the later grandiose de-lusion is effected is, I think, the farthest point of advance in Freud's conceptualising of the mental apparatus and adum-brates the work on cyclothymia in 'Mourning and Melan-cholia', while providing the jumping-off place for Abraham's last work and the developments of Melanie Klein. One must go back to the statement that 'paranoia resolves once more into their elements the products of the condensations and identifi-cations that are effected in the unconscious' to see that Freud held some theory of how the 'subjective world' is constructed in the course of development.

Thus we can see that the wonderful step forward, from the clinical point of view, represented by the Schreber case, is that of the conceptualisation of the inner world: the formulation of projection as a mechanism, and the introduction into the con-cept of narcissism of a new concreteness related to 'condensa-tions and identifications'; it is, nonetheless, somewhat attenu-ated by the restrictions imposed by the Libido Theory. The new theory proposed in 1920 in 'Beyond the Pleasure Principle' freed him from this restriction and enabled a new, more complicated approach to the comprehension of the perversions, by way of the phenomenon of masochism and its relation to destructive impulses. Here in the Schreber case he is hard pressed to account for the fact that the world destruction phantasy came *between* the delusions of persecution and the grandiose system. He falls back on the idea of a partial detachment of the libido and gets into something of a muddle in relation to 'ego-cathexes' and 'cathexes of the ego'. In the hedging about the 'fist' smashing the world to bits in paranoid fury, we can see Freud's chief difficulty and link it to his lack of conceptual equipment of a concrete inner or 'subjective' world that could be so smashed. Shaken by these difficulties, Freud ends his attempt at formulation with wryly noting the striking similarity between Schreber's delusions and Freud's theories in so far as the one lays so much emphasis on the 'rays of God' and the other on 'distribution of the libido'. 'It remains for the future to decide whether there is more delusion in my theory than I should like to admit or whether there is more truth to Schreber's delusion than other people are as yet prepared to believe'.

Chapter IX

Mourning and Melancholia
(Identification Processes)

I would like to discuss now that rather interesting period in the early years of the First World War when Freud had very few patients, since his students were mainly from abroad, and when he had time to think and take stock of the science which he had fathered – or mothered. He realized that there were great difficulties in every direction: in the training direction, in the theoretical direction, in the technical direction and also in conceiving its place in the world and what it might reasonably mean as part of the culture. He had been considerably stirred up earlier by the so-called defections of Adler and Jung and in the years from 1910 or 1911 onward there are outbursts against them in his writings every once in a while. They are interesting outbursts because their content often suggests that he is reviling them for just those things about which he is really troubled himself and with which he has not yet come to grips. For example, much of what he reviles Jung for will in fact later turn into his revision of instinct theory, although it is of course not quite the same as Jung's theory. He is reviling Jung for abandoning the central role of sexuality, the Libido Theory and so on in favour of something that he considered to be a watered-down, popularly acceptable product. Twelve or fifteen years later, it changes in his own hands into the new instinct theory, in which sexuality is not given this primary place but has to take its position within the life instincts and be opposed to what he calls the 'death instinct'. Similarly in his reviling of Adler, mainly for his masculine protest and his will-to-power theories, one finds the harbingers of Freud's later struggle with the whole problem of hatred and evil and destructiveness, which finally became the concept of the death instinct.

Therefore, even though it is rather annoying to see him stop and beat these fellows every once in a while as one goes through his writings, it is interesting to study the content of his irritation, which reveals something about his character. When he was at his most positive and authoritative – even authoritarian – he was often on the verge of having the greatest doubts and misgivings and throwing himself into the problem of revising his own thinking. A considerable amount of this sort of beating goes on in the period from 1911 to 1913, and then begins a whole series of 're-thinking' papers. I do not want to spend much time on the re-thinking and re-formulating papers and I am not going to discuss the technical papers, though these are interesting because one can see that when faced with the problem of training people to practise analysis he really had to think about his own technique. This brought him up against the problem I have been highlighting throughout these chapters: namely, the split between what he did and what he said or thought he did. In these technical papers he resolves this split quite substantially. There are papers on transference love and starting analysis, dream analysis, the new concept of 'working through'. These are important because they represent his realization that (as he said) just presenting the solution is not the end of the analyst's task. You remember that he earlier scolded Elizabeth and Dora because they did not accept his solution (and the dream of Irma's injection revolves around this problem). Now, however, he reaches the conclusion that these intellectual solutions in themselves do not constitute the analytical method; but that the whole economic task of enabling the patient to accept and to make use of these insights for bringing the unconscious into consciousness (as he was then thinking about it) is also the task of the analyst. One can not just throw the patient out once the jigsaw puzzle has been solved to the analyst's amusement or satisfaction. Therefore these technical papers are very interesting.

And then there is the series of 'metapsychological papers'. Not until this time did Freud decide that he was founding a quite new branch of psychology, which had to be distinguished from other psychologies because it was based on different kinds of data and method. Also, it was characterised by its concern with four different categories of mental functioning, which at that time he was calling: the topographic (or different levels of consciousness); the dynamics (mechanisms of mental functioning); the genetic or developmental; and the economic. So, although they are fairly theoretical, these papers are also of technical interest, particularly the paper on repression. And I would like to try to extract the changing view of the world and of life that is hidden and embodied in his theories of this time, when by virtue of coming to a conviction about the importance of the phenomenology of narcissism, Freud was just on the verge of a complete remodelling of his conception of the mind. The change from the so-called topographic model to what we now call the structural conception of ego, id and super-ego, was brewing.

It seems to have been the phenomenology of narcissism that most impressed and moved him; and the paper on narcissism is an attempt to gather together what he had already been saying for four – or perhaps five – years. Part of it had been stated in the analysis of the Schreber memoirs, yet more in the Leonardo paper, and now in this paper he draws it together with some of the ordinary life phenomena – as in his discussion of falling ill, falling in love and hypochondria. From them he abstracts a conception of the development of the capacity for instincts to seek objects starting with a period of primary narcissism (later 'auto-erotism'), in which identification with objects is almost indistinguishable from the choice of an object (in the first instance the body of the person himself).

In reading this paper one sees some very interesting aspects of the change in Freud's conception of the world. He is uneasy about his previous ambition, so much of which was previewed in the 'Project' of 1897. He is struggling still (as later in the paper on 'Mourning and Melancholia') with the whole question of mental pain and is still inclined to think of it as un-pleasure and in terms of excitation. In one place he even calls it 'painful unpleasure' – by which time he is at least acknowledging that it really hurts, and that it plays an important part in the processes of the mind. However, the whole issue of mental pain is thrown into a state of disorder in his mind by his coming at this time upon the tricky and difficult problem of identification: that is, the problem of 'whose pain is it really?'. It is from this angle that he discusses the question of being in love and particularly the question of hypochondria, which I think Freud handles with very canny intelligence, recognizing that it involves the problem of 'who is ill?' and 'who is suffering?' There is present in hypochondria the same phenomenon that he is going to discuss later in 'Mourning and Melancholia'. In the relation of mania and melancholia he saw a certain commerce in mental pain: that is, necessitating the questions 'who

is having the pleasure?', and 'what really happens to the pain?'.
Owing to the fact that he is becoming aware that pain is something that can be distributed – that the person in whom it
originates is not merely stuck with it, but can get rid of it in
some way – he is also aware that the neuroses which he has
been studying all these years are not just problems of a person
defending himself against having mental pain or unacceptable
ideas or repellent memories, but in so far as there is a problem
about mental pain there is also a problem about its distribution.
For although there are means (mainly by the mechanism of
repression) of remaining unaware of the pain that is going on
in oneself, there are also other methods of getting rid of it into
various objects in the outside world; there is a certain trans-
portation of mental pain, not simply defence against it. Its
location can be shifted, rather than its existence denied.

If we return to the Rat Man and the clinical notes on the
case, we will see that Freud was acutely aware that this played
an important part in the transference: that the transference
had not simply an ideational content (that is, phantasies that
were transferred on to the analyst), but that it also involved a
commerce in mental pain. In those notes it is apparent that
Freud was aware that his patient was causing him distress.
When he describes in his discussion of obsessional neurosis
what he calls the 'isolating of the affects' (separating the affects
from the phantasy and ideational content) he was quite aware
that these affects were going somewhere, particularly in so far
as they were painful. The patient was imposing on Freud very
painful affects; humiliating him, angering him by degrading
his love objects: his wife, his daughters and so on. He was
acutely aware that his carrying the transference was not simply
a matter of his being the object of the patient's erotic desires
or castration anxiety. One can but admire his impressive
patience and good humour. So it seems to me that by this time,
Freud at work was much more aware that his business was with
the economics of mental pain and that pain is not merely
absence of pleasure and the result of too much or too little
stimulation in the psychic apparatus.

I have already suggested how Freud became aware, particularly in the Schreber case, of the need to conceptualise a
person's world; and that this became necessary because he saw

how the world was either falling to pieces or being knocked to pieces for Schreber. We have Freud's brilliant realisation that it was this rebuilding, in a very bizarre way, of the 'subjective' inner world that had fallen to pieces, that created the noisy delusional part of the illness, the attempt at recovery. I suggested that in the earlier paper on Leonardo he had become aware of the necessity for trying to conceive of a person's life as a continuity and an entity; it was not possible as he had thought initially just to tease out little memories and little theories of events, and link them to symptoms; this was not a task commensurate with the stature of psycho-analytic thought and the expectations and hopes of those people who were attracted to it. Psycho-analysis had to become a discipline which undertook to try to understand and construct theories about all the evidence which it elicited. Consequently Freud became preoccupied not only with symptoms but with character. We have the paper on 'Character and Anal Erotism'; then a few years later a lovely paper called 'Character Types Met With in Analysis', in which he gives a round description of character types which we all know very well, having been all three of them ourselves at different times: one describes 'The Exceptions', who think that what applies to other people does not apply to them because they are special; another, 'Criminals from a Sense of Guilt'; and the third, 'People who are Wrecked by Success'. The people described here are all familiar: people in whose characters these different facets are such dominating and persistent features that their whole lives become coloured by them – whereas you and I only suffer from them every few minutes.

So one sees that Freud's interest was extending at this period: not only to character, but to anthropology, to the history of comparative religion, to the problem of art and creativity, to civilization as a process about which his 19th-Century optimism was waning. His interest in life and his wish to apply psycho-analysis to everything that came within his ken at this time is quite clear. Moreover, one receives the impression that the phenomenology of narcissism as he had met with it in the Schreber case and in his attempts to understand homosexuality on the one hand, and creativity on the other, in Leonardo; combined with the narcissistic phenomena that he had come upon in relation to such things as falling in love, hypochondria and people's behaviour during physical illness, moved him towards thinking of the mind in a much more organized way. It is only around 1915 that the view with which we are now so familiar, of the libido developing in progressive stages of organization (instead of there merely being trends in infantile sexuality) emerged as part of his thinking. The step of beginning to think of the mind in an organized and not merely in an operational way, was leading Freud to dissatisfaction with the topographic theory with its overwhelming preoccupation with levels of consciousness and its psycho-pathology. This was too narrow a framework.

Now I would like to turn our particular attention to the rather marvellous paper on 'Mourning and Melancholia' and, through both this and the paper 'On Narcissism', to focus upon three problems with which Freud tried to grapple. The most important of these, as already mentioned, and one which actually gave him trouble in his clinical work, is the problem of identification; secondly, the concept of the ego-ideal is beginning to develop and will become later the concept of the super ego; and there is, finally, the attempt to come more firmly to grips with the problem of mental pain.

Even before the Schreber case, in a sporadic way, it is clear that Freud felt the necessity of accounting for people's sense of being observed and watched. In a way, it is a remarkable thing that no inkling of the idea of conscience enters into his work for the first twenty years. It is only now, in 1919, under the pressure of these clinical phenomena, of people feeling themselves to be scrutinized, watched over and criticized in a rather paranoid way, that he feels the need to bring together two concepts which have been rather held apart in his thinking to date. He had produced the theory of the dream censor; then there was something called castration anxiety (which some unspecified figure of phantasy was mobilizing). Now he singles out these phenomena of feeling observed and scrutinized. But he is also aware of yet another phenomenon which needs to be accounted for and linked closely with the above, one that has to do with quite the opposite: namely, feeling encouraged and supported. His first attempt to deal with this is in the concept of the ideal ego. This is quite different from the ego ideal; the ideal ego is connected with a conception of the golden times of the past, of the time when His Majesty the baby was courted and enjoyed the megalomania, the narcissism and the omnipotence that is, as it were, the right of every baby. The conception of this idealized self, and the wish to recover that state of bliss and universal admiration, is formulated as the concept of the ideal-ego. And from this, by reversing the idea, comes the concept of the ego-ideal. It stands outside the ego or self and keeps pointing to the ideal-ego, saying, 'You used to be like that, so blissful, and you can become like that again'. Thus the ego-ideal is a rather gentle and encouraging figure, and Freud somehow manipulates the concept of narcissism so that the relation between the self and the ego-ideal begins to be something like a love relationship. Indeed, it is something very similar to what he describes in Leonardo's relationship to his boys, in which the artist is seen to be identified with his mother, loving and idealizing him as a little boy. Freud begins to think that this is within the realm of narcissism; that the ego and the ego-ideal (with the conception of the ideal ego in mind, as it were) can enter into a sort of blissful love relationship which, since it has to do with states of bliss or elation, is part of the phenomenology of narcissism. And he is thinking, perhaps, that this may be the core or substance of happiness.

This bears an important relation to his general idea of love at this time: because nowhere in his conceptions of it does loving develop beyond this seeking for gratification. And although he talks about loving, in libido terms, as the object being invested not only with the object libido but also with the ego libido, so that the ego becomes depleted and impoverished in favour of the object, yet to his mind this is always done with the aim of getting it back again. The move is thus a sort of capital investment aimed at obtaining a profit; you cannot exactly think of yourself as a benefactor of mankind when, by loving, you set up a factory, as it were, rather than endowing a charity. Freud's attachment to the Libido Theory, which must seek to explain things simply on the basis of the distribution of libido, binds him to the idea that mental pain is radically connected to maldistribution of the libido; that the absence of pleasure derives from either a dammed-up libido or – as he is thinking at this stage – from a drained-out and impoverished libido. And it is precisely because he is bound to this energetics theory that it is not possible for him to construct within its framework a conception of love that goes beyond enlightened self-interest. It remains really for Mrs Klein's formulation of the depressive position to carry psycho-analysis over that hump.

Now Freud keeps within this conception of an observing agency: one that stands outside the self criticizing or, as he was still thinking of it, encouraging; and he sees that it has something to do with identification processes. He actually calls them narcissistic identifications by this stage; and proceeds in the paper on 'Mourning and Melancholia' to the quite brilliant dissection of these four stages of mind: the melancholic state and its relation to the mourning state; the manic state and its relation to bliss, ecstasy and triumph over adversity. The discovery he seems to make – and one which I find most compelling myself – is as follows: though the melancholic and the person in mourning are strikingly similar in appearance, on careful examination one finds first of all that they are not in pain in the same way; that the pain of the melancholic has something to do with a depletion of himself, whereas that of the person in mourning arises because, owing to the loss of his love object from the world, the world has become empty. It would seem that the melancholic depletes himself through somehow becoming identified and completely mixed up with an object that is not experienced plainly as lost, but as depleted, denigrated, reviled and accused.

At this point in the differentiation it seems that Freud himself becomes very mixed-up, being unsure whether it is the ego accusing or, the ego-ideal turning against the ego. However, the relevant point is that he has come to realize that there is a question: 'Who is in pain?' – is it the ego or its object that is in pain; and 'Who is the one that is being reviled?' – is the person truly reviling himself or is he reviling the part of himself that is identified with an object that, at another level, he is really accusing. Freud comes to realize that while mourning states are terminable by virtue of the very painful process of relinquishment of all the memories, hopes, expectations related to the love object in the outside world, melancholia can terminate only when the object has been actually ground into the dust and is either dead or so completely denigrated that the ego can triumph over it. It is for this reason that melancholia tends to slip over into mania; and the mania is essentially a triumph over and a liberation from an object that was originally so superior that it commanded love, and then was disappointing or hurtful in a way that aroused terrible rage and hatred. Then through this process of attacking it while at the same time identifying with it, the destructive process is carried to completion. It was only a few years later that Abraham was able to describe how the completion of this process was a bodily act as well as a mental state; where defaecating out of the body an object that had now been turned to faeces was representative of defaecating out of the mind as well, and triumphing over it in its reduction to absolute rubbish. Abraham was then able to discover the next step in our understanding of melancholia, which Freud was not in a position to recognize: namely, that the identification with the object that Freud had described in melancholia recurs and the mania relapses into melancholia because this defaecated-out object is compulsively re-introjected (coprophagic phantasy). This has something to do with the way in which the destroyed object gets back inside and the way in which it becomes identified with once again, causing the mania to collapse into melancholia once more. Thus one sees a basis for a circular process in the cyclothymias.

The core of these discoveries is the realization that mental pain is the central problem and, quite apart from satisfaction or frustration of the libido, an article of commerce between the ego and its object; for once this is recognized one can no longer presume that the person who seems to be in pain is in fact in pain himself, but one must consider that he may be manifesting this mysterious process of identification with an object in pain. Of course Freud knew that identification could play a role in hysterical phenomena. You will recall that he was thinking of hysteria as being just a little thread of memory running through the personality, with a symptom on the end and a traumatic experience at the beginning. He had now to think of hysteria as a way of life and of an hysterical *person*, which meant a revision in his whole framework. It is interesting to observe that in certain of his writings of this period – such as the essays on war and those containing sociological and anthropological thought – Freud seems to be weighed down by an absolutely appalling and pessimistic view of the world. And while this was naturally a facet of everybody's reaction to the war, one must remember that Freud was seeing it fairly exclusively from the point of view of psycho-analysis at the stage it had then reached. That is to say, he was thinking that the difficulty with deformations of character originated in the repression of instincts and damming-up of the libido; and that from this ensued either anxiety – still seen as the consequence and not the cause of repression – or, in so far as the instincts were being frustrated and deprived of expression, soured love in the form of hatred.

I would like once more to stress this conception of love as being the desire to gratify these erotic instincts at whatever level they happen to be: auto-erotic, narcissistic or object-related, at whatever erogenous zone; and as a desire which, when frustrated, metamorphoses through ambivalence to hatred. For its immediate corollary is the naive and, indeed, presently popular, theory that all the trouble in the world is owing to people not enjoying themselves; that it is not evil in the world nor anything vicious, violent and destructive in human nature that makes us rather beastly to one another, but simply the unaccountable absence of a blissful happiness. The abdication from responsibility inherent in this idea, combined with the then current history of war, naturally eliminated any possibility that the world should seem to be getting better; it could only seem, of necessity, to be deteriorating. Indeed, in Freud's writing that primitive tribes did not suffer from this suppression which produces repression which in turn imposes restrictions upon their gratification – a theory quite incompatible with his talking about cannibalism – one is witnessing precisely this pessimism expressed in anthropological terms. His idea of 'primitive', in spite of his anti-religiosity, begins to sound like the Garden of Eden. One is led to imagine that it is as if things have been getting worse and worse since Adam and Eve were chased out of the Garden, or since the most primitive tribes began to be civilized and impose the necessity of making a living upon their children. I do not suggest for a moment that these are Freud's precise terms of argument, but wish to illustrate how the undervaluation of pain was costing him any hope about the possibility of health or happiness. He only found relief from this pessimism in his very last years when he began to formulate the question rather more properly to himself and to allow better for the terrific complexity of the personality structure. For the three-part structure that he begins to discern now and finally describes in 'The Ego and the Id' is in fact far more complicated than the earlier idea of an ego with instincts that it somehow had to manage in the face of an outside world which it had simultaneously to satisfy. Clearly this development with the discovery, inevitable to it, of the splitting processes and the understanding that health and illness can exist side by side in the same personality, allows for a more optimistic view. However, I think one has to realize that a truly optimistic conception would have to be one that thought of love as something beyond enlightened self-interest; and in order to get beyond this conception of love Freud was going to have to discard this energetics theory and the idea of un-pleasure, and really come to grips with a more purely psychological theory, in which 'pain' really was what it meant: that is, it really hurts and is not just the absence of something pleasant.

Chapter X   The Wolf Man (The Primal Scene)

The case of the Wolf Man is to my mind the most important case history in the whole of psycho-analytic literature and in all of Freud's work; for the Wolf Man was what might be called an encyclopaedia of psycho-pathology. Moreover, I believe this particular case was Freud's premier clinical experience because all the work that follows seems to be deeply involved with it. It opened up the phenomenon of the primal scene to him. Now this was something which Freud had in fact conceptualized very early on, but which – probably owing to his diminished interest in the idea of specific aetiology – he later put aside. It was not until he was faced with the Wolf Man and his extraordinary dream and the evidence of the impact of the dream on the child's development, that Freud took it up again. In a way it is this theory that gives proper psycho-analytic form to all of Freud's theories about sexuality; for although they had been, as it were, announced in the 'Three Essays on Sexuality', they were not built upon a foundation of psycho-analytic data, but merely from psycho-analytical modes of thought applied to ordinary medical and psychiatric data.

In the case of the Wolf Man, however, the data and reconstruction are purely psycho-analytical; and for that very reason it is convincing only in so far as one is already convinced. In other words, for people who view psycho-analysis from the outside it stands as a particularly ridiculous episode in psychoanalytic literature. From the evidence of a dream remembered from childhood, Freud reconstructs a scene of parents in their underclothes during the day, having intercourse three times from behind, witnessed by a child of one and a half years, who passed a stool. One can understand that it might seem ridiculous, but it is probably quite correct and, in the context of Ruth Mack Brunswick's account fifteen years later of her subsequent treatment of the Wolf Man, the dream is most enlightening. For during this second analysis – which was only of six months' duration – the Wolf Man produced the most marvellous sequence of dreams in the midst of a paranoid breakdown from which she helped him to recover; and these dreams are almost all concerned with the original wolf dream and its significance in his life. In point of fact, this writing is more 'convincing' than anything Freud wrote; furthermore a large body of subsequent literature has grown up about the Wolf Man: Muriel Gardner's account of his life after the treatment with Ruth Mack Brunswick and his life experiences during the Second World War; his own book – which came out in 1973 – about his analysis with Freud. It is an immensely well-documented case history and is, as I have said before, the premier case history of psycho-analysis.

The sudden development in Freud's thinking at this time was certainly influenced by this case. It started in 1910 and finished in 1914, interrupted by the First World War when the Wolf Man went back to his native Russia. There the revolution of 1917 swept away his fortune; he turned up impoverished and a little ill in Vienna and saw Freud for a few months in 1918 or 1919. It is worth noting that Freud collected money for his financial support for years in Vienna; for it was precisely this collecting of money that elicited from the Wolf Man a kind of parasitism of Freud and the psycho-analytic movement, and really precipitated his breakdown and the character traits associated with it in 1926.

It is therefore a case which throws a revealing light on Freud's character and on his relationship to his patients. For on the one hand Freud must have established this charity because he felt that this man's case history had made such a contribution to psycho-analysis that he deserved a kind of honorarium from the movement; and to my mind, this attitude, with its implicit understanding that psycho-analysis is the work of both patient and analyst, is fundamentally a correct one. Nevertheless on the other hand, I believe Freud in fact felt somewhat guilty towards this patient, largely as a result of the manoeuvre that he utilized for what might be called stampeding him into action. For with some three and a half to four years of desultory work behind him, and nothing to show for it but a continuing punctilious co-operation and utter absence of any feeling or involvement in the transference relationship, Freud became quite discouraged and set an irrevocable termination date. In the next six or nine months the most convincing reconstructive material was collected. As Freud indicated in a footnote in the case history, it was a tactic that he subsequently regretted.

However, in addition to the regret regarding technical procedure, I suspect there was another area of his work for this man about which he had misgivings; and about which the Wolf Man held a grievance that was to come out very strongly in his work with Ruth Mack Brunswick. For the prolonged illness had started out as a breakdown of a very hypochondriacal nature, during which he was terribly paranoid towards various people who carried the name 'Wolf': his dentist, his doctor; and indeed he was extremely paranoid towards Freud and, at one stage, probably quite dangerous to him. Now Freud was already ill with cancer of the jaw; a fact which must have weighed heavily in his decision not to take the treatment upon himself, and which also played some part in the hypochondriacal aspect of the Wolf Man's breakdown, as he had some inkling of it. However, his murderousness toward Freud was not based solely on an unresolved aspect of the transference; it was also related to the way in which Freud seems to have pushed the theory of sublimation very hard with this man, and urged him to sublimate his homosexuality by studying law and jurisprudence. This was quite contrary to the man's wishes and interests and he seems to have felt very coerced about it by Freud. Indeed I think there is probably much truth in the idea that Freud was still so utterly convinced by his theory that sublimated homosexuality was the source of the greatest cultural achievements, that he pushed for sublimation once he felt that he had satisfactorily analysed the infantile foundations of the homosexuality.

It is in this area, to my mind, that there was an exception in the technique used by Freud which was otherwise, by this time, purely analytical. That is to say, in the area of sublimation this concept was linked to the Libido Theory with its idea of there being a uniform mental energy dammed-up by repressions. At best, this energy could be prevented from release into a free flow that would emerge as infantile perversions and polymorphous sexuality, and could be channelled into sublimations to emerge as socially useful types of behaviour. Freud was almost totally convinced by this, basically owing to his commitment to the Libido Theory at that time. While this clinical work

91

was going on – between 1910 and 1914 – Freud was just in the process of realizing the area of narcissism and the phenomenology connected with it, and he was altering his instincts theory, but only to distinguish more between object libido and narcissistic libido, rather than between sexual instincts and life-preservative instincts; however, this did not really amount to an important shift in his thinking.

Finally, and before we come to concentrate our attention on the problem of the primal scene, I would like to mention other aspects which clarify its setting in Freud's mind. The most important issue is that of the dream. As I mentioned earlier, Freud placed dreaming in a rather trivial position in people's lives, assigning to it this rather unimportant quasi-physiological function of helping the dreamer to stay asleep by providing him with hallucinatory gratifications of his unconscious infantile wishes. However, in his clinical work, Freud never behaved according to this belief: take, for example, the emphasis on the repetitiveness of Dora's dreams; the attention paid to the Rat Man's dreams and their role in the elucidation of the transference, and the way in which the Rat Man's reaction to his dreams is taken as having important emotional reality for him. And when we arrive at this present paper, Freud is dealing with a dream of a child of about four years of age to which he attributes an absolutely crucial role in the child's whole development.

It is in fact somewhat puzzling to see just how Freud saw this dream as functioning, when one remembers that he considered it to be such a crucial event. Naturally, he is at first uncertain in his own mind and leaves quite open the question of the dating of the primal scene, to which the dream is supposed to be a reference and from which the primal scene is reconstructed. He thinks it is at one and a half but it could have been at six months, it could have been at two and a half: he derives, half-jokingly I think, the formula of $n + 6$ months. However, it seems to me that he hedges an important problem: namely, whether it was the primal scene itself that had the impact on the child, or whether it was the dream that he had between one and a half and three and a half years later which gave retrospective significance and impact to the primal scene. And owing to this indecision as to scene and dream, he also has to leave undecided whether we are dealing with a scene or with a phantasy. In this particular instance he seems fairly convinced that what he has reconstructed is a scene; but of course he leaves open the question as to whether it was the scene or the dream that had the impact or that organized the experience in retrospect. Then – from the point of view of developing the theory of psycho-sexual development, in which we are going to place a primal something – he has to leave open the question as to whether we are going to talk about a primal scene, or a primal phantasy. Thus, are we going to think of it as something constitutional, hereditary, a preconception carried with us from the primordal history of the race, etc.; or as something quite inevitable in the life of every child? To take the latter case, naturally we would have to deal with children who do not have both parents or are raised in hostels with a changing nursing staff and so on; but, needless to say, he does not have any data about these situations at this point.

There is some evidence for the first viewpoint. Let us take, for instance, the children of Anna Freud's 'Bulldog Bank' study, who were perhaps born in the concentration camp, passed around and in some mysterious way kept alive; having had nothing like parental care in any continuous way from their actual parents, they were then brought together in this home in Bulldog Bank, where it was found that as their primary defensive grouping broke up and they began to develop, they began to show ordinary oedipal manifestations. Such evidence does very strongly suggest that not only is the Oedipus Complex part of our constitutional predisposition and universally present, but that the expectation of the primal scene is so absolutely built into the apparatus of mental life that we consider it to be an ubiquitous phantasy. Being pressing, in any life situation where there are two parents in a child's life, it eventually produces for him a primal scene, even if it is not seen but heard, smelled or whatever: that is, an experience of being alone in the atmosphere of a parental intercourse going on somewhere.

Freud seems to think that the impact of actually viewing the parents in intercourse is probably greater and more likely to be traumatic than hearing or any other source of evidence from which the child construes that it is going on at that moment,

93

and which lights up his predisposition to this particular phantasy. I would say from my own experience that I do not see any compelling evidence that the viewing is more important in itself than, say, the hearing - which is what we find evidence of in the middle-class people with whom we are accustomed to deal. What we find evidence of nowadays is that where a child has been exposed to the viewing of a primal scene, he has, in our culture and the class of our culture with which we generally deal, been exposed also to a particular type of psycho-pathology in the parents who wish to expose their intercourse to the child, and behave therefore not with a special insensitivity but with a special inclination and determination to involve the child in the visual experience of the intercourse. So with the kind of patients whom we treat, when we find evidence of actual viewing, we expect to find evidence of parental psycho-pathology and not just fortuitous occurrence. Of course there are cases of the child toddling in in the middle of the night and so on, but even that is not the sort of thing that turns up in our material today.

In Freud's time however, things were really quite different: children probably always slept in their parents' bedroom for the first few years of their lives or until the next baby came along, or else slept in a room with servants, in wealthier families, and were exposed to their sexual activities. For Freud to reconstruct from his clinical material a primal scene as a visual experience in the middle of the day, is a far less unlikely event and far less likely to imply parental pathology than it would in our day. Therefore the reconstruction did not surprise Freud as a social phenomenon; what surprised him was the evidence of the immense impact on the child.

I think it is important to realize that at this time Freud's ideas on development were becoming much more complicated and more organized; he was not only thinking in terms of the 'vicissitudes of instinct' as he calls it, the development of erogenous zones from oral to anal to phallic to genital; he was thinking also in terms of the total characterological development of the child and of the individual. Although one has to say that Freud was not interested in children a few years later (directly: in their development as a phenomenon in itself; whereas he was mainly interested in reconstructing the childhood background of his adult patients' pathology), yet nonetheless he was at this time beginning to see the development of children in a much more unified form, and as something of great complexity. In the Leonardo paper we saw him trying to conceptualize a person as having a whole life which needs to be understood as an entity; in the Schreber case he was approaching the concept of a person who has to live in both the outside world and in his 'subjective' world which he can pull to pieces, or at least pull out something which holds it together so that it falls to pieces. Then there came the papers on character development, on anal character; and a few years later the papers on three interesting character types. Thus his whole view of mental life was really beginning to cohere and to cause him to conceive more fully of a person with a development which takes place in a particular milieu. Where in the cases of the Rat Man and Dora, one hears little or nothing of the mother, here in the Wolf Man case for instance, not only is she imminent in his adult life as someone who handles the money (she gives him a meagre allowance which causes them to row every once in a while like an unhappily married couple), but also one hears about the impact of his mother's personality on him as a child: how she tried to deal with his naughtiness by taking him to see the religious pictures, and how she succeeded in inculcating religion, which instituted his obsessional period. We hear about the impact of her menorrhagia and her gynaecological troubles, her saying to the doctor that she 'could not go on living like that', the family moving from one house to another, from the summer place to the winter place; the intricacies of the Wolf Man's relation to servants; the impact of his sister's character, how she seduced him sexually and tyrannized over him with her cleverness, and her very forceful and pathological character; and his reaction to her later committing suicide – the background all unfolds. One gets a much more complete, Tolstoyan picture of a whole community and people growing up in it, of a life being led amidst other lives. It absolutely springs to life. And just as Freud said his 'Studies on Hysteria' read like short stories, so does this read something like a novel, and leaves one with the same sense of having viewed a piece of life.

One might say that Freud was integrating his experiences,

developing not a theory but a psycho-analytic view, or point of view, about life and its processes; and this also made him aware of the inadequacy of many of the types of formulations that he had been using. Firstly, I think he was now aware to a great extent that his formulation about dreams was not quite correct: several papers written during the period in which he was treating the Wolf Man add a considerable amount to his recommendations about dream analysis and the clinical use of dreams. Secondly, the theory of narcissism really arose during the course of this man's treatment in the face of the Wolf Man's narcissistic phenomena – particularly his narcissistic identifications with his mother in the menorrhagia and feeling 'I can't go on living like this', and the narcissistic identification with his father mixed up with the old water carrier: his father's heavy breathing. And then there were the perverse tendencies of the little boy: the wish to be beaten and the phantasy of the prince being beaten on the penis, which led on to the paper 'A Child is Being Beaten'. Though published before this, it was written after it. Thirdly, there was the issue of the sexual theories which, when they were based simply on a conception of source, aim and object of instincts, were grossly inadequate. This earlier conception came nowhere near accounting for sexuality in action and people's sexual relationships. It made it sound as if people were simply using one another to masturbate, and did not allow either for any sort of description of the nature of their feelings towards one another or for the problem of jealousy or of masochism which runs so close to the whole question of pleasure and pain.

Now in this area Freud takes a great step forward in describing the primal scene; and he describes it with the intention of viewing it as a great universal organizing phantasy in the sexual development. In a way in this paper there is the preview to the concept of the complete Oedipus Complex, as it is later developed in 'The Ego and the Id' in 1923. The 'complete Oedipus Complex' is the first statement, one might say, of the realities of bisexuality: namely, that there are not just tendencies in the male child that could be equated with passivity, and not just tendencies in the female toward active participation that could be equated with masculinity; rather there really is something very concretely bisexual, male and female: not just active and passive trends but unequivocally male and female, from the very beginning of development, and they both have to find a way of evolving and expressing themselves. The complete Oedipus Complex encompasses both the masculine and the feminine Oedipus Complex in every individual, boy or girl. Although the truth of this concept was plainly visible to Freud in the Wolf Man, whose femininity is blatant and very strong, one has nevertheless to recognize that Freud does not make the distinction between his femininity and his homosexuality. In consequence, he does not recognize, for example, that the perverse tendencies (such as the desire to be beaten on the penis) and masochistic tendencies are not related to his femininity. He persists in dealing with everything masochistic as if it were passive and thus naturally part of the man's femininity. The patient's identification with his mother and her bleeding was to be equated with wanting to be beaten on the penis.

Nonetheless, a great step forward is clear, for Freud has evolved the foundations of sexual development in concrete and visual form: the basic situation consists of, somewhere, the mother and father having intercourse and, somewhere, the little girl or little boy watching, listening, thinking about it, feeling excited, resentful and whatever else: this is the scene. And it is a great step, for previously, with the talk about impulses, aims and objects, the only approach to emotionality Freud could make was in this rather simple arithmetic: love-turning-into-hate, positive-to-negative, various erotic impulses frustrated and becoming hate impulses, and so on – an approach that barely penetrates the question of affects. But once he has drawn a dramatic scene with dramatis personae in which something is happening in one place, and something else in another place, then the whole thing becomes flooded with feelings and springs to life. He is in a position to examine the emotionality of the situation. The difficulty with the discovery, of course, resides in the indecision as to where the impact comes from, in this equivocation between scene and dream. For Freud comes terribly close in the Wolf Man (much closer than in the Schreber case) to conceptualizing an inner world. If he had just made this step he could have leapt forward the way Melanie Klein's work leapt forward the moment she discovered that children were preoccupied with the inside of their mothers' bodies and the inside of their own bodies and that it was really a *place*, a world in which life was going on. If Freud could have made that step at this point, there would have been a terrific surge forward that would have led almost immediately to the concept of splitting processes which he could only reach – and even then only very hypothetically – in 1937. But he seems somehow unable to come to any such conception at this point; that is, to take the primal scene and find a location for it by placing it inside. And I think the reason was that he just did not have that kind of mind; it took somebody like Mrs Klein, listening to little children talking about the inside of their mother's body with absolute conviction as if it were Budapest or Vienna, as an absolutely geographical place, to realize that there really is an inner world, and that it is not just allegorical or metaphorical, but has a concrete existence – in the life of the mind, not the brain.

The result for Freud is that he is left with this equivocation; in the Schreber case he had equivocated in talking about the world's destruction and could not really come to the conclusion that Schreber smashed the world to pieces because he could not locate this world that had been destroyed. He had to talk about withdrawal of libido and withdrawal of interest instead, and the whole drama is thereby watered down. Now, similarly, in the case of the Wolf Man, it seems to me that because Freud cannot place the primal scene as an internal situation and allow that the impact goes on and on continuously, and because he cannot see the wolf dream (occurring at the age of four) and the other dream (at the age of twenty-three when he started analysis) as being the same primal scene going on and on inside and still having the same impact on the patient, he therefore cannot develop a sense of the immediacy of the infantile life. He is left not only with the equivocation between dream or phantasy and traumatic factor in the external world, but he is also left with the necessity of thinking about the analytical work that he is doing as reconstruction. One has the impression that a large part of the four years of this patient's analysis was spent analysing this one dream, although there must have been lots of other dreams relating to it and throwing light on it, detail after detail. But because Freud's model was of this reconstructive sort, putting the jigsaw puzzle together bit by bit and at

the end of the paper talking about the 'solution', his understanding and full use of the material was handicapped.

I think that the most cogent way of understanding his clinging to the reconstructive nature of the work that he was doing,
is to attribute it to his inability to find a place where it was all
happening in the immediacy of the transference, to see the
dream happening right under his nose. In fact this clinging to
the relic of the archaeological model seems to me to have had
the effect of attenuating the violence and the passion of the
transference situation. And while Freud does speak of the transference as the past returning and pressing to be put into action,
rather than to be investigated, he does always talk about it as
if it were a relic that returns 'as if' with a lot of feeling. He
speaks of the transference as 'unreal'; and I think one reason
for this is that his attitude towards the countertransference was
a very negative one. He thought of it as an interference with the
analyst's work rather than as a tool: just as when he first recognized the transference he saw it only as a nuisance. These things
are somehow connected with his reconstructive view, his idea
that it was the past returning, and not something present and
immediate; because he could not conceive of a place where it
was happening at the moment and then somehow erupting
from that place. For that reason, the affects connected with it
were in a way 'antique' affects: very precious and very interesting,
but not useful in the present, not alive and vivid at the moment.

This of course also affected his whole view of the nature of
the analytic method and its therapeutic effects. As I have said,
at first he thought that solving the riddle, the jigsaw puzzle,
and presenting the solution, was the analyst's work; then in the
paper on 'Remembering, Repeating and Working Through'
he states his realization that the analyst's work does not stop
there, but also has to help the patient accept the solution and
work it through. It is not quite clear what 'working through'
means, but at this point – around 1912 – it seems to have something of the same significance as his earlier idea that psycho-
pathology was due to experiences or ideas existing in the mind
in a sort of foreign-body relationship, unintegrated with other
ideas and therefore impossible to be worn away; thus, 'working
through' might be otherwise stated as working-away obnoxious
ideas and memories.

At this point, the consequence is that the attitude towards the therapy as a method is that it is fairly aggressive towards the patient; and this idea is in keeping with Freud's practice – which might be crudely described as giving the patient the solution and trying to get him to accept it, with the implicit reprimand which he felt toward Irma in the dream of the injection. Callousness of this sort in the attitude to the patient seems to manifest itself toward the Wolf Man in the irrevocable deadline that he gave him, and which probably contributed to his subsequent illness. And this aggressive attitude of 1914 or 1915 turned, by 1936 (when he writes 'Analysis Terminable and Interminable') into a terribly pessimistic attitude toward the analytic therapy; for here Freud in fact expresses quite a strong feeling of helplessness about the analyst's position: that he really has very little power to influence the patient in any way, but can only offer him the means or tools with which to influence himself. These two attitudes – the aggression and then the pessimism – are more or less opposite sides of the same coin; and they spring, it seems to me, from this relentlessly reconstructive view of the method, in which the analysis is seen to consist of the reconstruction: piecemeal at first, and eventually presented as a whole to the patient; and to find its solution in this. As I have said before, I think Freud was bound to this view because he could not make the step of conceiving of a more immediate and internal situation, of a place inside the mind, in a concrete way; and this was perhaps because he did not have the data for it.

And indeed I think that Freud could not, in any honesty, have made that step, given his material; he could have made it as a feat of imagination, but he was a person who stuck very close to the evidence and he simply did not have any evidence which he could see: and looking back on it, it would have been very difficult to see a concrete inner world. Even Schreber hardly provided it, for his own externalization of psychic reality is so complete that it would have been very hard to put it back into Schreber in one's mind without feeling that you were just imposing your theory and your solution upon him. Little Hans is perhaps a little different: the material about the stork box that he and his sister travelled in, the phantasies of breaking into a place with his father, evidence of claustrophobia and so on, would certainly suggest it. However, it is nothing like the material which Mrs Klein got from two and three year-olds when she started working in 1920; they just told her about it. And for some reason – not everybody would have – she took it seriously.

Chapter XI

The Child Being Beaten (The Perversions)

This is the most difficult chapter as far as I am concerned, because it touches on the real watershed period in Freud's work at the end of the First World War, and is followed by the great revolution in his thinking which was to build up during the 1920s and emerge as the Structural Theory. It is the most difficult chapter because it is extremely complicated: the evidence is difficult to comprehend and indeed I do not understand it very well, and so do not expect to be able to clarify it for anyone else. I would begin by emphasizing once more that the approach towards Freud in this book is through his clinical work and his clinical thinking, dealing with his theories – which are expressed as explanatory theories – as having essentially no explanatory power. It seems to me that the approach made to the mind which is based on trying to explain things, is a wrong one, and for this reason I shall take the theories as modes of thought which are intended to be useful in the consulting room and in thinking, writing and talking about one's clinical experience: modes of thought which are intended to gather together, to categorize and to help demonstrate the inter-relationships of the various phenomena that one meets in the consulting room while investigating people's minds. I am going to discuss a watershed period in relation to Freud's modes of thought, and it is very difficult to pick it out in the papers of this time; for we are in effect somewhere between the 'Wolf Man' (whose clinical work was carried out between 1910 and 1914 and written up during the war) and 'Beyond the Pleasure Principle' of 1920, which contains the seeds of the new Structural Theory.

Now while in the development of the concept of the ideal ego into that of the ego ideal, which I demonstrated in the chapter on 'Mourning and Melancholia' and the paper 'On narcissism', the formation of this Structural Theory was already under way, it was not yet dealt with as such, but rather as an *agency* in the mind. Freud does not remotely clarify the exact relationship of the structure to the developmental processes, nor easily convey his way of thinking about it. The period was during the war: he was fairly isolated from foreign and German colleagues alike

(Ferenczi was in Budapest, Abraham in Berlin); the patients he had being few, he was left with a great deal of time for thinking and writing. The result was a group of little but terribly interesting papers; for although he did not write large quantities, what he did set down was absolutely loaded with thought. And it is this evidence of the real struggling that went on at that period that I wish now to try to highlight.

'A Child is Being Beaten" is in my opinion the central paper in this process and will surely form the focal point of this chapter. However, in order to appreciate the full significance of the paper, not just as one on a psychological phenomenon that opened up an entirely new way for the investigation of masochism and therefore of the perversions, but also as embodying Freud's development of new modes of thought, it is necessary to deal with three other papers as well. They are very much more theoretical, and do not make much direct reference to clinical phenomena. In one, which I have already mentioned, on 'Character and Anal Erotism' (1908), he singles out three character traits – parsimony, stubbornness and orderliness – and for the first time describes the relation between character structure and the development of the libido and fixation of the libido. This was really his first excursion into character. In 1915 there followed 'Instinct and Its Vicissitudes' (a moralist title), and in 1917, 'Transformations of Instincts in Relation to Anal Erotism'. It seems to me that these two words – 'Vicissitudes' and 'Transformations' – which I still struggle to understand precisely, are a very important key to the changes in his modes of thinking; and I wish to investigate them a little before going on to 'A Child is Being Beaten'.

Firstly, however, I will recap some of the history up to this point. In the 'Studies on Hysteria', Freud had clearly set about studying simple phenomena (such as amnesia, conversion, anxiety), with the simple theory that they were the result of the repression of certain recollections. This in turn also involved some sort of damming-up of instincts, which were then converted into anxiety; and in turn the anxiety was somehow turned, with the repressed recollections, into symptoms. It was a highly simplistic theory which ran into trouble almost immediately when Freud began extending the field of his study to the obsessional neuroses, for he found that it could not be

103

dealt with purely on the basis of recollections. Somehow the affects became detached from these, with the result that the recollections were not repressed but the affects were: the recollections were available for memory but the affects had disappeared; he found that indeed it was pretty mysterious. He was quite convinced that it had something to do with sexuality and, discovering a great deal of confirmation for infantile sexuality in the course of his clinical work, that the Oedipus Complex as the central conflict situation in development was ubiquitous. Moreover, he was convinced that the whole thing *was* developmental, originating not in later life, but in infancy. Then came the case of Little Hans, which provided such lovely confirmation of the actual existence of the Oedipus Complex and of the infantile neurosis in children. The Rat Man case helped him to understand that there was conflict involved, and that it was conflict between love and hate in some way in the obsessional neurosis, not just conflict between ideas and desires that were unacceptable to the outside world and social standards. Then, as I said in connection with the Leonardo case, one can see that his ideas about psycho-analysis were expanding to try to accommodate the conception of a person's life as a unified thing which could be studied in a linear way from its beginning to its end, a continuous development in which progress and regression and other processes all had their place and were linked together in an integrated history. In the Schreber case, Freud seemed to discover that not only was there such a thing as a life, but there was such a thing as a world; and that everybody lived his life in his world, and that his world was in some way partly his own conception and in some way the world of his own particular mind, able to fall to pieces or to be torn or battered to pieces; he also seemed to discover that terrible things happen to a person when he has allowed his world to thus disintegrate.

So gradually the whole concern became something which could reasonably be thought of as a unified field of psychology, related to personality and personality development. At the same time in history, of course, other schools of psychology were growing up that were studying the same or different phenomena. The Gestalt school was studying psychology from an entirely different point of view, very phenomenological but having nothing to do with development and fundamentally nothing to do with personality. Other schools were much more sociological or anthropological in their orientation. But Freud pulled his own work together under the firm net of psychology with these four different categories: studying the developmental process and its genetics; studying its topography (that is, levels of consciousness and problems related to this: as he thought then, the crucial question related to psychopathology); the question of dynamics (that is, mechanisms of the mind by which the psychic energies were manipulated); and the economic aspect (that is, the attempt to define its quantitative aspects). At that time, by 'quantitative', Freud was meaning 'psychic energy', which he was then thinking of as a very concrete concern as if it were electricity or hydrostatic energy or heat. Therefore, the nature of Freud's modes of thought stemmed from this essentially hydrostatic energetics model; and his concepts related to affects were also almost purely quantitative, conceived of in terms of quantities of excitation in the mind. As the phenomenology that he and other people began to study extended beyond obsessional neurosis and the whole realm of narcissistic phenomena came into play in its relation to more serious illnesses such as manic-depressive states or schizophrenia, or hypochondria, it became increasingly clear that his modes of thought were just not tying the ends together and were not providing useful tools for comprehending the clinical phenomena. By this time the transference in the consulting room was no longer being dealt with merely as a resistance, but considered as something in its own right. This is evident to a certain extent in the Rat Man case, but still more clearly so in the Wolf Man, where the transference was seen as a communication with its own particular level of validity. And although it was still being used mainly for the purpose of reconstruction, this latter was no longer the simple serial delineation of a chain of mental events running back to a traumatic experience or a repressed incident that it had been in the early days, but had become (as seen in Leonardo and the Wolf Man case) an attempt to reconstruct a life and the entire development of a person: his personality, his interests, his relationships.

Now by 1915, Freud had finished with the Wolf Man case,

105

but I think that nevertheless it remained the crucial case in his subsequent development; he was busy writing it up and thinking about it, and at this time he was still very bound up with the Libido Theory. This is expressed very clearly in the paper 'Instincts and their Vicissitudes' (1915). What Freud means by the term 'vicissitudes' at this point, seems to be somehow connected with the context of a person's whole development: his character, his symptoms, what is healthy as well as what is ill about him. The 'Vicissitudes of Instinct' seem to mean something standing in specific relation to phases of development. Along with Abraham, he was thinking of personality development in terms of a series of organizations: and these organizations were at this point thought of as pregenital and genital. The pregenital organization was already considered to have different phases: oral – and (as Abraham was already thinking) anal-sadistic, as well as oral – and anal-erotic; but the main division was between pregenital and genital. Pregenital was also thought of as being the realm 'par excellence' of narcissism – this latter currently being considered by and large in these libido terms: that is, narcissism as a stage in the development of the deployment of the libido from auto-erotism to object relations in which the body of the person was taken as the object of the libidinal impulses, and then going on to object relations in which the bodies of other people are chosen as the object of the libidinal (i.e. primarily the sexual) impulses. Now the term 'vicissitudes' seems to have its roots of meaning in such a question as, 'What happens to the pregenital organization when development proceeds to the genital organization?' Where does it go? Obviously the erogenous zones are still there, the stimulation is still there, the phantasies and desires connected with it must be still somewhere in the mind: what happens to it? The answers to this seem to be given in terms of the ways in which the libido can be manipulated. And Freud thought of these manipulations at that point in a way that is fairly identical with 'defence mechanisms' as it has come to be used later in psycho-analytic history. He names these four in the paper: turning into its opposite, turning against the self, repression and sublimation; discussing not the last two since he has talked about them a lot before, but mainly the first two. And he does not use 'self' here as a technical term as we use it today (meaning a portion of the personality that has the meaning of 'self' and which contains both ego and id components integrated in some functional way); he is using the term in a purely descriptive way. In order to understand the idea of an instinct having vicissitudes of these four sorts, one has to understand that Freud was thinking of instincts as having qualities that tend to come in pairs; and the major pairs were the instincts relating to love and hate (that is, having the affects of love and hate connected with them): that of sadism and masochism, and that of activity and passivity. There is also the pair of masculine and feminine, but this he still reserves for the genital organization, not thinking of pregenital masculinity or pregenital femininity, but only of active and passive. Therefore, by the term 'inverting' an instinct into its opposite, Freud meant, for instance, that the instinct containing the affect of love can be converted into the instinct containing the affect of hate; similarly a sadistic impulse or instinct can be inverted into a masochistic one. He did not explain how it comes about, but simply said that this is something which can happen. Therefore, the turning-against-the-self is the equivalent of a return to narcissism: that is, the diversion of libido back into the self and making it into narcissistic libido. This is what Freud means by 'Vicissitudes of Instinct' at this point. He is still bound by the Libido Theory and to the idea that the explanation of human behaviour (for he is still trying to explain things) and of human feelings is to be found in the deployment of instinct; and the deployment of instinct is governed by these mechanisms or vicissitudes.

Two years later he was to write a paper called 'On Transformations of Instincts'; and I do not think that from these titles alone, one could tell why 'vicissitudes' and 'transformations' may not be interchangeable as descriptive terms. The fact is that in a very subtle way an entirely different mode of thought has come to be operative in his mind: and what he describes mainly in this paper concerns the anal instincts: the instincts connected with the anal erogenous zone and therefore essentially connected with the relationship of the anus and rectum to the faecal mass, and its meaning, significance and phantasy implications. It concerns the variety of ways in which this anal impulse relates itself to the faecal mass, of ways that have different meanings not clearly distinguished or differentiated from one another; and these meanings are, in essence, enumerated as follows (in what might now be called a 'confusional series'): faeces – penis – baby – money or gift. Now it is not at all clear why this is being called a transformation of *instinct*; for it does not seem to do anything to the instinct at all; it seems to do something to the way in which the instinct is conceived, and the meaning which is attributed to the action of the instinct: that is, whether the anal impulses and the anal excitements and phantasies are experienced as related to a faecal mass that has the meaning of penis or baby or faeces.

This, to my mind, is the beginning of ego psychology and tolls the death of the Libido Theory. I am sure many people would not agree with me, but I think that it dies at about this time, being replaced by ego psychology and object relations psychology – which are really the same thing, although they are talked about as if they were deadly enemies. Thus in moving away (quite decisively in this instance) from one mode of thought, Freud has moved towards another that is going to have a much greater organizing power in linking together phenomena, bringing them into understandable – as opposed to explicable – relation to one another. He has moved from thinking of instincts as simply body tensions requiring satisfaction (with the implication that happiness is something equivalent to a pleasant comatose state, so becoming known as the Nirvana Principle), to considering the mind as functioning primarily in relation to the manipulation of meaning. This movement away from an energetics principle, on to the study of the mind as an instrument for the manipulation of meaning, seems to me – as I said before – the beginning of ego and object relations psychology. And this is what we practise today.

It is interesting with reference to this that the only place (to my belief) in which the word 'energy', taken from the First Law of Thermodynamics, is replaced by the word 'entropy', taken from the Second Law of Thermodynamics, comes toward the end of the Wolf Man case. At this point Freud is using it in application to what might be called the stickiness of the libido: that is, the difficulty that people have in shifting their cathexes, their attachments, their interests, altering the balance of what is valuable and important in their lives. He is therefore talking about entropy as something essentially equivalent to inertia. But I think that it is a very important step in his thinking; for, with the help of information theory and linguistic philosophy, it has led to the development of our use of the idea of entropy. It is no longer peculiar to physics, describing energy running down or becoming unavailable as stated in the Second Law of Thermodynamics, but has been extended to include organization in general, and the progress from chaos to order. Now it seems to me that this is something that permeates and quite alters Freud's thinking from this point onwards. Although the trappings of the Libido Theory remain, and the language of cathexis, transformations of energies, hypercathexis and so on, still continues, yet the underlying mode of thought seems to me to have made a dramatic shift. The terms are no longer energy and its deployment, but meaning and the organization of meaning from chaotic modes of thought to organized and harmonious modes of thought. It is towards this that psycho-analysis has been directing its attention and development ever since.

While the little paper 'On Transformations of Instincts' (1917), mentioned above, is based on these astute clinical observations about the lack of differentiation in the deployment or organization of the pregenital and, particularly, the anal organization of the meaning and significance of the faeces (as penis, babies), it is primarily a theoretical paper. Our first glimpse of this new mode of thought actually being employed clinically is in the marvellous little paper entitled 'A Child is Being Beaten'. I feel I should preface my discussion of it by saying that no patient has ever said to me 'a child is being beaten', nor do I know of anyone else whose patient has said this: yet many of Freud's patients seem to have told him that they had this phantasy. It must have been a nineteenth-century phenomenon. Freud himself very interestingly points out that it does not in fact seem to be a phenomenon that can be traced back to a specific factor of children being beaten more in those days, or beaten more in Germany, or in Vienna, amongst the middle class, or amongst Jewish people; indeed the people who had this phantasy were generally middle-class people who had not been beaten and whose upbringing had been gentle.

But although we do not often meet with the phenomenon as such in practice these days, we do of course meet with plenty

109

of beating phantasies, beating perversions and flagellist fetishism. I would think the evidence is fairly convincing that the phantasy that 'a child is being beaten' – meaning, fundamentally, beaten to death – lies somewhere at the root of sexual perversions. Freud himself also comes to this conclusion: that is, that where you meet masochism you will somewhere find the phantasy that 'a child is being beaten'. Now this approach to masochism is entirely different from the one which had formerly been expressed in the 1915 paper on the 'Vicissitudes of Instinct'. At that point he was talking about masochism as the turning-against-the-self of a sadistic impulse.

But at this point he is investigating the transformations of a phantasy that 'a child is being beaten': whether the 'child being beaten' is the subject himself, or some other child; whether it is a male or a female child; whether it is being beaten by the father or the mother; whether it is a loved or a hated child? In short, what is the significance of the phantasy? He compares the experience he has had with male patients who have had this phantasy to that with female patients, tracing it to three different stages. In a way he does tie himself up in terrific knots about it; it is extremely interesting and very confusing. However, what eventually emerges – and this Freud pinpoints very clearly – is that the most important thing is the relationship of the phantasy to masochism: namely, that 'the child being beaten' is, at a certain stage in the transformation of this phantasy, the patient himself or herself. He then relates it back to the phantasy in the Wolf Man where the prince was beaten on the penis, and also to the man's masochistic anal tendencies as expressed in his need for colonic irrigations and so on. He relates it to a certain extent to his phobia of the wolf, tracing it – as he had previously done – to the fact that his fear of the wolf was related to his desire to be copulated with by his father and to his desire to be castrated and made into a female.

When one returns to that paper in the light of 'A Child is Being Beaten' and in the light of this shift from 'vicissitudes' to 'transformations' of instincts, you discover that there are two highly significant statements in it, which, to my mind, foreshadow the whole development of Freud's re-thinking about sexuality and sexual perversions: this great shift from energetics and distribution of the libido, to ego functions and thinking and dreaming. The two statements which are in a sense absolutely modern are: firstly, the defining of the phantasy, in relation to the Wolf Man's sexual peculiarities, to the effect that, in copulation, a person may be identified with a person inside the mother being copulated with by the father; the intercourse may have the meaning for him that he is really the baby inside being copulated with; and secondly, that a man may be identified with his own penis as a baby that is getting inside the mother. Of course, we are still today and have been for the last twenty years, studying precisely this kind of thing: namely, the way in which infantile phantasies are related to the inside of the mother's body. As I said, these two statements are highly significant in that they are, to my mind, the precursors of a mighty leap in the dark by Freud: to deal with the perversions as very complicated structures; to deal with the sexual life as filled with meaning rather than simply devoted to the mechanics of gaining satisfaction for instinctual tensions; to conceive the complexity of the phantasies that may underlie what descriptively may be called an ordinary act of sexual intercourse. Furthermore, one might put these two statements together: that of the person being identified with the baby inside the woman being copulated with by its father, and the person being identified with his own penis as the baby getting back into the mother's body or back into the womb; and one might see these in conjunction as a phantasy by which Freud has conceived of a sexual act, in which the entrance of the penis into the vagina is the child getting into the mother, and subsequently being copulated with there by the father's penis.

Now Freud does not make any specific reference to this in the paper 'A Child is Being Beaten', and we have to wait for a few years until he returns to the problem of masochism in 1924 with 'The Economic Problem of Masochism'. But we should keep in mind that he has already described these phantasies here in the 'Wolf Man'; that he has already made this shift from talking about vicissitudes of instinct and the energetics of their deployment, to transformations of instinct and transformations of the meaning of the act or behaviour or relationship. One can see that he has made a very great step forward in his approach to sexuality. Formerly (as I have said) one

111

would always have had to complain that his description of sexuality considered it as in essence a meaningless act, in no way differentiated from any other act for gratifying the body – scratching it, eating a plum or whatever – other than that it was the most convenient way – much better than masturbating. In other words, there had been nothing in his theory about sexuality to bring meaning into the relationship of the two people who were engaged in it. Now he has introduced into the whole field of sexuality rich possibilities for investigating the meaning.

Now of course one can object that this is what he has been doing all along; and indeed it *is* what he has been doing all along. If one goes back to the Dora case, or to the 'Studies on Hysteria', one will see that, as Freud says, they do indeed sound like short stories; he has been investigating the meaning all along. But to be investigating something and describing its phenomenology is a very different thing from having the conceptual tools with which to organize these phenomena so that they take on the significance of a body of knowledge which can then be passed on to somebody else for use in his consulting room. What an exciting and important period this is! It was made possible by his having a lot of time on his hands to think about the problems that were troubling him. And the problem which troubled him most at this time seems to have been the paradoxical one of masochism. It was paradoxical to Freud because it did not conform in any way to his central economic concept about pain; for the whole Libido Theory really rested on the concept that excessive stimulation, internal or external, was experienced as unpleasure or pain, and that relief of tension was experienced as pleasure or less unpleasure. Within the confines of that formulation, there was no way at all of accounting for masochism; that is, for the pleasure in being the object of the sadistic, pain-provoking behaviour of other people. Now even in 'A Child is Being Beaten', Freud does not make much progress with the problem of masochism itself. True, he pinpoints it in the series of transformations of the phantasy from 'a child is being beaten' to 'a child that I hate is being beaten', to 'I am being beaten by my father'; and somewhere in this transformation, the phantasy that 'I am loved by my father because he is beating that other child' somehow turns into 'I am loved by my father because he is beating me'. But there Freud is still just on the verge of recognizing something that has to do with identification processes.

And indeed he has constantly been on the verge of this ever since he began talking about Leonardo's homosexuality based on his identification with his mother and loving a young boy the way his mother loved him; since he began talking about Schreber's identification with his wife and how lovely it must be to be a woman being copulated with, and his relation to God as a woman; he has been on the verge of it all through the Wolf Man, in talking about the Wolf Man's identification with his mother's menorrhagia, and his identification with his sister with regard to the incident of his weeping at Pushkin's grave. In 'Mourning and Melancholia' of course, he is constantly on the verge of it, in raising the question of who is really in pain: is it the ego berating the ego ideal or is it the ego ideal berating the ego? And he almost brings it all together in this paper, in trying to investigate this paradox about mental pain. This seems to me to be one of the main obstacles preventing him from being quite satisfied with the Libido Theory as an explanatory one: for quite evidently masochism could not be explained in accordance with it.

The previous formulation of instinct-turning-against-the-self used in the paper on the 'Vicissitudes of Instinct' is simply a sleight of hand, and does not satisfy any requirements since it does not describe the process in any way, but merely puts the words to it. To define masochism as 'sadism turning against the self' is easy enough, but it does not actually say anything about it. In 'A Child is Being Beaten', Freud comes close to recognizing the central masochistic phantasy that 'I am identified with a child who is being beaten by my father because he loves me and hates that other child'. The identification is implicit. And when one couples that with those two statements from the Wolf Man about the copulation with a child inside the mother's body, you catch a glimpse of a process that Freud has almost grasped: so that instead of 'My father copulating with that child', 'My father beating that child', one should understand 'I am that child and I am being copulated with by my father in that painful beating way because he loves me'. There is masochism.

Chapter XII

Beyond the Pleasure Principle and
Group Psychology (The Ego-Ideal)

This chapter brings us to the very verge of 'The Ego and the Id' and the Structural Theory, which represents such an immense change in the conceptual tools with which psychoanalysts can try to understand and organize the clinical phenomena. In order to understand the importance of this change it is essential to see in what way Freud was in difficulty, both clinically and conceptually, and how he was struggling to find a way out of it. 'Beyond the Pleasure Principle' and 'Group Psychology' each in their own way attempt to solve the problem. Freud always, as he himself says, attempts to take the citadel by storm; and each of these papers endeavours to do everything at once. The first attempts to solve the problem by taking the Libido Theory and, as it were, standing it up on its ear: as if a change simply in the nature of the duality of instincts (giving them different names and a different type of significance) would solve everything. The second attempts the solution by establishing a concept of the ego ideal, which later of course in 'The Ego and the Id' turns into that of the super-ego. And both go some distance to enrich the conceptual tools with which he worked, as I now hope to explain.

In order to do this one has first to realize the nature of his trouble, and the kind of clinical phenomena for which his theoretical tools provided no help in comprehending or organizing. The main problem is that of mental pain, with which he had never had a satisfactory way of dealing conceptually, primarily because he was anchored to the neurophysiological conception of mental pain as a quantitative rather than a qualitative matter, as something having a quasi-physical significance, but no meaning. From the 'Project' onward, he has always thought of mental pain as unpleasure, and anchored it to such conceptions as Fechner's 'constancy principle' (later called the Nirvana principle), and other quasi-neuro-physiological conceptions, which reduced the aim of mental life to something equivalent to semi-coma: directed towards the reduction of mental tensions to a minimum, in a kind of stuporous comfort. Of course Freud knew this was wrong, but he could not find any way around it without jettisoning the whole conception that had been the inspiration of his younger days, in establishing a scientific psychology; and 'scientific' in the Germanic framework meant explaining things; and explaining things meant demonstrating causal relationships; and this in turn required quantitative statements. All statements other than quantitative (poetic, artistic) were fanciful, and therefore not scientific. A work like 'Beyond the Pleasure Principle' is a rather beautiful example of this split in Freud between the clinician struggling with the phenomena of the mind and their meaning, and the scientific theorizer trying to present a scientific theory which explains everything.

This then is the first of his difficulties: concerning the problem of mental pain and the question of affects and feelings, emotions, which had no place in his theory because they were dealt with as essentially meaningless, as by-products or the efflorescences of mental processes. Associated with this, he was in difficulty because his great economic principle was the Pleasure Principle, which more or less stated that pleasure consisted of the reduction of tensions, and unpleasure consisted of the increase or perhaps (he sometimes thought) their rate or acceleration of increase. But many phenomena made it quite clear to him that the attainment of pleasure and the avoidance of pain was not a satisfactory economic principle, in that it only covered a range of phenomena which could be subsumed under the category of wish-fulfilment (as in the dream theory). And many things going on in the mind simply could not be subsumed in that way. In 'Beyond the Pleasure Principle' he tries to bring to-gether these puzzling phenomena.

We have already heard about masochism; and Freud has already gone some distance toward coming to grips with it, through the recognition that the puzzle of masochism (like the puzzle of melancholia) involved a question such as 'Whose pain is it?', and that identification processes were involved in some way. But raising that question did not go any distance towards coping with certain other phenomena; and the one which came to the forefront at this time during the war, when there were so many cases of 'shell-shock', traumatic neuroses and so on, was the phenomenon of the traumatic dream. This seemed

115

the ultimate example to absolutely flaunt the Pleasure Principle, even when modified by the so-called Reality Principle.

The traumatic neuroses exhibited the following phenomenon: that the person dreamed over and over again of the situation of terror that had precipitated his breakdown: in battle or expectation of battle; as a result of explosions near them or without any explosion near them. The apparently ceaseless repetition of these dreams and the patient's waking in terror simply could not be subsumed under the dream theory about wish fulfilment, nor under the anxiety dream theory, in which the mechanisms for creating hallucinatory wish fulfilment were inadequate and the anxiety broke through. These dreams could not fall under that category, because they seemed to have no resemblance at all to dream structure: they seemed in their content to be simple factual repetitions of the experience or the expected experience that precipitated the breakdown. So they appeared to represent a phenomenon entirely different from any with which his dream theory had attempted to cope.

Freud had also noticed by this time that along with the repetitiveness of these particular dreams, went another phenomenon: namely the repetitiveness in children's play, and their endless desire for the repetition of the same story, the same game, the same experience in the minutest detail without modification. He suggested in this paper that there might be a more primitive economic principle (which is what he means by 'beyond' the pleasure principle: going back to the primitive mental processes beyond the establishment of that principle): a principle beyond this, which he called the Repetition Compulsion. This compulsion to repeat became linked with that other phenomenon which he had already called the 'compulsion to repeat' in relation to the transference: in which the transference as a phenomenon in the analytic setting seemed to manifest an inherent compulsion to repeat the events of childhood, in particular those events to which fixation had occurred, or which were traumatic experiences. From 'compulsion to repeat' to 'repetition compulsion' required only an inversion of language. And at the beginning of this paper it was these three phenomena which he brought together in order to formulate the idea that, at the most primitive levels of instinct, the instincts manifest an economic principle which is in essence a mindless compulsion to repeat: to repeat in a sense that is 'beyond' the pleasure principle, that is, having nothing to do with questions of pleasure or pain, but being simply the tendency to repeat endlessly the experience by which an instinct has manifested itself in the primitive organization of the child's mind and relation ships.

Up to this point, 'Beyond the Pleasure Principle' is a very clinical paper in which Freud has been trying to make these three clinical phenomena coalesce: the transference, the dreams of traumatic neurosis, and the play of children; and in this part of the paper occurs the famous passage about the child playing with the cotton reel. It has been up to now a paper dealing with clinical phenomena and enunciating an economic principle which may possibly be of use in trying to understand certain phenomena of the mind not approachable by means of the other economic principles – the Pleasure Principle and its modification in respect of external reality, the Reality Principle. One might say that here, the psycho-analytic part of the paper ends: and it swings back to the Project of 1897. The rest of it is an extremely elaborate speculation (Freud admits that it is highly speculative and even seems embarrassed about it) about the origins of life and the origins of sexuality and the way in which this compulsion to repeat is really the compulsion to repeat an inorganic state, and is therefore a death instinct. In other words, the instinct which he had previously been calling a life-preservative one is really (by a most tortuous tautological argument) the instinct to find one's *own* way to death, rather than being interfered with by others by being murdered on the way. And in effect the argument amounts to this: that a so-called life-preservative instinct (with its element of conservation) is now to be called a Death Instinct. In a sense its significance does not change, except that it is now being seen as a primary destructive impulse in which the aim is to destroy all the bonds linking together the cellular elements of the organism, and reduce them to an inorganic state – a sort of definition of death. In opposition to this, the sexual instincts are now to be called Eros or the Life Instinct, and to be seen as a constructive factor bringing together living units and making them into ever greater and more complicated structures, able to take on more complex functions. In none of this are the emotions of love and

117

hate mentioned, the emotions accompanying Eros and Thanatos (as it is called by Freud later on); again emotions are left out of the theory and therefore, given that there is a difference between meaning and significance, the meaning is also excluded. Freud enunciates the significance of a life instinct which is constructive, building greater units; and a death instinct which destructively tears them down, reducing life to an inorganic state; but of course this says nothing about the meaning which these processes have as they manifest themselves in mental life. Therefore it can be (and is) linked with biology and the behaviour of the protozoa; with the 'Project' 's scheme for the distribution of excitations and the reduction of tensions to a minimum; with the constancy principle and the Nirvana principle. The paper ends up with a theory implicitly linking itself to all these. And at the end of 'Beyond the Pleasure Principle', one is left in the dark as to how to make use of this formulation – of either the compulsion to repeat, or the life and death instinct, which is not supposed to mean anything very different from the life-preservative and sexual instincts, except in so far as it gives them a more biological foundation.

In one sense, however, 'Beyond the Pleasure Principle' is a great triumph, in that Freud has moved in the direction of rescuing violence, destructiveness and cruelty from a position of being tucked away in sexuality as a component instinct called sadism – having no necessary part in human life except in response to frustration, deprivation, or seduction. It is a great move forward, incorporating a conceptual vessel in which the meaning of primary destructiveness as an instinctual force is given a place, with the possibility of subsuming cruelty, violence, sado-masochism and perversity under the instinctual category; giving it a status in which (like the House of Lords) it has some say in the matter though not in the running of the country. Then the sexual instinct Eros is placed in opposition to it with the implication that it is going to win the day until senility sets in. This is more or less the picture one receives from Freud's attitude towards these two instincts: the death instinct exists, and its aim is to lead the organism through its life history to its natural death. But in this paper there is no picture of a continual conflict between life and death or love and hate, creativeness and destructiveness; because the whole concern is

118

placed in the context of bound cathexes and floating cathexes, and the way in which the destructive instinct is turned outward and away from its primary masochism, primary self-destructiveness; and projected. It therefore evaporates, and nothing much is changed by this paper except for the creation of a conceptual framework which Freud will begin to use functionally in later papers. In a way, however, he never made much of it; and I think never took it very seriously as a major modification of his viewpoint about mental functioning. It seems to me that Freud's view about life and death instincts was that they provided a neater and more inclusive way of talking about sexual and life-preservative instincts, owing to the wider coverage provided. Thus this new economic principle of the repetition phenomenon, provided a canopy under which the phenomena of masochism, the transference, and traumatic neuroses could all be gathered.

Imagining oneself as an analyst in 1920, however, one would not have known what to do with this principle, apart from having this slightly neater framework for discussion. And indeed everyone was terribly confused about life-preservative and sexual instincts: about how the life-preservative instinct could also be narcissistic and the sexual instinct could turn back on to the self as narcissism, and the two then seem to flow together; no-one could really tell where the other phenomena of violence, ambivalence and destructiveness, fitted in. But it is a fascinating exposition of this split with which I have been concerned; although I think that it is by this stage very much diminished; and although his enthusiasm is reminiscent of the boyish enthusiasm of the Fliess letters, he is also embarrassed and troubled about it, saying, in effect, 'now this is speculation . . . maybe next week some biologist will come up with something making it all sound like nonsense', but that 'anyway we must speculate, and not be bound . . .'. It is in this way very different from the 'Project', making very nice and interesting reading; it does not seem to have done any harm to psycho-analysis – except that a great deal of Lilliputian debate has raged over the question of the life and death instincts: much psycho-analytic politics has been staged in this tiny bit of territory.

The next paper, 'Group Psychology', is a different matter; because it is the first paper in which Freud really tried to come to grips with the problem of identification. As I have said, this has been touched on time and again throughout his writings; yet it is virtually never mentioned in the Index though you may look through volume after volume, except in relation to 'Mourning and Melancholia'; even in the Leonardo paper where the identification with his mother is absolutely essential, it is not in the Index; nor in the 'Wolf Man'. The omission is quite correct, for he was using the term descriptively, and not conceptually as yet. Up to this point identification has not really been a concept: not until this paper, when it is given some space and described at some length. In this very interesting paper Freud goes to work on all sorts of things, from the Church to the Army to falling in love to hypnosis to entropy to the problem of group formation and leadership and identification processes. What he is really working toward is trying to give some shape to the concept of the ego ideal, which he began to formulate back in the paper 'On Narcissism', and then in 'Mourning and Melancholia'. He realized that he had no definitive way of formulating it because he could not quite tell what it was that brought it about. Already he was talking about the ego and the separating-off of a part of the ego as a result of the process of introjection. This resulted in identification by a process analogous to eating one's father (i.e. cannibalistic) – although it was unclear whether he was eaten before or after he died. Freud could not quite achieve a formulation of what happened. A figure was seen as introjected into the ego, and then somehow this part of the ego was separated off to function as an ideal or love object for the rest of the ego. Some sort of spacial concept lay behind it. In this paper on Group Psychology he comes as close as he ever does in any of his writings to describing an inner world. For relating this introjection of an object into the ego, he connects it with the relinquishment of the relationship with the object in the outside world, until the whole operation of the object relationship is transferred to this new stage, on which the whole drama is re-enacted: the ego presenting itself as a love-object to the ego ideal, aspiring to become like it. In the background is always the lesson of 'Melancholia': that the whole process may turn sour and the participants start scolding and hating one another; or the ego may rebel against being scolded and expel the ego ideal, triumphing over it in its new freedom and becoming very manic. By this time Abraham had already begun to think that mania was connected with some sort of anal expulsion: getting rid of this introjected object or ego-ideal and triumphing over it, treating it like faeces; Freud was very fascinated by this idea, and began to realize it as something very active going on in some place: yet he could never quite formulate that it really was a 'place'; instead he speaks about 'imago', which seems to mean something equivalent to 'prototype', and again hedges the question of concreteness. This is, however, where he comes most close to describing what would later be called an 'inner world' in a concrete sense, in which internal objects and introjected objects have a life that stands in relation to the ego as external objects stand in relation to the personality or self.

The content of this paper concerns the understanding of Group Psychology; this is where Freud talks about the primal horde and the murder and eating of the father, and the competition between males for the sexual possession of the women; and where he places his theory about the origins of religion as an addendum to 'Totem and Taboo'. This is the main purpose of the paper, yet what is of greatest interest to psycho-analytic history, is this first organized description of the ego ideal and discussion about identifications. Now with identifications he does not seem to make much headway. He had already spoken of narcissistic identifications and of identification by introjection; and that distinction between regressive identifications (as he also calls them) and progressive ones is somehow lost here in favour of 'primitive' or 'primary' identifications, in which identification is seen as a very primitive process occurring naturally at the very beginnings of life, when identification and object relationship are indistinguishable from one another. He makes no attempt to explain how that comes about; again he implies (I suppose) that it is an inherent capacity, as it were 'beyond narcissism', earlier than narcissism, in which objects are identified with, or not distinguished from, the self. This may be what he means by 'primary narcissism', but it is never very clear.

Then there is a later form of identification which is specifically related to the relinquishment of an object in the outside world, and the introjection of this object into the ego, and the separating-off of the part of the ego which contains this object;

121

which separated-off portion assumes ego ideal function, or becomes the ego ideal. Freud is at this point talking almost exclusively about the father, and really only about the boy's relationship to the father and his introjection and identification. He states very clearly that this identification by introjection to form the separated-off portion of the ego called the ego ideal, is an identification very different in quality from the primitive form of identification in which the object is simply not recognized as separate, and the identification with it and experience of some identity with it is an immediate experience. He makes it quite clear that introjective identification, on the other hand, is an experience of confrontation with an admired object, which arouses aspirations and desires for emulation and development. This is very important; and although in this paper Freud does not penetrate very far into the nature of these types of identification (he is not really greatly interested in primary identification), yet he does distinguish between them.

Certain other aspects of this paper are worth noticing. He talks about hypnosis and more clearly than at any time since the 'Three Essays', about falling in love. It is important that his conception of sexual gratification is that it loosens object relationships; and the relinquishment of sexual aims or inhibited sexuality makes for durable and rich relationships. This has a rather cynical ring, but I think that Freud does not mean it to be cynical. He was thinking of sexuality in these energic terms; and since he was still bound to the energy theory at this time, it 'followed' (not as a matter of observation, but as a logical continuation of the implications of the Libido Theory) that once your libido has been discharged you feel fine and have no need of any further relationship with anyone until the tensions build up again. Just as sexual gratification is seen to deplete the ego of its vitality or tension, thereby releasing its tension and diminishing its need for an object, so is falling in love described as something which depletes the ego of narcissistic cathexis, and all the capacity for cathexis (that is, for relatedness and interest – for it is often defined as interest) is turned outward. Freud asserts that it does absolutely necessitate over-estimation and idealization of the love object, and that it is equivalent to a state of enthrallment or some very pathological state of mind, which he then equates with hypnosis and the relationship of the members of a group to its leader. And though this sounds cynical and repulsive, yet one has to remember that in this theoretical context Freud is not talking about Life, but rather about cathexes and libido – a different matter altogether.

This then was the position in 1920 or 1921. To this point the change in the instinct theory does not effectively give new meaning to anything; it simply provides new vessels for containing the concept of instinct, without adding much to their clinical usefulness. Freud has clarified to some extent the concept of identification and the ego ideal, in the paper on Group Psychology, with the separating-off from the ego of a special component; but he has not given the definition any sharpness because he is fundamentally uncertain about the central problem of the assimilation of an object into the ego, which seems to miscarry in some way. He cannot locate it exactly; he may refer to a 'stage', but cannot whole-heartedly accept it as a real stage with real actors upon it, and is therefore still in difficulty about giving it the concreteness which would truly set the inner world apart as independent from (though analogous to) relationships to objects in the outside world.

Chapter XIII

The Ego and the Id (The Advent of the Structural Theory)

When one attempts to take stock of the position of Freud's thought at this time, and to juxtapose it to the clinical data with which he was struggling, two basic factors present themselves. One is the residue of the 'Project', demanding restatement in terms of the new clinical phenomena; and at the other extreme there is evidence of the operation on his thought of the two masses of clinical data in his experience comprised in the 'Wolf Man' and in Schreber's extraordinary diary. One sees on the one hand his tendency to 'take the citadel by storm'and this by means to reduce the mysteries of nature to academic order and obedience; and on the other, his respect for an apparent galaxy of clinical phenomena thrown up by the psycho-analytical method, which defied such tyranny.

What were these phenomena? Schreber's hypochondria and persecutory delusions had revealed the world of narcissism, which Freud was seeing primarily in terms of the ego taking its own body as sexual object. By withdrawing cathexis from external objects on to the ego, early types of identification processes were invoked which antedated object relations. These could later be regressed to as fixation points (the stage of narcissism which followed auto-erotism in the baby's development). Then Schreber's 'world destruction' phantasy revealed the fact that in the mind a 'subjective world' is built up during development, from the 'sublimations and identifications' of the ego. The crumbling of this world was viewed by Freud as a relatively slow, non-violent process, resulting from the withdrawal of the libido from objects in the outside world. Just why this should produce a catastrophe in dementia or schizophrenia and not in melancholia he could not say, for he viewed the withdrawal of libido to be the primary operation in both situations. In any case, Freud saw this crumbling of the world of the mind as the event underlying the chaotic confusion of the dementia, from which a type of recovery was effected by building a delusional world from the fragments, 'not more splendid but at least one he could live in'.

This uncertainty, this hovering between 'sublimations' and

'identifications' as the foundation of character, is further illustrated in Freud's handling of the data of the 'Wolf Man', and appears to embody his uncertainty in abandoning the Libido Theory in favour of a more structural conception of the mind and mental events. The emergence in his thought of a 'special gradient in the Ego', a specialized part of the mind, at first called an 'ideal ego' and later on 'ego ideal', leaned towards a structuralization of ego-functions. He at first attributed such varied functions as censorship, the setting of aspirations, reality-testing and self-observation to this part of the mind, and saw it as being in some way linked to identification processes in melancholia. But he was undecided as to whether the alteration was in the ego itself: to which the abandoned object cathexis fell as an introjection – the 'shadow of the object' in melancholia and the 'radiance of the object' in mania; or whether it formed something quite separate from the ego. Did the ego ideal rant against the ego identified with the ambivalently held object, or did the ego rail against the object which it had abandoned externally by setting it up in the inside of the mind?

Since Freud's new theory of life- and death-instincts moved him toward perceiving conflicts of a new order, between the two classes of instincts and their derivatives rather than between adherence to the Pleasure Principle and the demands of reality, he realized that his central preoccupation with levels of consciousness was no longer either so mysterious or so crucial. Furthermore this topographic theory had run into great difficulties of a semantic nature, which Freud was at some trouble to sort out in 'The Ego and the Id'. At least three different uses of the term 'unconscious' could be recognized: a purely descriptive one related to mental phenomenology; a dynamic one connected with the theory of repression (which was already being broadened into the theory of the mechanisms of defence of which repression was perhaps of less importance than originally thought); and thirdly, a systematic usage. This last had been a move in the direction of structuralizing the model of the mind; as had, along with it, the conceptions of the stages of *organization* of the libido, which Freud and Abraham had been working out. But the mixture of topographic systems and developmental organizations did not coalesce into a unified theory; especially as Freud was now keenly aware that the

Unconscious and the *Repressed* could not be equated. The devious manoeuvre to hedge this issue, in the 'Wolf Man' case, by suggesting that the wolf-dream at age four had recathected with word-representations the thing-representations of the primal scene at age one and a half, thus making it available for thought and anxiety, could not really seal off the problem. Clearly there was an extensive period of early childhood which was not repressed but could nonetheless not be recalled. And clearly there was a vast amount of mental activity going on all the time to which the 'organ for the perception of psychic qualities', consciousness, was simply paying no *attention*.

It became necessary to consider that the unconscious was too vast and multifacetted a realm of mental activity to be contained in the fragile concept of the Repressed. Also called into question was the early imputation from the seventh chapter of 'The Interpretation of Dreams', and the later formulation of the 'Two Principles of Mental Functioning', that the processes in the unconscious were of an inferior order: being among other things timeless, illogical, subject to condensations and displacements, and lacking in negative ideas; this was all placed in doubt by such things as the recognition that dreams and sleep could be thought-full and problem-solving. Freud cites the example of mathematical problems being solved during sleep. The trouble lay partly in his attitude toward the dream itself: which considered its function in life to be such a narrow and defensive one – the guardian of sleep. Already the problem of traumatic dreams had contributed (along with the phenomenon of masochism) to the necessity of revising his basic idea of the economic, or quantitative, aspects of mental life; and had led to the formulation in 'Beyond the Pleasure Principle' of the Repetition Compulsion as an economic principle more primitive than the Pleasure Principle. But he was uncertain as to its point of impact. In 'The Ego and the Id', the problem seems to be by-passed in favour of a new idea: that of fusion and defusion of the two instincts, to account for the paradoxical aspects of instinct life – a move which is on the whole not successful. In general it would seem that the idea that the Repetition Compulsion can be so powerful that it overrides the Pleasure Principle and produces phenomena of the ego persevering in a painful position, is a more powerful explanation than the idea that fusions of love and hate – whereby the latter is neutralized in its virulence – come apart and liberate 'pure culture of the death instinct' (as in melancholia).

Probably much of the difficulty of formulation lay in the fact that Freud still lacked a theory of affects, even though his clinical material provides unmistakeable evidence for his dealing deeply and sensitively with the emotional relationships of his patients in the consulting room. It is probably the most impor- tant – though far from the most obvious – way in which Freud's clinging to the neuro-physiological and hydrostatic view of mental life of 'The Project', interfered with the formulation of a satisfactory theory for describing and partially explaining the very complicated phenomena of the transference process. The concept of 'quantities of excitation' as a basis for pleasure and unpleasure, left unformulated the whole area of mental pain; and tended strongly towards a view of life which was essen- tially denuded of meaning, or rather of meaningfulness. Accord- ingly, we find Freud returning to the idea of castration anxiety as the central pain; which leaves him in the lurch in cases where external threats cannot be demonstrated, throwing him back on vague phyllogenetic explanations. Also, of course, it leaves his approach to an understanding of female sexuality unconvincing, to say the least; and imposes on all his formulations the stamp of masculine arrogance, with the female sex taking on the significance of the second-class, 'faute de mieux'.

This weakness then finds particular expression in 'The Ego and the Id', when Freud comes to a definitive clarification of a structural hypothesis for the mental apparatus; dividing its functions into Id, Ego and Superego (or/and Ego Ideal). While he is able to make a definitive step forward in describing the Oedipus Complex in its 'complete' form – as consisting of both masculine and feminine conflicts for each individual – he is still left with terms like 'positive' and 'negative', 'direct' and 'inverted' with their penumbra of value judgment. Consequent- ly, as in the case of the Wolf Man, the 'Case of Homosexuality in a Woman', and in Schreber or Leonardo, the man's feminin- ity and the woman's masculinity retain their connection with the term 'homosexual'; in spite of his saying in many places that it is a complex and multifacetted term (much like his

127

confused definition of 'unconscious'); it tends to generate confusion rather than clarification. Furthermore, there are attempts to describe the Superego in its complete form as derived from 'the forming of a precipitate in the ego, consisting of these two identifications': that is, with both the mother and the father; but despite this, his consideration of the functions of the Superego *vis-à-vis* the Ego keeps returning to the father's figure as the central one, as the source of both the 'categorical imperative' of 'thou shalt' and the prohibitive influence of 'thou shalt not.'

In the fascinating section on the 'ego's dependent relationships' with Id, Superego and External Reality, Freud comes to take stock of the significance of his theory in its broad outline. And here he is forced in all honesty to recognize that he has put forward a picture of mental life which is pessimistic in the extreme. This will later find definitive expression in 'Future of an Illusion', 'Civilization and its Discontents', and 'Analysis Terminable and Interminable'. But the implication is unmistakeable already in 1923 and is very different from the Victorian optimism with which Freud had entered the arena thirty years earlier. The Ego is seen here as a poor creature indeed, 'serving three masters', despite its relation to the Id having been likened to that of a rider to his horse. Truly a horse may sometimes get the bit in its teeth; sometimes it must be allowed to go the way it prefers; its superior strength must be respected and its dangerousness acknowledged; but one can hardly say overall that the horse is the master. Likewise Freud has made it clear that the Ego, through its use of thought as trial action and by means of its exclusive access to the motor apparatus, is able to transform external reality to suit itself – within limits, of course. And finally he describes the Superego as having evolved from a specialized function of the Ego, through the introjection of the parental figures, just as the Ego arose from the Id through the exercise of its special perceptual capacities. A paradox is therefore created by the suggestion that it is 'higher' in the evolutionary sense, and derivative from the parental figures, who serve the helplessness of the child with their superior knowledge and strength. How can it be higher and nurturing in origin but a tyrannical master in fact? Here again one feels that preconception has interfered with learning from experience in the theoretical area of Freud's work, for he clings to the formulation that conscience is derived from the 'dissolution of the (genital) oedipus complex', coincides with the onset of the latency period. Moreover, it is virtually absent in the little girl, who is seen to remain bound to her external objects and be influenced more by fear of the loss of love than by castration anxiety like the little boy, by virtue of her sense of organ inferiority.

How then are we to understand this pessimism? Our concern here is not with how it may be viewed in the context of Freud's personality, his struggles and relationships. I mean rather: how are we to understand the evolution of his ideas so as to comprehend the position that he has reached by 1923? Why is he disposed to view the Ego as being so weak, and forced to employ all manner of deceptions like a politician? How is it that these thirty years of work have for virtually the first time produced for psycho-analytical consideration the question: 'How does a person remain well?', in displacement of Freud's constant pre-occupation with the problem of the 'choice of neurosis'?

It is striking that no sooner does he ask the question, than he finds in a stroke of astonishing brilliance, the answer which has guided future generations of analysts: though he only formu-lated the answer clearly, fourteen years later (and it was only applied twenty-three years later, by Melanie Klein). Only a few months after the publication of 'The Ego and the Id' he could write in the paper on 'Neurosis and Psychosis' (p. 152), speaking of situations of conflict from which the ego must emerge in order to avoid falling ill:

> In the first place the outcome of all such situations will un-doubtedly depend on economic considerations – on the relative magnitudes of the trends which are struggling with one another. In the second place it will be possible for the ego to avoid a rupture in any direction by deforming itself, by submitting to encroachments on its own unity and even perhaps by effecting a cleavage or division of itself. In this way the inconsistencies, eccentricities and follies of men would appear in a similar light to their sexual perversions, through the acceptance of which they spare themselves repressions.

Other aspects of the answer to the question of the sources of the pessimism inherent in Freud's theoretical construction at this time, may be found in two conceptions which he has touched upon but not yet utilized. The first of these is the quality of omnipotence, which he had clearly recognized in the clinical phenomena of the Rat Man, the Wolf Man, and Schreber. The second is the formulation of an 'internal world' or 'world of phantasy'. This played a large part in the understanding of Schreber's 'world destruction phantasy', and there Freud realized that it could be considered that the 'world' which fell to destruction from the withdrawal of libido from objects, had been composed of the 'sum total of sublimations and identifications' which made up the foundations of character. But he could not find a substantial place for it in his structural theory of the mind because he could not ascribe to it a constructive significance. In 1924, in the paper 'The Loss of Reality in Neurosis and Psychosis', he writes (p. 187):

> The sharp distinction between neurosis and psychosis, however, is weakened by the circumstance that in neurosis too there is no lack of attempts to replace a disagreeable reality by one which is more in keeping with the subject's wishes. This is made possible by the existence of a *world of phantasy*, of a domain which becomes separated from the real external work at the time of the introduction of the reality principle. This domain has since been kept free from the demands of the exigencies of life, like a kind of 'reservation'.

By this time he had returned the function of reality testing (earlier ascribed to the ego ideal) to the list of the ego's tasks and capabilities.

In bringing to a close this consideration of 'The Ego and the Id' and taking stock of the position which Freud had reached in his attempts to formulate conceptual equipment for describing (and in some measure explaining) the phenomenology of his consulting room, I suggest that one should bear in mind for future consideration, the defects in his approach. Firstly, he had no adequate theory of affects, and was still thinking of quantities of excitation. Secondly, the loci of conflict had not yet been pinpointed, partly because he was still inclined to a unitary hypothesis in this area. Thirdly, he had failed to make use of the attribute of omnipotence of which he had found abundant evidence. Fourthly, he was still inclined to attribute a trivial function to the dream as the guardian of sleep. And finally, he was disinclined to see in the 'world of phantasy' an aspect of the 'world' of the mind that had a reality of its own which rivalled in significance the reality with which the external world was apprehended.

Chapter XIV
The Last Years (Anxiety and the Economics of the Mind)

We come now to the rather sad last years of Freud's life: the last twelve years from the writing of 'Inhibition, Symptom and Anxiety' until his death. For despite being ill he seems to have worked a lot: in between a dozen operations he wrote three volumes of papers. His interest certainly turned very strongly toward retrospection on the implications of psycho-analytic findings for other fields – anthropology, sociology, and politics; and he produced these works: 'The Future of an Illusion', 'Civilization and its Discontents', and 'Moses and Monotheism', which I personally do not find very interesting. There is a change in his style of writing: it becomes very prolix and diffuse in many places; I think writing had probably become a necessary part of his life, and of course the people who followed him were interested in anything written by him.

However, I do not wish to discuss these works; rather, I propose to study the winding-up and tying together of his clinical ideas and the tools and equipment of psycho-analysis – developments in his attitudes rather than his technique: such as the problem of female sexuality; a more definitive view of the perversions; and a clearer shape to the concept of splitting of the ego and the mechanisms of psycho-pathology. All this makes a substantial though not perhaps a major contribution, such as occurred throughout the marvellous six years from 1920 to 1926, in which the whole theory was revised to become the Structural Theory, and with it the model of the mind for use in the consulting room. 'Inhibition, Symptom and Anxiety', or 'The Problem of Anxiety' as it is sometimes called, really reversed Freud's previous stand concerning anxiety. He tended earlier to consider it to be a kind of noise made in the mind as a result of the stagnation of sexual impulses and their transformation into mental pain. But here he decides that anxiety is really at the heart of the matter, and he uses the term not simply as a descriptive one (as previously), but as a general term for the kind of mental pain that functions as a signal of some impending disorder in the mind. This signal theory of anxiety is the one with which we actually work; although of course the theory of anxiety has undergone a considerable change in the hands of Mrs Klein, though her division of it into persecutory anxiety (corresponding to Freud's signal) and depressive anxieties, which corresponds more to a concept of mental pain.

In this way Freud came gradually to consider that the problems with which psycho-analysis was concerned were best stated in terms more closely related to the concept of affects. He seemed to come around to the view that affects and particularly painful affects, were at the heart of the matter; and that the pleasure principle was not simply a matter of avoiding unpleasure, but was really a matter of *dealing* with mental pain of various sorts. This really fitted in place the ultimate piece necessary for a workable model of the mind: one which, I think, has remained the model which we use in psycho-analysis. The structure of the mind – the Ego, Superego and Id – has been only slightly modified through the tendency to think more of 'self' than of Ego and Id: that is, to think of self as being composed of Ego and Id and split in various ways. Essentially, we still think of it as Ego and Id in its origins, but as 'self' operationally. There is great beauty in Freud's idea that the primordial personality, the primordial mind, was originally all Id, and that out of it evolved a separate organ of the mind – the Ego – from the impact of experience; and that from this evolved the Superego, as a result of introjective and other processes. His evolutionary view of the way in which the development of the mind recapitulates the evolution of mind in the species, has remained a happy model which most analysts find inspiring rather than useful.

In the years which followed the establishment of this model of the mind, Freud was very ill, and also very preoccupied with the applications of psycho-analytic thought; trying to understand what the psycho-analytic movement signified in the world. But he still continued to do clinical work and certainly a tremendous amount of supervision of his colleagues. By this time he was fairly convinced that the limitations of an analyst's work were imposed mainly by the degree to which he had made contact with his own unconscious 'complexes' (as he still called them): by his unconscious conflict. But he had also realized very astutely that an analyst's work was dependent on a continuation of the self-analytic process in the course of his work and of his daily life. He was also forced by various tragedies to realize that analysis, like most professions, or most jobs, carries an industrial hazard: analytic work was seen to be a danger to the analyst's mental health. And at this time he advised analysts to go back to analysis every five years. The training analysis at that time was a very cursory affair indeed, however; Freud (in about 1935) was thinking of it as something lasting only a few months, which was to be mainly devoted to the analyst getting a first-hand experience of the analytic method at work, and learning the rudiments of dream analysis and introspection. It was better than the walks in the park he had had with Ferenczi; but it was not a therapeutic view of the training analysis, which only grew up in the years following his death, when the third generation of analysts were to be trained. Freud was very specific himself, particularly in the paper 'Analysis Terminable and Interminable', that there is no complete analysis: that any analysis is, at its best, a preparation for a continuation of self-scrutiny and development, and it is not meant to protect people from having conflicts in life, but only to equip them to meet these. Analysis is the beginning, and not the end, of a process.

His interest in psycho-pathology lessened considerably during this time, it seems to me; and his interest in healthy development increased in two directions. The first is manifest in his changing views about female sexuality. The realization grew upon him that women analysts were able to get a different view of female sexuality, not just by virtue of being women and knowing at first-hand, but also because they elicited a richer maternal transference from their patients. This was true at that time, when male analysts did not know how to pick up the phenomenology of the maternal transference so well, and tended to work very much in the so-called 'father complex', recognizing mainly the paternal transference. Freud acknowledged his indebtedness to the women analysts of that era, and the changes in his views on female sexuality were I think very salutary ones; he partly gave up the differentiation of active and passive as if it were equivalent to masculine and feminine, and recognized the strong active trends that are present in femininity as well as in masculinity. This went a little distance toward the recognition

of passivity as a more pathological phenomenon, to be differentiated from dependence and receptivity. He did rather cling
to the view that the little girl knew nothing of her vagina and
had no vaginal sensations, although he acknowledges that
women may know more about this and that here he might be
wrong. He also acknowledged that perhaps his view that
women's primary difficulty stems from penis envy was an
exaggerated one; and that their penis envy (as Helene Deutsch
and others insisted) might be a very secondary thing, not at all
the primary manifestation of emerging femininity. Most importantly, he became aware that the little girl has a terrific task on
her hands in forming her Oedipus Complex – that is, her
feminine Oedipus Complex. Because the difficulty of changing
from her primary pregenital (which he still insists on calling
'preoedipal') attachment was so great, the formation of a strong
oedipal attachment to the father was a much heavier task than
the little boy's sexualization of his primary relationship to his
mother in his masculine Oedipus Complex. He devotes a lot of
thought to how it is the little girl manages this; and when he
lists motives which may drive her in this direction, they are
primarily grievances against the mother: that the mother did
not give her a penis, that the mother provided her with sexual
stimulation while changing her nappies but did not give her
full satisfaction; envy of the mother, castration anxiety and the
belief that she has been castrated at the mother's hands, anxiety
about being devoured by the mother, are all based on careful
clinical observation. But it is all rather negative motivation,
propelled by grievances on the one hand and anxieties on the
other, and generally conducive of a picture of femininity as a
rather unwholesome affair. What it lacks, and what is missing
generally from his theoretical views in these later years, is really
a use of the concept of identification. That is, he does not allow
sufficiently for the little girl's positive motivation of identification with her mother, through which she may turn to her father
in a loving way via the mother's love for the father. Therefore
he cannot allow for the intensity of the little girl's longing for
babies from the father; but thinks primarily of her craving
sexual gratification on the one hand, or the various motives for
revenge on the mother for disappointments, on the other.
Although the view of female sexuality makes a big step forward

135

in acknowledging the complexity and the role of activity, paying a tribute to the difficulty of the task of the little girl, it does not quite grasp the positive and tender motivation in her. Freud implies on the contrary that she is drawn to the father and to the penis, as the object of sexual desire, from primarily spiteful and negative motives. He speaks of little girls' attachment to their dolls, but tends to view this only as some sort of competition with the mother, and does not take into account admiration for the mother and the positive aspects of identification which play a role in the formation of the little girl's Oedipus Complex.

Probably Freud had forgotten along the way the ego ideal aspects of the Superego: those aspects of encouragement and nurturing and fostering which the Superego maintains toward the Ego. I think there is no doubt that his views about severity of the Superego hardened during this time, affecting his idea of the therapeutic task in analysis to the extent that he states quite unequivocally that part of the therapeutic task is to free the Ego from the domination of the Superego. In later psychoanalysts' writing, this is modified so that Freud's phrase 'the dissolution of the Oedipus Complex' becomes 'the dissolution of the Superego'. This reminds one of the joke that the Superego is the alcohol-soluble fraction of the personality – a wry joke indeed.

This would place psycho-analysis in a position to promulgate a value system devoted entirely to cultural adaptation, leaving no room for individual development and individuality or idiosyncrasy in values, for independence of one's culture and a healthy kind of rebelliousness. It is mainly from this point of view that Freud's late attitude toward the psycho-analytical method and its efficacy was pessimistic; and this pessimism is most clearly brought out in the famous paper 'Analysis Terminable and Interminable'. This attitude left the Ego with no ego ideal relationship to the Superego; it did not allow the Superego any function of promoting ideals and values and, in the absence of any internal source of ideals and values, these would really have to be absorbed from the external culture. This is related to the whole trend in 'Civilization and its Discontents' to the effect that adaptation to the culture is a necessity and that it is achieved at the expense of internal freedom. He does not conceive the possibility of freedom and a healthy maladaptation to a bad culture.

I suggest that the pessimism about analysis that percolates through 'Analysis Terminable and Interminable' is of a very peculiar sort. It seems to me that it is an outgrowth of Freud thinking of the analytical method and analytical theories as if they were complete (although he would absolutely deny this in theory); as if the method had now been brought to its perfection, and its efficacy could be evaluated in some final way. The weight comes down very much on the side of what psychoanalysis cannot do, because of the 'quantitative' or 'economic' factors. These economic factors were felt to be connected with the death instinct and destructiveness (primary sadism, primary masochism, secondary sadism and masochism); and the strength of these impulses was felt to create the negative therapeutic reaction in analysis. It manifest itself as what he called 'inertia' or 'stickiness' in the transference, and created the opposition to cure and the clinging to guilt. These three link together: the stickiness or the inertia of the libido as it is manifest in the transference; the tendency to negative therapeutic reaction to any step forward in insight; and the factor of the patient clinging, rather masochistically, to the repetition of his experiences of guilt.

One cannot escape the impression that he had had himself, and saw his colleagues having repeatedly, experiences of analyses grinding to a halt, long before a really satisfactory therapeutic result had been achieved. Freud considered these factors to be mainly constitutional; modified of course by the experience of the first five years of life which he considered to be so absolutely crucial. After these first five years, very little, if any, effect on personality structure could be expected. By the time the latency period was established, the personality structure and the fundamentals of character were likewise established.

The implications of that paper had a rather bad effect on the development of analysis. First of all, they tended to discourage character analysis; secondly, they tended to encourage analysts to restrict themselves to curing symptoms; and thirdly through the tone of the paper, to discourage technical innovation or experimentation. Freud had already spoken quite harshly of the experiments that Ferenczi had made in his last years with more active techniques; of other attempts to shorten the process; and of technical methods for dealing with resistances other than by interpretation. His attitude toward child analysis (although in two footnotes he gives credit to its developers) dismissed it from playing a serious role in the future of psychoanalysis either from the social or from the scientific point of view. This, I think, probably relates back to the relatively small yield that he drew from Little Hans: that case, in all its richness, was after all used almost exclusively to corroborate the evidence already drawn from adult analysis for the existence of the infantile neurosis and the reality of the Oedipus Complex.

In many ways Freud was right; but not for the right reasons. He was right because it has turned out that child analysis is so difficult, that not many people can do it well, that not many people who do it well can do it for many years, and that parents are not willing to make the sacrifices that are necessary for extensive analysis of children. The tendency is certainly for child analysis to gravitate to the child guidance clinics and into the hands of young people with low scientific status, too low for research accomplishment. I think it never occurred to Freud that the psycho-analysis of children would bring innovations to the technical aspects of the psycho-analysis of adult patients.

Finally there is another possible reason which may contribute to the pessimism of 'Analysis Terminable and Interminable', one probably more personal to Freud. Perhaps he was disappointed in the quality of people who were attracted to psychoanalytical work, whereas in the very early years, his optimism and enthusiasm had tended to cause him to idealize the people who gathered around him. Disillusion ensued when he discovered that naturally the people who were drawn to psychoanalysis were, by and large, people who needed psychoanalytical treatment. Because psycho-analysis was still in its early stages and its therapeutic efficacy was limited, it could not be expected to have the degree of success that would enable its students to do first class psycho-analytical work, or to withstand the industrial hazard. This pessimism was an outgrowth of Freud's tendency to view the method and technique as being far advanced, rather than rudimentary and in its infancy as a science. For instance, he always thought that psychotic illnesses and psychotic aspects of the personality would remain outside the possibility of psycho-analytic influence: such patients would be unable to form a transference neurosis. A transference psychosis of the Wolf Man's 1926 illness does not seem to have altered his view.

Because the psychoses drew their origins from such an early pre-verbal period in the history of the individual, so as to be beyond the possibility of recall, Freud was unable to formulate a therapeutic process comparable with recovery from the infantile amnesia. This brings us to another paper very closely tied to 'Analysis Terminable and Interminable': namely the little paper on 'Constructions in Analysis' – by which he meant what we would call 'Reconstructions in Analysis'. Here it is quite clear that his view of the analytical method still treated it as something of a jigsaw puzzle. Interpretation certainly is seen as a moment-to-moment activity of the analyst dealing with the bits of material as they come along; but the important and synthetic work of the analyst is considered to be the creation of the reconstruction of the history of the infantile neurosis, which the analyst then has to 'work through' gradually to enable the patient to accept and be influenced by it. Freud felt that the therapeutic task was very dependent on this intellectual activity of the analyst and the intellectual acceptance of it by the patient; for this reconstruction was supposed to assist in the relief of the infantile amnesia and the recovery of sufficient memories of the period of the infantile neurosis, to be convincing to the patient.

The very earliest year of life or earliest eighteen months prior to the development of the capacity to verbalize, did not allow the thing-representations to become word-representations which could become accessible to consciousness. Freud was in this way hamstrung by his own theories about how the mind worked; he could not conceive of the possibility that remembering could take place in action, simply as transference experience. This is partly because his idea of the truth continued to refer to the knowledge of external reality; which in turn may be seen as the consequence of his never fully conceptualizing (in spite of using the phrase 'internal world') a space in the mind occupied by figures of continuous existence, rather than by 'imagos'. And because his idea of an internal world never reached beyond this, his concept of truth could not become one

139

of the knowledge of psychic reality; despite his calling consciousness an 'organ for the perception of psychic qualities'. The accomplishment of a sense of reality, and the achievement of mental health, meant to him specifically the elimination of the tendency to infantile transference distortion: that is, the tendency of the past to distort perception and experience of the outside world in the present. This seems to me to have placed a very great limitation on his thought about the nature of mental health.

On the other hand he made a great step forward during these years in coming to think about mental health as a problem for psycho-analysis to investigate as a thing in itself, not merely as the absence or negative of psycho-pathology. In two papers: that 'On Fetishism' and that on 'The Splitting of the Ego in the Service of Defence', he does raise the question of how a person may remain healthy, and he immediately answers it in a very brilliant way. He suggests that the person achieves it by splitting his ego and relegating the less healthy parts of his ego to repressions, to being encapsulated by defences in some manner; and the healthy part of his ego, he turns towards the outside world. In arriving at this concept of splitting of the ego in relation to fetishism, and then applying it to the question of how a person remains healthy, Freud did provide an answer of a most useful nature. But it would be incorrect to assume that this is the same use of the term 'splitting processes' as that employed by Melanie Klein in her 1946 paper. There, she describes splitting processes as a 'schizoid mechanism': she means an entirely different thing from Freud. Freud referred primarily to a splitting of the attention, which thus brought about some sort of division in the Ego; attention to the outside world could be carried on by the healthy part, and attention to symptoms and to Superego could be carried on by those parts of the personality afflicted by psycho-pathological formations. Previously he had assumed that the Ego was a single synthetic organ of the mind; and in spite of all the evidence to the contrary (with Schreber, for instance) he never systematically questioned this, until he considered reformulating fetishism.

I will now summarize the development in these last years from the point of view of clinical psycho-analysis. It is important to understand the pessimism which afflicts these years somewhat, since it has had an immense influence in various ways on the development of psycho-analytic thought. This influence has consisted primarily in encouraging orthodoxy; in discouraging technical innovation; and tending to preserve to some degree the energetics concept of the Libido Theory, infusing this a little into the Structural Theory of the mind. For Freud himself preserved in this way his own preoccupation with with the quantitative aspects of things. I think that this category of meta-psychology (the economic category: the preoccupation with the quantitative relationships) is without doubt theoretically correct; but is is practically quite useless, and tends to serve for analysts the function of an escape hatch or rubbish bin into which analytic failures may be dumped. It discourages a more pugnacious attitude toward analytical failures; dissuades the analyst from full responsibility for his own failures; and encourages a tendency to blame the patient and assume that the failure of an analysis is that of the patient and not of the analyst. One of the unsavoury manifestations is the emergence of the term 'unanalysable', which comprises a sort of political conviction, a relegation to a psycho-analytical Siberia. This seems to me to have arisen in direct relation to the paper 'Analysis Terminable and Interminable', and to be the most unfortunate part of the legacy that we have received from Freud, glorious as it is in other ways.

PART TWO

Richard Week-by-Week

(A Critique of the 'Narrative of a Child Analysis' and a review of Melanie Klein's work)

Acknowledgements

I wish to thank Mr Eric Rhode, Mrs Catherine Mack Smith and Mrs Margaret Williams for their help in the preparation and proofing of the text.

Introduction

Any systematic attempt to teach Melanie Klein's work runs almost immediately into difficulties that are the exact opposite of the problems facing one in teaching Freud. Where the theoretical tail wags the clinical dog with him, hardly any theoretical tail exists to be wagged with her. This is not immediately apparent because all her earlier work (until the paper on manic-depressive states, but really only taking a clear-cut line of departure with the 1946 paper on schizoid mechanisms) is couched in the theoretical language of Freud and Abraham, shifting from the terms of Libido and Topographic Theory to the new Structural one.

One can hardly ascribe naïveté to such an astute woman; one must assume that the philosophy of science did not really interest her. The laws of evidence; the distinction between description, model, theory and notational system; the different classes of definitory statements – none of this concerned her. This was partly a matter of modesty, for she clearly considered her work to be merely a filling-out and clarification of Freud's and never recognized the huge leap she had made in method or model of the mind. She tended to be hurt and astonished by the hostility directed at her and thought of it only as antagonism to the ideas, much as Freud felt in his early isolation. But surely a great deal of this unfriendliness stemmed from very poor communication, linguistic snarls, further provoked by the dogmatic demeanor of her (and her colleagues') writing. These are the preconditions for political struggle over the 'mantle', Freud's, Abraham's, later Mrs Klein's. Although it now becomes a bad pun to speak of dis-mantling the Kleinian myth, that is certainly one of the main functions of these lectures.

In order to do this I chose to re-enforce Mrs Klein's own courageous attempt, embodied in that unique and fairly unread masterpiece (Henry Reed said it stood beside 'War and Peace' on his shelf), 'Narrative of a Child Analysis'. On the whole the adventure has been successful in its lecture-seminar form. Whether this can be carried over into printed form is uncertain for two reasons; one is that the lectures are meant to be virtually unintelligible unless the actual text of the book has been studied carefully, or at least very recently read. The second reason is more complex. The lectures were impromptu (though carefully prepared), recorded and the text edited. The result is very unsatisfactory from the literary standpoint but has been retained because of the personal flavour of my relation to Mrs Klein (internally). It is hoped that in this way it would be possible to maintain a critical attitude side by side with admiration and respect without generating an atmosphere either of reverence or iconoclasm. My discussion of the clinical work has a background in an exhaustive study of the book made by a group (Esther Bick, Martha Harris, Doreen Weddell, Claude and Elinor Wedeles) in 1962-64 for which Dr E. Wedeles kept notes. But the criticisms and praise of Mrs Klein's work are totally my own responsibility.

So the first purpose of these lectures was to help people to read, preferably to study, this important book. The second was to use the clinical work and Mrs Klein's notes as basis for a semi-systematic review of her method and ideas. This stock-taking, since it is partly determined in its sequence by problems which arise in the clinical material, is not orderly either in an historic (or chronological) sense nor in a systematic one. Nonetheless many of Mrs Klein's important ideas are reviewed and brought into juxtaposition to Freud's, with some resultant clarification on both sides, I think.

<table>
<tr><td>Chapter I</td><td>First Week: Sessions 1-6
Establishing the Analytic
Situation; Evolution of the
Concepts: Paranoid-Schizoid and
Depressive Positions</td></tr>
</table>

The book seems to have been written between 1958 and 1960, after *Envy and Gratitude*, which appeared in 1957. The clinical work, done in 1941, was first written up in *The Oedipus Complex in the Light of Early Anxieties*, (I. J. Psa. 1945) and then in 1946 came the paper which changed everything: *Notes on Some Schizoid Mechanisms* (I. J. Psa. 1946).

The first week of the analysis opens like a Chekhov play – immediately all the characters are introduced and all the themes and subplots are hinted at. An unlikely first week in the analysis of a ten year old. It is partly because Mrs Klein had already formulated some ideas in her mind, probably having taken a bit too much history from the mother. Consequently due to being in a hurry she makes mistakes which force things, mistakes in technique and interpretation which she has to make up for later. Her technique as she describes it in *The Psycho-analysis of Children*, was developed particularly with young children; and the technique with latency, pubertal and adolescent children was really an adaptation from this source. The basis of the technique aimed to *establish the analytical situation*, which meant getting some sort of transference going. Her way of getting it going was to perform some service to the child's unconscious by diminishing or modifying its deepest anxieties through interpretation.

Now Richard chronologically is a latency child, and you can see that when he comes to her, his manifest anxieties are at a minimum; whereas with small children her experience had always been that, in leaving the mother and coming to the playroom, the child would almost always experience severe persecutory anxieties which could be investigated with even minimal material. But with Richard it is quite different: there is very little manifest anxiety – she is not a doctor, she is not a man; he is quite used to charming and seducing women, and obviously has looked forward to seeing her. What can be seen

147

happening in the first week is that, whether intentionally or not, Mrs Klein has set about mobilising anxieties, rather than diminishing them. And the technique she employs for mobilising Richard's anxieties is really no different from one for diminishing them: that is, to go right into the depths.

In the very first session she has done this in quite a masterful way, with the material about the fear of his mother being attacked by a tramp. Immediately the stage is filled with characters: the primal scene is introduced and the cast builds up through the next three sessions – there is mummy, daddy, brother Paul, Richard; there is Bobby the dog; somewhere there is 'Cook', Johnny Wilson, his analytical rival; and somewhere there is Mr Klein, who is not dead despite Richard knowing very well that he was, and there is Mrs Klein's son. And in the background of the stage set is the war situation with accomodating maps on the wall and all the other paraphernalia of the Girl Guides' room. In that sense it was a very unusual setting in which to practice analysis; indeed there seems to have been enough material scattered round the walls for one to deal with it almost like a Rorschach. Anything Richard might select could be taken as having associative significance for him because it was taken from such a tremendous array of pictures and postcards on the walls.

In the very first session one sees Mrs Klein forcing the situation: forcing it, for instance, in a way which she would generally have considered a technical error; that is, by using her knowledge of the history to seek a specific piece of material, namely whether he was worried about his mother. The material about the tramp immediately came out. She is nevertheless very gentle with Richard regarding aspects of his character which are in evidence, such as duplicity, trickiness and treachery – a theme which appears very early on. She never really confronts him with bad aspects of his feelings and impulses without immediately balancing it with a recognition of the other side – of his desire to preserve and protect.

In this first week, in addition to the creating or evoking of the whole setting of the child's life, Mrs Klein also unfolds for Richard a considerable panorama of her own theoretical equipment: the splitting of objects between good and bad, the conflict between love and hate, between persecutory and depressive feelings. She hints at mental mechanisms like the denial of psychic reality, the difference between wishing, thinking, doing; she suggests such things as splitting on to the dog parts of himself; she speaks about splitting within himself and delegating, for instance, a bad part of himself to the monkey; about the primal scene and phantasies of involving himself in it (the material about the two dogs with the little puppy between them). She unfolds theories concerning the oral, anal, and genital erogenous zones in relation to the dog Bobby eating coal and Richard wanting to play with his 'big job'; and finally she introduces him to the concept of omnipotence.

Now it seems to me that in many ways she introduces these concepts to him in a hurry, in ways that are a bit in advance of the material. This is most clearly seen with the introduction of the concept of omnipotence a propos the monkey and the concept of tragedy, and whether the tragedy was really that Richard caught cold or that he realized that his destructive impulses were too strong to control. But I think that in general one sees her operating in a way which she never describes yet which is quite important to recognize: she sets about (not just by giving him the name of sexual intercourse) building up and establishing a vocabulary and system of communication with him which was in many ways specific to the analysis, and in that way, private to the analysis. It was different from any way he had ever been talked to before. This aspect of her technique establishes a certain sequestration of the analytic situation. By mobilizing his anxieties and showing that there are means of communicating about them, that she has equipment for dealing with these anxieties and pains (even though he says he does not want to hear about such horrid things,) Mrs Klein very quickly and deftly constructs the situation. Within a week it can be seen that an analysis – and a very intense analysis – is going on. By the end of the week (when his mother has to bring him) he has a severe aggravation of his fear of children in anticipation of the weekend breaks, (quite unusual, for children do not usually anticipate the impact of the first weekend.) She has already afforded him a brief period of relief, indicated in the sixth session when Richard reported being able to play on the beach with a child and had lost his trowel. One of his main difficulties was his near total inability to socialize with other children.

149

So this is a very dynamic first week, with the analysis set going very rapidly, first, by specific mobilization of his anxieties through evoking his fears at night (the story of the tramp); second, by interpreting in a way which establishes the means of communication, for instance, about sexual intercourse (which no one had actually discussed with him before as an actual event between his parents, although his mother had given him 'information' about the 'facts of life' on several occasions); third, Mrs Klein then proceeds very quickly to investigate the phantasies and their implications and to draw them into the transference. She has set the situation going in spite of his consequent suspiciousness towards her (his fear of being trapped like the fleet in the Mediterranean, his fear of being abandoned like the soldiers in Crete); in spite of all these anxieties being mobilized and flooding him, she has afforded him a temporary relief which he could experience in an actual external situation. She has also achieved the arousal of curiosity and interest in her in the transference (shown by the questions about Mr Klein, his suspicions about her being Austrian, what countries she has visited). His playing with the clock and going into her bag, with the associations thrown up, are clear indications of infantile transference in this rather poised child.

All this is extremely impressive; and is in a way different from the notes she has given for the different sessions, which partly describe and partly apologize for the technique which she has used (for instance, in giving him so much information about herself, which she said she later regretted). Perhaps by implication she is also apologizing for being in a hurry with him. The only serious mistake which I think that she made is of the same order as the first one, about his worries for his mother, namely, bringing the material about his circumcision. This had really the opposite effect, coming later in the week, when the transference was already set going. The first question opened up the whole area of his fears at night and worries about his mother and protectiveness toward her, leading to Mrs Klein's being able to interpret that he felt he could protect her, thus denying his father's existence and the parents' sexual intercourse. It seems to me that when she made that mistake again, it had the opposite effect, of letting him off from a situation in which he was beginning to feel that she was getting a line on him about his duplicity, the violence in his nature, the biting, the anal preoccupations, the identification with the Hitler-daddy, the wish to get involved in the intercourse and make it into something bad. He was feeling that she was beginning to see that he was not a trustworthy ally for her or for anyone else; and somehow by raising this issue about the circumcision (for she was, it seems to me, interested in getting a little closer to castration anxiety) she lets him off. He begins to show her the scars of his operation and the tension goes out of the session. The preparation for the weekend goes adrift. Feelings of depression and anxiety that had been mobilized and led to his difficulty coming to the session, seem to melt away. These extremely dynamic and relieving five and a half sessions peter out at this point. It ends on a friendly note but in a rather low key.

In order to follow this massive clinical data of work done almost seventeen years before its publication, one must keep in mind where Mrs Klein was in the development of her thought and experience at the time of doing the clinical work, as opposed to writing the book. In the seventeen years between the two, there appeared such landmarks as *Notes on Some Schizoid Mechanisms*, the paper on *Loneliness* and the major work *Envy and Gratitude*. During this time her conception somehow mellowed and altered as a result of her forming a clearer idea about splitting processes – splitting of the self (for it was really only after 1946 that she began speaking consistently of the 'self' rather than the 'ego', as being the structure that was split.) Although she never did clearly formulate the difference between the concepts of 'self' and of 'ego', it is fairly clear that she meant it as a structure and not as 'self-representation' in the manner say, of Jacobson.

I want to clarify the development of Mrs Klein's concepts of the paranoid-schizoid and depressive positions up to 1941 and subsequently. Her earliest writings were all focussed on the development of children with a very strong emphasis on the persecutory anxieties (which she also called paranoid anxieties). She repeatedly demonstrated that it was in the first two years of life, in pregenital development, that the fixation points for manic-depressive and schizophrenic illnesses existed. She asserted that children in the normal process of development went through phases of anxieties and phantasies characteristic

151

of these mental illnesses. Later, she changed her mind in many ways about that, but her attitude in 1941 was that the phantasies and anxieties were identical, and that these illnesses were simply efflorescences and elaborations of the normal developmental experiences of children. This implied that the fixations were not, as Freud said, fixations of the libido, but fixations of the whole personality, including ego functions, super-ego constellations, and libidinal or id fixations. But at that time, she did not see that these illnesses had a special structure of their own; she saw them as developmental stages. It was on this ground that she was strongly attacked, for saying that babies were psychotic: and although she said she did not mean this, she did in fact say that babies were psychotic in ways essentially identical to schizophrenic and manic-depressive psychosis.

She was studying the functions that had begun during the earliest feeding period as she reconstructed it from psycho-analytical evidence with young children. She first placed the crucial development from part-object to whole-object relationships (following Abraham) at about six months, later moving it back to three months, marking the onset of the depressive position. Her idea was that processes of introjection and projection commenced at the very beginning of life, as soon as there was sufficient differentiation between self and object for an inner world to be built up. This is in many ways her least spoken about and perhaps greatest contribution to psycho-analysis – this development of a very concrete conception of the inner world. It has become that aspect of her work which most differentiates her followers from others in psycho-analysis. Her idea was, that from the very beginning, the experience of satisfaction, deprivation or disappointment resulted in the splitting of the object into good and bad, both of which were introjected. In 1946 she added that it was also the self that was split into good and bad; that the bad part of the self and the bad part of the objects became immediately fused into the major persecutor of the personality, which then had to be separated off and kept at a distance from the good or idealized parts of the self and objects, which in their turn also came together to form the core of the personality.

Thus her earliest work was preoccupied with the description of the severe persecutory or paranoid anxieties and the phantasies in which they were embodied, and the kinds of defences that were used by the infant and small child in relation to them. It was only in 1935 in the paper *A Contribution to the Psychogenesis of Manic-depressive States*, that she began to talk about 'positions', a term which Fairbairn had already used, and I think she borrowed it from him. He had spoken of the 'schizoid position' and she spoke of the 'paranoid position'; later she fused the two into the 'paranoid-schizoid position'. While she felt that there was similarity with Fairbairn's views, there was also a difference. At the time when she first began to speak about positions, she did not only speak of 'paranoid position' but also of 'obsessive position' 'depressive position', and 'manic position'; and it is fairly clear that 'positions' first of all meant consortia of anxieties and defences. Thus her first idea of 'position' did not imply developmental significance, but pathological significance; it was not in any way a developmental phase, nor was it in itself a mental illness; it was a consortium or constellation of anxieties and defences and the impulses to which they related. She spoke of at least four positions to begin with. But by the time she wrote the paper on *Mourning and its Relation to Manic-depressive States* (1938), she had reduced these to 'paranoid-schizoid position' and 'depressive position', not thinking of them so much as constellations of defences and anxieties, as manifestations of crucial attitudes towards the objects. This change from paranoid-schizoid attitudes to depressive attitudes toward the object was felt to be bound up very specifically with the transition from part-object to whole-object relations – that is, the beginning of seeing the object as whole, unique, irreplaceable, and no longer exchangeable for other part-objects.

It was from this whole-object experience that concern, and what she called at this time 'pining' for the object, was felt to develop; and she felt that it manifested itself toward the end of the first year of life, specifically in relation to the comings and goings of, firstly, the breast and then the mother, as the breast-mother. Therefore at this point, she was talking of paranoid-schizoid position and depressive position as developmental phases and the fixation points for schizophrenia and manic-depressive psychosis respectively. But she had some difficulty in relating them to the developmental phases of the libido and the progression of the erogenous zones. She therefore speaks

153

not of 'entry' into the depressive position but of 'overcoming' the depressive position. I take it that by 'overcoming' the depressive position she meant learning to tolerate the depressive anxieties about the destruction of the good object, and being able to bear separation from an external good object, on the basis of developing greater confidence in the security of the internal object. At this point the emphasis was very much on this as a developmental accomplishment, although she says many times that it is never complete and the struggle to establish it has to go on over and over again throughout life. This nodal accomplishment enables the child to establish internal security on the basis of which intellectual functions, symbol formation, socialization, the ability to relate to people other than the mother, the development of the Oedipus Complex and relation to the father, both positive and negative, taking an interest in the other children in the family – were all dependent; and sublimations (of which she still speaks) also required this 'overcoming' of the depressive position. So at this time, what she seems to mean by 'overcoming' the depressive position is really this crescendo of pining anxiety: every time the child or baby was separated from its primary maternal object in the outside world, it was still vulnerable to attack from its persecutors because its internal object was not securely established. That seems to me to be the second stage in the development of the concept.

As the concept developed later (beyond the work with Richard) it was very different: Mrs Klein no longer spoke usually of 'overcoming' the depressive position, but rather of 'attaining' it, 'achieving' it, 'penetrating' it. She began to view it less as something to be accomplished than as something to be struggled toward with increasing mastery. It became something more like an area of life; so that the world of paranoid-schizoid object relations and the world of depressive relations were two different worlds which had a certain relation to internal and external but could be switched around: she speaks quite early of 'flight to internal objects' when external objects become persecutory, or 'flight to external objects' in manic denial of psychic reality when the internal objects are persecutory. So, as they later develop, 'paranoid-schizoid' and 'depressive positions' become areas of object relationships in which different

value systems prevail, having neither any particular significance as developmental phases nor as psycho-pathological
constellations. Their significance is rather that of economic
principles – though she never came to any clear statement of
it – which in a way transcended Freud's description of the
Pleasure Principle modified by the Reality Principle. From the
theoretical point of view, this is the main thing to keep in mind
à propos the work with Richard: that Melanie Klein did this
analytical work while thinking of the depressive position as
something that had to be overcome, and whose main characteristic was separation anxiety – the pining for the good object.
The elements in depressive anxiety connected with guilt, remorse and loneliness were satellites to the central position of
pining in separation, consequent to omnipotent (masturbatory,
usually) attacks on the internal object.

Second Week: Sessions 7-12
The Developmental Role of the
Thirst for Knowledge

This second week is a marvellous week of analysis. I said the
first week was like the opening of a Chekhov play with all the
characters and the stage setting, Mrs Klein introducing her
concepts and her language, and Richard being charming and
getting frightened. Mrs Klein was in a hurry and unused to this
setting, not knowing how to operate it. But the second week is
entirely different, she hardly puts a foot wrong and things move
on in the most astonishing way. If the first week sets the stage,
the second week really introduces the drama and produces the
first real formulation. I will try to describe it in phenomenological terms.

Richard's modes of representation become evident; the
geography for instance. It becomes quite clear that the inside
of the playroom is generally a very 'inside the mother's body'
situation and that he has a tendency to escape to the outside
to look at the hills. The exception to this is when he looks out
of the window, which often seems to have the meaning of being
outside looking in, and then he sees the children and the horse
and so on. It is a common phenomenon with younger children.
If you wear glasses, the child might come and look into you in
the same way. Thus the geography of Richard's phantasy begins
to come clear, inside and outside of objects. In the last session
another type of geography closely related to conscious and unconscious is suggested. It is represented in the drawing of the
ocean with the ship on top and the starfish and submarine and
so on underneath. Mrs Klein suggests to him that this represents
his desire to split these two levels. The division in the geography,
of inside and outside in relation to the object, is thus paralleled
by the geography of internal and external world in relation to
himself. Likewise his splitting of the self begins to be evident.
At least three divisions in his personality are fairly distinct; there
is a really nasty, rather fascist and primarily oral sadistic part
that bites his cap when he thinks about the ship's captain that
he admires, or wants to burrow its way into Mrs Klein's mind,

identified with the rats which used to be at his old school or in the laundry in X. It also has certain anal sadistic qualities that are connected with bombing and his preoccupation with 'big job', his laughing at the backside of the clock and laughing at the map when he looks at it upside down, or not liking the picture because it is brown. Secondly, there is a part of Richard which is affectionate and tender, that nuzzles the clock with his lips, that appreciates the beauty of the hills, likes the picture of the landscape, admires the tower and the sun shining on it. It obviously has a capacity for deep feeling but also utilizes these feelings in a very manic way, which Mrs Klein now notices. His relationship to beauty is attenuated by his manic use of it for the purpose of denying both the destructive feeling and the depressive anxiety about the damage that he may do. Finally Mrs Klein defines the sly, deceptive, seductive part of himself, the part that can easily change back and forth, that shows her how a Nazi flag can be changed into a Union Jack by just adding a couple of lines. Also his tendency to seek alliances emerges: with his brother, with his dog Bobby, with John Wilson. The wish for a sister and for other siblings as allies, both against the parents when they are bad and also against the destructive aspects of himself becomes a bit clearer.

Another category is the phenomena that begin to accumulate around the inside of the mother's body and its population, the representation of the father's penis in the electric bars of the fire that Richard turns on and off, the dirty children in the street, the girl with protruding teeth, the red haired girl, the wicked boy who was nasty to him, the little stools that he dusts so very vigorously and beats, and, in the drawings, the little starfish, which Mrs Klein at first interprets as the baby part of himself.

It comes out pretty clearly that Richard is a burrower-in and he tends to experience his closeness to Mrs Klein in the light of his intrusive voyeurism, a theoretical area we will return to shortly. The fact that she is not so seducible as the other women he has been accustomed to charm has the effect of drying up his chat so that he becomes more depressed and inhibited with her. In the last session of the week she introduces the drawing materials again which seems a bit surprising. She might have left it over till the next week but it was probably a part of her being in a hurry, feeling that he was drying up and getting slightly worried about what kind of weekend he would have.

Richard's curiosity seems to have the meaning of getting inside her. The inside of the room becomes very significant as the inside of her body, while the clock with its front side and backside suggest that the inside of the mother's body also has some structure corresponding to the external features of a front side and a back side, namely, a good clean place and a bad dirty place. In so far as it is occupied by the objects of his jealousy (the daddy's penis, the babies, the little foot stools, the other children that use the room, her other patients) Richard becomes very confused about good and bad and consequently has much anxiety about food, whether it is good or if it might be spoiled in any way.

Mrs Klein does not link this confusion to another phenomenon that appears in the first three sessions, that is, Richard going to urinate. It is a bit surprising that she does not link it with the way in which the oven seems dirty and the ink smells bad, and the foot stools are dirty and have to be beaten to make them clean. But what she does pick up and render as a beautiful formulation is that he cannot attack the daddy's penis and the babies inside the mother as his enemies without endangering the mother. This comes out in the material about attacking Hitler inside France.

Mistakes of the first week such as leading him by asking about the circumcision and about his mother's illness are not repeated. Asking him if his father is bald is not quite in the same category. When she has hints from the material she feels free to seek information about the child's life situation that might confirm or refute its significance. She seems to have become more comfortable in the room despite the nonsense about the key. Her technique settles down as she becomes more relaxed in the setting and feels that she is beginning to grasp what kind of a human being Richard is, that he is very frightened, very tricky and sly, and that he is very split and different parts of himself know very little about one another. But she also sees that he is urgently wanting help, as when he questions her about whether she had trouble when she was a child. Mrs Klein sees that he is always on guard, it becomes quite clear that he is miserable and furthermore that he knows that he is miserable. In a sense she helps him to a greater awareness of it by scotching some of his more psycho-pathic seductiveness. Probably the impact of the first weekend has already deepened the transference, in spite of his claim that he had a lovely time and the tragedy was hurting his leg. But he subsequently hurt his leg again before the next session. Mrs Klein only takes up the theme of castration anxiety that she was following in the previous week, but she does do a lot of linking.

One can see that she is constantly correcting her interpretations, quite unashamedly. If her interpretation proves useless she sweeps it aside and replaces it or rebuilds it or reconstructs it. She is constantly gathering the material together, making lists of the phenomena that are connected, like the horse's head and Turkey on the map, the little stools and the fire. Now that she has started to do a lot of linking, gathering bits together, one really begins to see Mrs Klein at work and to see in the second week what a diligent analyst she was, how hard she worked for the children, the richness of her imagination, her capacity to use the material, and to conduct experimentation in thinking. She could throw things out and try new things to see if they fitted better.

This second week conveys the sense of the relaxation with which she worked, whereas in the first week she was tense and in a hurry and, in a sense, placating and overdoing the emphasis on Richard's good feelings. After a mere twelve sessions a real analysis is going and a first major formulation has been made as regards the depressive conflict, that is, that you cannot attack the inside of the mother containing your rivals and enemies, without harming the mother herself. She picks up the connection between the black car with all the number plates (which must have been old number plates, 'dead' number plates) representing dead babies and the way in which Richard plays with the electric fire noticing that something moves inside it when he switches it on and then it stops moving and goes black and dead-looking when he turns it off. This will turn out to be the central theme of the whole four months of work.

Richard's urge to get inside the mother, both to attack and find out if everything is all right, illustrates a key concept of Melanie Klein's work. It is an intrusive voyeurism which is

159

looking for the dirt, laughs at the funny bottom and wants to beat the babies and bite the penis inside. But is is also an anxious, worried intrusiveness which wants to find out the truth about whether the mother is all right in spite of the attack. This is a differentiation which she does not really make clear anywhere in her writing although I think it is absolutely implicit in her clinical material. In her paper on *The Importance of Symbol Formation for the Development of the Ego* (1929), she wrote about a little boy named Dick who seemed very close to being autistic. She described beautifully how she got his treatment going but, what is more interesting, is the question she raises regarding symbol formation and how is it related to the thirst for knowledge or the epistemophilic instinct. When does it all start and how is it connected with the early stages of development?

Freud's idea about curiosity did not in any way distinguish between curiosity and the thirst for knowledge. He linked it specifically to what he called the 'sexual researches of children' which he thought arose somewhere around $3\frac{1}{2}$ to 4 years of age when the Oedipus Complex was set in motion. In his theory, the desire to know and understand was, at its foundation, the desire to know about the parental intercourse and in later writing was connected to the primal scene. (The Wolf Man case.) This desire to know about the sexual intercourse was in the service of the need to dispel castration anxiety. All other thirst for knowledge was in the nature of a sublimation of that quest and therefore Freud tended to assume that people who had a strong thirst for knowledge had never solved their Oedipus Complex and were inhibited sexually. This was in keeping with his whole idea about sublimation. In the Leonardo paper he rather assumes that genius and sublimation of homosexuality are absolutely bound up together.

Mrs Klein, almost from the very beginning of her work, in her first paper on observation of the development of a child, came to the conclusion that the epistemophilic instinct occurs at a very early age in connection with the conception of the inside of the mother's body. The desire of the child to know about it is highest when the mother is still the 'world'. The curiosity about the mother's body extended naturally to curiosity about the child's own body and played a part in the formation and creation of an internal world. It also naturally extended itself through symbol formation on to other people, other people's bodies and minds and then to the whole world. It did not require a process of sublimation but only an extension through symbol formation, which was a search for *meaning*. Sublimation, on the other hand, is a means of manipulating the libidinal impulses in the service of defence against anxiety.

That is a major philosophical difference between Mrs Klein's ideas about mental life and Freud's. He tended to look backwards through the lens of psycho-pathology whereas she looked forward through the lens of child development. In the late 1920s when she wrote the paper about Dick she thought that curiosity was, in the first instance, driven by the eruption of oral sadism. This, and the greed connected with it, linked with the conception of a combined object (although she does not at that time call it a combined object) – the father's penis inside the mother. It was this oedipal constellation that excited the baby's greed and its sadism and its wish to explore the contents of the mother's body.

That was her earliest formulation but it does not make any distinction between the possible difference of motives. That is, it does not distinguish between the intrusion for destructive motives, the wish to know as a primary satisfaction, and the wish to know driven by depressive or persecutory anxiety. Of course, she had not then formulated the depressive position, but by the time she was doing the work with Richard, she had done so. What can be seen in the material of this second week and this first major formulation is at least dual motivation for the curiosity; one aspect is the rat-like burrowing in, wanting to steal, wanting to spoil, wanting to bite; the other is wanting to get in, wanting to find out if everything is all right. When he finds an envelope full of pictures, he counts them; this is clearly linked to the number plates of the car and the concern with the seven little stools. It is, in effect, a defect in the formulation, that although she calls it an epistemophilic instinct, she does not treat it as an instinct, but as a defensive reaction. It is not quite the same impulse as in Freud's view, but none the less it is represented as having to be driven by anxiety and must therefore derive its meaning from its relation to anxiety. Not until Bion's work does the thirst for knowledge find a truly primary role in mental functioning and development.

161

Third Week: Sessions 13-18
'Envy and Gratitude' as the
Organizing Postscript to the Body
of Melanie Klein's Theoretical
Chapter III   Work

This week is a most astonishing one, rushed forward very much
by the fact of Richard's mother being ill, first of all from eating
salmon and later with a sore throat. The fact that she disappoints
him by not coming to 'X' with him and not visiting him, keeps
the tension up and drives the depressive aspects into the forefront of the material in a very premature way. In that sense it
is rather a misleading week and in a way it also misled Mrs
Klein into overestimating Richard's capacity for depressive
feeling.

It seems fairly clear that the coincidence of this with the
material of the previous week when he started doing the drawings of the starfish and the submarines, and thus the coincidence
of the revelation of his internal attacks on his objects with the
external situation of his mother falling ill and the canaries
going bald, really seems to have caught him in .a kind of
emotional vice that pushed him deep into hopelessness. It can
be seen as a little depressive *illness* from which Mrs Klein extri-
cated him with her interpretive work and enabled him to have
depressive *anxieties* instead. The circumstances surrounding the
secret that he defaecated in his pants and the way in which it
was connected with the bombings and torpedoings quite overwhelmed him. In at least three sessions of the week one sees
him, at least part of the time, quite depressively ill, absolutely
joyless, unable to take an interest, not wanting to talk, or play,
or draw . . . not wanting to do anything. Mrs Klein does manage
to pull him out of it very well.

The formulation, mainly centred on his jealousy, that, when
he attacked the father's penis inside the mother as if it were a
bad penis, he endangered his good object, the mother, undid
Richard's pretence of protecting her from the tramp penis.
This increased the fear that he would either destroy her or that
his love for her would turn to hatred, as towards Germany, or
that it would drive her into an alliance with the Hitler-father

and thus turn her into an enemy. That formulation launches the analysis and galvanizes it into a going concern from the point of view not only of the development of the material but also the development of Richard's participation, intellectually and emotionally. It is a bit interfered with because the external factor that propels him towards depressive feelings and despair tends also to enhance his paranoid response. For instance he asked the cook what she thinks is going on at home and she replied that they were having a lovely time, and Richard exploded inside at the thought of it.

This brings out a very different picture from the formulation Mrs Klein had made to him the previous week about his jealousy. At this moment clearly the central problem is envy. In her formulations Mrs Klein swings back and forth between talking of his jealousy and talking of his envy and has not quite centred on the envy, perhaps because of a certain reluctance to do so. The fact that she only has a short time with him may influence her judgment. She may have thought, even in 1941, that a problem of integrating envy would not be greatly forwarded in a mere four months.

The main thing is to understand the development of material in this week because it is particularly interesting. She had rather hastened the emergence of the drawing activity on the Saturday and Richard rather dived into it and was a bit dismayed when he discovered that she could analyse his drawings. The same thing happens this week in the second session when he asks her to bring the toys back and he sees that she can analyse his playing with toys as well. There is no keeping secrets from her! Finally he tells her that he has a secret but can not reveal it. Just as he said he thought he could retain his faeces and failed, out comes the secret. At the end of the week he brings her a dream ... final capitulation! There is no keeping anything from her. He is playing ... he is drawing ... he is telling her his dreams and associations ... he is co-operating in every way, even confiding that his mother sometimes accuses him of giving her headaches. One sees in this week relatively little of his trickiness and dissimulation, even when they are talking about the aeroplane drawings. He is saying 'Oh yes ... it could be this and this ...' and she is saying 'Ah yes ... but it could be that as well' and he says 'Yes ... but how about this.' Mrs Klein takes this up, and probably correctly, as alternative formulations, all of which have a certain validity. Yes, he is the only one who survives, and, no, the good family survives, and then everyone is killed. She sees these all as phantasies underlying alternative states of mind coming in rapid succession and in a very unstable relationship to one another.

Quite unlike the previous week, there is only one touch of suspicion, when she has to end the Thursday session a little early, and he asks her if she is going to see John a little earlier than usual. But otherwise Richard is in a much more trusting and much more dependent relationship to her, partly because he is in such trouble with his feelings towards his family, his mother in particular and anxiety about her illness. So that when he says he is so fond of Mrs Klein and she is so sweet, it seems to come through much more sincerely, even though one can see that it is a hedge against feeling anxious and persecuted by her or that she might desert him.

The drawings, as you can see, have already taken on the form that will characterize them throughout the four months. The empire drawings have their beginnings in the very first drawing of a big starfish (number nine) with all the squares filled in with different colours and then surrounded by a line and filled in in red. Mrs Klein links this back with the fish in the drawing two days earlier, when he had represented a mother fish who had eaten a baby starfish which was making her bleed by cutting and rasping a hole in her side. The empire drawings, the undersea drawings, the aeroplane drawings and later on some train drawings more or less embrace the main themes, varied in minute ways.

When he starts to play with the toys the main themes of his play immediately come up; parental intercourse and the child watching them comes out repeatedly; there are representations of a more part-object relationship with the trains coming into stations and knocking buildings over; the theme of childrens' rivalry with the parents, (the little girls and the dog; the children going to Dover, etc.). And then, of course, there is the central theme of the catastrophe that he can not prevent. Mrs Klein is very sensitive to the relationship of children to the play materials, apologizing for giving Richard two lorries that were

164

rather too definitive in their function, one carrying coal and the other timber. She is also very sensitive to the childrens' feelings about their lack of mastery over the toys, and mentions how children are dismayed by their difficulty in painting, and how they can not keep from making a mess, which distresses them. This is a bit true of the toys she has given Richard which tend to fall over; the woman falls off the swing, the buildings fall over, the minister and pink lady fall off the roof. He can not really impose his will upon them partly because they themselves are very unstable, and partly because his own dexterity is inadequate. She is very much aware of the way in which this can have an upsetting and oppressive effect on a child and probably can generate play disruption. Each successive time that Richard plays with the toys a disaster occurs and play is disrupted. He then either begins to draw or he becomes listless and wanders away. Mrs Klein recognizes that the play disruptions have something to do with the way in which the toys, by their own qualities, bring him into contact with his inability to keep things under control inside himself and in particular that he can not control his own destructive impulses. On the other hand, the train running amok and knocking everything over is mainly precipitated by the accident of the minister and pink lady falling off the roof.

It is probably a prejudice based on her work with younger children that the toys allow them somehow to experience the emotionality more vividly than by talking, drawing or even telling dreams. A modification of the formulation she had made to him the previous week now results. She sees in this assemblage (the play with the toys, the drawings and his relationship to her, all in the context of his mother's illness) a clear indication of envy, having to do with his feeling himself the outsider looking in upon his happy family consisting of his father, mother, Paul and the dog. It puts him in 'a blazing fury' as he says of the drawing about the Octopus, or 'wild' as he describes the starfish in a later drawing. He is a child who suffers quite a lot from envy of other people's happiness and the happiness of their relationship; the closest he comes to one is quickly spoiled by his seductiveness, his omipotence, his manic tendencies and his sexual excitement. His relationships end up in a disastrous way, just as the play with the toys ends up in disasters.

165

Mrs Klein begins to formulate to Richard now in this week that he really can not bear to see the happiness of the relationship of the good ones to one another, whether good ones consist of the father and mother in a good intercourse, or good babies inside the mother in a happy relationship, or good babies coming to the breast, or parents proud of their children. There is an envy of the goodness itself that wants to spoil it; not just to have it but to spoil it. It is this spoiling that she begins to see as an important feature of Richard's illness in this week.

As regards technique, this week is fairly flawless. A few times she seems to ask him questions that are a little beside the point ('Where did you get the gun? Whose gun was it?'). This is not really a good technique with Richard because any lead like that immediately produces material that has a fairly low order of validity. She makes some long interpretations to him. In spite of what she says in the introduction, it must be true that these interpretations, which are all gathered together and make up three quarters of a page, may have been interspersed bit by bit as the material was being produced. But it is not necessarily so, because she does at the end of the session often comment on how he behaved while she was interpreting. The impression is conveyed that, when she started, there was a certain suspending of action. He either listened or did not listen but did not do much else.

Perhaps she did make some very long interpretations to him in this week when she was under some considerable pressure to help him because of his severe distress. She realized that he was in a very despairing state about his mother's illness and could not get it in proportion in his mind. He clearly felt that something terrible was happening to her, all mixed up in his mind with the drawings of the submarines, the sinking of the Emden, the fish with the dreadful starfish baby inside her, rasping her open and making her bleed. Mrs Klein was in a very urgent state to give him some relief, but, oddly enough, not by drawing it into the transference, but by formulating it and giving him some insight into it. It does give him relief, at least from the point of view of helping him to get out of the feeling of being frozen by depressive illness and despair into being in contact with depressive anxiety and feeling ashamed and worried about himself and the problem of controlling his impulses.

In general, her way of working emerges clearly. She really meanders about in the material, formulating bits and pieces of it as she goes along, gradually, until something begins to come clear to her. Then she goes in more definitively and begins to formulate conflict and the structure underlying the conflict. Many of the things she says to Richard appear irrelevant, inimical to one another, or mutually exclusive. It is apparently a fairly true picture of how she worked, unashamedly in the dark, by serial approximation.

Although envy and jealousy are not yet clearly differentiated in the clinical work with Richard, one can see the germ of the eventual book, *Envy and Gratitude*.

The skeletal paper for this book was read at the 1957 Congress and it appeared in the following winter. It was the link that bound her work together, made it an integrated structure and set it on a different course from Freud's. In it she clearly distinguished between envy and jealousy, gave envy its correct status in relation to splitting processes, the therapeutic process, the negative therapeutic reaction and its relation to the future of psycho-analysis. This book stands in an interesting juxtaposition to Freud's *Analysis Terminable and Interminable*. Just as that was a valid but gloomy document in relation to psychoanalysis, this book seems to me to be an incredibly hopeful one. Both focus on the negative therapeutic reaction. Whereas Freud's pessimism stemmed from his loyalty to the Libido Theory, feeling that in the final result everything was a matter of mental economics, of forces impinging on the ego, balanced against one another, ultimately the life and death instincts, Mrs Klein acknowledged the constitutional factors in relation to envy and does consider it to be one of the main manifestations of the operation of the death instinct upon the ego. But what she emphasized was a structural viewpoint, namely that the role of envy in the personality depends less on quality of virulence or quantity of intensity than upon its location and distribution. In this book she talks about splitting processes and the differences between excessive or inadequate splitting on the one hand, or inadequate splitting-and-idealization on the other. Primal splitting-and-idealization has to be just right so that goodness and badness of self and objects are adequately separated from one another, but not so widely separated that they can not be brought into any kind of contact. The good self and the idealized object need to have a snug little time with one another until they get strong enough to admit the badness a little bit into their association. That model of the developmental process and the role of splitting-and-idealization and subsequent integration of the destructive envy made it possible to imagine that the envy might not merely be controlled but even ameliorated in its virulence.

Mrs Klein's advances in the concepts of splitting mechanisms and the nature of narcissistic identifications gave a new substance to Freud's structural concepts and brought them into the consulting room. The analyst could now begin to study not just in terms of the ego, the id and super-ego but also the bits and pieces of the personality and the bits and pieces of the objects to which they were related. The concept of projective identification made it possible to study just what we are beginning to see here with Richard, that is the inside of himself projected outside himself. By introducing the concept of envy and distinguishing it from jealousy, Mrs Klein started an important development in psycho-analysis, of finding words with which to dissect emotions just as she had earlier begun to differentiate different qualities of mental pain, persecutory and depressive.

| Chapter IV | Fourth Week: Sessions 19-24 Unconscious Phantasies as Mechanisms of Defence, with Special Reference to Obsessional Mechanisms |

This fourth week of analysis is also rather a splendid one and raises some interesting theoretical problems regarding obsessionality. The question of obsessional mechanisms is a puzzling and difficult aspect of Mrs Klein's work, since it is nowhere particularly set out. This is a week again punctuated by a disturbance in the setting. The mother's illness interfered in the third week. This week, in the second session, Mrs Klein has to take him to her lodgings and this also interferes in some way, although it is not so clear how and she takes it up very little.

The analysis is already going quite smoothly; she is working very confidently with him, sorting things out and throwing things away, and turning up new ideas. The changes in the formulation are changes in her ideas and attitude about the meaning of the material, but a lot of it has to be attributed to the deepening of the transference relationship so that it is more clearly differentiated from Richard's relationships at home to his parents, brother and Bobby. This is reflected very clearly in the way Mrs Klein interprets to him. The mode of presentation of the material keeps changing; he brings the fleet and then he draws, he plays with the toys and squeezes the football, he wanders about the room. In between he talks to Mrs Klein, confiding in her little things John said (that he wished she were dead), telling her a dream in the fourth session and being very confiding also about the paranoid suspicions about her. These are now becoming much more intense because they are also juxtaposed to the building up of a much more genuine positive transference. One still feels Richard to be disingenuous at times. It mainly comes out with regard to the drawing, when he starts saying why there are two of this and three of that, or one of the other. His sincerity is not so convincing but most of the time he works closely with her. Anecdotal material from his life outside the consulting room begins to enter, like the business of whether he could stay in the cinema in the evening or whether

169

he had to run out because he felt sick from the noises of the sing-song. Altogether, as far as material is concerned, there are hardly any doldrums. Richard seems most of the time to pay attention to what Mrs Klein says, even when he is suspicious and is questioning how she can know what goes on in his mind. She explains to him how she works and examines the material, what it may mean about his unconscious and so on. Even at times when there is great suspicion and doubt he is really working with her. It is rather a joy to see this sort of thing from a little boy who seems to be able to tolerate very little in the way of discomfort. Yet, when it comes to mental pain he is not too bad about it. He does soldier on somehow, better than one would perhaps have expected in the first couple of weeks.

The fleet material is of particular interest, probably partly because he brings it in himself and with his precious ships he does represent things that are different from his play with Mrs Klein's toys. The fleet play bears more on the organization of his family and the attempt to weld it together harmoniously, so that there would not be outbreaks of violence and chaotic running amok, whereas with the toys and trains all hell is let loose as soon as masturbation is represented by the swing in motion or the dog wagging its tail. With the fleet Richard is somehow trying to construct an idea of the possibility of a family where things are balanced, equal. No one should be saying I'm more important than you are. Paul need not be grabbed by Cook and Bessie because he is screaming and yelling that Mummy is with Richard, nor are the children engaged in homosexual activities because they are so furious about mummy and daddy being together.

All these different situations that disrupt the harmony of the family are rather beautifully represented in the fleet play, perhaps in a more convincing way than the drawings of the submarines, fishes and starfishes. This may be due to the equivocal quality of the drawings like that little argument about whether the torpedo was going to hit the ship or not. Somehow with the fleet he is more in control and can manoeuvre the relationships and represent them more accurately. Mrs Klein describes what emerges as obsessional mechanisms. Richard attempts through the fleet play to figure out a method of carefully balancing the privileges, pains and pleasures of each member of the family in such a way that harmony reigns and all the enemies are outside the family. This is a very important part of the obsessional mechanism, the attempt to achieve stability by balancing. But it is also very clear that to effect this balancing another technique is also required, omnipotent control and separation. It comes out particularly when he manoeuvres Rodney and Nelson to represent the daddy courting the mummy, very gently (not quite touching). These two mechanisms, the attempt to achieve a balanced situation and to effect it through omnipotent control and separation of the objects are described by Mrs Klein in the notes to this week and are probably her most advanced statement about obsessional mechanisms. She has used the term many times and in many different ways throughout her writing.

These obsessional mechanisms would, if they succeeded, enable Richard to establish a latency period in the ordinary sense. But it is also fairly clear that he is not able to stabilize things, partly because Mrs Klein is interfering by interpretation, but one also feels that he is not really able to manage the violence of his impulses by mechanisms of this obsessional sort. Instead what happens is that the material of the analysis begins to deepen into what one would call more psychotic levels that require a rather different formulation from those Mrs Klein found herself making in the first three weeks. There, after all, she was, in one way or another, interpreting first his castration anxiety in relation to his Oedipus Complex, then something more related to obsessional despotism and conflict between love and hate with envy and jealousy coming into it, all on a rather whole-object level, not very much connected with projective identification or with part-object relations.

This kind of formulation would imply ordinary neurotic difficulties, that his fear of the other children might be connected mainly with his jealousy of his sibling, Paul. In the first three weeks there was abundant evidence of claustrophobic anxiety and of phantasies related to projective identification. The drawing of the fish with the starfish inside it, making a hole and causing it to bleed; the material about the Mediterranean with ships being trapped there, or troops being trapped on Crete, or his going out of the playroom: all these bits of evidence of claustrophobic anxiety were not quite in the forefront of the material. But in this fourth week, as a result of Mrs Klein interpreting to him the attempts to establish a quietus in his internal situation by means of these obsessional mechanisms of omnipotent control, separation and balancing, and thus disabling him, so to speak, from establishing this somewhat phoney quietus, the material deepens.

First of all clear material marks the emergence of his homosexuality on an oral level referable to preoccupation about sucking the penis and his playing games in bed with Bobby. Then there is the marvellous dream about the fishes. In a way it seems that Mrs Klein does not make as much of that dream as she might, mainly because she does not relate it to the drawing where the starfish were in a rage and were pulling the octopus out from where it was hiding and eating the grass. She recognizes the octopus as the father's penis inside the mummy, being attacked by these greedy babies who wanted to have the mummy all to themselves. But for some reason she does not interpret the fishes that invited Richard to dinner, and particularly the very insinuating and ingratiating manner of the chief fish, in a way that connects with the homosexual material that has just come previously, about Bobby and about Richard sleeping in Paul's bed. Have the fishes invited Richard to join them in devouring the father's penis inside the mother, or do they intend to devour Richard when he is in projective identification with this penis? Mrs Klein interprets it in terms of a claustrophobic anxiety, a fear of being trapped, as she had interpreted before the evidences of claustrophobia in relation to herself and the room, or like the ball he wanted to get out of the cupboard. Her work with this dream is not quite as powerful as it might have been, had she linked it to the homosexual material and the evidences of a collusive alliance with Paul or Bobby against the parents and their heterosexuality. It would thus have lent itself to connection with his identification with Hitler in the material in which he tells the boy to go away and gives the Hitler salute and later stamps up and down and goosesteps. The gang would eat up the father's penis and in that way assimilate its power and take over the world. What she does emphasize, however, is the theme of betrayal when he flees from the fire leaving his family behind. Richard is very uneasy about this interpretation and confabulates an addendum to the dream in which he puts out the fire and restores the fertility of the ground that has been scorched.

The theme which will become the main focus of the analysis begins to be represented this week by the empire drawings. These are an elaboration of the starfish drawings and particularly the multi-coloured one in the red circle. (No. 9) It links also with that picture of the fish containing the starfish, (No. 7) and touches on a very important theoretical problem that must have been exercising Mrs Klein at the time of the treatment, namely the interplay of projection and introjection, and of the identification processes they set in motion. By the time she was writing the book and the notes, she was tremendously interested in problems of structure: if a part of the self was put into an object, was it ego or was it self? did it in itself have internal objects? were those objects the same as the internal objects of other parts? if this was projective identification with an internal object, how could that have internal objects? She found herself elaborating some kind of Russian doll model of the mind.

The other part of the material which begins to develop now is the squeezing of the football which goes through various stages accompanied by cock-and-hen noises and phantasies. As the empire drawings relate more to processes of rivalry for the external mother, the football material and its later elaboration as the 'baby-tank' relates more to Richard's experience of internal objects, and thus connects with his hypochondria. For instance, the phantasy that the egg is laid as the chicken's neck is wrung, is connected with anxieties about birth and Richard acknowledges that birth can be dangerous and painful to women, as his mother had told him. But in his phantasy it is connected with his concept of a sadistic penis, that goes in and does damage inside the mummy. On the other hand, the mother and the penis can come together to form the 'wicked-brute' object.

The clarification and differentiation of the transference situation from his relationship to his mother brings out Richard's ambivalence to Mrs Klein, or rather his split relationship to her, to the 'sweet' Mrs Klein for whom he evidently does begin to feel some love, and the Austrian Mrs Klein who has the dead Mr Klein's penis inside her and is terrifically mistrusted. He wants to know whether they were on the other side in the

173

previous war and asks her to read some 'Austrian' to him: he does not want to call it 'German'. As a result of that clarification of the transference and differentiation of it, and because she blocks his attempt to balance with obsessional mechanisms, the material deepens and the claustrophobic material begins to come forward. It is highlighted by the dream of being invited underwater to have dinner with the fishes, and is made current by his being unable to stay at the cinema because of his fear of the children there, of their attacking him. This is amplified by his questions to Mrs Klein about whether the big boys would hurt him if he went to boarding school.

This deepening of the material, with its preoccupation with the inside of the mother's body, his desire to penetrate into it, the greed for what it is felt to contain, the feeling that the father's penis is in possession and has to be eliminated somehow, all has the structure of a much more psychotic level of anxiety and preoccupation than she had been dealing with in the first three weeks.

A word should be said about the impact in this week of Mrs Klein seeing Richard in her room. Of course, at first he was quite excited and this seems to lead on to the feeling of being admitted, as it were, to the club. Now he is one of the select that comes to her room and therefore he is one of her men. Since she does not have intercourse with him she probably does not have intercourse with anybody and therefore everybody is equal: a happy analytical family. On the other hand, he is also very evidently disappointed, as when he scolds her a bit at the end of the Wednesday session for having left the window open previously. It gives impetus in one direction to the obsessional mechanism because he has been admitted to the intimacy of her rooms, but it also gives some thrust to the more paranoid feeling of being tricked, seduced, enticed. In that way it has a relation to the fish dream and the feeling of being invited in order to be devoured or in order to be lured into some bad alliance against his good object.

So much for the material of the week. Regarding the theory of obsessionality, a large conceptual difference from Freud's use of it must be noted. It has never been made very explicit anywhere in the literature although it has obviously caused terrific confusion and agitation all round. Freud's conception of defence really starts from two points: one is his recognizing repression as it operated in hysteria, in amnesias, in slips of the tongue and parapraxes and the ordinary amnesia for early childhood. But the concept of mechanism has another root in the formulation of the dream work, that is, the work done by the dreamer to change the latent content into its manifest content for the purpose of evading censorship. The latent content has been given a twist by logical or linguistic techniques such as condensation, displacement, reversal. In this way the dream work, in so far as it is equivalent to mechanisms of defence, consists of manipula- · tion of the meaningful content of the latent dream. But when Freud talks about mechanisms of defence starting with repression, and then later adds further mechanisms such as projections, introjections, withdrawal of libido, introversion of libido and sublimation, then he is not talking about mechanisms operationally but rather phenomenologically. He is gathering under the rubric of repression all those phenomena which he thinks must be caused by some neuro-physiological mechanism, the working of which he does not know. 'Repression' in that sense is truly mechanical. The sense in which Mrs Klein spoke of projective identification or splitting, as mechanisms was purely operational, and therefore merely a description of the unconscious phantasy, like Freud's description of dream work. The reason for Freud's use of the term was his dedication to the Libido Theory and to the concepts of the manipulation of quantities of excitation. Mrs Klein's work from the very beginning was bound to unconscious phantasy and its content. Therefore in her work the unconscious phantasy *is* the defence against anxiety.

Early in her work, Mrs Klein tended to use the term 'obsessional mechanism' as Freud had used it, phenomenologically. He spoke of obsessional mechanisms being in operation whenever obsessional phenomena were in evidence, as for instance in the Rat Man case. She recognized as early as *The Psychoanalysis of Children*, that obsessionality had something to do with controlling other people or controlling the objects. A brilliant footnote links it with catatonia, as perhaps the ultimate in the sadistic employment of obsessional defence.

The other great difference between Mrs Klein's use of the term 'mechanisms of defence' and Freud's use of it lies in his

175

contention that particular mechanisms of defence were very specifically related to what he called the problem of the 'choice of neurosis.' Now Mrs Klein seems not to have thought that, or, in a sense, to have neglected this aspect of Freud's work, partly because of moving the whole Oedipus Complex back into early childhood in relation to part-objects, and partly because of having a more developmental view rather than psycho-pathological view of things. It was her idea that a mechanism of defence could be utilized at different stages of development in relation to different developmental problems and would therefore have different consequences depending on what sort of conflict it was deployed against. She also had the idea that a particular mechanism could be deployed on a spectrum varying from the most sadistic employment of it to the most sparing or even reparative use. In this sense, of longitudinal application and of variable spectrum of sadism, she developed the concept of obsessional mechanisms in a flexible and powerful way in relation to clinical phenomena.

If one turns to the instance here in Richard's fleet material, one can see that Mrs Klein thinks he is employing the obsessional mechanism, which she defines quite clearly as attempting to achieve a kind of balance through omnipotently controlling and separating, and that he is using it in relatively gentle and tender ways. It is an attempt to establish a quietus, a sort of Pax Romana, you might say, in which, under his benevolent despotism, everyone will be equal and happy. And that would be a very benevolent use of it, bordering on manically repara-tive use, of obsessional mechanisms, and it would typify the way in which these are generally used by children in the estab-lishment of a more or less healthy latency period. But she also sees that Richard tends to employ the same mechanisms in a much more sadistic way, that is, a bit earlier when he attempts to keep everything motionless. This of course is more sadistic and its ultimate extrapolation would be to the motionlessness of suspended animation that is imposed upon objects in cata-tonia. It will come again towards the end in the 'Black Island' drama (85th session). Her most comprehensive descrip-tion of obsessional mechanisms is to be found in the paper 'Mourning and its Relation to Manic Depressive States', but it is also a very confusing paper.

Fifth Week: Sessions 25-29
The Anxieties of the Paranoid-
Schizoid Position: Paranoid
Anxiety, Persecutory Anxiety,
Persecutory Depression

Chapter V

This week of the *Narrative* is an important one and brings up some very interesting problems, giving us the opportunity to investigate the history of the paranoid-schizoid position. It is again a week that has certain outside interferences. The mother is ill again and she goes home to visit Paul, while the nurse comes to look after Richard. He is furious about it, and by the end of the week he is ill himself and misses the Saturday session, and the next three sessions up to Thursday of the following week. It is a week in which his seductiveness and his placation and his trickiness are fairly in abeyance. Instead, what emerges is something very paranoid in the boy. In the context of much greater co-operation with Mrs Klein, he is able to admit to her something that must have been quite unknown, not only to Mrs Klein, but to his mother as well, absolutely secret, namely his paranoid fears of being poisoned by Cook and Bessie.

The material develops on the heels of the previous week's work, with its extremely valuable dream about the fishes inviting Richard to dinner. Somehow the tension was lost a bit toward the end with the Empire drawings. But he returns this week more deeply involved in the transference, although Mrs Klein's technique does not quite take into account the increased engagement. She is still inclined to relate the material back to his mother and father and Paul and not to acknowledge its gathering towards herself. This gathering and intensification partly results from her planned trip to London hanging as a threat over the sessions. She has not given him a date yet. In contrast, his mother's illness seems to have very little impact on the material in spite of that little dream in which Richard is having his throat operated on three times.

What impact his mother's illness does have, along with her going back home to see Paul, is switched quickly to compound an increasing preoccupation with Mrs Klein, the danger of her being bombed, her relationships with John, and her son, and the dead-but-alive Mr Klein. Richard now discovers that there is also somebody living at her lodgings with whom she might have dinner, 'the Grumpy Old Man'. The intensity of the jealousy is very much gathered together in the transference and the material plunges into far more part-object relations and far more primitive emotionality. This comes out very forcibly in his behaviour, gnashing his teeth, being very defiant towards Mrs Klein, muttering things against her, squirting water at her, throwing the pencil shavings at her, saying he was going to leave the room if he wished. But his feelings of resentment come out, also, because they are less under the sway of his omnipotence and can emerge in a more straightforward way in the transference. The result is that Richard can also be more confiding with Mrs Klein. It is in this context that he confides to her his fear of being poisoned, after she had picked up in a very astute way his distrust of her in the little incident about the Fifth Columnists and its addendum, the problem of confidentiality in the analysis.

Richard himself seems to experience this symptom as pretty mad. But he confides to her that he has had the delusion that Cook and Bessie were spies, that he has spied on them and listened to see if they were talking German, that he smelled the condiment bottles to see if they smelled like poison. This must also be connected with the question of the smell of ether versus the perfume his mother gave him to take to his tonsilectomy. His primitive reliance on the sense of smell is indeed very closely connected with paranoia and the use of non-social cues for making social judgment. The paranoic characteristically uses as evidence things other people would never consider to be evidence: the use of senses rather individually and rather omnisciently to pick out social cues.

This is the sort of thing Richard seems to acknowledge to Mrs Klein at this point, that he has used his ears and eyes and nose in this rather paranoid way, trying to determine whether Cook and Bessie were spies and then whether they were out to poison him. In the first session of the week he had mentioned the three children that made their mother sick on the tram or bus, and Mrs Klein connected this with his feeling that he was such a nuisance with his questions and his nagging that he was making his mother ill, and might do the same to Mrs Klein.

Several threads of material become tightly interwoven at this point to form the background of the paranoia. First there is the jealousy material already mentioned, along with the Empire drawing where the three men, Daddy, Paul, and Richard, grab all the best territory and leave the mother with very little. Second, there is the noxious, invasive nuisance material which implies that the Mummy or Mrs Klein would wish to be rid of him. Finally there is the contamination material about the dirty water; how it gets dirty and how the water goes out of the sink and flows out of the pipe to the outside. It is all this that seems to be split off and projected into the bottle of poison that Cook and Bessie, who are in with German spies, would use to poison him and get rid of him because he is such a nuisance.

It is in effect a transformation of the earlier formulation Mrs Klein had made about the parents joined in intercourse against Richard. In this context of awareness of being a noxious baby with his nagging, his urine, his faeces, his continual questions and probing voyeurism, that the projection of that noxious quality on to the mother, really on to the breasts, represented by Cook and Bessie, generates his paranoia towards the breasts and the fear of being poisoned. There is also arising now in the material the theme about the dead baby. It emerges in the material about the sinking of the Hood, where Richard murmurs to himself under his breath 'Richard . . . Richard . . . Richard . . .' later 'Daddy . . . Daddy . . . Daddy . . .' and Mrs Klein so intuitively interprets to him that these were the drowning sailors calling for help. In the next session Richard was able to consider very seriously whether he would have been able to rescue all of them, or any of them, or whether he would have needed to be rescued himself and would have joined the others in calling for the daddy. In conjunction with this dead-baby and the drowning-baby material we also learn of Richard having an irrational fear of ghosts and of his nocturnal anxieties, for which he reports that his nurse or nanny used to have to sit up with him when he screamed in the middle of the night.

In a way Mrs Klein tried to relate these two bodies of anxiety, the persecutory anxiety, related to the dead baby turned into ghosts which would attack him in the night, and the paranoid anxiety about the breasts that had turned poisonous and had turned against him in alliance with the bad penis and were going to poison him. At this point of the analysis she is not able to separate them from a third situation, the anxiety that he himself might poison the breasts with his noxious urine and faeces, his insidiousness and trickiness. Mrs Klein was beginning to erect three different formulations, whose relationship to one another is not at all clear. It is not clear partly because Mrs Klein did not have a clear theoretical basis for distinguishing them. One is this severe anxiety about dead objects and ghosts, perhaps the most severe of the persecutory anxieties. The second is a moderately severe persecutory anxiety which is more in the nature of a suspension of trust in the goodness of the object. When there have been sadistic attacks upon the breast, particularly if these attacks have been made out of possessiveness of the breast and a wish to spoil it and poison it so that others can not enjoy it, there follows a reflux of anxiety that the subject has poisoned the breast for himself as well. These two persecutory anxieties can be discerned and in some way in between them is this other anxiety that has a resemblance to them but is also different in a way that is not at all clear at this point, paranoid anxiety.

Paranoid anxiety is not just a suspension of trust in the goodness of the object; its core is a really severe confusion between what the paranoid feels and what he thinks. In his feelings he is drawn to the attractiveness of the object: in his thoughts he is frightened of its malevolent core. And this is the situation that is presented about Cook and Bessie. Quite clearly the two of them also represent part-objects. Here Mrs Klein makes the clearest formulation anywhere in her work about the nature of the combined object at part-object level, that is, the penis in the breast. This combined breast and nipple somehow creates confusion between good and bad. The division between feeling attracted to the breast and thinking that the nipple is not to be trusted creates the atmosphere of paranoid anxiety. The Thursday starts as a very defiant session and ends quite tenderly with Richard admiring the scenery, going out because he cannot bear the playroom at this point, feeling it to be a horrible, filthy place. He admires the hills and talks about climbing them with Mrs Klein. I think she lets him off quite a bit when she interprets his digging the stick into the ground as some sort of reparative intercourse. By the Thursday session he must have already been a bit ill. He did not come for the Friday session and went home till the following Thursday.

In the beginning of her work Mrs Klein used paranoid and persecutory as synonyms. Here in talking about Richard she does not make a clear distinction between them although later on in the book she does clarify this. Now the point is that in her very earliest work she described an essentially biologically determined efflorescence of sadistic impulses in the baby toward the breasts, attacking them in fact and phantasy, primarily out of greed, perhaps a little out of envy, but mainly out of greed. The modes of attacks were essentially biting and scooping, which were intended to rob the breasts, as part-object, of their food, and when extended to the mother as a whole object, to rob her of her beauty, food, babies and internal penises. But the earliest was the part-object relationship to the breasts, scooping them out in the greed to possess the food and to have absolute access to the breasts at any given time. The anxieties which this produced followed the Law of Talion – what you do to the breasts, they will then do to you; a logical operation, very much in keeping with Freud's views about how love turned to hate.

Mrs Klein at this time, was also thinking mainly in terms of logical operation, but as her work developed it became clear to her that the child was persecuted by the damaged object. That was during the early 1920s and she did not find a solution to this problem of why the damaged object was a persecutor until 1957 when she discovered that the damaged object was felt to be envious of the intactness of other objects or the self. Many of the attacks which were earlier described as sadistic, biting, cutting, tearing, and so on, could be later seen to be attacks by projective identification. This made a very big difference in her views, that it was not simply 'if you're nasty to me, I'll be nasty to you'. The mental operations were much more complicated when the attack was in a concrete form and that the biting or scratching or spitting or urinating merely implemented the mental mechanism of projective identification. An object was wounded essentially by thrusting into it a part of the self which was in pain and contained vicious or destructive impulses. By this projection, the object then took on the malevolent characteristics.

181

As a consequence, Mrs Klein was very inclined to think of internal persecution as being equivalent to hypochondria and spoke about persecutory hypochondria and depressive hypochondria. Although in a sense this is a simple view of hypochondria, it was nonetheless an advance over Freud's work. His most developed idea was that hypochondria was a narcissistic disorder and stood in a certain relation to paranoia, equivalent to the relationship of conversion hysteria to anxiety hysteria.

This was fundamentally Mrs Klein's position on persecutory or paranoid anxieties until the 1946 paper on splitting mechanisms and projective identification which added a whole new dimension of complexity to the investigation. Although her early theories included splitting of the object into good and bad, it did not include a parallel splitting of the self into good and bad. The bad objects were somehow feared, but if you follow the clinical description, the persecutory anxieties that she describes in the children mainly come from damaged good objects rather than from bad objects. Of the objects that have been split in this splitting-and-idealization, it is the attacks on the good objects which result in persecution while the bad objects mainly produce frustration and deprivation. It was in this way that she discovered phenomena related to the early stages of the Oedipus complex corresponding to Freud's description of the harshness and primitiveness of the super-ego which he attributed to the distribution of death instinct.

Notes on some Schizoid Mechanisms, with its description of splitting mechanisms and projective identification, brought a new complexity to the field. For these splitting mechanisms dismembered the unity of the self as a structure, opening up the prospect of intra-systemic conflict. If the self could be divided, either by splitting-and-idealization, or on other planes of cleavage, the segments could be in conflict with one another. For instance, persecution could come from directions other than retaliation from objects that have been damaged by the child's sadistic attack. That is, the persecution of the idealized part of the self by bad parts of the self could be recognized and this gradually developed into later insights about narcissistic organization. But it also brought about the possibility of seeing the operation of projective identification, for instance, in a fusion of the bad part of the self with the bad objects, producing a quite

182

malignant 'self-object', as Michael Fordham has called them.

What is still muddled in the clinical work of 1941 is clarified in the notes this week, which were written in the late fifties, when a further advance was made, as Mrs Klein began to recognize something more about confusion between good and bad. This is related to two possibilities. This area of confusion was described in *Envy and Gratitude* as attributable to an inadequate splitting-and-idealization, which does not sufficiently separate the idealized from the bad object or the idealized part of the self from the bad part of the self. But confusion can also be brought about by bad parts of the self intruding into good objects. The first of these, that is the inadequate splitting-and-idealization, is reflected a bit in Richard's material. In order to function as a prelude to normal development, splitting-and-idealization must apparently create mirror images, that is, objects that are complete in themselves but mirror images of one another, one being the idealized and the other the bad one, distinguishable not in their form but only in their qualities and performances.

When splitting-and-idealization functions along other planes of cleavages, for instance where an attempt is made to make the bottom half good and the top half bad or the front good and the back bad, or the breast good and the nipple bad, great difficulties are generated because of the tendency of these splittings-and-idealizations to collapse or for confusion to arise when attempts at integrating the good and bad are brought to bear. This is clear in Richard's case, that splitting and idealization has been attempted along sexual lines, causing the Oedipus Complex to be fraught with confusion. The frightening intercourse seems to be a consequence of Richard having attempted to keep the daddy or the penis bad and the mummy or the breast good, so that every time any conjunction of the masculine and feminine object occurred, it produced a confluence of goodness and badness, generating confusion in Richard's mind.

But the other thing that this week reveals is the paranoid anxieties – and demonstrates how different they are from persecutory anxieties. The paranoid object, represented by Cook and Bessie, arises from projective identification, where the split-off bad part of the self penetrates into the good object. It then seems to be good but is in fact malignant and vicious. This

183

is the paranoid object, the breasts that secretly speak German, while on the surface they look like a nice English cook and maid.

Unfortunately, we do not have two words for distinguishing between *being* confused and *feeling* confused, like we have 'hopelessness' and 'despair'. They are two words which seem to be very much alike but become useful once they are used to express the difference between a hopelessness that is still grasping after hope and is very painful and a despair that has given up hope and is no longer in pain. But we do not have a good way of distinguishing between confusion that is fraught with uncertainty and confusion that is solidified in an object that looks good but is bad, as when there is a beautiful appearance but malignant intentions. The paranoid object is of this quality. This approach therefore takes 'persecutory anxiety' as a general term under which 'paranoid anxiety' would be subsumed.

We can therefore describe at least six different kinds of persecutory anxieties. *First*, one can be persecuted internally or in an externalized, projected form by a bad part of the self that can tyrannize, corrupt, frighten, seduce, threaten, propagandize to magnify jealousy and distrust, and in these ways to attack the relationship to the good object. *Secondly*, one can be persecuted by bad objects which seem primarily bent on tyrannical control, frustration, enslavement, the equivalent of Freud's Super-Ego, (not the kind of daddy Schreber had, who really seems to have been sadistic to children, but the good puritanical mummy and daddy who think 'spare the rod and spoil the child').

There is the *third* type of persecution that comes from damage done to good objects by sadistic attacks upon them. Mrs Klein saw this as mainly related to masturbation attacks of various sorts. This persecution by good objects seems fairly clearly what is now called 'persecutory depression'; that is, when recognizing the damage one has done to good objects, one feels persecuted by these damaged objects because of being unable to bear the depressive feeling, despairing of reparation.

Fourth, there is the severe persecutory anxiety that comes from the formation of a rather malignant bad object through projective identification and fusion between the bad part of the self and the bad object. It produces the bad uncle figure, the bad big brother who is confused with the big daddy. This is the tyrant, the really sadistic tyrant, as distinct from the puritanical and harsh parent or super-ego. Perhaps it is Bion's 'super'-ego.

Fifth is the paranoid object that seems to be due to projective identification of a malignant part of the self into the good objects, especially the breast. This is closely related to Richard's material, of phases of the moon filled in with black, the circle on the paper with the pencil almost shoved through it, Cook and Bessie speaking German, the poison in the bottles. It is also related to his distrust of himself and the bottle that he gives his mother, distrust of his own capacity for love, his secrecy, his tendency to conspiracy.

Finally, sixth, there is a special terror of dead objects, becoming apparent in the material about the sinking of the Hood, the uncertainty if dead people can come back to life and about ghosts. It is also important to remember that when confusion is added to persecution, there comes a tremendous tendency to act out, that is, to test in action what cannot be rationalized in thought.

Sixth Week: Sessions 30-33
The Development of the Concept
of Reparation: True, Manic and
Mock Reparation

Chapter VI

These four sessions bring into focus an important aspect of the development of Mrs Klein's work, the concept of reparation. It has a very confusing beginning and winds gently through her work, never really drawn together anywhere, in spite of the book she wrote with Joan Riviere in 1937, *Love, Hate and Reparation*.

Again in this week, we meet a contaminated field, because Richard missed the first three sessions, and after his unusual extra session on Sunday became ill again. In a way the week is split into two, the first two sessions being devoted to his recovery from the terrific paranoid and hypochondriacal reactions to his illness and those sessions of the previous week which probably precipitated it, and then the last two sessions devoted mainly to the excitement of having an extraordinary session that arouses both his jealousy and his curiosity. The outbreak of paranoia is particularly linked to his having a sore throat and becomes connected with his hostility towards his father and Paul and the wish for the hook to stick in their throats, like the salmon which might die because of the hook.

The transference context of that material is devoted to mistrust of Mrs Klein, his hostility to her, not just to the 'brute' Mrs Klein. He wants to swear, using the word 'bloody' to assault her. She seems very relieved when he specifically indicates his wish to assault her. She is probably a bit wrong in the beginning of the first session when she takes up the 'Melanie' as a feeling of having a good mummy inside him. Quite likely it is a bit of cheekiness and patronization, treating her as a servant, like Cook and Bessie. She corrects herself quickly enough to pick up his paranoia. She is able to link it back to that confession of his fear of being poisoned by Cook and Bessie and she says quite promptly that he is feeling poisoned by her the moment he has pain in his tummy, feeling that she is really feeding him a fish hook.

He recovers quite nicely, which she tends to attribute almost entirely to her interpretations, but something important has changed in her demeanour towards Richard in response to his asking her for help. He asks repeatedly that she put out the lights, fill in his drawings for him, and finally says 'Do something for me', and Mrs Klein realizes that he does not know what it is he wants her to do. He is acknowledging his helplessness and his dependence upon her, after having previously told her rather courageously, that he thought 'the work' would do no good. However, in the second session, he tells her that it *is* doing him good, and later on in the week there is more feeling in it. He needs her help but does not know what he needs, except that it has something to do with his feeling so frightened of other children and that his fear somehow provokes other children to violence towards him. When later in the week he tells her that he has gathered a little more courage, it is immediately consecrated to do terrible things to all his enemies after the war. But being able to think about after the war also means that he has recovered some hopefulness, not only about his internal war, but of the external war as well. It contrasts with his mood when he told his mother that he would commit suicide if the Germans invaded.

There is a very marked change in his hopefulness and his trust in Mrs Klein, along with an increased interest in her work. This change seems due, not to the interpretations which were not very different from previous ones, nor is the material much different, but largely to his asking her for help and her responding in a way that seems to mark a change in her feeling for him. These eruptions of his hate, of violence and cruelty, of terror and paranoia have generated a more serious conception of the severity of his illness and the nature of his constitutional problems. Mrs Klein seems now much more impressed that he has a really difficult temperament to cope with and that there is something very brutally sadistic and cold in him, augmented by possessive jealousy. Its eruption absolutely sweeps him along and there seems to be nothing he can do about it. This change in Mrs Klein produces a marked increase in Richard's trust and hopefulness about the treatment. However, this beneficial shift is interfered with by his excitement about seeing her on Sunday. Why does she not always see him on Sunday? Who does she see on Sunday? Her son and grandson? His usual intrusive jealousy tries to ferret out this information. All in all, it is a very satisfactory week and mobilizes his constructive and reparative tendencies.

In *the Psycho-analysis of Children*, and the early papers, such as the one on criminality, Mrs Klein used the term 'restitution' not 'reparation'. Generally this stemmed from her studies of the pregenital period and particularly those aspects she later called the paranoid-schizoid position. She was greatly impressed by the greed and stealing; the child robbing the mother of her faeces, her internal penises, babies, and other phantasied riches. If the child could tolerate guilt and was not so persecuted by dead or damaged objects, it could begin to try to restore some good relationship. This often resulted in the child attempting to give back what it had stolen, to make restitution. In *The Psycho-analysis of Children* she speaks much more cogently of the omnipotence with which this is carried out; not only the attacks but the restitution as well, are carried out by omnipotent means. But the importance of this issue tended to be lost for a number of years. This is reflected at many points in her interpretative work with Richard. Her mode of presentation seems to lay stress on his active attempts at restitution, later called 'restoration' and finally 'reparation'. Her recognition of the omnipotence by which these active measures are carried out by the child seems to get lost until *Envy and Gratitude* (1957), although there is some mention of it in the 1946 paper on schizoid mechanisms.

The difference between true reparation and various forms of manic activity (later called 'manic reparation' and 'mock reparation') carried out by omnipotence, does not really become clear before the very end of Mrs Klein's work. Some notes in this book are her most succinct and advanced statements on the subject. The shift from calling it restitution to calling it restoration and finally reparation is not simply a shift based on recognitition of the role of omnipotence. The greater complexity of the child's attacks on the mother's body, both its motives and its means, were defined first in *Notes on Some Schizoid Mechanisms* and later in *Envy and Gratitude*. For instance, the jealousy of the internal babies arose on two scores, first of all jealousy of their imagined blissful existence inside the mother and secondly the jealousy of them as potential new babies that would be born to take possession of the breasts. Also, there developed a greater complexity in her thinking about the nature of the attacks. Smashing to pieces calls for different means of reparation from stealing. She interprets to Richard that he feels he wants to put together all the pieces but feels incapable of doing so. Richard clearly reacts with feelings of being overwhelmed by the task that she seems to be presenting to him. She seems to require that he perform such onerous tasks as putting together all the smashed and broken objects, giving the mother more babies with his good penis, as well as fighting and defeating this Hitler part of himself. Her response to his plaintive breakdown, asking for help, later accompanied by his touching her neck, which she recognizes means touching her breasts, links back to the little paper on art, about the operetta of Ravel with the libretto written by Colette. In citing the libretto, Mrs Klein refers to her concept of reparation as an illustration, describing the child as having a temper tantrum of smashing. He becomes persecuted by all the broken furniture which had come to life to threaten him. But finally a squirrel that is dying moves him to pity and he tries to bandage it. At that moment all the persecution disappears, the animals and the furniture that had come to life are very sympathetic to him and say he is a good boy. At that time he calls for help, saying 'Mamma'. Somehow the importance of his saying 'Mamma' tends to be a little bit lost in the admiration that Mrs Klein, as well as the animals, feel for the bandaging, so that the fact of his feeling utterly helpless to repair all the damage, and being able to call for help is perhaps undervalued. It became a bit lost in her general theory about reparation.

To begin with then, reparation was seen as a very active process with the mental significance of reversing all the damage. But Mrs Klein recognized that, when children attempt to put into action their reparative impulses, they experience a terrible incapacity and frustration. They discover that it is terribly easy to break things and terribly hard to put them together. Her ideas about reparation were set in flux. As a purely internal process the child can in his phantasy and feelings omnipotently repair all the damage that is done, but only at the expense of being caught on the manic treadmill, Sorcerer's Apprentice fashion.

It is important to note that around this time when she was developing a concept of reparation, Mrs Klein used the concept of sublimation in a very integrated way in her theories, but very differently from the way Freud had used it. She puts forward the idea that the drive to reparation is the main stimulus to sublimation and therefore sublimations are in fact reparative acts. She cites the woman doing the painting, suddenly and impulsively, having been in a state of mental anguish because somebody had taken a painting off her wall and the empty space was tormenting her with depression. She painted a picture herself of a naked negress, demonstrating an extraordinary talent, although she had never painted before. It was entirely different from Freud's idea that sublimation was a rather tricky way of directing one's polymorphously perverse infantile sexual impulses into action in the outside world in a socially acceptable and desexualized way.

She also distinguished at this time between 'reactive tendencies' in a manner again very different from Freud's use of 'reaction formation'. He conceived a manipulation of affects to alter the direction of impulse into its opposite. Mrs Klein used 'reactive tendencies' to describe forms of activity which are intended either to prevent the damage of assault on the objects or to reverse the damage in some way particularly connected with reparation. This seems to be her position with reference to reparation until the 1946 paper on schizoid mechanisms.

First of all she began to differentiate the motivation: between manic reparation as defence against persecutory or depressive anxiety; and something much more genuinely in the service of the objects. Secondly, as a result of the discovery of splitting processes and projective identification, her conception of the mechanics of reparation moved to a deeper level. Whereas previously her descriptions of unconscious phantasy had a very concrete quality to them, there was less emphasis on the meaning of the child's masturbatory phantasies of assaults on his objects. At the height of his sadistic period in the oral and anal phases he chopped them to pieces and burnt them, etc. The recognition of splitting processes and projective identification implied the understanding that these assaults were not simply raw impulse run wild, nor simple revenges or robbing, but that they have a meaning in psychic reality related to the structure of the personality. From this point of view, the meaning of these assaults was seen as twofold. One is a splitting type of assault and the other is a projective type of assault. That is, one type of assault creates a split in the object; something that was a single object before is now two objects. So splitting attacks result in a multiplication of objects. The other kind of assault by projection has the meaning of taking something from the self and putting it into the object. This brings about the psychological state in which your own self seems now to be lacking in something and the object to have something added to it.

From this viewpoint reparations can also have a structural meaning, not merely the concrete sense of putting broken bits together again or giving back the goodies. How was the structural alteration and its meaning for self and object to be undone or reversed? What could the self do and what would have to be done by the objects? And what would be the mental economics of such recovery? Such questions began to produce the realization that the child could not put the bits together, he could not give mummy new babies, he could not heal the splits. Perhaps he could take back a projective identification as the active component that the self can perform in reparation.

But on the whole, reparation began to take on a more mysterious meaning, something that happens in the depressive position. That frame of mind of depressive feeling, guilt or remorse or just regret, or wishing it had not happened, seems to make possible the process by which objects repair one another. The distinction between the active and passive components immediately galvanizes the understanding of the difference between manic reparation and true reparation. The true reparation is something that happens when the mental condition, the mental atmosphere is conducive to the objects repairing one another.

This gave an entirely new meaning to the concept of the primal scene; not simply mummy and daddy enjoying one another or making babies. A specific function of repairing the splitting infused a new urgency to the parental coition: mummy must repair daddy's penis and daddy's penis must repair mummy's breasts and thus reconstitute the combined object. These two components, a part which the self can perform by taking back its projective identifications through accepting its depressive feeling, and a part which the objects can do for one another in their coition when infantile dependence is acknowledged, restore the damage that has been produced primarily by masturbation attacks. Mrs Klein's work with Richard marks a turning point in her views on reparation. The sessions this week bring a change in her orientation to him. She is much more helpful and nurturing to him in his greater acknowledgement of helplessness. Her helpfulness is largely centered on the interpretive process, but also emerges in little services at his request.

Seventh Week: Sessions 34-39
Concepts of Confusion – Their
Absence in the Work with Richard
and its Consequence

Chapter VII

An interesting week, but again it is a week that is interfered
with because, on the Tuesday, Mrs Klein tells Richard that
her trip to London is to start at the end of the week. He does
not really react to this information until Thursday, and then
on Friday and Saturday it strikes him terribly. So it is another
one of those weeks in which the setting has been interfered with
– the mother's illness, Mrs Klein going away, the playroom
being locked so that she has to take him to her lodgings. There
is hardly a week that has not been interfered with in some way,
but it is very instructive to see how the interferences and the
analytic process somehow mingle with one another.

By this time in the analysis almost all Richard's insincerity
has dropped away, at least temporarily, and this is a week in
which there is very little resistance to the analytical work. His
participation has become somehow less formalized; although he
plays with the fleet and draws a few empire drawings, the really
important things that happen just erupt – suddenly he digs
in Mrs Klein's bag; he rushes out of the room into the kitchen
and squirts the water; emotionality pours from him, looking
up at her eyes, saying how he loves her. This analysis is going
at full pace, and Richard is passionately involved in it, already
feeling that it has benefited him. He tells her so, and his mother
confirms this, that some of his fear of school children has diminished. He is beginning to be able to think of himself as possibly
grown up someday.

With all this the attachment to the analysis and to Mrs Klein
in the transference is becoming very manifest. It is true that
she continues her mode of interpreting, rather unlike her
general technique, continually referring to Mummy and Daddy
and Paul. When she does that quite a lot she meets strong obstacles in him, indicating that he would much rather deal with
the transference, about Mrs Klein and Mr Klein and her son
and grandson, about what is happening in the war, to act it

out there in the playroom, and not have it pushed back into his home situation where things are much less clear to him.

Our main approach has been to study Mrs Klein's work historically and to follow the development of her technique and theoretical equipment but it is also instructive to notice the theoretical equipment she was not yet working with and the ways in which it left her in the lurch. That is probably the way psycho-analysis develops, that an analyst has the feeling of being left in the lurch by his framework of understanding, and begins to search for some other way. The formulations he is using just are not containing the situation and helping it develop. In 1941 Mrs Klein did not as yet have a workable concept of confusion, as a close examination of part of a session will show. Even when confusion is not central, Richard's material can be difficult to follow because various threads of material move rather simultaneously and interweave. It is incredibly interesting and one can imagine how challenging it must have been to work with this child who kept shifting his modes of representation – one minute rushing out of the room onto the steps, the next minute the fleet play, then telling her dreams or bits of information, and then back again to the fleet play. It is questionable how to understand this continual shift of mode of representation. The shifting comes about in a way that tempts one to say, as with earlier sessions, 'play disruption'. But now one is impressed that the shift in the nature of the material has much more the significance of changed mode of communication. It is as if Richard said, 'No, you don't get it yet. Suppose I jump down the steps; now do you get it?' This continual shifting of representation, although it is taxing for Mrs Klein, also allows her, just as continually, to rectify her interpretation and reach better approximations in her understanding.

By this week it is very clear to her that Richard is constantly asking her for help, mainly by his attitude but sometimes in concrete requests such as the time he puts the stools on one another, knocks them over and asks her to help him build them up again. The interpretations also veer towards emphasis on his helplessness in the fact of the violence of the impulses which produce the catastrophes. She is more pointedly investigating his masturbation and even presses him to acknowledgement, which is rather relieving to him. She has a particular way of talking about masturbation simply as a fact and relating it a bit to the kind of material that will illustrate for him the sort of unconscious phantasies that accompany his masturbation. She does not seem to link the masturbation to the functions and phantasies about his penis, which emerge in the concreteness of the material. She does not, for example, interpret to him that his penis *is* his hand digging into her bag, or that his penis *is* like his hand digging into the dirt, or his father's penis *is* like the crane that handed the jack-in-the-box to him. Instead of making the masturbation phantasy very vivid to him by linking it strongly with the material, she seems to be introducing him very gently to the idea that these are phantasies that accompany masturbation, implying that it is not the masturbation itself, but the meaning of the masturbation that is important.

Regarding the development of the material of the week, the very striking thing is the intensity of relationship with the breasts that is beginning to show through. It comes out parti-cularly on the Thursday and Friday, somewhat under the pressure of her imminent holiday, but the impression created is that although the breast material may be increased in in-tensity by the imminence of the holiday, it has not been propelled out of sequence, as was, for example, the intense de-pressive feeling forced forward by his mother's illness in the third week. Mrs Klein going to London and the threat to her of being bombed or the possibility of his having to go to her funeral are all very vivid to Richard and stir concern for her but mainly for himself in his need for analysis. He handles it in a manful way, asking, should she die, who could continue his analysis. Clearly he feels that there is something quite unique going on in his relationship with Mrs Klein that will not easily be replaceable. He makes her promise to go to the air raid shelter and to give his mother the name of another analyst. This is very impressive. For a young boy, in the midst of feeling attached to Mrs Klein and leaning his head against her, to whom she looks beautiful like the hills outside, to be able to grasp that it is the analysis he needs and that in this respect she is potentially replaceable, shows surprising discrimination.

Of course Richard does not take it all in for the first two days but continues in an obviously manic way with the fleet play in which somehow peace is to be kept in the family. But this time it is not the peace of everybody having equal shares, as in the Empire drawings and in the fleet play where no one was to touch the mummy ship or was to have any special intimate relation. In this material, particularly in the harbour gate episode, and Richard laughing about the pigs trying to get into the pigsty and his account about the chickens – how the cock had his head in the hen house and how their bellies shook – the emphasis has shifted from everybody having equal shares to one-at-a-time. The good stuff is down there in the harbour/genitals and all the men – Mr Klein, he, Paul, Daddy – get their turn and get what they need, which is not necessarily the same as what they want or equal. So there has been a considerable advance in his concept of justice – the progress from egalitarianism to each-according-to-his-need. The mummy is a rich mummy, the rich machine from which he got the jack-in-the-box, the woman who gave him the liquorice.

In this context, Richard's second experience in Mrs Klein's lodgings is not very exciting. He is much more in awe, frightened that the 'grumpy old man' would be about and a bit worried that this was not the right place for his analysis. He does not really like that session very much and is very relieved to get back to the play room the next day. This seems a good indication of progress with his greediness. This piggy greediness that was mainly attached to his penis is coming up into his mouth and being directed to the breasts. It is at this point that he becomes very confused and Mrs Klein does not have the conceptual equipment to help him. The problem of confusion which he represents variously by the jumping down the steps, by going in and out of the house to watch the water drain away seems to involve various dimensions of relation to the maternal object – inside/outside, upstairs/downstairs, frontside/backside, and all in the matrix of uncertainty about the good and the bad in his object.

To illustrate how the lack of a piece of conceptual equipment could interfere with her grasping things about the material, we must examine the session itself. This is from the Thursday session, towards the bottom of page 177 – 'Richard had become restless, he walked over to the map and studied how much there was of occupied and unoccupied France. He again wondered how the allies were getting on with Syria. Then he went outside

196

and, as usual, called Mrs Klein to come too. He looked round and said he did not like seeing the sky overcast. He repeatedly jumped down from the steps, which were fairly high, and said it was fun. He said he was looking forward to playing croquet with the Polish soldiers.

'Mrs Klein interpreted that the soldiers stood for the nice Daddy who would help him become potent, would teach him (croquet) and treat him like an equal, which also meant that he would also help him to be equal in sexual matters – to have sexual intercourse with Mummy and give her children'. [That is the theme she is on, of his wanting to be potent and his concern about his penis and masturbation. She has not picked up the greediness of the penis and its function of getting in like a hand in her bag, that is, its prehensile capability. She is thinking more of his desire to use his penis to give babies to Mummy, to thank her, repay her, protect her.] His pleasure in jumping well had the same significance.

'Richard kept on running up and down the foot path. Suddenly he asked Mrs Klein to go quickly back into the room with him; he had seen a wasp. (He was not really very frightened of the wasp, but was dramatizing.)

'Mrs Klein followed him into the room and interpreted that the footpath represented her inside and genital, running up and down and jumping from the steps meant sexual intercourse with her; the dangerous wasp stood for the hostile Daddy and Paul inside Mummy, or Mrs Klein's son or Mr Klein inside Mrs Klein.

'Richard played with the stools and piled some of them on top of each other. He pointed out to Mrs Klein that he had again made a big tower' [As he had on the Monday session when it had fallen down and he had asked her to help him put it up again] 'and the way in which he said it plainly showed that he was thinking of the tower which had to be dynamited'. [his reference to the Crystal Palace tower, 34th session.] 'He knocked the stools down and said, "Poor Daddy, here is his genital tumbling down!" ' [He tried to go along with her interpretation quite sincerely. But there is some considerable difference between falling down and getting hurt, and jumping down quite skilfully.] 'Then he remarked on a man passing by on the road, said he was nasty and might do him some harm. He

197

watched the man, hiding behind the curtain until he disappeared from sight. [That seems a bit of genuine anxiety. connected with his trying to go along with her interpretation of dynamiting Daddy's penis, and in consequence, becoming persecuted by the daddy again.]

'Mrs Klein interpreted that though he was sorry for Daddy if he attacked Daddy's genital, he also felt that Daddy would turn into an attacker and injure Richard's genital, (mixture of depressive and persecutory anxiety). That was why he was suddenly frightened of the 'nasty' man, (the wasp) and had been so afraid of children in previous sessions. The boys not only stood for Daddy and Paul and the attacked babies, but also Daddy's attacked genital.

'Richard had gone back to the table and looked at the drawing, reminding Mrs Klein to date it. He said he would like to see all the drawings next day. Then he pointed at the blue section which had no coastline because he had divided it off by a pencil line and asked Mrs Klein whether she knew what this represented. But he answered the question at once himself: "it was Mummy's breast".' [This is how he goes to another representation as if to say 'Wait a second, you didn't get it; now I'm talking about jumping down from Mummy's breasts to Mummy's genitals and how, when I do that, the wasp comes. But up at Mummy's breasts it is much better'.] 'He mentioned for the second time that a lady at the hotel had given him liquorice – she was very nice. He now looked happy and very friendly, and putting his arm very lightly round Mrs Klein's shoulder and leaning his head against her, he said "I'm very fond of you".'

'Mrs Klein interpreted the connection between her, as helpful and protective, and Mummy's feeding breast – the lady's liquorice. Also, by co-operating with Mrs Klein and asking her to preserve the drawings he wished to return to Mrs Klein what she had given him'. [One can see how she allows herself to be corrected.] 'Richard particularly felt that she was good to him, and fed him with her good breast because the work she was doing with him had made him less frightened about his genital.

'Richard replied that he thought so too. He ran into the kitchen, turned on the tap and made the water squirt by putting his finger inside the tap and listened to the noise it made'. [It

198

was very impulsive, she mentioned the word genitals and he's off]. 'He said that this was Daddy's genital and that it sounded very angry. Then by putting his finger into the tap in a different way he made the water squirt differently and said that this was himself – he too was angry'. [One can not escape the impression that he is angry with her for having mentioned genitals, about her making him frightened of them, when it is quite clear that he is feeling that to be the baby at the breast has made him less hostile to everybody and therefore less persecuted by other children, wasps, and grumpy old men. But it is not his genitals being preserved that has brought relief. His general persecutory anxiety has been relieved because there has been some diminution in his own general feeling of hostility to everybody.]

'Mrs Klein interpreted that he had shown that his own and his father's genitals were fighting inside her, (the tap); he expected Daddy or Mr Klein to be angry with him if he put his genital inside Mummy or Mrs Klein.

'Richard went outside and asked Mrs Klein to pull the plug out of the sink so that he could see the water running away. Then he found a bit of coal and crushed it with his foot'. [In the last session he had crushed the female doll with his foot in reaction to Mrs Klein going away. He had put his Hitler boot on it, but carefully, under the instep, so that in effect he did not crush it. Now he does actually crush the piece of coal.]

'Mrs Klein interpreted that he was destroying his father's black genital'. [By bringing him back to the genitals, and in that way reminding him of the father's genitals, she has functioned as a breast which flaunts the nipple and reminds the infant of the father's penis and of the mother's intercourse with him. This is seen as black and bad and arouses a pregenital oedipal attack on the breast and nipple as a combined object.]

'Richard fetched the broom, swept the floor and said he would like to clean up the whole place.

'Mrs Klein suggested that if he felt he destroyed Daddy's genital inside Mummy, he would also dirty and injure her, and then would wish to put her right again'. [The point is that when he found the bit of coal and crushed it he was outside and now he wants to clean up the room inside. Probably inside the room has the same relation to outside at this time as the top of the steps has to the bottom of the steps – up at the breasts

and down at the genitals. Richard seems to be saying again here that it is the daddy-penis outside that he attacks but if inside or up at the breasts he feels very helpful and would, as it were, like to lick the breast and make it lovely and clean.]
'Richard went back to playing with the tap. He said he was thirsty and drank from the tap. Then he asked Mrs Klein if she knew what he had been drinking, and again without waiting for a reply, he said, "Little Job",' [that is, urine. He shows extremely clearly at this point that he is struggling with some confusion between nipple and penis, and whether this tap is a nipple which gives milk from the breasts or is it daddy's penis which is presiding over, or possessing, the breasts and urinating into his mouth.]
This material gives the impression of Mrs Klein being in-adequately equipped to understand what Richard is struggling very hard to tell her, that something is going on in his relation-ship with the breasts. He distrusts the feeling that he has when his arm is lightly around her and he says he's fond of her because the moment she mentions genitals he becomes confused, as if instead of milk, urine had come into the baby's mouth. Seeing such difficult material tackled with inadequate con-ceptual equipment helps one to understand a little bit the historical perspective in psycho-analysis. It is not like saying 'What did they do before TV?', but more like wondering how people ever tolerated loving children when they knew that more than half of them were going to die in childhood. Mrs Klein at that point in 1940/41 was struggling to understand some-thing about a child's approach to the breasts and the way it was being interfered with by Richard's anxieties about her going to London and the fear of her being killed. At the same time, her going off to London means to him that she is going to see her son and grandson and that it is indistinguishable from her going on holiday. This in turn means the same as going to see Mr Klein and having intercourse with him, although Richard knows Mr Klein is dead. It confronts him with this Oedipus Complex at a pregenital level, which Mrs Klein knows a lot about. But what she does not know much about at this point is how it is that the genital oedipus complex impinges itself on a baby's relationship with the breasts. She does not know any-thing about these kinds of confusion, that the two breasts can

be making love to one another, the two nipples can be homo-
sexuals sucking on one another etc. Consequently she has to
struggle with this sort of material with still fairly inadequately
equipped. But by the fifteenth week you will see that she has
worked it all out with Richard's help. Both he and Mrs Klein
seem suddenly to realize that four months of analysis is not very
much. He has already had almost two months with her and
there are only two months more. He is getting the wind up
about it and she is realizing also how much needs to be done
for this boy and how little she is going to accomplish. Mrs
Klein writes a sad little note about what the mother told her —
how much better Richard is. While it is true, both he and she
were feeling pretty desperate about having only a few months
more. Perhaps it helps one to understand this other aspect of
her technique in this case which seems to be different from that
which she usually followed, that is, referring back to the family
situation instead of drawing it all into the transference. Mrs
Klein may quite reasonably have been afraid of involving him
in the depth and intensity of transference that would make the
ending not only terribly painful but possibly insupportable to
him.

Chapter VIII

Eighth Week: Sessions 40-45
The Phenomenology of
Hypochondria: its Differentiation
from Psychosomatic Phenomena
or Somatic Delusions

This is the week following Mrs Klein's return from her nine days in London. It starts on the Tuesday and goes through to include Sunday and is a week that is very sharply divided. In the first session Richard is very persecuted about coming back to X and persecuted also by Mrs Klein. He does not really regain his relationship to her until the next session when he confesses his infidelity or, really, betrayal of her during the break. He had apparently seduced his mother by telling her she was a better analyst than Mrs Klein because she was his mother. Once Mrs Klein has related this to the breast-transference, contact is restored.

In the week before Mrs Klein went away she seemed to be emphasizing castration anxiety and only sporadically recognizing the infantile transference to the breast and the horizontal splitting of the mother into the breast-mummy upstairs and a very sexual and potentially bad and seductive mummy downstairs. This is the material that presents itself immediately in the Tuesday session, where he seems to have externalized that split on to his good mother at home and Mrs Klein as the bad mummy, surrounded or filled with poisonous nettles and toadstool babies. Again he stamps on his rivals and again the phantasy of being poisoned comes out when he gets his sore throat. That theme of the splitting of the mother into the idealized light blue breast-mummy who gives him his shredded wheat and this bad old woman genital spitting yellow stuff now also invades the empire drawings so that it looks like a horrid bird which has black stuff falling out of it. (This is the material Mrs Klein used for her 1945 paper *The Oedipus Complex in the Light of Early Anxieties*.) When he can not keep the split going, Richard either gets a sore throat or feels that he has poison dripping down inside him. It is instructive to note how different is this confusional and persecuted state from the paranoid

202

delusion of being poisoned by the secret German spies, Cook and Bessie.

The manic material which follows the confession of seducing his mother seems to have two determinants. One of these he confessed to on the Saturday – that he was sleeping in the same room as his mother because of limited hotel accommodation. It was also determined by Mrs Klein letting him off much too easily, by not making it quite clear to him that during the separation there had been an element of betrayal, leaving her to be bombed and killed in London. Her excessive gentleness often has the consequence of Richard becoming rather manic, feeling that 'Larry the Lamb' has triumphed over truth.

The next few sessions are very much influenced by feeling that now Mrs Klein has become the good, light-blue as well as his mummy, whom he has both day and night. He and Mummy are the king and queen and his Daddy and Paul are reduced to babies, little piggies trying to get into the pigsty. The manic triumph is also represented by the long red thing going all the way through the Empire drawing (No. 27), which Mrs Klein astutely ties up with his lining up his ships and seeing they are straight. She interprets a manic acquisition of all the rival genitals and appending them to his own penis. In a way the mania does not so much break down as a result of Mrs Klein's interpretations; somehow it just seems to collapse very suddenly as bits of persecution appear. There are two men talking outside and he is spying on them and they are spying on him; a horrid old woman is spitting this nasty yellow stuff, and then he comes back the next day with a sore throat and persecuted. There is no doubt in his mind that it is tied up with this semi-delusion that Cook and Bessie are poisoning him. When Mrs Klein recognized the implication that she and the mother had become the two idealized breasts which now suddenly turned into these very bad and poisonous buttocks [the horrid bird], she is able to afford him very great relief.

The next day, of course, he is filled with gratitude and admiration for her in her silver dress and her lovely hair. The idealization builds up again, represented by the shredded wheat that he has had from his mother, which allayed his gnawing hunger and protruding bones. It was from material like this that Mrs Klein built up her concept of persecutory and depressive hypochondria as the mainstay phenomena for the concept of the concreteness of psychic reality.

Freud, when he wrote the paper *On Narcissism* cited hypochondria as one of the general evidences for narcissism as a stage between autoerotism and object relations. In hypochondria, the libido regressed to narcissistic libido, was concentrated on the body and this produced the hypochondriacal symptoms, which Freud took mainly as obsessional.

In *The Psychoanalysis of Children*, Mrs Klein noted hypochondriacal symptoms as one of the very common complaints of children. In the 1920s and early 1930s, her ideas were still very attached to the Libido Theory, but had been modified now by her concepts of projection and introjection as continual processes. Her view of hypochondria was in a way similar to Freud's: but where Freud expressed the dynamic in terms of withdrawal of the libido from objects onto the ego, she tended to express it as withdrawal of the libido from external objects onto internal objects. In a certain way, this seemed to imply that she was talking about narcissistic phenomena in Freud's sense of narcissistic libido. This first attempt to formulate hypochondriacal phenomena in terms of Libido Theory and the interaction of projection and introjection only qualified as narcissism because it involved the cutting off of the person's interest in the outside world, corresponding to Freud's idea of withdrawal of object libido.

By 1934, in the paper on manic-depressive states, when she was already further along in considering the interplay between paranoid-schizoid and depressive phenomena she was in a position to recognize and describe two different types of hypochondria. She first delineated hypochondria of the type she had talked of in *The Psychoanalysis of Children*, in which the person feels attacked internally, attacked in the self by bad objects, but she also described a depressive kind of hypochondria in which the good objects are being attacked, internally, by the bad objects and the id. If she had gone back to it later after the paper on schizoid-mechanisms she probably would have described the two types of hypochondria differently, one that was dominated by depressive concern for the objects represented by the organ that was afflicted, the other dominated by persecutory guilt, in which the person wanted to get rid of the afflicted organ. This takes hypochondria as a single phenomenon, in which parts of the body are seen to be identified with internal objects that are suffering in some way, and one may either have a depressive relationship to the suffering or a persecutory one. She would not have had the means of distinguishing between hypochondria and somatic delusion or psycho-somatic phenomena. The phenomena Richard reports this week seem to be a mixture of all three, a sore throat as a depressive psycho-somatic phenomenon, a somatic delusion of internal poisoning and persecutory hypochondria about his gnawing hunger and protruding bones.

The mechanisms that produce hypochondria were becoming apparent to Mrs Klein at the time she treated Richard, but she did not have the equipment to elucidate it. Note I (p. 216) goes some distance in doing that, since she recognized that it had something to do with identification processes, that it was linked to Freud's and Abraham's conception of melancholia. She saw that hypochondria stood very close to melancholia through identification with damaged objects and that the struggle had to do with the way the identification processes altered emotionality, so that instead of feelings of guilt on the one hand or persecution on the other, the person tended to feel self-pity, projected as clamorous demands for reparation of the self, or to be rid of the damaged object by surgical means. The only very significant addendum to that conception of hypochondria that one could add from more recent works is most plainly described by Dr Rosenfeld. The hypochondriac, like the melancholic, is in a rather double bond of identifications; he is not only projectively identified with the internal object that is damaged (and partly it is damaged as a result of the projective identification) but is also identified with this object introjectively. Thus he is caught in a rather double system of identification from which it is extremely difficult for him to liberate himself.

The other issue that Mrs Klein discusses at some length in her notes on this week (Note 2, p. 216) is the business about integration. The notes about it are really too poorly related to the material to be at all convincing at this point. That whole topic about integration and what she meant by it and how it relates to concepts of splitting are better illustrated in later sessions.

	Ninth Week: Sessions 46-52
	Splitting and Idealization–its Role
	in Development and its Defects'
Chapter IX	Contribution to Psycho-pathology

This week's material springs from the themes of the Monday session, the most important session in the book as regards Richard's disturbances about the shortness of the analysis. This was becoming very real and vivid to him, and to Mrs Klein, for she is again seeing him on Sunday. It is another seven-session week. The previous Sunday, which was the sixth session of that week because she had not seen him on the Monday, brought material about her silver dress and lovely hair, and his golden shoes. The atmosphere of the session, which Mrs Klein did not pick up sufficiently, was one of incipient mania which burst on the Monday.

The way in which these Sunday sessions are impinging on him becomes very clear during this week and she finally notes it in the Sunday session itself, when Richard raises the question about her not going to church but seeing him instead. He has a strong suspicion that it is because of greed for money, for he has discovered the facts of her fee, and confronts her with it in rather a devastating way. The other factor in the setting of the week is the expectation of the arrival of his father. Although Richard is looking forward to going fishing with father, the thought of being expelled from his mother's bedroom, which has really been the source of the mania, drives him quite wild. In the Thursday session, the very interesting 'go away Mr Smith, go back to work' material appears, certainly referring forward to his father's coming. All the railway drawings seem under the sway of the expectations of his father's arrival, but are woven into the transference: people crossing, Mr Klein going away sobbing, Richard and Mrs Klein meeting secretly. And there are the various interesting names which she makes use of, 'Valing' 'Roseman' and so on. The 'Roseman' quite clearly referred to the hotel manager scolding him for picking the roses. Mrs Klein relates that mainly to his craving for the father's penis, which comes out quite clearly, following on from the earlier material about the 'delicious monster', or the yellow pencil being crammed into every orifice, mouth, ears, nose, in biting the pencil, and in the very interesting phantasy about the mouse in his parent's bedroom. It ate the two biscuits, ran up his father's fishing rod and both father and mother were afraid of it. There is probably a bit of the truth in it, that there was something about the violence in this boy that did intimidate his parents, and made it very difficult for them to maintain any constant curb on his naughtiness, his exhausting his mother, or doing as he pleased.

The collapse of the mania comes on Wednesday with the fascinating Kafka-esque dream about his being tried at a court but not knowing the charge against him. In the Thursday session it transpires that he was charged with breaking a window, and Mrs Klein spots immediately that it is connected with a window being broken in the playroom, although not by Richard. Presumably one of the girl guides had broken it. Nevertheless it is certainly connected intimately with his phantasies because he admits in the Friday or Saturday session that he was very cross in the morning and felt like breaking a window. The idea of breaking a window is closely connected with his Hitler identification, with the bomb that had fallen near his home, smashing the glass house and frightening Cook and Bessie.

The dream reflects the curbing of his manic tyrannical phantasies and helps Mrs Klein to focus on a problem which she says herself was only to be discussed fully some fifteen years later in *Envy and Gratitude*, the problem of splitting-and-idealization. The notes to the Thursday and Friday session about splitting-and-idealization are some of the most important theoretical-technical notes in the book. Mrs Klein has come to recognize through Richard's material how quickly and easily good objects turn bad for him. He loses his judgment under the slightest stress, and becomes not only persecuted but persecuting. She had already interpreted that if he attacks the father's penis as a persecutor inside the mother, he also attacks and harms the mother. His confusion and difficulty in distinguishing between good and bad in his objects and himself is illustrated by the blackness of his father in the Empire drawings which contrasted with his actual love for his father. Now the quickness with which Mr Smith turns bad and then is a quite nice man a few minutes later in the session astonishes Richard.

One might think that this was a problem about which she was very clear for it goes back into her earliest writings, when she talked about the baby splitting the breast into the good and bad breasts. But she did not realize until much later that this critical operation for the establishment of the conditions for growth and development was most difficult and could go wrong in many ways. In this note (III, p. 249) she discusses mainly the two ways it could go wrong quantitatively: inadequate or excessive splitting-and-idealization. In her later work there are hints that she was also aware that it could go wrong in qualitative ways; that is, the plane of splitting could be basically faulty. There is, for instance, the splitting-and-idealization with respect to the mother and father, for one to be idealized and the other to be the bad object. This goes on a bit here – also at part-object level between breast and penis, or between the breast and nipple. A horizontal plane of splitting between the top of the mother's body and the bottom, or between the front and the back, can be attempted, each giving rise to a situation in the child that is unsatisfactory for development.

In this note Mrs Klein explains that it is necessary for the splitting-and-idealization to be sufficiently 'wide' to diminish the persecutory anxiety. That is, the badness must be sufficiently split off so that it is not constantly crowding into and spoiling the secure relationship between the idealized part of the self and the idealized object. On the other hand, it must not be so widely split off as to diminish the anxiety below the level which is necessary for development. This necessary level, probably different in different children, had become apparent to her, mainly by examination of the analytic situation, discovering that patients in analysis needed to maintain a certain level of anxiety in order for the material to come, and for working through to take place.

This problem of inadequate splitting-and-idealization of self and object will henceforth be central in Richard's analysis. He could not keep the destructive and Hitleresque part of himself from crowding in on and taking over the good part. A very clear description of the consequent hypocrisy in his character is brought to light by the Larry-the-Lamb material, how he acts like a lamb while secretly causing all sorts of difficulties. A bit of confusion enters these notes because Mrs Klein has introduced the concept of externalization as well. She felt that the transference was mainly based on externalization of the internal situation. The patient's desire to externalize his internal situation was a way of putting it into the outside world, partly as an evacuation of internal persecution and partly as a way of ridding himself of the complete responsibility for the preservation of his internal objects. She has introduced this concept of externalization into her discussion of splitting-and-idealization in relation to Richard's locating his persecutor in the outside world, as in the 'Now I can kill Hitler' material, when he was holding all these sharpened pencils in his hand, and feeling that he now had the weapons with which to kill his persecutor. That his persecutor could be felt as a real figure in the outside world is an aspect of the externalization and seems to Mrs Klein to be helpful to his development because of the way in which it locates his persecutor and places it at a distance from himself, thus representing a widening of the splitting-and-idealization. She connects it with his being able to be more open himself, which is perhaps not very convincing. The material in the previous week already indicates that Richard was more confiding, more open in his communications, less secretive and less omnipotent in his secrecy. For instance his asking Mrs Klein personal questions about going to church or about her fee, although sprung on her in a slightly tricky way, all represent an improvement in his honesty.

This brings into focus another aspect of her notes, about integration. Although Mrs Klein saw the thirst for knowledge as essentially a thirst for knowledge about the mother's body, representing the child's world and later extended to the world in general, she also saw evidences of a thirst for knowledge about the internal world, psychic reality. She noticed the amount of pleasure that patients could take, and Richard here takes, in discovering things about the unconscious, despite the fact that the discoveries may bring elements of mental pain. She felt this to be the pleasure of integration, of the discovery of little-known parts of oneself, repressed, split off, or not realized in one way or another. This pleasure in the coming together of parts of the self, and feeling more whole, was, in her view, one of the great benefits of the analytical process. In her notes she attributes Richard's pleasure to integration, where he says now he's an American, he feels he's a new man. It may not be a quite correct understanding because he seems a bit manically optimistic at that point, celebrating his transformation. But the idea is certainly right. You can see his pleasure in discovering things. It goes along with his being a bit puzzled and asking Mrs Klein if she enjoys her work, and trying to construe what is at the heart of psycho-analysis. He is an intelligent child, and he seems to suspect that the discovery of the truth about yourself and the world is a source of some very considerable pleasure, a pleasure which had been relatively unknown to him before. It may have contributed to his fear of being a dunce, for he not only could not learn but could not take any pleasure in learning.

These two notes are probably the best statements in her written work of these two aspects of her thinking about integration and about splitting-and-idealization. Taken together they describe the developmental stages that she envisaged, to which the primal splitting-and-idealization is a precondition of development. This split had gradually to be brought together as persecutory anxieties diminished and finally was given a very strong impetus for integration under the pressure of depressive anxiety.

With that discussion in hand, it might be useful to examine the Monday session in detail. This is the 46th session, Monday. 'Richard presented a very different picture'. [The Sunday session had ended with his golden shoes and her lovely hair.] 'He was lively, but over excited and his eyes were very bright. He talked constantly and incoherently, putting many questions without waiting for an answer, was restless, continuously, in a persecuted way, watching passers-by, and apparently quite incapable of listening to any interpretation. Mrs Klein interpreted there was no response. He was clearly in a state of strong manic excitement and much more openly aggressive, even directly towards Mrs Klein, than he had been for a long time. He said at once that he had brought the fleet and was planning a big battle. The Japanese, the Germans and the Italians were all going to fight the British. (He suddenly looked worried.) He asked Mrs Klein what she thought about the war situation but went on talking without waiting for an answer'. [It seems at this time the war situation was impressing itself upon him.] 'He said he felt very well indeed, there was nothing more the matter with him. He had been writing to his friend Jimmy who was the second most important person in his game – Richard himself being the most important – about plans for battle against Oliver. Then he put out the fleet. The British were stronger than all the others together and were stationed behind rocks, represented by Mrs Klein's handbag and clock'. [This is again a very good indication of the nature of his mania, how it was connected with sleeping with his mother on the one hand and Mrs Klein seeing him on the Sunday on the other, how much he felt he really had these big indestructible objects as his armaments.] 'Suddenly the Italians appeared, but soon turned tail. Other enemies started to fight but one hostile destroyer after another was blown up. Richard said, while putting them aside, "They are dead".' [This putting aside of the dead had happened before.] 'A small British destroyer fired at a German battleship and at first was supposed to have sunk her; then Richard decided that she had surrendered and the destroyer brought her back. In between, he repeatedly jumped up, looked out of the window and watched children. He knocked on the window to attract their attention, made faces at them, but quickly withdrew behind the curtain; he behaved similarly toward a dog; he said of a young girl that she looked silly. He was particularly interested in all the men who passed by ... He looked at Mrs Klein, admired the colour of her hair, touched it quickly, also fingered her frock to find out what it was made of. Then he spoke of a "funny" old woman who had walked past the house. When he had started the fleet play he made, as usual the noise of engines, something like chug, chug, chug. He interrupted himself and said, "What is this? I have now got it in my ear". After having sunk the enemies' fleets, Richard suddenly became "tired" of playing and put the fleet aside. He took the pencils out and at once put the yellow pencil into his mouth, biting it hard. Then – which was unusual – he pushed the pencil into his nostril and into his ear, put his finger to one nostril and made various sounds. At one point he said the noise was like the whirlwind in "The Wizard of Oz" which blew Dorothy away, who was a nice girl; she did not die as a result of the whirlwind. Meanwhile he asked Mrs Klein whether she liked his light-blue shirt and his tie.' [That is another indication of the light-blue mummy and getting all mixed up with her,] 'but did not seem

211

to expect an answer. He took out his handkerchief to wipe his nose, although he did not need it, but he looked at it and said "My mucous hanky".' [He must have said this with some sort of affection.]

'Mrs Klein interpreted that he particularly wished her to admire his shirt and tie, which also stood for his body and his penis, because he felt that he was mucous, actually had poison inside; with it he meant to attack the internal parents and they would retaliate with poisonous attacks on him. Mrs Klein also pointed out that by biting the pencil he had attacked and taken in Daddy's hostile penis and that the noises Richard had made went on inside him, he had said he had heard the chug, chug, chug, inside his ear. In his mind the fleet battle went on internally and these fights would injure not only himself but the internal good mummy, just as the whirlwind blew away the nice Dorothy. This meant he was the magician who had arranged all these battles'. [That is an interpretation intended to stop the mania cold, by warning him that he is carrying out something that is dangerous to his internal situation, of the anxieties implied about Dorothy and of the chug-chug going on inside him. Such an interpretation has too much of an action in it rather than a communication. Richard is in no mood to be put off in this way.]

'Richard had been grimacing, biting the pencil violently and asked whether Mrs Klein would mind if he broke it or bit it through. Not waiting for an answer he asked whether Mrs Klein liked her son. He was scribbling his name all over a page, nearly illegibly, and then covered it up with further scribbles'. [Further evidence that the interpretation had not yet touched him.]

'Mrs Klein interpreted that, in the fleet play, the little destroyer fighting the battleship stood for Richard fighting against his mother.

('Richard had got up, was running about not listening at all and continuing to make noises.)

'Mrs Klein suggested that the "silly" Mummy-fish which in the drawing of the previous day had got in the way of the torpedo and stood for Mrs Klein who exposed herself to his attacks, was today represented by the "silly" girl who passed by. He had recently expressed his aggressiveness more openly and had said today that he had written to Jimmy his plans for an attack on Oliver. He wished to be able to have an open and external fight'. [Here she brings in the theme of externalization.] 'When he had decided to attack Oliver he had said he was happy (33rd session) and had hated his pretence of friendliness when he loathed his enemy. But he nevertheless had expressed his hate by secret attacks, by "big job" – the scribble hiding his name and the fleet battle which he felt was going on internally represented by the chug-chug in his ear. His jealousy of his parents, and now of Mrs Klein and her husband or her son, again and again stirred up his hate; and since he felt he had taken them into his inside, he could not help feeling that the fight went on internally and not only externally'. [She has got down to work with his duplicity, and his contempt for the object that he feels he can possess and control. This really touches him.]

'Richard had been sniffing and swallowing'. [That is, he had become rather more anxious and hypochondriacal.]

'Mrs Klein reminded him that two days ago he had said that his mucus was running down into his stomach; he felt he was attacking the enemy parents inside his stomach with poisonous mucus which also stood for poisonous urine and faeces. He expected that they would do the same to him. This internal battle would make him feel he had dead people inside him, whom he could not put aside like the fleet, and he was particularly worried about the injured or dead mummy inside, represented by the "silly" fish or by Dorothy in "The Wizard of Oz", blown away by his own faecal whirlwind.

'Richard, while Mrs Klein was interpreting, had begun to draw a battleship'.

The mania is under control by now. The first interpretation that she made to him, which in many ways was substantially correct, did not get at the duplicity and the contempt for his object which is such an important part of the mania, that is, the triumph over Mummy and Mrs Klein whom he feels he has seduced and brought under control. He was sleeping in Mummy's bed and he was having Mrs Klein on the Sundays and everything was under his control, as he felt with the pencils in his hand that he could kill Hitler. He could be Hitler, as it were, for if you could kill Hitler you could take his place. This seems to be a very important illustration about the problem of mania and the problem of interpreting mania. When Mrs Klein interpreted to him something equivalent to 'How can you treat your mother like that?', that is really the question that needs to be answered, that you can indeed treat your mother like dirt, when your internal mother has become dirt by yielding herself to your seduction and has thereby demonstrated to you that she does not know the difference between good and bad herself. This is the substance of this session, and the substance of his mania, which had its origin in the previous session, a Sunday session. He felt very strongly that Mrs Klein was utterly swept away by his admiration of her silver dress and lovely hair and on Monday expects her to admire his light-blue shirt. The two of them would be cohabiting in mutual idealization in the same way he and his mother are by their sleeping in the same room.

It is a very beautiful illustration not only of Richard in his more destructive and more violent moods but is also an illustration of how ineffectual an interpretation can be in relation to mania when it does not get at this nub, the contempt of the object and the contempt in the transference for this Mrs Klein, whose bag and clock were the rocks behind which he could hide and attack everybody.

Tenth Week: Sessions 53-59
The Composition of Intolerance
to Frustration—Review of the Ten
Weeks' Work

Chapter X

Since this week rather marks the beginning of the end, it might be useful to take stock of what has happened in the $2\frac{1}{2}$ months of the treatment so far. It is a week fairly full of suffering, mainly related to the father being in 'X' and Richard being expelled from his mother's bedroom. But it is also filled with the beginning of his suffering about the termination.

There is a very interesting episode about the catching of the 'salmon parr' and the killing of it. Richard has an authentic response of anxiety and guilt on the one hand and regret about it. It links with the episode where for a moment he was confused between the three women who were present at the river when he caught the 'parr' and the three 'silly' women who were outside the consulting room in the session with Mrs Klein. She takes it up only in terms of anxiety about killing mummy's baby, which is certainly correct. It comes up again in a more reparative form in the material about the kitten, as evidence that he has also good feelings towards other children/mummy's babies. Mrs Klein does not however take up his identification with this little 'salmon parr', feeling himself to be the baby who is hooked away from the mummy. It comes up in the drawings about the mother fish and all the little fishes, and the bait that is being let down into the water. The feeling is unmistakeable that one of the baby fish is going to take the bait and be hooked away. Perhaps she does not pay much attention to that aspect because of still being a bit preoccupied with the genital conflict and the castration anxiety.

In the Thursday session the central issue is one of jealousy and anxiety about the other men in Mrs Klein's life, starting with Mr Klein, her son, grandson, Mr Smith, Mr Evans, the 'Grumpy old Gentleman', the 'Bear'. Her men are all objects of extreme suspicion and jealousy. This central problem, which she has focused on very sharply, is his distrust of his mother, how easily she turns bad in his mind. He is not able to split-and-idealize and keep the good and bad aspect of his objects well separated from one another. The moment the combined object is formed, the moment the mother comes together with the father, the moment the breast is apprehended as coming together with the nipple to form a combined part-object, it becomes an object of paranoid mistrust. Cook and Bessie are going to poison him. Father is felt to be a Hitler father, a greedy father who takes the good things and puts in the bad stuff instead. It comes out for instance in his saying he was drinking 'little job' when Mrs Klein saw him drinking two bottles of lemonade. It comes out in the drawing with the anti-aircraft gun shooting at the dot in the middle of the circle (43). She recognizes this as the breast, but does not pay attention to the dot as nipple at this point. She is however very much focused on the problem of his mistrust of his object and its relation to his own trickiness. The 'Larry-the-Lamb' material comes up again in relation to the tricky 'Chinese Ambassador' in the aeroplane that was being struck by lightning. The duplicity on this 'Larry-the-Lamb' is dealt with mainly in Freudian form, of projection as attribution: being tricky himself, he is naturally prone to attribute trickiness to his objects.

In 1941 Mrs Klein was not yet actually utilizing her concept of projective identification. Perhaps more important, she was not equipped for seeing the material at a part-object level, as a combined object. She is very aware of the coming together of the parents, their forming this combined object. But she is not able to link that with the increasing attention to the breast material in the transference, manifest for instance in his regular drinking from the tap at the beginning of the session, or drinking the two bottles of lemonade and expressing it as 'little job'. The strong emphasis on greed and urgency seems to indicate that the material is coming to the infantile level of relationship with the breasts. This rather strengthens Richard's omnipotent trends and his wish to be able to control his object, as in the material about his playing with the rope, putting it between his legs, being God with the lightning in control of the whole situation. One can see very clearly in the material that what is driving him now increasingly is his anxiety about the ending of the analysis, of being hooked from his object like the little fish, of his objects being taken away from him by the daddy, who is going to fill the mummy with all the new babies. Mrs

Klein's emphasis on the role of frustration in her reconstruction of his babyhood is not one-sided. As always she insists that the developmental difficulty is not due to frustration alone. The ways in which the child experiences frustration, for instance as a punishment for his own aggression, or as a result of making his object bad in some way, through projections, cause the frustration to be not just a deprivation but a persecution.

In addition to the environmental situation pressing on him this week, that is the father's presence in 'X' and Richard's expulsion from the bedroom, there is also hanging over their heads this difficult issue about the Sunday session. Mrs Klein is now fairly convinced that it is having a disturbing rather than a helpful effect upon Richard. She tries to leave it up to him but finds he can not make a decision not to have any more Sunday sessions. It is very striking how they have impinged upon him. Mainly he has felt that he was being allowed to exploit and empty and damage his object with his greed. This tended to mobilize quite excessive quantities of depressive anxiety, but also insecurity, for an object that would allow him to do this might also allow rivals to do the same. If he is allowed to parasitize and empty the breasts, what was daddy doing down at the genitals, and what were the other babies doing inside the mother? It is very noticeable this week that there has been some lessening of Richard's hostility and fear of children on the road, even toward the little red-haired girl who asked him if he were Italian. It might be because he is more preoccupied with the adult figures and less with the children, but also because he has moved 'up' in his transference, less preoccupied with the genital and abdominal contents of the mother, as reflected generally in his undersea drawings. He is now much more preoccupied with the breast situation and with the combined-object.

This progress is shown most clearly in the Thursday session, which is extremely intense: 'Richard went to meet Mrs Klein much nearer her lodgings than usual. [As a rule when he was early he waited either in front of the playroom or met Mrs Klein at the corner of the road, which meant he walked for a minute or two with her.] He was very excited because he had brought her a letter from his mother, asking her to make two changes next week, so that he could spend more time at home with his brother who was coming on leave. He also asked Mrs Klein what she had decided about the Sunday hours after the following Sunday, after which his father would have returned home. Richard was delighted when Mrs Klein replied that she would change the times and would not see him on Sundays after the next one. He was obviously relieved about Mrs Klein's decision. He put his arm swiftly round her shoulder, saying that he was fond of her. He suddenly remembered that he had left the fleet at home; he said he had meant to bring it. [Usually when he did not bring the fleet he gave definite reasons for having left it behind, or merely said he did not feel like bringing it.] Richard noticed, after a quick glance, that Mr Smith was coming along the road and would therefore have met Mrs Klein by herself if Richard had not been with her. Richard pointed this out casually, saying "There is Mr Smith", but went on at once talking about the change of sessions [presumably to absorb her attention].

'Mrs Klein, when they arrived at the playroom, referred to what Richard had said recently about her meeting Mr Smith and that Richard, by waiting for her at the corner, might have wanted to find out whether she met Mr Smith sometimes on the way to the playroom. He had repeatedly, and again on the previous day, expressed his jealousy and suspicion about Mrs Klein going to the grocer's and to Mr Evan's shop'. [– the mother taking her genitals to the daddy's genitals to get her supplies from him.]

'Richard looked searchingly at Mrs Klein and asked whether Mr Evans was very fond of her, and whether he "gave" her many sweets.

'Mrs Klein interpreted his jealousy of every man whom she met or might have known in the past. He was still jealous of Mr Klein although he knew he was dead. But when he referred to him as if he were alive, this not only meant he felt Mrs Klein still contained him, but that Mr Klein stood also for all the men with whom Mrs Klein in the present might have sexual relations. He also seemed to be very suspicious of Mummy in this respect.

'Richard sat down at the table and asked for the pad and pencils. Mrs Klein discovered that she had left the pad at home'. [In the earlier session she had brought a yellow pad, having been unable to get a white one and he had been terribly disappointed. The next day she had a white one and he was thrilled.] 'She said she was sorry and Richard tried to control his feelings and said he was going to make his drawings on the back of earlier ones. He first drew three flags next to one another – a swastika, the Union Jack, and the Italian flag – and then sang the National Anthem. Then he drew a few musical notes and sang a tune to these notes; he wrote $3 + 2 = 5$ but did not give any associations. Then he began scribbling on another page, making dots with quick, angry movements and in between he wrote his name and hid it again under the scribbles. Now his anger and sorrow which he had been trying to restrain had become quite apparent, both in his movements and in his facial expression. He looked very much changed – white and suffering – and it was clear that his anger about Mrs Klein not having brought the pad was coupled with misery'. [That is very important. He was miserable for being so overwhelmed by anger toward her.]

'Mrs Klein interpreted that her not bringing the pad was felt by Richard as if the good Mummy at that moment had turned into the hostile and bad one who was also allied with the hostile Daddy – now Mr Smith. This was shown in the drawing of the flags; the British flag, representing himself, was squeezed in between the hostile German and Italian flags'. [A slightly strange idea! She is really interpreting that the mother squeezes him in between the hostile men, Mr Smith/Klein/Evans.] 'Richard also felt that Mrs Klein and Mummy had turned hostile towards him, because when he was frustrated and did not get enough milk and love and attention from Mummy, he soiled her secretly with his urine and faeces; therefore in turn he expected her to frustrate him as a punishment'. [Lacking the concept of projective identification, she must attribute persecution to expectation of retaliation. She can not suggest that with his urine and faeces he splits off a hostile part and projects it into her in order to be rid of the misery he feels about being so hostile.] 'Mrs Klein also suggested that when he was jealous of men in connection with her – Mr Smith, the grocer, Mr Evans – he tried to believe that they were nice. At the same time he suspected them of being insincere and "rascals" towards her and towards him. The "nice" Mrs Klein and the "light-blue" Mummy also seemed in his mind to be sweet, but he could not trust them either; as soon as they withheld love and goodness – now the pad – they turned into enemies'. [This is the focus of the work now.]

'Richard had been scribbling angrily, spoke for a moment like "Larry-the-Lamb", but quickly returned to making angry noises. Meanwhile he had been sharpening all the pencils, and, swiftly, with a glance to see whether Mrs Klein saw him do it, he bit the green pencil, which had often stood for mummy (and which, so far, he had not bitten or injured) and put its rubber end into the pencil sharpener, therebye damaging the rubber'. [There is the nipple material.] 'He scribbled over Drawing 43 which represented an anti-aircraft gun shooting at a round object and which had been interpreted by Mrs Klein as Richard shooting at Mummy's breast'. [He is shooting in fact at the dot in the middle, the nipple.]

'Mrs Klein interpreted that Richard's biting the pencil and secretly using the sharpener on the rubber end expressed his feeling that he had secretly bitten up and destroyed Mummy's breast as well as soiled it. These feelings came up again every time he felt frustrated. But he also felt every disappointment and deprivation as a punishment for having attacked or destroyed Mummy's breast'. [That is, she is interpreting a circular system of conflict. The more he attacks, the more he experiences deprivations as punishments and retaliations.] 'Now he had expressed this in relation to Mrs Klein – the pencil representing her as well as Mummy; he had been careful that she should not see what he was doing to her'. [Again emphasizing the secrecy.]

'Richard went outside', [the claustrophobia] 'and noticed a man in the garden on the other side of the road (which was at a distance at which he could not possibly hear what was being said.) Richard said anxiously, "He watches us, don't speak"; then he whispered, "Please say 'go away'." Mrs Klein said this'. [This was her technique; at one point she gives him her penknife, which is a little surprising.] 'But since of course the man did not go, Richard went back to the playroom. But even there he walked on tiptoe. He found a quoit on a shelf, threw it against the stools and up to the ceiling. He said under his breath "Poor old thing".' [Here is the crucial mixture of his sadism and his depressive concern for the breast.] 'When it rolled toward the cupboard (which formerly Richard had closed so that the ball would not fall into it) he took it quickly away' [separating the objects].

'Mrs Klein pointed out that the "poor old thing" represented her breast and genital, pushed violently against the genitals of various men, (the stools) – Mr Smith, Mr Evans the grocer, – of whom he had been jealous. In that way he meant to punish and ill-treat both parents, was suspicious of both and became very sorry for them.

'Richard was writing something and read it out in defiant tone: "I'm going back home on Monday to see Paul. Ha-ha-ha-ha, ho-ho-ho-ho. Haw-haw-haw-haw".

'Mrs Klein interpreted that Richard wished to show her that he was pleased to leave her', [the separation situation] 'and could turn to Paul, because he felt frustrated by her (not bringing the pad) and jealous, believing that she preferred Mr Smith or Evans to him. But he also wanted to show that he did not care, that he felt triumphant and punished her by deserting her. He might also have had such feelings when he allied himself with Paul against Nurse, standing for Mummy. He had just written "Haw-haw-haw" which meant that he was like Lord Haw-Haw, of whom he had spoken repeatedly as the worst traitor to this country. Richard felt he was like him if he turned against his parents with secret biting and bombing attacks'. [Mrs Klein has succeeded in improving Richard's splitting-and-idealization again.]

'Richard went to the window and looked out. He said under his breath "Why don't you keep me for two hours every day?"'

'Mrs Klein asked did he mean twice daily?

'Richard replied "No, two hours at a time".

'Mrs Klein interpreted that he had been deeply upset because she did not bring the white pad, which stood for his good relationship with her and for her good breast, and yesterday had been linked with the Milky Way'. . . .

The breast material has come absolutely into the forefront in spite of the fact that Richard was expelled from his parents' bedroom and the complication of the Sunday session which had aroused a lot of castration anxiety, and resentment at the genital level. The movement of the transference is toward the breast and the central anxiety is one of being hooked away, deprived, being weaned prematurely, (he was weaned to the bottle at a few weeks as a baby). The feeling that this weaning was a conspiracy between nipple and breast or between father's penis and mother's genitals to fill her with babies who would take the breast away from him, is connected with his fear and hatred of other children. This is in a sense his main symptom, his main incapacity for life. It makes him unsocialized and unable to go to school.

It might be useful to spend a little time in trying to see where the ten weeks of work has brought the analysis. This Thursday session, the 56th, seems a bit of a watershed, for Richard has reached a fairly intense experience of the breast. The first thing to note is the way in which the material has changed. In this week the fleet play is more authentic than ever before, experienced no longer either as a diversion to keep Mrs Klein busy nor as a device for controlling his objects omnipotently to make a happy family. The fleet play gets very much at the heart of the conflict of possession of the object in the rivalry and ambivalence towards the object. On the Friday a terrific confusion arises about what is happening, who is fighting whom. The empire drawings which were quite important at one time are fading out now, tending to be replaced by more pictorial drawings, the air combat ones, those of the planes being struck by lightning and the railway drawings with their interesting names. He gives Mrs Klein a lot of material verbally now, transference material in every way, relating directly to her. He is seldom fighting the interpretations, but rather thinking about them and even amending them and improving them sometimes, as when he made a link about the searchlights – ('You search, don't you?'). He goes out of the room much less and is very little occupied with those intrusive elements in this peculiar playroom, which earlier on had disturbed him so much and had been used quite a lot as a diversion. The stools seem to have become a fairly stable part of the equipment of representation. His dreams are coming at fairly regular intervals, not very frequently, but most of them are fairly pithy and the last one, the one about his trial, seems to be particularly important for highlighting the problem of his duplicity and trickiness (the Larry-the-Lamb material). The undersea drawings, which have related mainly to his intrusion inside the mother, and to hypo-chondria – his catching cold and his fear of being poisoned, also seem to have made an advance. The whole phase that was concerned with intrusion inside the mother (the submarines, the fishes, the starfishes, attacking the father's penis inside the mother, the fear of being trapped, the claustrophobia, the hypo-chondria connected with it) has been rather left behind. What replaces it is preoccupation with the genitality of the situation and the castration anxiety which Mrs Klein probably took up excessively, for it gradually became a bit clearer that it was not the genitality itself that caused the trouble. Confusion of zones of the mouth, genital, anus, of bombing and biting, began to highlight Richard's helplessness. Dependent material came forward and now, by the tenth week, it had begun to sort itself out, with this strong emphasis on his oral needs, his hunger, his intolerance of frustration and the ease with which frustration of his oral needs gives rise to distrust of his objects and to secret attacks.

The whirlwind progress of this treatment up to the tenth week seems to be the consequence of both patient and analyst being under terrific pressure, knowing they have only four months. One must not look upon it as therapeutic triumph attributable either to the obvious brilliance of Mrs Klein's work or of Richard's intense co-operation. It is better under-stood in terms of the very great flexibility in the analytical method and process. Whatever is available is made use of in the same pattern, whether in a session, or a month or ten years. The same fundamental pattern of the process is made use of but, as Mrs Klein emphasizes repeatedly, one can not expect that reaching this transference situation with her in ten weeks can possibly have the same therapeutic significance for the child as the same process having been worked through over and over again in, say, three years. The transference has reached this point in rather a headlong way but nothing has been worked through. Mrs Klein is very worried about whether, at the end of four months, he will be left with anything that can not immediately be thrown away, as for instance, his threat to go to Paul, ha-ha-ha. In the next six weeks Mrs Klein will be seen to try very hard to consolidate some foothold in relation to his capacity for depressive feelings.

223

	Eleventh Week: Sessions 60-65
	The Clinical Manifestations of
	Splitting Processes and the
	Structural Meaning of Integration,
	with Special Reference to the
Chapter XI	Concept of Ambivalence

This is a week that presents us with a very interesting problem about analysis, the one that arises from Richard's father becoming ill. It produces a very different response from the time when his mother was ill, which threw him into something of a panic and an attempt to split and idealize in a very frantic way. Richard's father's illness occurred dramatically and it seems that Richard found him collapsed, presumably from a heart attack or some aspect of heart disease. It came after the Monday session which had the fascinating material about Mr and Mrs Bluebottle and Richard's savage attack on the moth, following which he became very persecuted. He was very anxious when Mrs Klein referred to it as a beetle instead of a moth and all this was in the context of his fear of thunderstorms.

That session was very dominated by the prospect of Richard's father, who had been staying in X, going away again, and it was still, as the previous week had been, under the sway of the Oedipus Complex, although at a more pregenital level than Mrs Klein was inclined to think. However, when his father then became ill, Richard developed a psychotic depressive state in miniature. Its manifestation was focused on his knife, the same knife with which he had attacked the moth. It now became virtually a suicidal instrument. He put it in his mouth, he hit his teeth with it, he pointed it at himself and Mrs Klein was worried enough to warn him of the danger.

This seems to be a very important analytical problem that has to do with questions of omnipotence. Analysis functions not only to bring up infantile problems from the depths but also to stir and intensify them. If, when infantile problems are stirred up in this way, they then encounter fortuitous events in the outside world which set up a terrible reverberation, the potentiation of omnipotence can give rise to very dangerous problems. This is, I think, illustrated very dauntingly here. Richard acts very concretely, as if his knife had got into his father's heart. There is a bit of material later where he is poking around in the water tank in the kitchen and he says, 'This is the inside of my father's heart'. He is not poking round with his knife just then, but with the poker, yet it certainly links clearly with the material two days previously when he was scratching the poles of the tent, equipment belonging to the Girl Guides, and later on going about with an axe and hitting the flue of the stove. Mrs Klein is worried and lets him off rather easily, perhaps slightly conspiring with his manic-reparative tendencies, (clearing out the soot). But she did not get away with it because he became extremely persecuted on the Saturday when he discovered that the splashing of water on Friday and Saturday had caused spots of rust to appear on the stove. Mrs Klein had to clean them off for him.

We can not suppose that Richard drove his father into his illness. It functions as a fortuitous event that meshes with his outburst of savage omnipotence with his penknife and the moth in the context of the thunderstorm and his fear of it. How has Mrs Klein taken this up with him and what sort of conceptual equipment did she have at that time for dealing with such a thing? One can see that her attitude towards omnipotence at this point in the 1940's was still very closely linked to Freud. Omnipotent wishes, the omnipotence of word and gesture, magic – these seem to be her conceptual tools, in spite of the fact that she has been taking up with him problems of internalization, of internal persecution, attacks on his internal objects and the mother's internal babies. It clearly implies that at the time of this clinical work she still hedged the question of omnipotence and the concreteness of the experience of psychic reality. She speaks about the guilt and anxiety as manifestations of his imagination and his feelings 'as if' he had done such and such. It seems characteristic of her work after the 1946 paper on splitting and projective identification that the 'ifness', the distinction between phantasy and reality which characterizes Freud's work, tends to disappear. It is replaced by an insistence on the concreteness of psychic reality. Objects are really damaged in the inner world: they really become persecutory; they really do have to be repaired; no manic pretence of doing it really accomplishes the job. The later work, in this way, places acknowledgement of psychic reality at the centre.

Very interesting things happen in this week as a consequence of Mrs Klein's handling of the suicidal impulse that was acted out with the knife. One of the things she notices is that there is an increased splitting-and-idealization in his relationship to her, reversed at this point, not by her being the bad one and his Mummy being the good one, but the other way round. Mrs Klein is the dark-blue mummy in one session and the light-blue mummy in the next session. But she also notices that he is only listening to half her interpretation. A fascinating observation! He is in a dreamy, far-away state while she interprets his depressive anxiety and his guilt, but as soon as she begins to interpret his reparative tendencies he is right there. It is very amusing that he should ask her the question 'what are you thinking of?' because you can see he is immediately in projective identification with the object and carrying out the analytical reparative work.

The interesting and important thing about her being the dark-blue mummy and then the next session the light-blue mummy is that it brings home very clearly the integration of the experience. Richard is now beginning to give evidence, in a quite remarkable way for the eleventh week of an analysis, of his ability to experience the oscillation in the quality of his object, from being good to being bad, it becomes so rapid that he is almost able to feel ambivalent. Ambivalence is a term that seems to be used very loosely by Mrs Klein. It was not used so loosely by Freud and certainly not by Abraham in particular, who considered the achievement of the experience of ambivalence the beginning of mental health. It is not experienced where the love and hate for the object are kept very wide apart. For Richard to be able to experience his love and his hate for Mrs Klein, his trust and his distrust, his pleasure to be there yet his hatred of coming, so closely together that they just oscillate back and forth, is very akin to experiencing his ambivalence itself. It would make one think that his progress in the analysis is fairly substantial at this point in terms of the experience of his emotionality. On the other hand, one has to look at how little feeling he seems to have about his father's illness. Apparently, from the evidence, he is really quite unable to feel this event as a problem of the potential loss of a loved object either for himself or for his mother and brother. His dramatization when he reported the matter initially is pretty thin emotionally. When Mrs Klein does bring him more into contact with his feelings they are almost entirely primitive infantile ones towards his father as a part object, which then gets tangled up with the killing of the moth.

However, the infantile area of his emotionality is coming through very strongly now; he tells Mrs Klein that he loves her in the Saturday session and it is true, not at all like his seductiveness at the beginning or his manic admiration of her silvery dress or her hair; love seems to gush out of him when he suddenly kisses the drawing he made and kisses the breast. It is as authentic in its love as his attack on the moth was authentic in its hate. So the work of carefully analysing the Larry-the-Lamb aspects, his insincerity, duplicity, trickiness, seems to be paying off at this point, in the limited area of his infantile emotionality. However, it is important to notice the paradox that there is not by any means an accompanying improvement in the emotional depths of his relationships at a more mature level, as manifest by his reaction to his father's illness.

This paradox is perhaps clarified by the drawing of Mrs Klein with the big V and the little V for Victory. Children's drawings in analysis, especially those of latency children can be quite uninteresting in their manifest content. The classical thing is patterns. There are almost always interesting items in the drawing, but hidden so carefully from the child himself that their presence in the drawing is clearly unconscious. It requires a great deal of looking, just sitting and gazing, before any hidden meaning might suddenly leap out from the page. If the child will let you, it is very important to watch the process of drawing to see the sequence in which things are done and also to be gazing at previous drawings, especially those that seem in any way related. There was probably no secret intention in putting drawings nos. 54 and 55 on the same page, but one of the things that they illustrate is the strong artistic similarity they bear to one another – as, for instance, in different periods of Picasso's work – the realistic drawings of the Blue Period and suddenly the Cubism. Drawings nos. 54 and 55 have a very strong relationship to one another, one abstract and the other representational. The two smaller circles of the railway drawing turn into the head and breasts of the portrait of Mrs Klein. The railways have a link back to the recent series of railway drawings, but the circle also has a reference back to the anti-aircraft gun which was firing into the air in drawing 43, which in turn, is the converse of 42 and 47, of the lightning striking the aeroplane.

One can begin to see that the same phantasy has many different iconographic representations, just as Richard has often shifted his play representations. In retrospect, it gives strong hints that all of the station drawings with the trains going through between the two stations, had to do with, on the one hand, the breasts and the baby between the breasts, as well as the penis going into the vagina. The conflict between the two situations was most clear in drawing 50 where the father was coming through in one direction and Richard coming through in another. Who was going to get to the station first? Also the baby's victory was indicated when Mr Klein was to go away, sobbing. Previous drawings of this sort can now be seen as representations of the mother's body, the father's penis as a train, the baby's tongue also as a train. The confusion about which is going to get to the breasts and which to the genitals can be seen by juxtaposing the anti-aircraft gun drawings with the lightning-striking-the-plane drawings. Being down below, shooting up at the breasts has something to do with the feeling that the bad penis gets into the vagina and shoots poison into the breasts. This conflict and confusion is temporarily resolved in drawing 55 when the transference to Mrs Klein and her body produces the two V's for Victory, the big victory up above for the baby at the breast and the little victory down below for the daddy at the genital. This horizontal splitting has enabled the baby Richard to feel that what he is getting at the breast is protected either way, or at least not disrupted, by whatever the father is doing down at the mother's genital.

This week also raises a technical problem, about answering questions. Richard asks Mrs Klein why she has not brought the old folder for the drawings and she says she got it wet. He asks what she did with it, and she says she salvaged it. In the note, she says this is contrary to her technique, that is, in so far as it was a reassurance against his suspicion of her Austrian origins.

She might explain about its getting wet. Probably the urgency of the counter-transference situation, related to the shortness of time, and Richard's frightening playing with the knife on the Tuesday pressed her towards reassuring him. It is very convincing that her response was experienced by him as reassurance and that it had an effect of splitting the transference at that point. Ordinarily one would not have thought that it would be a very impressive piece of reassurance at that time when everyone was salvaging everything. Nonetheless she is right in thinking that it was a reassurance to him in the face of his distrust of her, thinking of her as foreign, admiring her jacket and asking if they wear such colourful jackets on the continent. Since he is still keenly aware of her foreignness and very distrustful of her, it does stand as reassurance and immediately the girl with the curly hair who happens to be passing by, looks like a monster. Why should giving a reassurance about this particular item immediately bring such splitting? The point she makes about it is a very cogent one. The reassurance that brings about this increased splitting-and-idealization does not represent an increase in trust but quite the contrary. It represents a loss of trust in her as if Richard were to think 'If she were honest, she would not have to say how honest she is'.

The note 1 on page 267 raises important questions about integration. There is a great deal of evidence in the material to indicate the coming together of the split in Richard's object and of his being very close to ambivalence and the pain of it. Mrs Klein tended to distinguish between 'integration of the self' and 'synthesis of the objects', but it is not clear what distinction is implied by employing the different words. 'Adequacy' of splitting-and-idealization implies psychological distance between split parts of the self or objects. In excessive splitting, for instance, the fragments might be at such a distance that they have no knowledge of one another; or they can be at a lesser distance where they have knowledge but are not able to communicate with one another; or they can be at a still lesser distance where they can begin to communicate but not influence one another; or they can be so close together that one dominates the other; or so fixed as to become indistinguishable from one another. This is probably the meaning that Mrs Klein wishes to infuse into the concept of integration which is otherwise a very loose and airy one. In Richard's material a fairly concrete and precise application of the concept to the clinical phenomena is possible, both as regards the splits in his self and in his objects. The concrete clinical application of concepts of structure which the 1946 paper were to make possible are all adumbrated here. Other dimensions are hinted at, such as planes of splitting – up and down, front and back, inside and outside. The degree of sadism of the splitting process seems to determine the depressive price for its reparation.

All these lines of development are hinted at in various notes. Thinking about splitting processes in this very concrete way is extremely difficult if one is still hedging about psychic reality in its absolutely concrete sense. It requires an immense shift in one's view of the world to think that the outside world is essentially meaningless and unknowable, that one perceives the forms but must attribute the meaning. Philosophically, this is the great problem in coming to grips with Kleinian thought and its implications. It is only from that point of view that the depressive position acquires the concreteness and the hardness as a concept that makes it an invaluable tool for understanding clinical phenomena. Do people *really* suffer because they have *really* damaged their internal objects? In this week there is the beautiful example of the incident about the moth on Monday and the father's illness on the Tuesday. One can see that the father's illness has had an impact on Richard that stands very specifically in relation to this killing of the moth the previous day. Pointing the knife towards himself and hitting his teeth with it had real suicidal significance and were later clarified when he spoke of probing his father's heart. (Note II, page 304, 61st session.)

Twelfth Week: Sessions 66-71
The Role of Interpretation in the
Chapter XII   Therapeutic Process

Richard returns to playing with the toys for the first time in two months. Mrs Klein has some notes at the end of the session which are of great technical importance. Just to recall the setting: Richard's father is ill and Richard is travelling back and forth between Y where his family is living and X where the analysis is taking place, travelling on the bus. He has started living at the Wilson's, which he does not like. He seems to be managing quite admirably and is rather proud of himself, 'doing his bit'. In connection with his father's illness, he certainly is trying to spare his family. In that way he contributes to holding the analysis and the family rather separated from one another in his mind, which Mrs Klein seems to realize more fully now and states it quite clearly in one of the notes.

There is some additional technical interference during the week other than the disturbed background setting. The first is the somewhat gratuitous information Mrs Klein gives Richard on Tuesday about his very limited breast feeding and early weaning. This has a terrific impact on him, which she justifies a bit in her notes on the basis of the mother having neglected to give this information, despite Mrs Klein's request. Why she picks this point to give it, and why she thinks it necessary to give it at all is a bit mysterious and she is rather apologetic about it. The second and third sessions of the week are dominated by the consequences of that information which excites a terrific flurry of distrust in Richard, distrust of mothers, of breasts, of Mrs Klein and his mother's collaboration with her. This is worsened by the end of the week because there is to be a conversation between the two adults the following Monday. Richard is terribly anxious that they are going to discuss his future, particularly the future of his schooling. He begs Mrs Klein to advise his mother to have a tutor and not to be sent to school and then he settles for a small school, clearly quite terrified still of the prospect of going to a big school, which seems to mean a school full of big boys. The anxiety centres on both the size of the boys and the number of them. A bit of material at the end of the Thursday session shows this when he asks Mrs Klein about all the people in X crowding at the top of the hill. It comes up later about the bus. There is something about the 'crowding' in his concept of a big school that stirs his anxiety about there not being enough attention for him or being crowded out of contact with his good object by these big boys. It is very interesting that his immediate response to Mrs Klein's information about his premature weaning was to ask if the mother had given the breast to Paul, then also to daddy. It seems to him immediately that the breast, if it had been taken away, must have been given to somebody else.

Another technical intrusion affecting the week's work, and interfering a bit with his trust, surrounds Mrs Klein's bringing extra toys on Saturday (the little figures). It seems most unusual as she also admits in the footnotes. She usually leaves broken toys and then replaces them at holiday periods but it is a bit peculiar to have done this at the end of the week. Probably the pressure of the approaching ending of the treatment is affecting her technique. She is hoping to be able to make some arrangement with Richard's mother for the continuation of the analysis in the foreseeable future, but this never actually comes about. It is certainly very clear that Richard is getting more and more desperate about it. But on the other hand, it is mobilizing some fighting spirit in him. He speaks with determination about how he is going to return to his home at Z, and to his fort, and how no-one is going to stop him. There is some sort of spirit mobilized in this boy by the restored relationship to his good objects and he is in consequence less confused and less distrustful.

It might be useful to try to dissect the various types of material that run through the week because it can be very instructive to see how the themes they present interact with one another and what themes they seem to isolate. Mrs Klein writes a very interesting note about how children's material shifts back and forth and in a way, settles the problem about the difference between a shifting of representation and a play disruption. Now, this first theme is about jealousy, which becomes focused on Mr Smith and his meeting with Mrs Klein. Richard is monitoring her, jumping out at her, questioning her, having to run out of the house after Mr Smith passes, to see if he could look in. He never notices, as Mrs Klein of course does, that Mr Smith

232

is taller than Richard and would have a somewhat different view into the playroom. Richard is afraid of people knowing what goes on in his thoughts and feelings in the treatment situation and this is related to the theme of Mr Smith that runs through the whole week and is related to the way 'G' for God keeps coming up in the drawings. His anxiety about the daddy monitoring and attacking him is increased because Mrs Klein insists on his genital desires rather than his oral greed, namely his wish to get inside the mummy and take everything.

This theme of his greed emerges more clearly in his repeatedly playing with the money. This is for his bus fare mainly, but there is quite a lot of material that runs through the week about the money in his pocket, his greed for it and handling of it, links with his anxiety about whether he dirtied it when he scribbled on it, the difference between silver and copper money and spinning the two half-crowns as breasts. It links back with the theme of Mr Smith and the radish seeds for which Richard is very greedy. It is not quite clear what these radish seeds are intended to be, although Mrs Klein takes this mainly in terms of genital desires, to have the seed to give babies to mummy as reparation. Probably the radishes are more connected with the nipple. The strawberries have come up as nipples and suggest that Richard is much more concerned with being able to fill the mother with the kind of seeds which would produce the kind of foods he likes to eat. It is through his feminine attachment to Mr Smith that its significance as seeds for babies arises.

Another theme is the line of drawings which continue the big and little V for Victory, ending with a drawing of himself and Mrs Klein putting their genitals together. It appears in the figure of eight railway track that has a big siding going out of the top and another little siding going into the loop at the bottom. Mrs Klein examined this in terms of Richard's wish to put a big V for Victory up at the breast, not only getting the food but putting his genital near the breast and having some sort of genital/breast gratification.

The fleet play hardly comes into the week except at the beginning. It seems clear that Richard is rather reluctant to bring the fleet. It belongs more and more to his home life with his family which he desires to keep quite separate from the analysis. As the fleet stays at home, in comes the use of Mrs

233

Klein's toys again. It starts very shyly, bringing out the swing which seemed to represent his masturbation. It is extremely interesting that the first thing to come out of her bag is this wretched swing that always started the trouble and the disaster in the earlier toy play. There has not been a word about masturbation for weeks. Mrs Klein apparently did not think it necessary to mention the actual masturbation when she was dealing with the phantasies underlying it. She might very well be right but probably some of Richard's anxieties, feeling spied upon, and his distrust about his mother and Mrs Klein talking together had something to do with the fear that they are exchanging information.

Nevertheless the toys come out and the play scenes that existed in the earlier toy play are reconstituted and disasters occur, but they are much more controlled disasters at this point and the emphasis is very much on survival. Concern about the breast enters into the play in a way in which it certainly did not before. The trains going round in a circle; the two goods trains are watched by the children who are enclosed in a pencil fence and are allowed to watch the breast and seem to enjoy that. The emphasis is again on trying to establish peace and trying to prevent catastrophe by means of equality, shared experience; nobody should have the breast all to himself. This leads to the phantasy of people crowding up on to the mountain. Fear of deprivation brings the bit of material in which Bobby goes down a rabbit hole, a very oral kind of penis that gets into the mother in a greedy way, all part of the disaster. The other part of the disaster is always the rage and this is represented particularly by the land mine drawing which is connected with Richard gritting his teeth, scribbling and making dots all over the page. When he notices that the dots go through and make dents on the paper below, he tries to fill them in a little bit. These dots become enclosed and become the landmine and then they turn into the strawberries, first three, then two, and four green leaf-babies. Those leaves are very akin in shape to the starfish-babies and the strawberries look very much like under-sea mines. Landmine and undersea mine; strawberry leaves and starfish babies; undersea and above surface are still in many ways confused in this material, implying that internal and external situations are still not very well differentiated. But what does come out so clearly is the preoccupation with the nipple. The main theme is delineated by the strawberries and the radishes and the wish to have all these seeds, millions and billions of them, in order to be able to inseminate the mother with the seeds that produce the food for which Richard is so greedy.

Under the sway of the distrust of his mother and Mrs Klein meeting, which is represented by his caricature, Melanie and Henrietta, the old hen and the nasty old woman, how quickly these hostile elements emerge. In spite of that, the feeling of being able to differentiate good and bad, and being able to trust his objects, is certainly very greatly strengthened by insight into the consequences of his attacks. When he bites the little doll with the red hat, connected with the red haired girl who he said was choked with rage, he does not like the taste. It certainly connects with the blue ink, which is 'light-blue' Mummy, and a bottle of smelly ink connected with Cook and Bessie's poison, the poisoned breast. This is a very clear indication that he understands that the breast becomes bad when he projects something into it. When the nipple, this little red haired nipple, becomes the head-of-a-child bit of Richard that has got into the breast and is felt to be soiling the breast, urinating and defaecating into it, that is what makes the breast turn bad. And the same result is brought about indirectly by projection into the father. Richard begins to comprehend that it is his own badness, the rascal in himself, which gets into the daddy's penis, which then becomes the Goebbels penis, like a rat and like Bobby going after the rabbits. When that rascal penis gets into the mummy that is what spoils her and changes her into the brute, the wicked brute mummy, the breast that can not be trusted, that might be poisoning and speaking German.

That whole theme seems very greatly clarified and has strengthened the emotionality of his participation in the transference. When Richard caresses Mrs Klein and tells her he loves her and wants to be her husband – when he grows up, mind you – it is with great feeling and very little seductiveness. The seductiveness does come earlier when he begs her to go to the cinema. His jealousy is behind it and his distrust of what she is doing at night, wishing to keep an eye on her. But at the end of the week when he is worried about her being lonely and talks

235

about how lonely his mother would be if his father died, this brings forward his wish to marry Mrs Klein and his acknowledgement that her husband is really dead. There is some differentiation between the dead Mr Klein in the outside world and the live Mr Klein and his penis inside Mrs Klein. Richard's concern about the end of his analysis is not merely influenced by consideration for his own welfare, but also about Mrs Klein going back to London and the dangers to her there.

These are the themes that come out mainly through the return to play with the toys. Direct interaction with Mrs Klein is very intense now. The other interesting theme is the one about the baby-tank, the cooking stove and its soot. Where did the water run? It had come up as a sequence in earlier weeks: filling up the sink and wanting Mrs Klein to let the water out while he rushed outside to see where the water escaped. This material, with the soot and dirtiness of the water, shows that he is reaching for some understanding about the functions of the parental intercourse in keeping the milk clean and not allowing the urine and faeces of the babies to contaminate the inside of the mother's body. It will come out even more clearly with the dead flies and reaches its resolution in the dream of the Black Island. Mrs Klein notes that he is now regularly drinking water from the tap. He does not seem to use the lavatory much, judging from the text, although he urinated two or three times in an earlier session and in one of the current sessions he speaks of being unable to urinate though wanting to.

In a general way, then, one might say that in the drawings Richard is clarifying the problem about the breasts and nipples and the competition, the big V for Victory at the breast and the little V for Victory at the genital. Separation anxiety and the anxieties about the ending of the analysis are being worked out more directly with Mrs Klein, while the tendency of jealousy and envy to produce disasters and to engender his worst anxieties and despairs are being worked out in the play with the toys. The fleet is staying at home as a way of separating his home life and, in a way, the more mature part of himself, from the infantile transference situation in the analysis. Finally the problem of contamination and preservation of the goodness and purity of the breast is being worked out largely with the stove and 'baby tank'.

At that time Mrs Klein did not have a concept of confusion. Consequently her interpretations tend simply to delineate the separate phantasies and the particular anxieties connected with them without much sorting out. Her concept of the therapeutic process, as she emphasises over and over again in the notes, rested upon the importance of interpreting the immediate material. Where it was coming up thick and fast, as in the play with the toys, her emphasis was always on selecting the most pressing, and by this she meant generally the 'deepest', anxieties that are available to view. She certainly did believe that the interpretation itself somehow diminished the anxiety. While she often organizes the evidence, it is only very occasionally that she makes an interpretation that links themes together. These interpretations seem rather staccato descriptions of separate phantasies, often overlapping, sometimes seeming mutually exclusive, but her feeling was that these phantasies were all existing at the same time, at different levels, and it was the delineation, and, in Freud's sense, the elevation into consciousness that diminished the anxiety. As persecutory anxiety diminished, depressive anxieties were able to come forward. She did not have a concept of persecutory depression. So it is not surprising to see her misunderstand the ice rink material in the second session. Probably that is the one piece of material in the week she may have genuinely misconstrued. Otherwise, one may not agree with all the different phantasies that she sees operative, but one can see what an extraordinary and fruitful imagination she brought to bear, her excellent memory and ability to link the evidence. Her response to the material is almost always interesting, never pedestrian. Her capacity to move from internal to external, from inside to outside, is fairly remarkable. From the therapeutic point of view the sorting of this deep confusion between good and bad in self and objects is a major accomplishment and is bound to make a major difference to his mental health. Already some benefit is in evidence, mainly manifested at this point in the material, but also in his adjustment outside the analysis, being able to travel alone, being able much of the time to be relatively unpersecuted by other children, improved friendliness for people, for instance, his being able to go back to the hotel to visit the people he had left. Previously he could not even say goodbye to them when he left. An improvement appears in his sense of reality and in his regret about his debilitated state. Towards the end of the week he speaks again of his fear of being a dunce and an imbecile and his regret at not playing the piano. It is really very touching evidence of the strengthening of his capacity to experience depressive anxieties.

Thirteenth Week: Sessions 72-77
The Relation of Ambivalence to
Chapter XIII   the Experience of Depressive Pain

It is rather a beautiful week, influenced on the outside by Mrs Klein meeting Richard's mother and his anxiety about the kind of school she would recommend. Also the question of plans for the possible continuation of the analysis are in the air. His suspicions and anxieties about these issues more or less dominate the first two sessions. Richard's father's illness casts an influence which threads through the week and there is also the problem about staying with the Wilsons which he does not like. He finds Mr Wilson much more authoritarian than he is accustomed to; he is used to being treated as an only child, nor stinted of sweets. The Wilsons are a more disciplined family than his own. He finally begs Mrs Klein and his mother to make other arrangements for him, which they do. He is also jealous of John, who is with Mrs Klein in analysis and is older, about fifteen. He probably feels rather pushed aside when John will not take him for a walk with a friend, or will not climb a mountain with him. Then there is a big disturbance in the setting on Friday, when Mrs Klein brings the oranges which absolutely drives Richard wild with jealousy.

But in spite of these external factors disturbing the situation, the main themes that have developed through the week are coherent in a very impressive way. Mrs Klein is seen working in top gear and in several places pulls things together very definitively. Finally in the Saturday session she reaches her most advanced formulation of his psycho-pathology by means of the 'baby-tank' material and the killing of the flies.

It is instructive to tease out the themes and to see how they orient themselves to the different kinds of material. He is playing a lot with the toys again this week, especially in the first three sessions, centering on the problem of the disasters. They mainly take the form of the two trains competing, representing himself and his father in competition for the position of the leader, the husband in the family, and, in part-object terms, the fight of the penises inside the mother which Mrs Klein has spelled out very clearly. Again there is not a direct word about masturbation the whole week. On the periphery of the disaster play there are all the themes having to do with people watching each other, expressing Richard's need to try to control everybody in the family in order to keep his own destructive impulses in check. It never quite succeeds but the disasters are more controlled, and somebody always survives. Reparative impulses take the form of a hospital block where damaged figures may be repaired. Mrs Klein plays into that by actually repairing some of the toys for him.

The fleet comes in briefly to express similar themes at a part-object level, for the fleet play and the toy play have come together, but also diverge. The fleet play is more preoccupied with the genitals while the toy play clearly now represents the breast, providing milk for the children. The theme of Richard's greed which lies at the root of his destructiveness and his hatred of other children is thus made clearer. The theme of the competitions with the babies inside the mother for possession of the mother's riches, first expressed in the starfish drawings, now comes out very clearly in the play of the giving of milk to the children. First they are allowed to watch the breast, then they are actually given milk and then the thing goes wrong because of the competition between the goods train and the passenger train, that is, the nipple and the penis. It explodes on the Friday because of the intrusion of the oranges. It is very interesting, for Richard acknowledges that he neither likes oranges nor milk but the infantile meaning of milk and breast arouses his greed and rage.

Richard has not brought any dreams for about six weeks. Next week, the fourteenth, there is a dream, and then in the fifteenth, a real bonanza of them. But Richard is doing a great deal of talking with Mrs Klein and this shows up the transference particularly clearly. It centres on the termination of the analysis and the feelings of abandonment and anxiety at two levels, being deserted by Mrs Klein as analyst, but also as breast. A series of incidents runs through the material, holding her hand, asking her to speak a little German as if she were talking to her husband, wanting to come and see her at her lodgings, asking her if she will ever come and visit his home. Finally in the Saturday session, rather touching material appears in which he expresses his desire to sleep in Mrs Klein's bed, to snuggle up to her, to caress her, to cuddle her, but not to have any genital contact. On this basis, she finally formulated the horizontal splitting, the separation of the breast mother from the genital mother, relating it also to the situation with his nurse and his mother in early times and the difference between the light-blue mummy and the dark-blue mummy. His ambivalence finally emerges towards the figure of the pretty conductress, who says, 'Half fares stand up', which Richard so much resents. She says this when the bus becomes crowded and it is this crowding in on his relationship with his good objects that is the focus of his more persecuted, not paranoid, feelings. These latter were really tied up with his being confused between the good and bad objects.

The splitting-and-idealization has been very well delineated now, with the result that Richard's ambivalence to his object, the internal object, is much more held together but splits again easily. It appears as a split between Mrs Klein and his mother when she does not want him to go swimming and he turns against her briefly. He turns viciously against Mrs Klein about the oranges. He turns against the bus conductress when she says, 'Half fares stand up', but he admits she is very pretty, much prettier in ordinary clothes than in uniform. This very quick oscillation is not between the idealized light-blue Mummy and the black Mummy, the bird with the crown and the faeces dropping out of its bottom, not the malevolent 'wicked-brute', poisonous Mummy, but this dark-blue Mummy who frustrates him, disappoints him, who has the mysterious genital activities that do not include him. The distinction between this bad mummy who frustrates and disappoints him in sexual ways and the malevolent one who is mixed up with the Hitler-penis and Richard's own projected violence and destructiveness is now sharply drawn, mainly thanks to the dream of the trial and the jack-boots with which he was kicking all the buildings down and kicking them up again.

The oedipal theme is a bit in abeyance now, probably partly due to his father's illness and his being like another baby who is being nursed, has two nurses in fact. Even Mr Smith has dropped out a bit, but Mr Klein is very vivid in his mind and he would really like to know what kind of relationship she had had with Mr Klein and what sort of Mr Klein she has inside her. Is she a happy person with a good husband or a good penis inside her, or was it an unhappy relationship? Does she carry round in her a bad Hitler-kind of daddy?

The theme about his fear of children has begun to give way and Richard has begun to look at them with interest. Although he is suspicious and very frightened of them, he can admire a little girl and say she is pretty and looks rather nice. He keenly wishes John to be friendly with him. Along with that, his boastfulness, his provocativeness towards other children and his contempt for them seems on its way to diminishing rather rapidly. This relief from his hatred of other children seems directly related to the murderousness and anxieties expressed in the 'baby-tank' material. For weeks Richard has been drinking from the tap and examining the water tank which he calls a 'baby tank'. He also repeatedly examines the stove and the soot in it, tears up bits of paper to throw into the water, drains out the water into buckets which Mrs Klein has to empty into the sink so he can find out how it runs out of the house. It all gives an impression of systematic research into the metabolism of the mother's body in relation to good and bad substances. How does the mother manage to get rid of all the bad substances that the baby evacuates into her? That problem becomes clearer than ever before on the Saturday, with the killing of the flies. This links back to the incident of his killing the moth and the bluebottles. Clearly, the trouble is not the baby's evacuation into the mother, but that his evacuations have a hostile, destructive intention towards the babies inside her. It is made explicit by his squashing the flies and links with his tearing up the bits of paper, which Mrs Klein had mistakenly interpreted to him as giving babies to the mummy. Later on he tries to share the blame with the father's penis; he says he only killed two of the flies, the pipe killed the others.

This might be a useful point to turn our attention to the matter of Richard's depressive feelings. Early in the *Narrative* Mrs Klein seemed very impressed with Richard's capacity for love, but perhaps mistakenly at that point, because his expressed love for his mother, his wish to protect her from the tramp, his love for the beauty of nature, all turned out to be primarily connected with his concern for his own comfort. His love for the dog Bobby turned out to be related to sexual collusion and the projection into him of his own naughtiness and faecal dirtying. The very possessiveness and controlling nature of his loving was manifest. Now the intensity of his love for Mrs Klein as the breast mother in the transference relationship resists her technique of interpreting, which tends constantly to push things back to his mother and back to the nurse and back to the past. The intensity of his transference attachment to her and the genuine warmth of it is certainly tied up with a very desperate need of her, but the genuineness, the authenticity of it is very instructive in comparison with the vanity, the use of flattery and seductiveness which characterized his earlier relationship to her.

Now this capacity for love is most certainly tied up with an improved splitting-and-idealization of self and object and the overcoming of the paranoid trend that came out most clearly in the Cook-and-Bessie material. His inability to distinguish between malevolent objects and bad objects produced an intolerance to frustration, disappointment or authority. It was epitomized in the dream of the trial which turned out to be a trial for breaking the window, which in fact he had not broken. But he had wanted to break windows on many occasions and in the dream he smashed all the buildings with his jack-boots and then manically kicked them up again. The light-blue mummy who was idealized as a possession has become a much more separate object and therefore stands in a more oscillating or, at times, ambivalent relationship to the dark-blue mummy. This figure is represented in the material mainly by the pretty bus conductress in the blue uniform who says, 'Half fares stand up'.

This achievement of differentiation between malevolent objects, frustrating objects and idealized gratifying objects brings with it the possibility of depressive feelings. A real desire now appears to repair the object for its own sake and not merely to put a stop to the persecution by the damage when it can not be distinguished in its qualities from the malevolent object. Giving babies to Mummy or kicking the buildings up again was part of the defence against persecutory anxieties and was thus *manic* reparation. When he said to Mrs Klein very early in the analysis that his mother could have plenty of babies, she was not too old, he was quite insincere. But at this point he has a real feeling for babies that comes from some considerable degree of integration of his femininity. This aspect of his personality enters into the sessions now, bit by bit, over the last four or five weeks, sometimes in competition with the mother for the father's penis, which easily turns into homosexuality and contempt for women. His genuine feeling of warmth for babies first came with the kitten material and is seen a bit more this week. As a result of this improved contact with his femininity and related capacity to care for babies, he is also able to look at little girls on the street and see one of them as being rather pretty. He is not even being terribly venomous towards his enemy, the little red-haired girl, although she turns up as one of the flies he squashes. His antagonistic feelings towards girls and his thinking of women as haughty or horrid, those women with yellow sputum and the terrible girl with the buck teeth who asked if he were Italian, have simmered down considerably. What does remain is his fear of big boys, for very little of the analytic work has so far thrown any light on this fear.

The depressive feelings that are able to emerge as a result of the improved contact with his femininity and a greater capacity to identify with the mother, seem to show themselves in this one sudden little bit of material in which he said his nurse had died, and died of pneumonia, her milk froze. That seems to come as a consequence of his being terribly sensitive at this point to the slightest rebuff to the emergence of genuine feelings of warmth from him. When Richard asks Mrs Klein to help him stretch by holding his hand, he feels very rebuffed by her, very hurt, very much like the boy who cried wolf – the touchiness of the recently reformed criminal. Having simulated love so often, he is terribly frightened that this genuine love will be misunderstood, undervalued, thought to be the same old falseness. The material about the nurse seems to be an important indicator, in projective form, the pneumonia, the milk freezing, of his own liability to depression now. There was material two weeks before which Mrs Klein did not grasp about the drawing of the ice rink when he said 'ice, ice, ice'. She did not pick up the first time that he was talking about feeling depression as freezing and here is a second reference to it.

As we approach the last few weeks of treatment this particular indication of a growing capacity to experience depressive feelings in their most essential form, as freezing, helps one to gain an idea of why his manic trend was so strong previously. Richard certainly has been brutally controlling with his objects and experienced them as dead objects which needed to be brought to life, like the black car with the many number plates, or the black bar on the fire. The inner feeling of coldness is in many ways the prototype of depressive pain. Richard is beginning to be able to suffer from it, although only in passing, and in the material about the nurse it is projected outward as a result of his feeling rebuffed and wounded by Mrs Klein. His response to depressive feeling is also very much improved. All through these sessions in one little way or another, he is asking Mrs Klein to help him, to hand him things, to empty the bucket. He is very concerned when he jumps from the step and touches her face that he might have hurt her. His whole relationship to her now is a constant appeal for help, which is the central theme of Mrs Klein's little paper about Colette's story in Ravel's operetta. The moment the child who has destroyed everything in rage can cry 'mama' and ask for help, the reparative process swings into operation in some mysterious way. This ability to ask for help is now really quite established in Richard's relationship to Mrs Klein and it begins to extend to his mother, when, instead of making demands on her, he can phone to ask if she could make other arrangements for him because he does not like staying at the Wilsons.

Chapter XIV

Fourteenth Week: Sessions 78-83
Technical Problems Related to
Countertransference

This is a terrible week. Why it is such a bad week is hard to
say. Somehow Mrs Klein is not in such close touch with Richard
and even loses her temper with him a bit on the Friday. It
might be instructive to review the Thursday session in detail to
to see what went wrong and why it is a rather heartbreaking
session. The theme of the 'baby tank' which began developing
five weeks before has become central now. The water tank in
the kitchen has become not only the 'baby tank' but the 'milk
tank' as well. The very central issue is the killing of the flies
and putting them in the milk and whether the milk is dirty and
poisonous. In this week Mrs Klein has lost the formulation she
found the previous week, the one that seems to be the climax
of the treatment. Instead she keeps going back to the problems
of castration anxiety and the competition with the father, all
of which is quite true, but not central any longer. It is a complicated week. The threat of the ending hangs over the whole
procedure and Richard can often hardly bear to think about
it. But it is also very complicated in other ways concerning
mainly the two bus conductresses, the pretty one who says,
'Stand up' and the other one who does not, and the dark-blue
uniform.

To the Monday session he brings the weekend dream that he
changed analysts, to a dark-blue analyst, the woman in dark
blue with her dog named James. When Richard insists on
Mrs Klein's prettiness she notes that he was really placating her
like an unfaithful lover. It arises again about his tie which was
tied for him by a maid at the Wilsons. It is a little difficult to
tell what this theme is, but one strongly suspects that his mother
was a rather pretty woman. His attachment to her beauty and
the infantile attachment to the beauty of the breasts as an
aesthetic object, has entered into the treatment in a very powerful way that tends to replace the dichotomy between the light-
blue mummy and the dark-blue mummy. It has some reference
to his looking at the sky and saying that it is light blue, although
it is quite clearly cloudy. He says at another point that it is

cloudy but it is going to clear although there seems to be every indication that the weather is worsening. The light-blue mummy who gives him this peace and quiet becomes juxtaposed to the disturbing dark-blue mummy, the cloudy sky, the storm breaking over the mountain, the combined object which insists that he stand up, develop and go to school. He does not like the dark-blue uniform on the pretty conductress because it has a masculine quality, representing the beautiful mummy who also has strength and the good penis inside her, related to the nipple. At one point he asks her again, 'What is this part of the breast called?' and she has to tell him again that it is called the nipple. But Mrs Klein keeps forgetting about the good penis and the combined objects and goes back to talking about his fear of the bad penis that makes mummy into the 'brute-mummy'. This seems to upset Richard because he is very keen that they should be in accord as the end approaches. In several sessions he wishes to synchronize their watches and to make sure they are keeping exactly the same time. At another point, he is very affectionate and cuddles her clock. She does note the desire for this unity of mind, although she speaks of it as though it were mainly a defensive process.

It is also present in his wish for her to be the milk maid and he will be the milk man; together they will milk the baby tank. In the face of repeated disappointment at her failure to follow him and after she has lost her temper a bit with him on the Thursday, he is extremely distrustful of her in the Friday session and will not look at her and says, 'Hitler said "my patience is exhausted" '. Early in the treatment he had said that one of his main difficulties was that he exhausted his mother's patience by endless questions. Bouts of this behaviour appear, as when he begins asking about the bad dream, questions her about her son, her grandson and what she will do in London, will she be in the heart of London? It is very interesting to see his recovery when he says 'the heart of London', 'Oh, the heart again'.

In fact Richard is working extremely hard and even when he seems to be out of control, the rapidity with which he recovers and shifts his ground to other material seems to indicate that there is a very strong element of dramatization and communication present. At no point is he terribly out of control, but is, rather, terribly in distress. When he is flooding the floor or hitting it with a hammer, or kicking the stools he never once attacks Mrs Klein. He has at other times actually thrown something at her and also abused her verbally. She seems to underestimate the intensity with which he is trying to work with her to evoke a clarification about the 'baby tank' being the same as the 'milk tank' and how the dead flies get into it. This problem appears also with the lobster he has in his suitcase, reminiscent of the 'delicious monster'. But he also attacks it with his knife as he had attacked the moth. Clearly one minute it is a delicious penis, next, it is a horrible, hated penis or a baby.

The Thursday session brings up clearly the element of fear that the analysis will fail. It comes up with the photographs that he wants to take of Mrs Klein, which she allows, and is connected at that point with the photographs of the landscape, one good, the other a failure, which he tears to pieces and puts the black bits in his mouth and spits them out, saying that they are poison. Very clearly this refers to the dead flies and the bits in his mouth. Fear of the analysis failing is very closely related to his fear of being a dunce, of going to school but not being able to learn. He is obviously intelligent and has already learnt quite a lot at school. She tends to think of his fear of school as being primarily a school phobia, a claustrophobic anxiety, and probably underestimates a bit how intense is his competitiveness and how unbearable are failures to him. Let us examine the Thursday session.

(Session 81) 'Richard was again waiting at the corner of the road. He asked whether it was sixteen days until Mrs Klein's departure. In the playroom, he adjusted his watch to her clock. He opened the clock, inspected it, set the alarm going, and went on opening and closing the leather case, also caressing it with his hands. He said that even if his watch was a little slower than others, yet it was "going its way", and he drew his finger round the face of the watch'. [There is something rather admirable about these sessions, although it is desperate and unsatisfactory in other ways. He wants something from her and is quite determined to get it.] 'He said that nobody, and certainly no other watch, could command that it should stop . . .' [It was as if he had said to Mrs Klein, "You may be stopping the analysis, but I'm not. I'm going on even if I have to go on without you".] 'He quickly looked round the kitchen, glanced uneasily at the "baby tank", and was disturbed because he saw some rust on it. He tried to scrape it off and seemed grateful when Mrs K removed the rust with a brush'. [It is not clear why she does this unless he asked for help, to which she usually responds now.] 'He quickly went back to the table and again looked into the clock to see whether it was still working . . . He told Mrs K that he had a secret which she did not know. He had cycled to the end of the road last evening, and had passed her house. Where did the little path at the end of the road lead to? What was Mrs K doing at about 8.45 last evening (which was the time when he had passed her house)? Would Mrs K have been angry if had looked in? He did not wait for answers to any of these questions but went on speaking. He explained that he had borrowed the bicycle the day before and had cycled all over the village'. [Really quite adventurous of him.] 'Unfortunately it had been too late to go farther out to the next village as he had intended'. [Connected with his plan to climb a mountain with John and his friend.] 'He went on describing his exploit in detail and said it had been fun and he had enjoyed it very much. When he went downhill he made noises to himself, as if he were a bus'. [Containing the dark-blue pretty conductress-mummy.]

'Mrs K interpreted, as often before, that when Richard investigated her clock, this meant looking into her inside and reassuring himself about her still being all right'. [This is the line on which she keeps working.] 'The same applied to his looking around the kitchen. Both were connected with his killing the flies on the previous day, the mess he had made in the kitchen, and his fear of the harm he had done in this way to Mrs K. His cycling tour showed that he was less afraid of other children and also served as a means to satisfying his curiosity. Cycling past Mrs K's lodgings meant the exploration of her inside. The little path represented her genital and he wondered where it would lead if he puts his penis – the bicycle – into it'. [Thirst for knowledge or intrusive curiosity?] 'He seemed to be less afraid of his penis being a dangerous weapon and could therefore use the bicycle'. [This little path was something like a delivery entrance and he was curious about it, curious about the structure of the mother's body and the connection between the side entrance and what was going on in the main part of the house. In that way the connection between the sexual relationship of the mother to the father's penis and the breast with its supplies and thus the connection between the 'baby tank' and the 'milk tank', is illustrated.] 'All this meant that his fear about his hatred and destructive wishes taking effect had lessened. His watch "going its way" though slowly, stood for the smaller, less potent, but uninjured genital. He seemed to accept that it was only a boy's genital, but he hoped he would be a man in the future'. [This is her desire, to get him into the latency period and quieten him down. One can not blame her.] 'Making his watch agree with Mrs K's clock meant that they would understand each other and he could keep her as a friend, also inside him'. [Here she gets at it.]

'Richard, again manipulating the clock, said with strong emotion, "Must we two part?" He went outside, looked at the sky, and said under his breath, with feeling, "It is heavenly". Back in the room he looked round, found the hammer, and hit the floor hard. While doing so, he mentioned that his canary, the one that was left', [after the other one had died,] 'was coming home, and he was looking forward to that. (The bird had been at his nurse's house, who, as mentioned previously, lived with her husband in the neighbourhood and whom he frequently saw.)

'Mrs K interpreted that he had intended by his hammering to open the floor, to take out the dead babies, and to find the live ones, the bird which was coming home'. [A rather puzzling interpretation.]

'Richard went to the piano, which had been turned to the wall, and on which a number of things had been put, and said he would like to try to play'. [He had given up playing the piano after having reached quite an advanced development, playing sonatas and so on.] 'In the course of the analysis, Richard had occasionally looked at the piano, but until then he had only once opened it and played a few notes (Fifth Session.) Now he attempted to open it and asked whether Mrs K could help him' [again, she must help him] 'to move it and to take the things off the lid. She did so. There was a big Union Jack in the corner by the piano. Richard said that he was going to keep an eye on it, meaning that it might fall down. He first very hesitantly played on the piano with one finger only, then he stopped again. He said it was dusty. Could Mrs K help him dust it? She did so, and he tried playing again', [as though dusting, like cleaning the rust or dusting the little footstools, would improve his playing] 'looking sad and saying that he had forgotten the sonatas he knew; then he tried something else, fetched a chair, sat down and played some harmonies of his own. He said, in a low voice, that he used to do this a lot. After a while he asked whether Mrs K would play something, and she did so'. [Puzzling! And dangerous?] 'Richard was very pleased, went back to the piano and, again trying some harmonies, said under his breath that this would be a great pleasure when he went home'. [Back to the house at Z after the war.] 'He opened the top of the piano', [like opening the top of the baby tank] 'and asked Mrs K to touch the keys while he looked "inside". He suddenly became aware of the word he had used and, glancing at Mrs K significantly, said, "Again the inside". Then he hit the keyboard with his elbow and trod hard on the pedals. He seized the Union Jack, enveloped himself in it, and noisily sang the National Anthem'. [A rather gorgeous example of projective identification with the daddy's penis.] 'His face was flushed, he was shouting and was trying to counteract anger and hostility by loyalty'. [She is not quite right about loyalty. Probably he is trying to counteract hostility by the promise of having a man's status some day.] 'He looked out of the window, saw the old man opposite, and said "There is the Bear".' [Externalization of the penis invaded by projective identification.] 'After a pause he asked whether Mr Smith had passed. So far he had paid hardly any attention to passers-by, but now tension and suspicion had set in and he began to watch out for them'. [The situation probably turned bad because of the juxtaposition of his incapacity and her capability. In playing for him she, as it were, exhibited the penis that she had inside her.]

'Mrs K interpreted the piano as standing for her inside, as Richard himself recognized, and his playing on it stood for his putting his genital into hers and for caressing her with his hands, as he had done earlier with the clock'. [The clock very clearly represents her mind and also the breast and probably the piano also has quite a lot to do with being in harmony with her and their minds working together.] From this point on the session goes progressively wrong as she pushes the theme of reparation to the Mummy by giving her babies with his penis. The photograph material follows, apparently accompanied by hammering the floor and flooding the kitchen. The fiasco of Friday ensues, barely rectified by the fragmented material of Saturday.

Fifteenth Week: Sessions 84-89
The Concept of the
Combined Object and its
Impact on Development

Chapter XV

This fifteenth week is the least satisfactory of the whole analysis from the viewpoint of Mrs Klein's work. Richard is absolutely preoccupied with the approaching end, and attempts to work out the various possibilities, sometimes in quite a matter-of-fact and rather grown-up way. If she dies would somebody else be available? Could he not go to London, stay in a hotel? It seems to cause Mrs Klein great distress during the week and perhaps makes her work less well than usual. I would think that she must have been considering in her mind the same possibilities. She did call his mother, and try to discuss the question of the continuation of the analysis. Although she firmly took it upon herself that the decision to come to London was too dangerous for him, one assumes that she must have tried to investigate this with the mother and found her quite adamant about it. In a way Richard is better than Mrs Klein in this week, produces dreams and new play material but does not get much in response. The previous week she had lost track of the formulation about the breast and the nipple and the upstairs and downstairs of the mummy's body. Things went wrong when she played the piano and later she lost her temper. But she was struggling.

Some of the notes to this week indicate conceptual limitations or difficulties she was having at that time. One such limitation is illustrated by the theme of the three conductresses, not only two, not just a pretty face and a not so pretty one, but now a painted-faced one as well. This third figure has to do with Richard's distrust of Mrs Klein and of his mother and his suspicion of hypocrisy. This is mainly a projection of his own hypocrisy and trickiness and slyness. The charm and seductiveness of the early weeks has been replaced by urgent clinging. He can hardly keep his hands off Mrs Klein now. He touches her and looks at her in a way in which his eyes are touching and clinging. The whole concept of clinging and sticking (which Mrs Bick has been investigating for the past few years) was unavailable to Mrs Klein. The difference between a baby hold-ing on to the nipple in order to control the breast and a baby holding on to the nipple for fear of being dropped into the abyss seems to be very clearly illustrated by the situation with Richard at this point. At an infantile level he is in mortal dread of the end of his analysis as a precipice.

At the same time as being much more in contact with this very primitive anxiety which makes him so clinging, he is also noticeably more mature. His maturity shows not only in his actual social behaviour, like the cycling, his friendliness with John and John's friend, and in his way of dealing with the problem of trying to sort out the possibilities about the con-tinuation of his analysis, but at one point he does actually think over the improvement that the analysis has brought into his mental life and he talks about it precisely and in detail. So these two can be seen to co-exist, infantile terror of being dropped and the beginnings of the young man who knows that he needs analysis if he is going to develop properly and does not want to be a dunce. A 'dunce' begins to take on the meaning of being unable to perform any useful function in the world, as illustrated in the material about the merchantmen carrying supplies to Alexandria.

The other way in which his anxiety is illustrated is the heart-breaking little bit where he says, in despair, that he does not want to do anything, that it is lovely to do nothing. Mrs Klein is obviously hurt to hear this little boy express such apathetic cynicism. He does come out of it very quickly and by contrast is at his most hopeful when he is reporting his dreams. Mrs Klein's analysis of it suggests that she thought it a somewhat manic hopefulness that tended to collapse again. But it is very interesting to see how important his dreams have become, implying that the acknowledgement of psychic reality had been re-established in him. The play with the keys, the darkening of the room, his reaction to the rain, are all a bit reminiscent of the early sessions and none of it has much substance in com-parison with the dreams. It is noticeable that he shows very little reaction to the man coming in to read the meters. That spark of humour in him has an important link, as Mrs Klein points out, with the fact that there is always somebody who survives when there is a disaster. There is always a bit of life left. In the dream of the Black Island there is a little patch of green. Richard's capacity for humour is very closely linked with Mrs Klein's own spark, and is part of what saves him, whereas lapsing into apathy, 'it's lovely to do nothing' seems a bit connected with his father's state, which overshadows the week, with the renewed fear that he might die. Certainly Richard's tiredness seems very intimately connected with the father again being very tired.

But the main material of the week centres on the three conductresses, and the dreams are accordingly about buses and ships and cars. In the Tuesday session (page 430) Mrs Klein was talking about the three conductresses and describing the one with the painted face. 'Mrs K suggested that the conductress he liked stood also for Nurse. When he felt uncertain and suspicious about Mummy, he had turned to Nurse, who at that time was not married, which meant she had no husband as Mummy had. The pretty conductress stood for Mummy, who was prettier than Nurse; but there was a time when Richard loved Nurse more than Mummy, and he felt guilty about that'. [She is interpreting the conflict of loyalty in terms of the historical background.]

'Richard said that Nurse was quite pretty – not at all ugly. He had seen her on the previous day when he changed buses on his journey home, and she had given him some sweets. (He now seemed to realize how fond he still was of her.) He said that Mrs K was not the one with the "painted face"; she was very pretty too, but not as pretty as Mummy'. [Trying to balance it amongst these women – the Judgment of Paris.] 'Then he asked whether Mrs K felt hurt.

'Mrs K suggested that she represented a mixture of Mummy and Nurse.

'Richard said that he had had a dream which was frightening but thrilling at the same time. A few nights before he also had a dream about two people putting their genitals together. He greatly enjoyed reporting the more recent dream and described it vividly and dramatically, sounding sinister at the frightening points, while at the climax his eyes were shining, and happiness and hope were expressed on his face. "*He saw Mrs K standing at at the bus stop in the village where the bus leaves for 'Y'. But the bus was going to some other place; in the dream it went to 'Y' only once every fortnight. It passed by without stopping.* (Here Richard made vivid noises like the bus passing by.) *Richard ran after it to catch it, but the bus had gone. He went after all, but in a caravan. With him travelled a very happy family. The father and mother were middle aged; there were quite a lot of children, and all of them were nice. They passed an island. With them was also a very big cat. First the cat bit his dog, but then they got on well together. Then the new cat chased his actual cat, but they also got to like each other. This new cat was not an ordinary cat, but it was very nice. It had teeth like pearls and it was more like a human being.*

'Mrs K asked whether it was more like a woman or like a man.

'Richard replied it was both like a gentleman and a nice woman. He said "*the island was on a river. On the bank of the river the sky was quite black, the trees were black, there was sand which was sand-coloured, but the people were also black. There were all sorts of creatures, birds, animals, scorpions, all black; and all of them, people and creatures, were quite still. It was terrifying*".' [The stillness, not so much the blackness, was terrifying.] 'Richard's face expressed horror and anxiety'. [In the Wolf-Man's dream it was also the stillness of the wolves in the tree which was so terrifying. Freud interpreted that as representing in reverse the violent motion of the parents in intercourse.]

'Mrs K asked what the island was like.

'Richard said *the island was not quite black, but the water and sky around were. There was a patch of green on the island and the sky over the island showed a little blue. The stillness was terrible. Suddenly Richard called out, "Ahoy there", and at that moment everybody and everything became alive. He had broken a spell. They must have been enchanted. People began to sing; the scorpions and other creatures jumped back into the water, everybody was overjoyed, everything turned light, the sky became all blue*'.

Mrs Klein's interpretation of the dream emphasizes the reparative impulse from the manic viewpoint and the light goes out of Richard's eyes. She does not see a link to his calling for help so frequently nor its resemblance to the child in the Colette-Ravel operetta calling 'Mama'. Clearly she thinks the 'Ahoy there' is similar to his kicking the buildings up again with his jack-boots. She does not think that his new-found friendliness is breaking the spell, friendliness generated by the happy internal (caravan) family and the earlier (by two days) Adam and Eve dream. The dream may be representing the possibility that when Mrs Klein goes away as a external object (connected with the buses and the conductresses and the bus not waiting for him) that an internal experience of family may continue to generate friendliness and happiness in him.

The puzzling notes to this session go some distance to explain the difficulty on a conceptual basis, relating to the interaction of internal with external situations, with special reference to the combined object. (Note II, p. 433.): 'Richard had at that point shown a step in development: he was able to feel that he and I, representing his mother, could be together without his internal object or my internal object interfering. A good balance between internal and external situations and relations is of fundamental importance. In Richard's case this meant that the combined parent figure – and his internal persecutors – had at least temporarily lost in power'. [It is not clear whether his 'internal persecutors' stand in apposition or in contrast to 'combined parent figure'.] 'This was an indication of progress, although I am aware that these changes were not fully established'.

What Mrs Klein seems to be saying is that in order to have a good relationship to an external object, there has to be a balance between it and the relationship to the internal object and that the internal object should not interfere too much. In ordinary terms that would mean something like 'your conscience should not bother you too much' but also must mean 'your internal object is not always clamouring for attention'. Now, if it is clamouring for attention it is a little bit hard to see how it manages to be a good combined internal object. It shows that at the most advanced point of her work at the end of the 1950s she was still not really decided about the role of the combined internal object and whether this combination – which meant father and mother together in intercourse, vagina and penis together, breast and nipple together as a sexual combination – whether this functioned as a good object or whether it functioned as too powerful an object that flooded the personality with sexual excitement, overpowered it with its activity, stirred envy and was in that way a disorganizing influence. In *Envy and Gratitude* she seemed to consider the combined object as the core of strength in the personality, but here in the notes I think she reveals that she was still quite uncertain about it because of the intensity of the envy that this combined object is felt to arouse. Richard's Adam and Eve dream, a primal scene dream, visualizes the parents and their genitals but he does not seem to be shocked with envy or overwhelmed by sexual excitement. In fact, seeing their genitals looking so huge like the monster he described, is unpleasant. This dream is an important prelude to the 'Black Island' dream with its hopefulness about this destruction being reversible in psychic reality, that dead objects, dead babies can be brought back to life by goodwill towards the good, creative intercourse of the internal parents.

Now this is related to Mrs Klein's uncertainty about the conceptual status of the depressive position. She had never absolutely crystalized this in her mind, for sometimes she speaks of 'penetrating' the depressive position, 'overcoming', 'surpassing', all of which have a different implications regarding the meaning of 'depressive position'. This is brought out in note no. 4, on page 434. 'Here we are touching on one of the important anxiety situations inherent in the depressive position. If Richard felt himself to be full of attacked and therefore bad objects (for instance, the dangerous, attacked flies and the lobster) and dangerous excrement, as well as destructive impulses, then the good objects inside him appeared to be endangered'. [Are these attacked, damaged objects different from bad objects produced by splitting-and-idealization?] 'This meant in states of great anxiety that everything inside him was dead. Richard tried to solve this problem by taking out the bad and dangerous elements (the soot). But when he felt more secure, he resorted, as in the dream, to reviving and improving the bad objects'. [Omnipotently? It is not clear.] 'It is interesting that the island had not been altogether black, but that there had been a patch of green and a bit of blue sky in the centre. This centre of goodness, which enabled him to keep hope going, thus represented the good breast, the good analyst, and the good nurse, as well as the good parents, in harmony'; [Intercourse?] 'and from this core of goodness life and reparation could spread'. [Life and reparation would seem then, to spread from "the core of goodness", the internal object not the self.] 'The play with the train and the baby on the swing had shown that the good baby also stood for regaining and preserving life. (As mentioned before, Richard was extremely fond of young babies and often asked his mother to have a child. When she replied that she was too old, he said that this was nonsense, of course she could have babies, and there is little doubt that he assumed the same of the analyst.)

'The good breast as the core of the ego I take to be a fundamental precondition for ego development. Richard had always maintained his belief in the light-blue Mummy. The idealized mother co-existed with the persecutory and suspect one. Nevertheless, idealization was based on a feeling', [not a psychological fact] 'of having internalized the good primal object to some extent, and this was his mainstay in all his anxieties. In the present stage of the analysis, Richard's capacity to integrate the ego and to synthesize the contrasting aspects of his objects had clearly increased and he had become more able, in phantasy', [not in psychic reality,] 'to improve the bad objects and to revive and re-create the dead ones'; [All of this sounds like an active process by the ego and not something that happens to it through the mysterious agency of 'the core of goodness'.] 'this, in turn, linked with hate being mitigated by love'. [Mitigate by love implies something *meaningful*, rather than mechanical as in Freud's use of 'neutralize'.] 'In the dream, Richard could also bring the two parents together in a harmonious way.

'These processes were, however, not fully successful, as was shown by my being left behind when I was hidden behind the man, which represented Richard's doubts as to whether the union of the parents would actually be good. (This indicated again the combined parent figure.)'

Clearly Mrs Klein was not really decided whether this combined parent figure represented the core of the ego and of ego strength or whether 'in harmony' meant two parents with a possibility of combination. Therefore she remained uncertain about the breast and the nipple being in itself essentially a combined object. Her approach to the dreams seems, therefore, to hedge a little bit in favour of hauling Richard into the latency period, that is, rather encouraging him to desexualize his objects, to have the nice middle-aged parents in the nice caravan with the nice children and the cats love each other and so do the dogs, even if they occasionally bite each other.

The whole thing is being suburbanized with niceness. In the same way she wants him to play the piano. Everyone wants him to play the piano but that was not her technique. At this point in the analysis, in this week in particular, she was not at her best. She does not make much of the poppy and the little fir cone. She does not make much of the dreams. She has missed the opportunity to show him how frightened he is of dying and that the end of the analysis means, for the baby part of him, the danger of blackness spreading everywhere. Perhaps she could not bring herself to frighten him that much. But, more important, Mrs Klein did not have the conceptual equipment. The issues about which she was uncertain are still unclear, or perhaps essentially mysterious: the clinging; the fear of blackness; the 'dead end'.

Sixteenth Week: Sessions 90-93
The Achievements of the
Analysis, with Special Reference
to Dependence on Internal
Objects

Chapter XVI

The material that Richard brings in these four days is less dramatic than the previous week with exception of the lovely piece about the umbrella with which Mrs Klein works so beautifully. He tends mainly to peregrinate round different types of material that he brought earlier on in the analysis and a little bit of a dream or really the extension of the dream that he brought on the previous Saturday. In a sense there is nothing very new, no expectation on either part of discovering anything else during these last sessions.

It is all a rather sad reviewing of what they had accomplished and some attempt at making more explicit what thay have not accomplished. Richard can not keep his hands off Mrs Klein and these hands that are caressing and touching her also turn into the crab's claws waiting to fasten on her. This is the clinging material which Mrs Klein had no conceptual framework for developing, but the fear of falling comes out in the parachute material and is discussed in the notes connected with it. It gives an insight into a fundamental insecurity of an extremely primitive sort, underlying the weakness of Richard's ego and his distrust of his mother. This distrust is connected with the dark-blue mummy, this pretty conductress whom he says he 'wouldn't have'. But one can see that his mother, like the conductress who is accused of saying 'stand up', is the mother who expected too much of him in some way, expected him to be too independent, too manly, too potent. Mrs Klein also has tended, in emphasizing his genital conflicts, his castration anxiety, his wish to put his penis into the mummy and explore her inside, expected too much masculinity from him. Something very strongly feminine has not been allowed to develop and perhaps has not fared much better during this analysis, although he has had an opportunity to express it occasionally. At the end of the Saturday session there had been the dream of the empty bus, to which Richard brings more detail on Monday; again the eerie stillness, as in

261

the Black Island dream, is central. The bus slowed down when Richard rang the bell and he jumped out while it was still moving, which is a very clear indication that the analysis is still a going concern for him. He feels it to be cut off at a time when he is probably making his greatest progress.

Beside the bus in the dream there was a flattened car in which a little girl was lying next to her father, but then she turned into a spaniel. The flattened car seems to link with an earlier piece of material in which Richard closes the frame of Mrs Klein's clock, so that it almost collapsed, and then, saying that he was still supporting it, opens it quickly and says 'Now she is all right again'. I think that is a very important link to the dream. The little girl in the flattened car has something to do with his own femininity which in this brief analysis had very little opportunity to come into much contact with Mrs Klein but has remained in the projected state, in his mother or Mrs Klein or perhaps even the little red-haired girl or the bus conductress. It would thus have the significance of an unborn sister.

These seem to me to be the indications from the dreams and from his attitude towards the conductress, that there has been too much expectation about his masculinity and not enough recognition of his femininity. On the other hand, the extraordinary progress at infantile level is beautifully tied up in the umbrella-parachute material on Tuesday. (p. 455).

'Richard appeared not to have listened to Mrs K's interpretation. But at this point he again emphatically confirmed that he did not want to hurt Mrs K in any way. Yet a minute later he threw all the buses except the "electric train bus", which stood for himself, down from the table, saying that it was a "precipice".' [Here is the falling theme, the abyss.] 'His face was flushed and he was very excited. But he was at once concerned when he saw that the two front wheels of the engine had come off, and asked Mrs K whether she was angry and whether she could mend it.

'Mrs K said that she could mend it and interpreted Richard's wish to know whether he had actually done harm to her children and friends, and if so, could she make them well again and forgive Richard for his hate.

'Richard went into the kitchen, drew several buckets of

water, and said that this water was not very clean; but apparently he did not mind this. He added that he wanted to draw all the water so that the tank should become clean. While drawing water, he kept on looking into the tank to see how the water whirled into the pipe and took the dirt with it.

'Mrs K interpreted that Richard was expressing his desire to clean her inside and Mummy's inside from bad "big job", babies, and genitals. His attacks on Mrs K, represented by the goods train, were meant predominantly to free her from the bad Hitler-Daddy – the ammunition which was put on top of the train – and to save and protect her. But he was also jealous of her, just as he was when he thought of Daddy being in bed with Mummy while he was left by himself. This was why he had thrown the buses down the "precipice". The rival buses stood for the rival Daddy (also the good one) and for Paul and all the children who he thought might yet be born'.

'Richard had during the last few minutes played with Mrs K's umbrella which he had opened. He made it spin round and said he liked it. Then he used it as a parachute with which he was supposed to float down. He looked at the trademark and stated with satisfaction that it was British made. Then, again, holding it open, he turned round and round with it and said that he was dizzy, he did not know where it was taking him. He also said over and over again that "the whole world was turning round". Then he let the umbrella drop gently; he once more said that it was a parachute and that he was not sure whether it would go down the right way. He told Mrs K that he had completely wrecked Mummy's best umbrella when he had used it as a parachute on a windy day. She had been "speechless with rage".

[Here comes a gorgeous interpretation.] 'Mrs K interpreted the umbrella as her breast; that it was British made meant that it was a good breast, and that Mummy's breast was a good breast too. She referred to his doubts about what Mrs K contained – a good or bad Mr K. The open umbrella stood for the breast, but the stick in it stood for Mr K's genital. Richard did not know whether he could trust this breast when he took it in because it was mixed with Mr K's genital, just as in his mind his parents and their genitals were mixed inside him. The question where the umbrella would take him expressed his un-

certainty whether they were controlling him inside or not'.
[This is her point about the combined objects being too powerful and controlling.] 'The world which was turning round was
the whole world he had taken into himself when he took in the
breast – or rather Mummy mixed with Daddy, and her children,
and all she contained. He felt the internalized powerful Daddy-
penis – the secret weapon – as something which made him
powerful if he used it against an external enemy. But is became
dangerous if it attacked and controlled him internally. Nevertheless, he trusted Mummy and Daddy – the umbrella – more
than previously, both as external people and inside him. That
was also why he now treated Mrs K's umbrella more carefully
than he had formerly treated Mummy's'.

That is incredibly condensed and really pulls together the
whole treatment of this boy. In the second note to this material
she writes: (p. 457)

'During the present session, apart from watching Mr Smith
when he passed, Richard had hardly paid any attention to
people on the road. He was deeply concentrated on an internal
situation and in that respect he felt more secure than formerly.
This more secure internal situation included a stronger belief
in the good protective breast expressed by the parachute
which had helped him in an emergency. Although it soon
appeared that the good breast was mixed in his mind with the
penis, nevertheless it seemed more reliable than on former
occasions'. [But surely the umbrella would not function at all
without the central stick-penis] 'More recently Richard had
become able to direct his aggressiveness more consistently
against the bad, the Hitler-father and to unite with the good
mother and help her to defend herself. Instead of quickly turning his aggression against the breast when anxiety came up,'
[very crucial with this boy,] 'he could in a relatively more
stable way maintain his trust in the breast and in the mother,
and face the fight with the father', [that is the bad Hitler-
father.] . . . 'The change from stronger depression in the previous session to greater security in the present one was also due
to a manic element in his mood. He used the stronger belief in
the good internal Mrs K and mother, and the good father, to
ward off the fear of parting and his depression'. [This is part of
what she means by the use of manic defences as a modulating

device in relation to depressive anxieties. A certain manic over-estimation of the internal situation as a defence against being overwhelmed by external difficulty can also be reversed when external situations are good, to overcome anxiety about the internal situation, such as in the face of illness.]

The next bit, which is so interesting, shows how Mrs Klein worked with internal situations. (p. 458). [This is just after Richard has been making some demands about changes of time because he wanted to go with John Wilson. Mrs Klein could not accomodate him.]

'Richard, at one moment when both trains were standing in the station, suddenly said he felt unwell and had a pain in his tummy. He looked pale.

'Mrs K interpreted the station as Richard's inside. He expected all the time a collision inside him between the electric train, containing Mrs K and the good Mummy, and the hostile goods train, standing for all the angry patients and children from whom Richard wanted to take Mrs K away and run with her to his home town'. [That is her foundation for the interpretation of his illness, that he has been pursued in this play, as in the outside world, by all the daddies and all the children from whom he has taken the breast and mummy as his exclusive possession.] 'Therefore he also wanted to change the time of his sessions, which meant taking Mrs K away from everybody else. While Richard was striving to avoid a collision between the trains, because he did not wish to hurt Mrs K and Mummy, and their children and wanted to finish the analysis peacefully, he did not seem to believe that he could avoid the collision internally'. [Here she should be linking it with his masturbation, which, for some reason, she always leaves out.] 'This meant that he and Mrs K would be hurt or damaged by his rivals. Therefore he had seemed so tense during this play and had a tummy ache'. [She is interpreting this as an internal anxiety situation, experienced as an actual pain in his tummy, not a hypochondriacal situation.]

'Richard said, looking at Mrs K in surprise, "The pain has now quite gone – why?" The colour had come back into his face'.

Finally, on page 461, note III declares Mrs Klein's understanding of the structure of Richard's illness as well as the

265

dynamics of his anxieties. 'I had already interpreted that one part of his self', [not ego] 'felt to be good and *allied with* the good object, was fighting his destructive part combined with' [not merely 'allied with' – that is, in projective identification] 'the bad objects'. [*The* bad objects produced by splitting-and-idealization.]

This was the nature of his conflict with the Hitler-Daddy. But Mrs Klein was not able to differentiate that persecution from the paranoia towards Cook and Bessie. The paranoia had the structure of a destructive part of the self combined with, in projective identification with, the idealized part-objects, the breasts. This is perhaps the classical structure of paranoia.

There remains the task of briefly recapitulating the treatment of Richard. He started as a child who presented difficulties both characterological and symptomatic. We know that he was ineducable by virtue of being riddled with agoraphobic and claustrophobic anxieties and fear of other children. His character was freighted with insincerity and hypocrisy and pseudo-charm. At the start of his analysis, his illness seems to have him in its grip and casts him back in his development, mainly during his schooldays in connection with his competitiveness with other boys, which resulted in his being bullied. It was undoubtedly aggravated by the war situation and by the bombing of the home, their moving and Paul going into the army.

During the course of this analysis, the transference process seems to have moved through a genital seduction period which quickly deepened into voyeuristic jealousy, [the starfish drawings] and catastrophic masturbatory phantasy [the toy play.] The struggle with rivals for the possession of the mother, [Empire drawings] began to generate depressive anxieties, and a period of intense oscillation of depression and persecution ensued which gave promise of an unresolvable distrust of the mother. This was surprisingly broken by the revelation of a focus of paranoid confusion between good and bad at the oral level, [Cook and Bessie material] and the transference moved into high gear as Mrs Klein began to respond to the helpless baby in Richard. Splitting-and-idealization of self and objects [the trial dream and lightning drawings] began to improve in clarity as the end of the analysis hove in sight. Desperate clinging to the breast [touching and drinking behaviour] and acceptance of it as a combined object [parachute-umbrella] strengthened his hopefulness about the strength and goodness of the internal situation, so long as he could be friendly to the other babies and not kill them [the milk-tank material and the Black Island dream.]

PART THREE

The Clinical Significance
of the Work of Bion

Acknowledgements

I wish to thank Mr Eric Rhode, Mrs Catharine Mack Smith and Mrs Martha Harris for reviewing and proofing the text. Mrs Barbara Forryan graciously produced the index at very short notice.

270

Introduction

Although this book can be read on its own, clearly its intention was to link the work of Bion, particularly in its clinical application, to the line of development in psycho-analysis leading from Freud through Abraham to Melanie Klein and on to Wilfred Bion. In the two earlier volumes a selective attention was given first to the clinical writings of Freud, with emphasis on the evolution of his methods of observation, the clinical data thrown up and finally the formulations that were reached, treating them not so much as scientific theories as metaphoric devices for organizing description of phenomena. Next the 'Narrative' was examined in detail, week by week, as the clinical reference point for describing the evolution of Melanie Klein's formulations of mental development and psychopathology, highlighting along the way the evidences of her clinical methods of observation, thought and communication.

The first two volumes therefore followed different methods of exposition: the first chronological, the second focussed, looking both backward and forward on the history of Mrs Klein's thought. In the present volume the chronological method is taken up again, with respect to the date of the clinical work if not always the date of publication. Thus, for instance, the papers republished in 'Second Thoughts' will be dealt with earlier than the second thoughts themselves. The emphasis of the book will be on Bion's methods of observation and thought, again, as with Freud and Melanie Klein, rather neglecting the theories as an explanatory system. This should not be taken as value judgment, dismissive of the theoretical aspects, but rather as a manifestation of the method of exposition being followed and the underlying purpose. The intention in these three volumes has been to trace the continuity of clinical method and thought from Freud to Bion in order to establish on firm ground the conception of the 'Kleinian Development'. This view is not tenable in the realm of theory, where a very marked dis-continuity is clearly in evidence, both from Freud to Klein and from Klein to Bion. Freud has constructed a quasi-neurophysiological explanatory system which never departed in its foundations from the preconceptions of the 'Project for a Scientific Psychology'. Melanie Klein constructed a quasi-theological system in which internal objects have the significance of deity. Bion has constructed a quasi-philosophical system where thought sits amazed in Plato's cave straining itself to apprehend the noumena of the world. Each of these systems, *qua* system, has its area of interest and appeal but scant clinical application. In studying the work of Bion, then, the stress will be laid, to borrow his words, on those elements which are 'meant for use in the consulting room'.

The present volume was presented as lectures to the fourth-year students of the Tavistock Child Psycho-therapy Course, along with other members of the clinic staff and guests, in 1976-77 and 1977-78. They were constructed on the assumption that the audience would have read the relevant work of Bion in the week prior to presentation and thus have the text clearly in mind. For this reason the book cannot be very profitably read by anyone who does not follow the same discipline. In contrast to the lectures on Freud and Klein, which were delivered extemporaneously, with the exception of rare direct quotations, the present lectures on Bion, because of the intricacy of the argument and the frequent need for quotation, were read out and followed by a period of discussion.

'Experiences in Groups' is the work of three different periods in Bion's life: military psychiatric, in wartime, age 40, (preview), civilian psychiatric in peacetime (experiences) age 50, and psycho-analytic (re-view), age 60. Never task- or result-oriented, the key word is always 'experience', later to be formalized as the basis of 'learning from experience' as against 'learning about' things, and finally formulated as 'transformations in O' and 'becoming O'. The military psychiatrist who had to form a training wing for the rehabilitation of neurotic soldiers saw his task as one of restoring these men to integration in a disciplined community from a state of subjugation to the 'helplessness' of neurosis. His thesis was that the restoration of discipline as an internal fact required participation in an external discipline, which in its turn depended on two factors: (1) the presence of the enemy and (2) 'the presence of an officer who, *being experienced*, knows some of his own failings, respects the integrity of his men, and is not afraid of either their good will or their hostility'.

It is of interest to note Bion's emphasis on the qualities of the person in responsibility, for at no point in this little paper does he minimize for the sake of the appearance of modesty the impact of his personality on this group of 300-400 men. And he seems able to do this without immodesty by virtue of this assumption: 'being experienced, etc'. While at no point does he enlarge on this extraordinary assumption that 'experience' produces these valuable qualities of self knowledge, respect for others and fearlessness in the face of others' emotions, one can only suppose that he already had in his mind a quite idiosyncratic usage for the word.

But what of this 'presence of the enemy'? It is characteristic of Bion's playfulness that he should use ambiguity to allow the reader both to misconstrue his meaning and to remain puzzled and uncertain for some time before clarification arrives. It is evident that these men are in a hospital and not in the 'presence of the enemy'. We have to wait for the bottom of the page to find out that the enemy is 'neurosis as a disability of the community'. Reading Bion is perhaps not very different from being in one of his groups, where his fearlessness takes the form of a playful patience in the interest of allowing others to have experiences. The reader is so exposed to these experiences that he has not the slightest difficulty in believing in the impatience and exasperation of the members of the groups when faced with this immovable body.

These two contrasting usages of language, ambiguity and idiosyncracy, are essential tools of Bion's methods of both investigation and exposition. The search for ambiguity will lead him to more and more mathematical formulations as the years go by, while his idiosyncratic use of language will achieve a poetic syntax quite distinctive; so distinctive in fact that his impact on other peoples' modes and content of thought can be traced, like a radioactive compound, circulating in the stream of their language usage.

When we turn to the ten year older Bion of the therapeutic groups we find virtually the same elements at work as those employed to institute discipline among the soldiers of the training wing. His humour is not just a matter of literary style, even if literary style is used to amplify it. 'It was disconcerting to find that the Committee seemed to believe that patients could be cured in such groups as these. . . . Indeed the only cure of which I could speak with certainty was related to a minor symptom of my own – a belief that groups might take kindly to my efforts'. It is a humour that emanates from a very particular position as observer-participant, compounded of the qualities that he had enumerated for the 'experienced' officer plus an ability to see the situation from many different angles. This will later be formulated as the concept of Vertices, the necessity for 'binocular vision', and the phenomenon of 'reversible perspective'. But in this early work it manifests itself in two particular ways. For instance: 'Most members (of the group) had been told that I would "take" the group; some say that I have a reputation for knowing a lot about groups; some feel that I ought to explain what we are going to do; some thought it was going to be a kind of seminar, or perhaps a lecture. When I draw attention to the fact that these ideas seem to me to be hearsay, there seems to be a feeling that I am attempting to deny my eminence as a "taker" of groups'. Or, '. . . it would be very useful if we could feel that when we have made observations of this kind they corresponded to facts'. This first manifestation, the differentiation between hearsay and observation of facts, runs through Bion's work and will result in an emphasis on the role of the 'selected fact' for creative thought.

The second manifestation of his capacity to see things from different angles, and with consequent humour, is his alertness to paradox and 'surprising contradiction'. The qualities of mind which make for this alertness are not in evidence in this early work but will be investigated by Bion later in his preoccupation with the psycho-analytical method, resulting in the emphasis on the moment of experience needing to be guarded from 'memory' and 'desire' in order to be apprehended in its uniqueness. This has an important link with his attitude towards language: that it can be either a powerful and irreplaceable instrument of thought, or its greatest deterrent. '. . . we have to recognize that perhaps the members of the group assume too easily that the label on the box is a good description of the contents'.

But the humour is not the only emanation coming from this ability to see things from many different angles. It is probably also the basis of the modesty of presentation which can easily strike the reader as affected in a man of such eminence. 'The articles printed here aroused more interest than I expected', or ' – the fact that the interpretations would seem to be concerned with matters of no importance to anyone but myself' could appear facetious if one did not comprehend Bion's awe of the complexity of the phenomena he sets out to investigate and describe. He is clearly sincere when he indicates that his intention is 'to provide as much material as possible for the reader to use in reaching his own conclusions'. It is not clear whether Bion in fact considers that the complexity inheres in the phenomena themselves or whether it is a function of the complexity of the mind that studies them, that it can only see them in the round and in full emotional colour when it employs its imagination from different points of view simultaneously. In any event his modesty is deeply rooted in respect for both phenomena of the mind and the difficulty of gaining and transmitting knowledge of them, ' – phenomena whose existence I have only been able to indicate by descriptions of facts that bear less relationship to the object of our study than the lines of a monochrome print do to the colours of a painting in which colour is the all-important quality'.

We will have many opportunities in the course of our study of Bion's work to amplify this initial appraisal of the particular qualities of mind and character which he has brought to bear on the phenomena of the analytical consulting room, but it seems of special interest to gain some view of the pre-analytical Bion and of the equipment he brought into the field, to distinguish it from the techniques and modes of thought he developed from the special experience of psycho-analysis. So we may now turn our attention to modes of thought that are exhibited in 'Experiences', recognizing that these cannot sharply be distinguished from character and qualities of mind.

Early in the 'experiences' we meet a mode of thought which Bion, on the model of the use of a microscope, calls 'altered focus'. This is not to be confused with binocular vision, which seems to refer particularly to the points of view natural to the different mentalities involved in any situation. Altered focus would seem to imply that the instrument of observation, comparable to the microscope playing upon a thick section, is a variable model of the structure of the situation being observed. The example he gives involves two different models: in one there is a group of people meeting and interacting, from which group two members are absent; in the second model there is a group of people interacting, some of whom are present and two of whom are absent. These two foci seem to be able to throw light on one another if they are seen also to reveal systems of thought, feeling and behaviour that interact. This is a mode of thought because it is a device that can be used for enhancing observation and reflection, while the binocular vision is an expression of character in that it is the natural mode of experience of an individual who, by contact with different parts of his personality, is able to identify with different roles in human interaction and perception.

Another characteristic mode of thought for Bion is the framing of hypotheses as instruments of observation, to be tested for their utility in widening the field of scrutiny and thereby its phenomenological comprehensibility. This differs significantly from the use of the hypothesis in Baconian science as a framework for the construction of experiment and of eliciting proof or refutation. 'I shall postulate a group mentality as a pool to which the anonymous contributions are made and through which the impulses and desires implicit in these contributions are gratified ... I shall expect the group mentality to be distinguished by a uniformity that contrasted with the diversity of thought in the mentality of the individuals ... If experience shows that this hypothesis fulfils a useful function, further characteristics of the group mentality may be added from clinical observation'. In other words the utility of the hypothesis will not only be manifest by clarification of the phenomena it is meant to assist in observing, but will also lead to observations which will make possible the expansion and clarification of the hypothesis.

Very striking is Bion's use of negative evidence and his trust in it as a guideline to the formation of hypotheses. For instance: '... I shall assume nevertheless that unless a group actively disavows its leader it is, in fact, following him ... I dare say that it will be possible to base belief in the complicity of the group on something more convincing than negative evidence, but for the time being I regard negative evidence as good enough'. This is more reminiscent of Jesus than Pasteur, but this is not surprising when one remembers Bion's later repudiation of the medical model for psycho-analysis. The point about negative evidence in the field of psychological research would seem to rest upon the thesis that a function of which the mental apparatus is capable cannot be simply absent or suspended, as can physiological, including neuro-physiological, functions; only manipulation of its relationship to other functions, including the function of consciousness, can be effected, simulating absence.

Having briefly investigated Bion's qualities of mind as they are revealed in this book and then some of his characteristic modes of thought, it might be useful to turn to the type of experience to which his reader is exposed, for the stressfulness of reading his work is not to be minimized. It is easy, under this stress, to assume that his modes of thought are difficult or that his methods of exposition are obscure. But I think that neither of these is particularly true, and furthermore that, even if they are to some degree, they are not the source of the stress. It is to be found in identification processes, that is identification with members of the groups he is treating (and in later papers with his patients in analysis) and in failure of identification with

Bion himself. Let us examine these two in turn, for recognition of their role may both lessen the painfulness of the reading and thereby increase the ease of comprehension.

Identification with the members of the group is conducive to exasperation for a simple reason: that Bion's primary thesis in work with groups is that he is 'not concerned to give individual treatment in public, but to draw attention to the actual experiences of the group'. While this may have been difficult for the members to bear, it is doubly difficult for the reader who is alone with the book and not in a group atmosphere. The frustration becomes seasoned with humiliation when told that 'the exasperation, at first sight so reasonable, of the patient whose pressing personal difficulty is being ignored, is dictated, not so much by the frustration of a legitimate aim, as by the exposure of difficulties the patient had *not* come to discuss, and in particular his characteristics as a group member . . .'.

On the other hand identification with Bion as leader is constantly blocked by feelings of inferiority. For instance, '. . . if the psychiatrist can manage boldly to use the group instead of spending his time more or less unconsciously apologizing for its presence . . .' or '. . . it may be helpful for the psychiatrist who has a taste for trying my methods in a group to remember that few things in history have aroused a group's feelings more powerfully than controversy about the characteristics of the deity whose cult is at the time flourishing' (referring to investigation of the psychiatrist as leader and deity of the dependent basic assumption group). The certainty of not having the requisite 'boldness' and therefore of having no 'taste for trying (Dr Bion's) methods' crowds in upon the reader in a daunting way.

Perhaps the next useful step in our investigation of this early work of Bion, since our aim is to outline the special equipment he brought with him to psycho-analysis, might be to trace some of what might be called his postulates, for he does sometimes call them this himself. They are perhaps, in relation to the research being described, in the nature of preconceptions rather than realizations growing out of the experiences in groups. They throw a useful light on his approach to problems of the mind.

Perhaps the most important one is the idea of a 'proto-mental' level of function, an idea which appears in this book but not, to my recollection, anywhere explicitly in his later work. As always in reading Bion it is important to remember that, in proposing this postulate for understanding the way in which the emotions connected with the basic assumptions are bound inextricably to one another, he is not suggesting a theory or solution but only proposing a model because it might prove 'convenient' and 'useful', and furthermore that there is 'no harm' in so doing, provided it is not taken to describe a cause and effect series. The idea is that there is a proto-mental level at which physical and psychological events are not differentiated, where the emotional components are fused because incipient as observable psychological phenomena. This has a strong link to Freud's concept of primary narcissism as a level at which object relation and identification are undifferentiated and where the ego is still purely a body-ego. But it is also different, for Bion is approaching groups on the assumption that man is a herd animal and that his most primitive mentality is overwhelmingly concerned with his membership of groups. From that point of view individual relationships would derive their meaning from their origin in pairing groups.

This leads on to a second postulate, namely that the group phenomena he is studying are radically different from those of the family. This is fundamentally different from Freud's approach in 'Group Psychology' where he assumed that the family was the basic model and that the roles of individuals could be extrapolated for groups from those observed in family life. The liberating effect of Bion's postulate is the best evidence that it was a postulate indeed, rather than a realization, for it first of all clearly liberated Bion from having to play any of the roles that the group wished to impose upon him, whether under basic assumption or in the work group. This perhaps needs to be grasped in order for the reader to be freed from identification with the group members in their exasperation, and to grasp the magnitude of achievement it made possible. Of course having such a postulate may have armed Bion against the acceptance of roles imposed by the group but it is clear that long struggle was required to learn to implement it. The consequence was a field of study for group phenomena in every way comparable to the field of the transference in psycho-analysis, where participant-observer could employ the binocular vision of simultaneous inward and outward scrutiny.

Taken together these two postulates imply that man's primitive heritage makes it necessary for him to be a member of a group and that he has mental equipment for doing this of two different sorts, making possible his participation in two contrasting groupings: the basic assumption group (ba) and the work group (W) (at first called the 'sophisticated group'). Involvements in the ba group are managed at the proto-mental level, where emotional reactions are undifferentiated from physical ones and where impulses express themselves in directional tendencies (he calls it 'valency' and likens it to tropism) rather than in phantasy or planning. The capacity of ba states for instantaneous spread in the group is matched by their deeply unconscious position, making them far more easily evident to an observer than to the subjects themselves. In contrast, participation in the W group is managed by phantasy with easy access to consciousness; it is bound to reality and therefore to development through learning from experience. Despite its handicaps of cumbersome procedure and disunity in comparison with, and in conflict with, the tendency to basic assumption organization, 'it is the W group that triumphs in the long run'. A comforting message, despite lack of specificity as to the duration of this 'long run'!

In this scheme it would seem that individuality arises from experience of the work group, paleontologically speaking; that is, out of the emergence of the family from the matrix of the tribe. This is an important implication of Bion's point of view, but must be taken as part of the system of postulates that makes up the point of view or vertex from which he is approaching mental phenomena. He then uses it as one focus to juxtapose to the focus adopted, say, by Freud, in order to frame the hypotheses he wishes to use, and to test for usefulness, not for correctness. It should be kept in mind that Bion's conception of human science is phenomenological and, as will be clear in his later work, mystical. The widening of consciousness, and thus of observation and thought, is his aim, not proof and explanation.

The hypotheses which grow out of this postulate ground revolve about the nature of conflict in groups, that is between ba and W as well as among the three different ba groups, dependent (D), pairing (P) and fight-flight (F). The description of the uses of this hypothesis and the phenomena they reveal forms the body of 'Experiences in Groups' and need not be summarized here. What is needed instead, with a view to our study of Bion's later work, is to trace further the implications of this structure of hypothesis for a vertex on the individual mentality as it is studied in psycho-analysis. One implication is that the psycho-analytical method consists of two operations, one being the formation of a two-member W group for studying the phenomena of the other the baP (basic assumption pairing) of the transference. This baP has its origins in the child's experience of the family in the light of the Oedipus conflict, in which the pairing couple (primal scene and combined object) is the centre of interest. It stands in contrast with the child's experience of the family as W, a work-group of two parents met for the purpose of raising children, for instance.

A second implication would be that the study of the transference would involve noting the fluctuations from oedipus conflict (baP) to other ba groupings, baD (infantile dependence, splitting and idealization, narcissistic self-idealization, etc.) and baF (paranoid-schizoid position, delinquent narcissistic organization, delusion formation, etc.). This point of view could enrich the analyst's study of acting out and of the interaction between the analysis and other areas of the patient's (and analyst's) life. The notion that these ba functions can simmer on at a proto-mental level could add a new dimension to the analyst's scrutiny of dreams, one quite different from elucidation of unconscious (latent) meaning. It would add a new dimension to the concept of conflict. Where would one place it? Inter- or intra-systemic, for instance.

In closing this first chapter it is necessary to emphasize the chronology of our study. It will have been evident that thus far only the pre-view and the seven papers on 'experiences' have been discussed, as the aim was to draw a baseline of the pre-analytic Bion. It is true that he was already studying psychoanalysis at the time of the actual work of 'taking' the groups, but the conceptual framework and language are not strictly psycho-analytical. The 're-view', written several years later, will be left for consideration along with one of the early psychoanalytical papers republished in 'Second Thoughts'. In drawing this base-line, attention has been paid to a number of aspects: the qualities of mind and character, modes of thought, language usage, scientific method (and by implication, philosophy of science), literary style and its impact on the reader, structure of postulates and use of hypotheses. Very little attention has been paid to the actual theory of groups or therapeutic method with groups, as that will have been evident to the reader and is somewhat aside from the purpose of this book.

Chapter II   Re-view of Group Dynamics and The Imaginary Twin

In the first chapter an attempt was made to draw out the pre-psycho-analytic Bion by the use of the first two sections of 'Experiences in Groups', the clinical work for which probably extended from 1942 through 1950. Some evaluation of the special equipment he brought into the field of psycho-analysis was attempted, bearing on his character, his modes of thought, the background of his special humour, his philosophy of science, his use of language and his basic differentiation between individual and group mentality.

In the present chapter we are concerned to examine Bion's transition into the field of psycho-analysis, which occurred through his association with John Rickman and his training analysis with Melanie Klein. The review of his work on groups in the light of the work of Freud and Melanie Klein should show us something of the impact of psycho-analytical experience and thought on his previous ideas and attitudes. His first clinical paper in analysis, 'The Imaginary Twin' might be expected to show him working in the consulting room so that we can compare the man in these two therapeutic settings, group and individual. It is perhaps worthwhile to remember the historical setting of his work. For instance, Melanie Klein's great paper on projective identification and splitting processes ('Notes on Some Schizoid Mechanisms') had appeared in 1946 while the 1950s were characterized by the opening up of the phenomenon of the counter-transference for clinical use by such figures as Winnicott, Paula Heimann, Money-Kyrle. The severe disputes in the British Society over issues of theory and technique raised by Mrs Klein's work had settled down to a 'gentlemen's agreement' which held the society together and created a fairly electric atmosphere for research and discussion. Bion became Director of the Clinic a few years after qualification and stirred great interest by his papers on psychosis.

The first problem vis à vis the psycho-analytical community raised by his work with groups was that of the highly subjective nature of the observations, (p. 148), 'It can be justly argued that interpretations for which the strongest evidence lies, not in the observed facts in the group but in the subjective reactions of the analyst, are more likely to find their explanation in the psycho-pathology of the analyst than in the dynamics of the group. It is a just criticism, and one which will have to be met by years of careful work by more than one analyst, but for that very reason I shall leave it on one side . . .' But Bion is not content to forestall criticism, for he has a very positive and original contribution to make to the study of counter-transference and its relation to projective identification which is hidden here and not taken up elsewhere in the literature until the work of Racker in the 1960s, and Grinberg in the 1970s with his concept of projective counter-identification. Bion writes (p. 149), 'Now the experience of counter-transference appears to me to have quite a distinct quality that should enable the analyst to differentiate the occasion when he is the object of a projective identification from the occasion when he is not. The analyst feels he is being manipulated so as to be playing a part, no matter how difficult to recognize, in somebody else's phantasy – or he would do if it were not for what in recollection I can only call a temporary loss of insight, a sense of experiencing strong feelings and at the same time a belief that their existence is quite adequately justified by the objective situation . . .' These criteria for identifying an experience of being the object of a projective identification: namely a temporary loss of insight during an emotional experience whose quality seems unquestionably justified, followed by insight and the feeling of having been dominated by someone else's phantasy, make a satisfactory scientific instrument of what promised to be a technique for wholesale self-justification by analysts. The key is the experience of having been manipulated to play a role in someone else's phantasy, the realization of which is accompanied by anxiety and humiliation leading to retaliatory impulse.

By means of this conception Bion makes the link between his work with groups and with individuals quite compelling and gives substance to the hope of bringing a binocular vision to bear on mental functions. The basic technique of psycho-analysis of examining the transference from a position which is both inside and outside the relationship is made applicable to groups through this recognition of the possibility of losing and recovering insight. But it is not quite clear what position Bion adopts regarding the essential relationship of group mentality to individual mentality. In the earlier papers where the postulate of a proto-mental system was put forward as a tool for examining the observations it seemed likely that the two systems were quite separate but with a linkage. This linkage seemed to be forged in the unconscious at a juncture of narcissistic organization (though Bion does not directly suggest this) and the basic assumptions that are in abeyance at the moment and held at the proto-mental level. In this psycho-analytical re-view he brings the two together by way of the Oedipus conflict and the concepts of primitive splitting and identification processes at a part-object level, (p. 162), 'On the emotional plane, where basic assumptions are dominant, Oedipal figures . . . can be discerned in the material just as they are in a psycho-analysis. But they include one component of the Oedipus myth of which little has been said, and that is the sphinx'.

Here is an instance where one suspects that the special qualities, sphinx-like, of Bion have obtruded themselves on the material, but he insists that this is inevitable where the group includes anyone with a 'questioning attitude'. The fears thrown up by this attitude 'approximate . . . to very primitive phantasies about the contents of the mother's body' and sets in motion defences 'characteristic of the paranoid-schizoid position'. The pairing group is consequently seen as bound closely to the primal scene at a primitive level, the dependent group to the breast relationship as partial object, the fight-flight group to paranoid anxieties connected with splitting-and-idealization. Consequently a continuous spectrum of degree of disturbance now is seen to link the basic assumption group to the work group and 'the more stable the group, the more it corresponds to Freud's description of the group as a repetition of family group patterns and neurotic mechanisms'. This has the appearance of a climbdown from a more radical position. The emotional colouring of the basic assumption group is no longer a manifestation of valency but can be described with the words used for individual emotions, for 'there is much to suggest that these supposed "basic assumptions" cannot be regarded as distinct states of mind'; by which he means distinct from one another but also from the individual mentality, probably. Again the equivocation sounds rather like a climbdown in the face of the intimidating impact of the psycho-analytical basic assumption group.

If viewed in this way the brilliance of Bion's rapprochement to Freud's views is quite disturbing. His assimilation of the church, army and aristocracy to the dependent, fight-flight and pairing groups respectively leaves open the possibility of considering psycho-analysis, for example, a special instance of the pairing group and thus naturally preoccupied with sex. In this way group and individual mentality are brought absolutely together as merely 'special instances' of one another, (p. 169), 'The apparent difference between group psychology and individual psychology is an illusion produced by the fact that the group brings into prominence phenomena that appear alien to an observer unaccustomed to using the group'. That sounds a very sophisticated apologia and recantation. The impression is reinforced when Bion asserts, 'I have been forced to the conclusion that verbal exchange is a function of the work group' and that the basic assumption group communicated its valencies and generates its unanimity by 'debased' rather than 'primitive' methods, that is, its efforts lack symbol formation and are more in the nature of actions than communications. And here he brings in the myth of the Tower of Babel, which he will come back to twenty years on.

Bearing in mind the suggestion that the impact of psycho-analytical training upon the community concerned with this had an intimidating effect temporarily, we must turn to Bion's first clinical paper. From the outset the Bionic atmosphere is in evidence in the terse description of selected facts and pithy observations, with a clear evidence of patiently waiting for phenomena to make their impact upon the analyst. And when they do, the binocular vision is immediately evidenced, 'as if two quite separate scansions of his material were possible'. Also Bion's feeling for language is searching out the ambiguities, paradoxes and equivocations with an acuteness very reminiscent of Freud. But listen to him speak to the patient who has just suggested that the analysis is fruitless: 'I replied that although estimations of progress in analysis were difficult to make there was no reason why we should not accept his evaluation as correct'. He goes on to examine the meaning of 'treatment' and its implications, one of which being

286

'that the alleviation of symptoms was sometimes achieved by factors incidental to analysis; for example the sense of security obtained from feeling there was someone to go to'. The impressive aspect is the representation of the 'questioning attitude' which does not shy from serious consideration of un-pleasant possibilities threatening the very foundation of the undertaking. But note also that Bion is willing to consider that the 'security obtained from feeling there was someone to go to' was 'incidental to analysis'.

This is worth noting because it is linked to the report of an incident in the analysis which shows that his view of the pro-cedure was very closely bound to the concept of the 'mutative interpretation' (Strachey) and Mrs Klein's trust in 'correct' interpretation. The way in which Bion has construed the patient's association about the complaining woman (S.T. – p. 7), which followed the silence attendant to his statement about factors 'incidental', is impressive as a possibility. But he may also have felt himself 'packed off' by Bion and experienced the rhythm of 'association-interpretation-association' as inter-pretation-association-interpretation: that is, being held under Bion's control and packed off with soporific interpretations of a so-called tramline sort, as suggested by statements such as: 'There was plenty of Oedipal material, produced on a most superficial level, which I duly interpreted'. Duly and dully.

This suggests that Bion was experiencing a sort of psycho-analytical latency period in which dutifulness was indeed dull-ing his creativity – and perhaps his critical judgment. It strikes one as strange to hear him say such vague catechistic statements as, 'When I had recovered from my surprise, I remembered that we had often had reason to suppose that he felt he had a poisonous family inside him but that was the first occasion on which I had had such a dramatic exhibition of himself in the act of introjecting objects'. It is puzzling to find no 'second thoughts' about this section (14) in the commentary of twenty years later.

The dream which followed the session in which the 'twin' was first interpreted confirms that Bion was felt to have blocked the patient's egress from analysis in a cleverly spiteful way but does not cover the earlier operation in which the patient in his car 'kept abreast' of the other car, 'conforming to its movements', which might suggest, for instance, that, when the breast-feed stopped, the nipple became split off and turned into a persecutor, perhaps indistinguishable from a bad part of the self. The point is not to plead that this would improve Bion's interpretation but to remove the dazzle from his work, induced by his use of language, so as to notice the drop in his creativity of thought that this paper represents. It is a paper devoted to the already familiar subject of split-off-bad-parts and is a confirmation of Mrs Klein's findings dressed up in Bion's unique style.

Similarly in the 'curled up or rigid' material (p. 10), Bion displays a typical indifference to the critical aspects of the patient's material (for instance that the big bill of the dream might refer to his making such long and prolix interpretations), typical that is of psycho-analytical papers and so uncharacteristic of Bion himself. But in the midst of this disappointing paper in which a preconceived theoretical framework is imposed on rather recalcitrant material, that is, the central theme of the imaginary twin, sparkling bits of material appear giving evidence of Bion's restiveness under the restraint of psycho-analytical theory (much like his patient's feeling about being curled up and in danger of the cramp).

It seems fairly clear from most of the paper that Bion had been learning to practice analysis properly – listening, observing, interpreting. But it is also clear that his interpretations in analysis now, unlike his work with the groups, were explanatory rather than descriptive. 'The fear of his aggression, closely linked in his mind with faeces, caused him to retreat to a position in which he felt constrained and confined and thus secure from . . . etc.'. It is only quietly, as if on tiptoe, that the uniqueness of his approach begins to assert itself. It can be seen in an operation that is characteristic of his work but will not be made explicit for another twenty years. This is his capacity to observe the transactions in the consulting room as if they were all a dream and to listen to a patient's account of his life in the outside world as if it were the account of a dream.

The material that demonstrates this relates to what he calls 'the manner in which the patient was able to bring his material into consciousness'. Bion clearly treats the patient's reports 'in terms of play therapy with a child', that is as phantasy or dream-equivalent. The result is a fascinating account of the patient's attempts at reality testing by means of unisensual scrutiny, first with the eyes, then the nose, the ears, the mouth, etc., over which series the intellect is then to preside and judge. At this point Bion is inclined to consider this a tenable method, but later in his work ('Learning from Experience' – 1963) he will recognize the fallibility of the serial testing in comparison with what he will puckishly call 'common sense'.

Finally, a point about the 'two speculations' (p. 20), which grow out of this thesis of the imaginary twin. The first has to do with the connection between the personification of splits in the personality and symbol formation, suggesting a 'capacity' that is variable from person to person and from time to time. Both of these items, the personification, and the role of symbol formation, are very closely bound to Mrs Klein's work, and are not the most creative aspects of it. This is, or can easily be taken for, apostolic behaviour.

The second speculation about the role of vision in the material of the three patients terminates weakly. 'For myself, I have found it impossible to interpret the material presented to me by these patients as a manifestation of purely psychological development divorced from any concurrent physical development. I have wondered whether the psychological development was bound up with the development of ocular control in the same way that problems of development linked with oral aggression co-exist with the eruption of teeth'. What a far cry from the boldness with which he could postulate a proto-mental system!

In summary then, a fairly unmistakeable impression results from taking these two papers, the Re-view and Imaginary Twin, together; namely, that psycho-analytical training has had an oppressive effect upon Bion. It is perhaps one of the great limitations of this sort of training that the personal analysis takes so long to 'recover from', to use a phrase Bion employed in 1976 in his lecture at the Tavistock Centre. In this regard one should note that all Bion's major publications came after the death of Mrs Klein in 1960.

It is perhaps difficult for people unaquainted with the use of the concepts of splitting and projective identification, as well as for those who have become perhaps a little blasé about them, to realize the electrifying impact of Mrs Klein's 1946 paper, 'Notes on Some Schizoid Mechanisms', upon the analysts who were working closely with her. With the notable exception of Bion's later work it could be said that the history of the next thirty years of research could be written in terms of the phenomenology and implications of these two seminal concepts.

Thus in approaching the papers written by Bion in the years 1953 to 1958 one immediately is struck by this aspect of the content in its application to the phenomena of the psychotic, and especially the schizophrenic patient. The 1950s were in a sense the heyday of psycho-analytical interest in the psychoses and the literature swells with contributions to their metapsychology and reports of successful treatment by psychological methods. In the latter category, especially the work done in America at that time by people like Frieda Fromm Reichmann, John Rosen, Milton Wexler; or in France by Mme Sechehaye, turned largely upon the modification of the psycho-analytical method to the treatment of these disorders. While this was intended to be an adaptation in the technical sense, by which means the analytical method had been made suitable to the treatment of children by Mrs Klein and Miss Freud, for instance, a great deal of methodological confusion reigned. It was not perhaps realized that, at least as far as Melanie Klein's adaptation of the method was concerned, the intention had been to alter nothing in the method, but to facilitate the means of communication available to the patient. This was not so true of Miss Freud's early work, largely on the basis of an assumption that the child would not be able to form a transference in the same sense as the adult patient. That assumption was based in turn upon a view of the transference that stressed its 'transfer' from the past under the sway of the repetition compulsion rather than viewing it as an externalization of internal object relations under the pressure of the immediate operation of impulse and anxiety.

The confusion of method that resulted from the gross modifications of the setting: in the behaviour of the analyst, the substitution of action for verbal interpretation (non-verbal interpretation), rendered results incomparable and generated a fragmentation of the psycho-analytical community which was trying to adapt the method for use in mental hospitals as well as to widen the scope for out-patient treatment. Added to this was another dimension of confusion based upon the use of a nosology borrowed from descriptive psychiatry which was far too gross to differentiate categories of illness relevant to a method based on meta-psychology. Accordingly the term schizophrenia, for instance, was so variously used in clinical reports that evaluation of the utility of technical modifications became virtually impossible.

Bion, along with other people such as Rosenfeld and Segal who were working with psychotics at that time, chose to follow the technical tradition of Mrs Klein in adapting the method by altering nothing but the means of communication available to the patient, and this they did in fact by widening the scope of their powers of observation. Naturally this took the form of paying greater attention, as in child analysis, to the actions of the patient in the consulting room. But it also extended to a new area of phenomenology, the uses of language. Here psychoanalysts such as Bion, who had had a classical as well as medical education, were in a position to profit from the great developments in semantics, linguistics, communication theory and mathematics that had commenced in the 1920s (Russell and Whitehead, the Vienna Circle, the later Wittgenstein, etc). This in turn focussed attention on problems of symbol formation, notational systems, modes of thought, uses of ambiguity, the meaning of silences, the role of the musical versus the lexical level in communication, etc.

In this historical context, inside and outside psycho-analysis, the papers of the 1953-58 period (a meagre production and in many ways repetitive) are significant in two directions which may be most profitably and lucidly discussed separately; the direction of research into the schizoid mechanisms and the phenomenology of the paranoid-schizoid and depressive positions in the psychoses, and, secondly, the application to the psycho-analytical method of concepts borrowed from philosophy, mathematics and linguistics, enhancing both the scope of observation and the complexity of thought applied to them, both in and outside the consulting room. Bion the apostle and Bion the messiah, taking these terms as applicable to daily life in no exotic sense.

One must also, therefore, in discussing the apostolic aspect of these papers, remember where the development of Mrs Klein's thought had reached at this time. The description of schizoid mechanisms came as an investigation of the details of the paranoid-schizoid position at a time when she was still considering these two positions as the fixation points respectively for schizophrenia and manic-depressive psychosis. They occurred in the baby's development in the first year of life characteristically and meant that the infant suffered from states of mind that were in all their essentials equivalent to the adult psychoses, taken as regressive states in Freud's sense. Although she denied that this was tantamount to saying that babies are psychotic, it is difficult to see how this implication could be escaped. Only gradually did this view of paranoid-schizoid and depressive position as developmental phases give way to their application as economic principles, finally tersely summarized by Bion himself as Ps↔D.

Therefore the view or model of schizophrenia that Bion is using in these papers in not really consonant with Freud's construction in the Schreber Case, of a quiet 'world-destruction' phase of the disease followed by the noisy 'recovery' phase of delusional system formation in which the 'world' (not quite clearly formalized as 'inner world') was reconstituted along delusional lines 'not so grand but at least one in which he could live'. Bion is taking schizophrenia to be a severe consequence of the employment of projective identification and splitting of ego and objects where the attacks, under the influence of excesses of destructive impulse (perhaps connected with jealousy and envy), produce fragmentation of the personality, carrying to destruction with it the capacity for verbal thought. The consequence is that the patient in Bion's view finds himself imprisoned, not in a delusional system, but in 'a prison which seems sometimes to be me (Bion), sometimes psycho-analysis and sometimes his state of mind which is a constant struggle with his internal objects' (p. 27).

One effect is that Bion's approach is mechanistically oriented,

292

but of course not in a mechanical cause-and-effect way but a phenomenological one. Nonetheless it must be recognized that the apostolic aspect of these papers leaves much to be desired regarding exploration of the meaning of the patient's experience in favour of exploring the mechanisms that produce the clinical phenomena. This of course is very far from the messianic Bion of later work. However, putting aside this disappointment, one can see the brilliance with which the conceptual tool of 'schizoid mechanisms' is employed by him to dissect out the phenomena. It should be noted that Bion, like Segal in her paper on 'Depression in a Schizophrenic', was keen to flesh out the skeletal concepts by demonstrating how they operate in life situations, especially in the consulting room. He was not, like most workers, content to take the description of 'omnipotent phantasy' applied to splitting or projective identification as meaning that these operations occurred merely in phantasy. In fact, of course, Mrs Klein's first description of projective identification envisioned it as operative with external rather than internal objects, its latter employment only being made clear some twenty years later, as in my study of anal masturbation. If it operated with external objects, serious questions arose regarding the means by which it was brought about, the actual impact on other people, including the analyst, and the ultimate fate of split-off and projected parts of the personality.

To implement this intention Bion has made an intensive use of the counter-transference, undoubtedly using the technique that he outlined in the re-view for the recognition of the operation by the patient of the mechanism of projective identification with, or really *into*, the analyst. But the same is true of the operation of splitting processes. He has used the counter-transference and close scrutiny of the *structure* as well as the emotive and phantasy content of his own state of mind in response to the patient's productions, for recognition of the operation of the mechanism of splitting the object, (p. 25), 'The patient comes into the room, shakes me warmly by the hand, and looking piercingly into my eyes says, "I think the sessions are not for a long while but stop me ever going out". I know from previous experience that this patient has a grievance that the sessions are too few and that they interfere with his free time. He intended to split me by making me give two opposite interpretations at once and this was shown by his next association when he said, "How does the lift know what to do when I press two buttons at once".'

This compelling example of his clinical method and mode of thought illustrates the surging creativity that Bion was trying to curb from its tendency to break out of the existing structure of psycho-analytical theory and model of the mind. But the result is a stretching of concepts to the breaking point, with attendant confusion of exposition. The existing concepts will not cover the bizarre phenomena he is trying to investigate. Thus his loyalty to Freud's position about the two principles of mental functioning and the interaction of pleasure and reality prin-ciples requires an attitude toward verbal thought which views it as being *the* essential instrument, the 'apparatus of awareness that Freud described as being called into activity by the demands of the reality principle' (p. 38), i.e. that consciousness was dependent upon the transformation of 'thing-representations' into 'word-representations'. Ten years later Bion will propose a more adequate tool, the concept of alpha-function. But at this time this idea of the dependence of consciousness on verbal thought gives to the schizophrenic patient's attack on his own capacity for such function a central position in the mechanics of the pathology and elbows unconscious phantasy out of the picture. The result is that splitting processes and projective identification are seen to operate on the words, as in the example of the patient splitting the word 'penis' first into its syllables and then into its component letters (p. 28), in a way that is indistinguishable from splitting of the ego that contains these functions.

The result is great confusion when Bion tries to investigate the 'bizarre objects' with which the schizophrenic's world abounds. The minute fragmentation of the apparatus of aware-ness and the subsequent projective identificatory expulsion of them into objects in the outside world leads at one place to their 'penetrating, or encysting, the object' and in another to their 'engulfing' the object which is then seen as if to 'swell up, so to speak, and suffuses and controls the piece of personality that engulfs it: to that extent the particle of the personality has become a thing' (p. 48), rather than the thing assuming qualities or attributes characteristic of a part of the personality. Similarly re-entry of these expelled fragments has to be explained as 'projective identification reversed'. This is meant to be different from introjection or re-introjection, but that concept too has already been stretched to the breaking point by being equated with perception, as in the description of 'the smooth introjection and assimilation of sense impressions' (p. 41). The use of these inadequate conceptual tools results in a poetry that is at once evocative and incomprehensible. For instance, when describing the state of mind in which the schizophrenic is imprisoned by the 'planetary movement' and 'menacing presence of the expelled fragments', now containing bits of objects to become 'bizarre objects', Bion writes (p. 39), 'In the patient's phantasy the expelled particles of the ego lead to an independent and uncontrolled existence outside the personality, but either containing or contained by external objects, where they exercise their function as if the ordeal to which they had been subjected has served only to increase their number and to provoke their hostility to the psyche that ejected them'.

Now clearly this way of speaking, if it is to be taken as a conceptualization rather than a poetic metaphor, is in no way compatible with Freud's model of the mind and his view of ego-functions, nor is this idea that verbal thoughts and the words they involve can be treated as things, equivalent to pieces of the personality, compatible with the view that words are ordinarily 'smoothly introjected' since introjection is a term referrable to the taking of objects into the mind. Similarly 'having thus rid himself of the apparatus of conscious awareness of internal and external reality' has not sufficient explanatory power, you might say, to account for a phenomenon such as when 'the patient achieves a state which is felt to be neither alive nor dead'. Compare it with Freud's description of Schreber's delusional system in order to grasp its conceptual pallor.

We need not labour this image of Bion's adolescent-like surge of growth bursting out of its latency-period Freudian-Kleinian clothing. But before turning to take stock of the burgeoning originality that is half stifled in these papers it is necessary to note certain rather idiosyncratic features which can be very confusing to the reader. In the first place Bion is using 'psychotic' in his differentiation from 'non-psychotic' as if it were synonymous with 'schizophrenic'. This is perhaps the consequence of his allegiance to Mrs Klein's view of the paranoid-schizoid position as the fixation point for schizophrenia. As in 'The Imaginary Twin' he is intent on tracing the significance of splitting processes as a concept for understanding personality structure and its phenomenology, a contribution to the development of a psycho-analytical nosology of mental disorders. The need for this was felt keenly by everyone working with psychotic patients and a notable start in this direction had already been made by Edward Glover in his well-known paper in the Journal of Mental Science. But Bion's use of 'psychotic part of the personality' in this way seems clearly, in its reference to splitting processes, i.e. 'part of the personality', to suggest that every psychotic part is schizophrenic. Yet the paper itself is a major contribution to establish the complexity of the disease. Mrs Klein could never have meant to include such bizarre processes as Bion is describing as part of the paranoid-schizoid position when she was considering it as a normal developmental phase of infancy and early childhood.

On the other hand it is not clear whether Bion thinks that this part of the personality is ubiquitous or only present in the person who actually presents a schizophrenic disorder. The list of predisposing personality factors: preponderance of destructive impulses, hatred of reality, unremitting dread of annihilation and premature object relations, makes it sound a quite selective disorder. This brings into view the second idiosyncratic element, namely Bion's use of the term 'reality' as in 'hatred of reality' to mean both internal as well as external reality. By this he seems to imply that there is something left over which is not hated, but one can find no reference to it, except perhaps implied in the idea that the schizophrenic exists in a state of mind that is neither alive nor dead. This is perhaps as close as he comes to indicating the delusional system as an alternative to external and psychic reality. But if the schizophrenic perhaps loves his delusional system or his 'imprisonment in a state of mind', which part of the personality wishes to escape from it? Clearly all these questions are too difficult for the conceptual framework to which Bion is being so loyal and the result is powerful descriptive poetry and conceptual confusion.

With this image of Bion's position in mind we can now turn to examine the content of his bursting originality, which finds its expression most clearly in the paper on hallucination. This paper is heavily dependent on the previous one for its conceptual framework, but the difficulty is that this framework has been worked out by an attempted compromise between Freud's concept of thinking and Mrs Klein's of unconscious phantasy. Because Bion wishes to describe and investigate phenomena which seem to imply a destruction of the patient's capacity for thought and his habitation of a world that is neither internal nor external reality, he wishes to be able to describe attacks which damage the very functions which make thought possible. This cannot be managed by the use of splitting processes and projective identification operative in an omnipotent way in relation to unconscious phantasy in Mrs. Klein's sense because she has never envisioned these functions as finding discreet representation in phantasy. On the other hand Freud had no concrete conception of psychic reality that could have made use of such an idea as attack on functions, not even as late as his paper on 'Splitting of the Ego in the Service of Defence' where he was concerned to show how illness and health can coexist in the personality.

The result is a plea for the use of 'ideographs' and 'attacks on links' as conceptual tools which is neither Kleinian nor Freudian. He will have to develop his own theory of thinking before ideas such as 'attacks on linking', extensions of the primal scene to include the 'conjunction of objects' in symbol formation or 'verbal intercourse' can become comprehensible as theory. But this is the area into which his originality in observation and thought is breaking; an area untouched by Mrs Klein and unimplemented in clinical activity by the theoretician in Freud. Just why it was that Freud paid so little attention to the implications in this direction in Schreber's memoirs is quite as mysterious as Bion's lack of reference to the same case.

It is also clear that this effort toward a theory of thinking is accompanied by dissatisfaction with the Freudian evaluation of dreams, both as regards their significance for mental life and their structure. Bion is on firmer ground than Freud in being able to consider dreams as an aspect of psychic reality, so that his grappling with the problem of the loss of reality in the schizophrenic is far less confused than Freud's attempt to differentiate between neurosis and psychosis on the basis of libido theory and withdrawal of cathexis. Bion can see that a theory of narcissism based on libido distribution or even different types of libido, or even on the later dual instinct theory will not cover. The patients he is investigating are deeply concerned with objects, but with bizarre ones whose nature he tries to describe. Conceptual attempts such as 'the unconscious would seem to be replaced by the world of dream furniture' is incomprehensible as he cannot yet give us any idea of that 'furniture', having indicated only what it isn't, (p. 40), 'The patient now moves not in a world of dreams, but in a world of objects which are ordinarily the furniture of dreams'. This 'ordinarily' makes it sound a universal phenomenon of dreaming but we cannot discern what it is.

The paper on hallucination is an attempt to bring these two concepts of dream and hallucination, and at one point also the concept of delusion, into conjunction with one another, (p. 78), 'It is a short step from what I have already said about hallucinations to suppose that when a psychotic patient speaks of having a dream, he thinks that his perceptual apparatus is engaged in expelling something and that the dream is an evacuation from his mind strictly analogous to an evacuation from his bowels'. In other words, he cannot bring together ordinary dreaming and hallucination because he cannot feel convinced that the dream of the psychotic is ordinary. The central idea of the paper that the process of hallucination is dependent on the use of the sense organs for the expulsion of perceived (introjected?) objects is in itself highly original. But as an idea it is probably not really new. What is new is Bion's capacity for observation of hallucinations as phenomena of the consulting room, (p. 67), 'When the patient glanced at me he was taking a part of me into him. It was taken into his eyes, as I later interpreted his thought to him, as if his eyes could suck something out of me. This was then removed from me, before I sat down, and expelled, again through the eyes, so that it was deposited in the right hand corner of the room where he could keep it under observation while he was lying on the couch'.

The immense concentration which can discern small quiverings, read the meaning in a glance, note the equivocal use of language and make links with what the patient had said 'six months ago' is fairly staggering to anyone acquainted with the rigours of analytical work. This power of observation, outward and inward, is the fountainhead of Bion's originality, struggling at this time to find a conceptual framework for assembling meaningfully the masses of new observations. His loyalty to existing theory constricts him and the reader is of course deeply disappointed to find such highly novel phenomena squeezed into the constricting formulations at the end of the paper (pp. 82-85). But the clinical material is scintillating! It reveals in action the opening up of new territories of phenomenology in the consulting room which, although they seem to refer at this time to schizophrenic patients, will inevitably find representations, as yet unnoticed, in the analysis of patients of every degree of disturbance, even the 'healthy' candidate.

Chapter IV   Approach to a Theory of
                  Thinking

The historical approach to Bion's work which we are following
seems to reveal something of a latency period in his creativity
contemporary with his apprenticeship in psycho-analysis proper,
standing between the brilliance of his work with groups and the
full-blown emergence of his thought in the books commencing
with 'Learning from Experience'. This period of re-orientation
was followed by the period of the papers on schizophrenia which
reveal him more fully than in any other of his writings deploying
his extraordinary capacity for concentration and observation.
The result was his uncovering a plethora of phenomena as yet
unnoticed in the consulting room, at first with frankly psychotic
patients and later with the 'psychotic part of the personality'
of less ill people. The consequence was a kind of adolescence
of reborn creativity in which his expanding thought was struggling to stay within the bounds of existing concept, both Freud's
model of thinking and Mrs Klein's model of the structure of the
personality in conflict. The areas of incompatibility of the two
and their fundamental inadequacy to cover the phenomena
with which he was dealing was revealed in the manner in which
concepts such as primal scene, splitting of the ego, projective
identification and verbal thought were stretched to the breaking
point.

The three papers that followed in the years straddling Mrs
Klein's death in 1960 reveal the germs of the new theory. These
three, 'On Arrogance', 'Attacks on Linking' and 'A Theory of
Thinking' have to be read against a background of the clinical
data of the earlier four in order to gain any credibility, for, in
themselves, very little description of the analytical situation is
contained to help the reader make connections with his own
experience in the consulting room. In addition the idiosyncratic
features of Bion's writings are often rather exasperating: for
example a section headed 'Curiosity, Arrogance and Stupidity'
in which these three terms find virtually no use whatever. This
stylistic aspect of Bion's writing is one which will increase rather
than diminish as he goes along in the following fifteen years,
making heavier and heavier demands upon the reader for an

300

intimate knowledge of his prior works as well as an ever greater capacity to follow the high level of abstraction at which he eventually moves.

For instance, the six examples that he cites in the paper 'Attacks on Linking' reveal the analytical situation in such a transcendental half-light that they seem almost a cursory obeisance to the usual technique of analytical exposition and fail to clarify the discussion following. This brings from Bion an unusual outburst of Freud-like defiant apologia, (p. 104), 'To some this reconstruction will appear to be unduly fanciful; to me it does not seem forced and is the reply to any who may object that too much stress is placed on the transference to the exclusion of a proper elucidation of early memories'. This seems rather disingenuous to a reader who has been struggling to understand what he is describing when the difficulty is not the failure of 'elucidation of early memories' but rather that the 'stress – placed on the transference' is based to such a high degree on the ephemeral and 'inchoate' – and thereby indescribable – aspects of Bion's counter-transference. Probably most people who have been deeply influenced in their clinical practice by Bion's work have had the same experience, of initial irritation and suspicion followed by a long period during which they have only gradually discovered the evidence of his impact on their own observations and thought. Perhaps the time will come when such an initial reaction of exasperation will seem as strange to the future reader as most people feel when informed that the first playing of a certain Beethoven quartet left the audience shocked and hostile. Certainly, for instance, the reading of the paper 'On Arrogance' at the Paris congress struck many people as a shocking display of the very 'hubris' Bion was describing.

In approaching a critique of these three papers it will probably be more satisfying if we follow a sequence dictated by the internal logic of psycho-analytical theory rather than taking the papers chronologically. It is necessary to try to elucidate the moves that Bion is making to free himself from strictures on his thought. The most germinal of these is perhaps his expansion of the concept of 'part-object' beyond the bounds that could have been meant by Freud and Abraham, and used by Melanie Klein, in a concrete way, in her pursuit of the content of 'unconscious phantasy' as the premier material of the analytical situation. Bion writes (p. 102), 'The conception of the part-object as analogous to an anatomical structure, encouraged by the patient's employment of concrete images as units of thought, is misleading because the part-object relationship is not with the anatomical structures only but with function, not with anatomy but with physiology, not with the breast but with feeding, poisoning, loving, hating'.

Such an attitude seems utterly reasonable and interesting, but it is going to require an apparatus of representation quite different from that of the predominantly visual unconscious phantasy, so akin to dreaming in its composition. Bion's move to solve this problem seems to be a new concept using a deceptively old and simple word, 'link'. This is to be the unit which will be attacked or established. So the problem is moved on, so to speak, to the difficulty of discovering how the links are themselves represented. We are wondering if these links are also to be taken as the 'dream furniture' which was suggested as something different from the dream or dream-world, (p. 102), 'I employ the term "link" because I wish to discuss the patient's relationship with a function rather than with the object that subserves the function; my concern is not only with the breast, or penis, or verbal thought, but with their function of providing the link between two objects'. We are none the wiser after this tautological statement, but rather puzzled that 'verbal thought' can be placed on the same level of conceptual abstraction as 'breast' or 'penis'.

Some clarification comes when we remember that Bion is also extending Freud's concept of the Oedipus conflict by pointing to the importance of the sphinx in the myth and suggesting that beneath the problem of incest is that of 'hubris', taken as meaning the insolent pride that is determined to discover the truth at all cost. By this extension Bion is bringing together an important gap between the thought of Freud and Mrs Klein, namely the importance of infantile curiosity, or the 'epistemophilic instinct', as she liked to call it, in the child's development. But he is also modifying her concept, which viewed curiosity as primarily directed toward the contents of the inside of the mother's body out of sadism (later specified as envy) and consequent greed, modified in the depressive position by concern about the safety of the good object. Nowhere does she, any more than Freud, despite calling it an instinct, acknowledge the thirst for knowledge as a motive in itself, seeking food for the mind. Bion comes closer to this when he speaks of 'the impulse of curiosity on which all learning depends' (p. 108).

But nonetheless Bion is able to point to a very interesting aspect of the problem of learning, the ability to ask 'why' something is taking place, either in the object, the relationship or the state of mind, and not merely 'what' it is, (p. 102), This he identifies with questions of causality, by which, as already mentioned, he does not mean mechanical determination but phenomenological relatedness. In this sense he is thinking of mental phenomena in a way quite different from Freud's idea of 'overdetermination', which simply hedged the question of casuality by multiplication of the factors into a field theory.

By this move of including the connection between baby and breast as a 'link' analogous to that between penis and vagina in the genital oedipus conflict he has at least given a location to the prototype of what he means by link and filled it with a function at a mental level, 'learning'. But again it is stretching Mrs Klein's concept of the function of the breast relationship beyond its bounds, for in her view the functions of the breast as the prototype 'good object' were limited to its protection of the infant from the excesses of persecutory anxiety engendered by the death instinct (diminished by splitting-and-idealization) which were the major threat to its achievement of integration in the depressive position.

One could therefore say that Bion has evaded, at this point, the problem of representation of linking in favour of citing the infant-breast relationship as its prototype and giving it some specific function, learning, that has a promise of including the area of 'verbal thought' by embracing 'all the perceptual apparatus including the embryonic thought which forms a link between sense impressions and consciousness' (p. 107). Here is the task which he sets himself and will try to acquit in the years to follow; the exposition and elucidation of 'embryonic thought which forms a link between sense impressions and consciousness'.

At this point he is able only to establish that thought has some connection with the developmental process and the means of communication between mother and child. Falling back on Freud's concept of introjection, the mechanics of which have always remained mysterious and virtually unexplored, and the extended concept of projective identification as described by Melanie Klein, he is at least able to investigate the failure of learning pursuant to the 'excessive' use of this latter mechanism. Unlike Mrs Klein he is not content with this quantitative statement but explores the emotive content and motivation for its employment, the 'hatred of the emotions' from which it is 'a short step to hatred of life itself' (p. 107). Here he must fall back also on the predisposing factors, in particular the excesses of death instinct, involved in the formation of the psychotic part of the personality, even though he makes real headway in defining the nature of the environmental failure, namely the failure of the mother to be able to receive and modify the infant's projection of those parts of its personality which are at the moment suffused with the fear that it is dying. Since he is still considering the paranoid-schizoid position as a 'phase of development', it is not clear when he speaks of the 'psychotic infant' whether he means to refer to the states of mind characterized by the formation of bizarre objects and their projection and re-introjection to form the 'persecutory superego' as a ubiquitous one or present only in those infants where the environmental failure is compounded by an unfortunate predisposition of temperament.

This then is the distance Bion has come in the first two papers in both locating and trying to solve the conceptual limitations of existing theory as tools for exploring the phenomena thrown up in the consulting room by the 'psychotic part of the personality'. He is viewing the whole thing as a 'disaster' which may be uncovered in the course of an analysis, a disastrous failure, that is, in the early development of the capacity for 'embryonic thought'. Out of this failure, he suggests, there arises fragmentary splitting of ego and objects and 'excessive' use of projective identification that forms a world of 'dream furniture' composed of bizarre objects and a persecutory superego which, together with the impaired capacity for thought itself, comprises the essential phenomenology of the schizophrenic disorder or of the 'psychotic part of the personality'.

In this chapter it does not seem useful to take up fully the content of the paper 'A Theory of Thinking' but only to view it as a preliminary statement to 'Learning from Experience'. We can take stock of it to see the new moves that he is making in order to try to grapple with the problem he has recognized inherent in the phenomena he has observed. His most important move is to 'restrict' the meaning of 'consciousness' from its phenomenological sense to an operational one, following Freud's early description of it in the VIIth Chapter of the 'Traumdeutung' as a 'sense organ for the perception of psychic qualities'. This is a Platonic view of knowledge. Whether it is to prove compatible with the more Aristotelean view of knowledge as a mating of internal expectations (Bion's pre-conceptions) with external facts (his realizations) to form conceptions is a question I am not qualified to answer. But certainly it is congruent with Bion's flexible approach to sense organs and their functions as described in the paper on hallucination.

By viewing consciousness as essentially turned inward upon the self, he can then formulate the infant's mental helplessness and dependence on the mother (later on the internalized breast and mother) as primary for thinking and not merely secondary to its need for modulation of its fear of dying. This service to the infant he will call 'alpha-function' to indicate its mysteriousness. This apparatus is to be viewed as creating the elements, thoughts, which are necessary for manipulation in a process to be called 'thinking'. This is the second move, the reversal of the ordinary assumption that thoughts are the product of thinking. He is going to view them as the building blocks for constructions of thinking that will eventuate in concepts.

The third move is to bring into play concepts of omnipotence and omniscience in a meaningful, not merely a quantitative way, for he is going to view them not merely as hypertrophied functions but as qualitatively different from reason, (p. 114), 'If tolerance to frustration is not so great as to activate the mechanism of evasion and yet is too great to bear dominance of the reality principle, the personality develops omnipotence as a substitute for the mating of the pre-conception, or conception, with the negative realization' (frustration). 'This involves the assumption of omniscience as a substitute for learning from experience by aid of thoughts and thinking. There is therefore no psychic activity to discriminate between true and

305

false'. Instead there takes place a 'dictatorial affirmation that one thing is morally right and the other wrong'. We are perhaps left unclear as to whom the dictator is dictating, but the differentiation between science and morality is clear. Just how this relates to the whole area of values introduced by Mrs Klein into psycho-analysis with the concepts of paranoid-schizoid and depressive position must remain unanswered for the moment.

The final move attempts to grapple with the question 'why' which we all, as non-psychotic personalities, are supposed to be able to ask. Why is an apparatus for thinking necessary in the first place? Bion of course will tolerate no tautological or teleological argument. Instead he stuns us with, 'If the conjoined data harmonize, a sense of truth is experienced. The failure to bring about this conjunction of sense data induces a mental state of debility in the patient as if starvation of truth was somehow analogous to alimentary starvation', (p. 119). He means what he says apparently, that the mental apparatus is constructed on the model of the digestive system.

We are startled also to realize that we have come full circle (by the end of the third paper) from where we had started with the first. There we learned that Oedipus' crime was his insolent pride in being determined to know the truth at all costs. Now we learn that lack of truth-function causes a debility of mental starvation. The suspicion we must entertain and hold for the future is that the differentiating features lie somewhere in the realm of 'insolent pride' and 'dictatorial assertion'. But what this means in terms of a formalized theory of mental structure and function is difficult to see.

Chapter V   Alpha-Function and Beta-Elements

In the previous chapter we examined the approach to a theory of thinking that had been forced upon Bion from two directions, one coming from the torrent of new phenomena that he was observing in his application of the strict psycho-analytical method to the treatment of schizophrenic patients and the other coming from the manifest inadequacy of existing theory to cover these phenomena. By 'cover' it is not meant to convey 'explain' as much as 'organize' for the purpose of coherent description. As Bion says in 'Learning from Experience', (p. 14), 'It appears that our rudimentary equipment for "thinking" thoughts is adequate when the problems are associated with the inanimate, but not when the object for investigation is the phenomenon of life itself. Confronted with the complexities of the human mind, the analyst must be circumspect in following even accepted scientific method; its weakness may be closer to the weakness of psychotic thinking than superficial scrutiny would admit'. This is very reminiscent of Freud's statement at the end of the Schreber case to the effect that there might be more similarity between his theories and Schreber's delusions than he would like to recognize.

The point about this inadequacy in our ability to think about mental phenomena is, by extension, applicable of course to the language in which it can be framed, which has, after all, been developed at the lexical level for describing the 'world' as objects in motion and in relationship, more or less as if they were purely mechanical in their principles of operation. This is the problem that Bion sets out to master in 'Learning from Experience' to implement the nine moves which he had made in the previous papers in preparation for a frontal assault, so to speak, on the task of framing a theory of thinking that could really be used in the analytical consulting room. These nine moves, you will recall, were the following: (1) extension of the concept of part-object to include mental functions; (2) erection of the concept of 'linking' as the thing 'attacked' when the person seeks to destroy his capacity for thought and emotion; (3) extension of the Oedipus complex to include the action of 'hubris' upon the functioning of the epistemophilic instinct; (4) definition of the prototype of the linkage that generates

307

'learning' as the baby-breast link; (5) giving substance of a qualitative nature to Mrs Klein's idea of 'excessive' projective identification, namely the motive of 'hatred of emotions' and therefore of life itself; (6) limiting the concept of consciousness operationally, as the 'organ for the perception of psychic qualities', after Freud; (7) reversal of the usual idea that 'thinking' generates 'thoughts', so that 'thoughts' in existence require an apparatus for 'thinking' them; (8) giving a new substance to the concept of omnipotence, functioning in the realm of thought as omniscience, the 'dictatorial assertion that one thing is morally right and the other wrong'; and (9) finally the suggestion that the mental apparatus needs truth as the body requires food.

If we think of these nine as the forces he was mobilizing for his assault, we may, to follow the metaphor, consider that the key to his strategy is contained in Chapters 3-11 of 'Learning', those in which he develop the 'empty' concepts of alpha and beta elements and functions. It is more useful to think of these as his strategy than to mistake them for theories. That would be to misunderstand quite completely the nature of Bion's work for the next fifteen years, which is devoted to trying to fill these empty concepts with meaning. 'Learning' is in that sense both the seminal work but also the opening skirmish of his assault, the master plan and the first attempt to implement it. Our task therefore in these two chapters is to take stock of both the progress of his assault on this mysterious fortress and the ways in which he fails to take it by storm.

His procedure may seem to you a novel one more applicable to the physical sciences, which can be mathematized, and Bion certainly had in mind, from the point of view of the philosophy of science, Mendelleyeff's achievement with the periodic table of elements as the model upon which he wished to operate. It is used again later in a more global way in the construction of the 'grid' of the 'elements of psycho-analysis'. But in fact this is probably only a particularly self-conscious instance of the method by which psycho-analysis has proceeded in its major moves forward from the very beginning. 'Beyond the Pleasure Principle' posits two 'empty' concepts, Life and Death instincts; 'Notes on Some Schizoid Mechanisms' does the same with splitting and projective identification. These great seminal papers were exercises in intuition to which armies of analysts have had subsequently to give substance by clinical findings derived by their use. We are still in the process of discovering what projective identification 'means', not that we assume that Mrs Klein necessarily 'meant' all that in 1946, consciously or otherwise.

So one need not be intimidated by the mathematical forms, the talk of 'functions' and 'factors' by which Bion attempts to give precision to his purpose of being as imprecise as possible. 'The term alpha-function is, intentionally, devoid of meaning – it is important that it should not be used prematurely to convey meanings, for the premature meanings may be precisely those that it is essential to exclude.' (p. 3). But it is difficult, having in hand as reader all the data of earlier papers, to obey this injunction once he starts to describe the apparatus of his imagination. He wants to describe a mythical apparatus which could perform the function of processing 'emotional experiences' (which may occur in either the waking or sleeping state) in such a way as to generate 'dream thoughts' which can be stored as memory or used for thinking. He wants to imagine ways in which this mythical apparatus could go wrong, either failing to function or function in reverse, and the possible clinical consequences. So he is going to call the whatever-it-is that appears in the mind when alpha-function fails to operate by the un-name, beta-elements. Furthermore to give its consequences structural firmness he is going to imagine a continuing alpha-function turning out a membrane of thought which will function as a 'contact barrier' between conscious and unconscious, while, when it operates in reverse it will throw out a beta-screen which prevents such differentiation.

Now how are we to examine what he, Bion, means without transgressing his injunction against prematurely investing it, the concept, with meaning? Let us see if we can indeed usefully examine this mythical machinery of the mind, (p. 6), 'An emotional experience occurring in sleep does not differ from the emotional experience occurring during waking life in that the perceptions of the emotional experience have in both instances to be worked upon by alpha-function before they can be used for dream thoughts'. Now he is not saying they are the same but that they do not differ *insofar* as they both require alpha-function, etc. in relation to the 'perception' of the emotional experience. So alpha-function does not operate on the experience but on its perception, which we learn embraces both the 'sense impressions and the emotions', 'of which the patient is aware'. The 'aware' takes us by surprise. But we must remember that he is not describing the ego, or consciousness but has the right to assume these exist by virtue of his limiting the operational significance of consciousness to 'an organ for the perception of psychic qualities'. Apparently then alpha-function is operating on what consciousness, the organ etc, has perceived, awake or asleep. Well, we must have forgotten that this limiting of the concept 'consciousness' to an operational sphere implied that, of course, sleeping is not the same as being un-conscious but only that the psychic qualities being perceived are mainly limited to intrapsychic events, as the organs of exteroception have (relatively) closed down for the night.

We must note for future reference, perhaps with some disappointment, that Bion is not proposing to tell us anything at this point about the emotions themselves. Clearly, unlike Freud who in his theories persisted in treating emotions in a James-Langean way as bodily states attending the vicissitudes of instinct perceived *as* emotional states, essentially therefore archaic, Bion is intent on treating them as the very heart of the matter of mental life, in keeping with Mrs Klein's implications. But alpha-function is going to operate on emotions already in existence as part of the 'experience'. It may strike us as difficult to take in, this ranging side by side, as at the same level of function (or abstraction, from the point of view of exposition) of the three, sense impressions, emotion, experience. Clearly by 'impression' he does not mean 'data' in the neuro-physiological sense. He may seem to be talking about processes on the border between brain and mind but he would, surely, consider this border to be marked by an unbridgeable gulf at least as wide and deep, probably wider and deeper, than that separating animate from inanimate. Presumably the 'sense impressions' are impressions of the mind operating upon sensory data already neuro-physiologically ordered by all those processes studied by neuro-physiologists, experimental and gestalt psychologists. We must go back to 'Groups' in order to understand Bion's meaning. The (equally empty) concept of a proto-mental apparatus included functions of the mind in which emotions and bodily states were not as yet distinguished from each other. This is borne out by the example: (p. 8) 'A child having the emotional experience called learning to walk is able by virtue of alpha-function to store this experience. Thoughts that had originally to be conscious become unconscious and so the child can do all the thinking needed for walking without any longer being conscious of any of it'. He calls this 'learning a skill'. Learning, suppression and repression are thus to be linked, becoming perhaps synonymous, thus erasing the significance of the difference between the systematic unconscious and the repressed unconscious drawn by Freud in 'The Ego and the Id'. In this way we begin to see that the 'empty' concept of alpha-function has implications which, if found to be useful in practice, would begin to fill the empty vessel.

In fact Bion's description of the products of alpha-function (alpha elements), that they 'resemble, and may in fact be identical with, the visual images with which we are familar in dreams', strongly suggests that his model of the mind is going to replace Freud's 'primary' process with 'impressions of emotional experience', and 'secondary process' with 'dream-thoughts' and thus create an entirely different approach to the analysis of dreams. It would imply that 'the elements that Freud regards as yielding their latent content when the analyst has interpreted them' would no longer have 'latent content' which had to be discovered through reversal of the 'dream work', but *meaning*, which would need to be understood by thinking. The vessel is filling up certainly, for many analysts would agree that they think about, rather than decode, dreams, discerning their meaning and construing their significance by a process having no resemblance at all to Freud's alleged 'jig-saw puzzle' method.

But we are leaping ahead of our intention to stay in Ch. 3-11 to try to understand what Bion means, which must be in historical context, before tracing his own attempts to fill the concept of alpha function with clinically useful meaning. The next question that arises is: how does the model of alpha function operating on the sense impressions of emotional experience, such as learning from experience to walk, generating a continuous 'membrane' of dream thoughts which can function as a contact barrier between conscious and unconscious (both as immediate experience and as mental system) compare with

Mrs Klein's and Susan Isaacs' concept of unconscious phantasy? Does it displace it to the same extent that it supersedes Freud's ideas of primary and secondary process, which, after all, he viewed as having implicit the differentiation between rational and irrational (primary process knowing nothing of negation, being timeless, etc)?

First of all it is necessary to remember that Mrs Klein was in no sense a theoretician. She was not concerned to develop a theory of the mind but was purely a descriptive clinician using Freud's model of the mind as the basis for description of the phenomena that she discovered in her playroom and consulting room. For this reason the evolution of her theories, so-called, follow a smooth line of development determined by the internal logic of discovery. At no point does she seem greatly aware of the immense changes of implicit model of the mind that her discoveries indicate. The concreteness of the inner world; the geography of mental spaces; the central role of affects; the crucial function of values – all this is an addendum to psycho-analytical theory that cannot really be contained by the basically energetics model, operating even upon the structures of ego, id and superego, suggested by Freud.

The concept of a continuous stream of unconscious phantasy in waking and sleeping states is taken as a fact not requiring explanation of its genesis. It seems implied that it is produced by mental mechanisms intrinsic to the apparatus of the mind; principally by projection and introjection, managing a commerce between the spaces of outer and inner world of objects and self. It is a great advance over Freud in that it provides, by this interaction of mechanisms, a theatre where meaning can be generated (the internal world) and thus makes this arena primary for emotional relations. We see the external world *as*, that is as a reflection of internal relations from the point of view of meaning and significance. There is no such apparatus in Freud's model, the distinction between Pleasure and Reality Principles being so bound to body sensations and gratification of instinctual needs, the alternative to which is hallucinatory wish fulfillment. Primary process derives its irrationality from this purpose and any thirst for knowledge would arise only secondarily to the requirements of the Reality Principle. Consequently the epistemophilic instinct which Mrs Klein envisages as so important a factor in development, and which Bion will place alongside love and hate as the third great motive force in mental activity (K), could find no crucial role in Freud's model.

If we take it then, historically, that the concept of unconscious phantasy superimposes itself upon that of primary process in order to allow for the development of a concrete inner world as this theatre for the generating of meaning, bound in emotionality, we can see that the phenomena of disorders of thought for which Bion was seeking a model required an additional modification. The processes of projection and introjection, even amplified by ideas of minute fragmentation, the extension of part-object concept to cover mental functions, and the idea of agglomeration of fragments to form bizarre objects, could not be used to give order to such phenomena as the existence of thoughts that could not be used for thinking, of hallucinatory phenomena and of concreteness of thought where words become things. So Bion's idea of alpha-function is intended to envisage a hypothetical function and an apparatus for performing it which could be imagined to produce both digestible and indigestible elements, assuming that the functions of the mind have been developed on the model of the experience of the functions of the alimentary canal. (It is left open, whether Bion is using this only as analogy or whether he thinks that the evolution of the mind has employed this analogy.)

From this point of view then we can say that the idea of alpha function only *seems* to throw Freud's primary and secondary process out the window. As a second echelon modification, superimposed on Mrs Klein's implicit modification, it is merely a more complex model which allows for the inclusion of more complex phenomena. Freud was trying to describe the distribution of the libido and its vicissitudes, Mrs Klein was bringing these into the sphere of object relations and Bion is attempting to account for the development of thought and learning within the confines of object relations, and thus for their pathology. By erecting an apparatus which could be imagined to function to produce thoughts that could be used for thinking he is giving substance to the word 'experience' which, as we have seen in studying the work on groups, was central to his preoccupations from the pre-analytic days of his work. The 'experienced officer'.

So we should be able to turn now to the negative aspect of the myth of alpha-function in order to understand its meaning, as an empty concept. Bion is going to use the label beta-element for those 'sense impressions of emotional experience' which are not worked upon by alpha-function. This means that he is not envisioning a beta-function in itself. Beta elements are the raw materials of thoughts, indigestible by the mental apparatus, that can not be stored as memory but only as accumulations of facts. He must leave it open whether such storage does in fact take place and, if so, whether this accumulated debris of emotional experiences can be recycled through the alpha-function. Now this begins to sound a lot like early Freud, in his theories of hysteria, where traumatic experiences were somehow imagined to be lodged like foreign bodies in the mental apparatus and not 'worn away' by some process that linked them with other memories. Just as, in keeping with this idea, the therapeutic process turned upon the recovery from amnesia of these events and their subsequent 'working through', we would be justified in assuming that the idea of beta-element storage as random facts would also imply a therapeutic process of their recycling for inclusion in memory.

Bion's vision includes other possibilities, in keeping with the digestive model. They may be evacuated, but where? They may be used as weapons, but how? They may be treasured and hoarded, but with what consequences? They may be recycled but without alpha-function. We are immediately struck by a similarity between these possibilities and phantasies in the sphere of anal erotism at a part-object level. But we must obey Bion's injunction against premature attribution of meaning to the mythical apparatus. Nonetheless, the immediate impression of anal phantasy does remind us that, in assessing the value of the construction, alpha-function, we must ask ourselves if it really enables a new approach to phenomena unmanageable by previous theory or is it a disguised application of existing theory to the new phenomena.

The final novelty of this apparatus, the idea of alpha-function operating in reverse, that is of its cannibalizing alpha-elements or dream-thoughts to produce beta-elements, enables Bion to double back on himself and suggest that this may be an alternative method of producing the bizarre objects he had pre-

314

viously accounted for by minute fragmentation and agglomeration. The mechanistic and mythic nature of his conception begins to resemble a Ronald Searle cartoon, and we begin to imagine the old machine broken down, its leaky pipes tied together with the old school tie, churning out beta-elements and filling the attic of the stately old home with unusable archaic rubble. But this impression has been created here because the clinical references have been screened out of Bion's discourse in order to bring before you the apparatus in its historic context of theory-building. In subsequent chapters it should be possible to trace the ways in which Bion fills it with clinical facts, measuring the success and failure of his first assault.

Chapter VI
Container and Contained
the Prototype of Learning

To complete our critique of 'Learning from Experience' two major tasks seem to present themselves. The first of these is to build upon the description of alpha-function by examining its relation to the three functions, love (L), hate (H) and knowing (K) which Bion selects as the three major types of emotional experiences to whose 'sense impressions' alpha-function is applied for the generating of dream-thoughts and the membrane of the contact barrier differentiating conscious and unconscious, thus making possible the binocular vision which psycho-analysis exploits in its method of study. The second would be to examine the prototype of relationship, namely the baby-breast as container-contained, in which learning from experience is conceived to come into existence as a possibility (phylo- and onto-genetically, one supposes), to see if Bion has succeeded in laying the foundations for a theory of the emotions for the first time in the history of psycho-analytical thought. It certainly is one of his intentions.

Before embarking on these two critical tasks it might be useful to put to one side for future consideration an aspect of the mode of presentation of the ideas in this little book which does almost universally stir every negative feeling. This is the quasi-mathematical form in which the ideas are presented, with Greek letters whose names most people never knew, plus signs, dots, erotic symbols, and letters of various sorts. In Chapter Five the use of the 'empty' concept of alpha- and beta- was defended as a methodological proceedure. But it was also suggested that this is an inevitable part of the movement in any science, that a theory should begin relatively empty, at least, and gather its meaning as it snow-balls along – or, of course, fail to do so. That methodological fact was not seen in itself to justify the use of Greek letters. But the wish to avoid 'premature' filling of the emptiness by virtue of the employment of words for a name, which words would in themselves carry a preformed 'penumbra' of meaning from earlier usages, seemed cogent. In this field in particular it would seem to be superior to the compounding of neologisms from the Greek or to deriving names from myths.

This, however, is not the rationale for the general mathematical form in which Bion has chosen to present the main ideas of this book. That derives from an aspiration toward precision of description as the basis for precision of thought which aspires to place psycho-analysis on a footing with astronomy, say, for the purposes of intra-disciplinary communication. From that point of view 'Learning' is also the prelude to 'The Elements of Psycho-analysis'. Bion writes, (p. 38), 'As an example of an attempt at precise formulation I take alpha-function and two factors, excessive projective identification and excess of bad objects. Suppose that in the course of the analysis these two factors are obtrusive to the exclusion of other factors that the analyst has observed. If psycho-analytic theory were rationally organized it should be possible to refer to both these factors by symbols which were part of a system of reference that was applied uniformly and universally. The Kleinian theory of projective identification would be referred to by initials and a page and paragraph reference. Similarly, Freud's view of attention would be replaced by a reference. This can in fact be done, though clumsily, by reference to page and line of the Standard Edition even now. Such a statement could lend itself to *mere manipulation*, more or less ingenious, of symbols according to apparently arbitrary rules. Provided that the analyst preserves a sense of the factual background to which such a formulation refers, there are advantages in the exercise in precision and rigour of thought that is exacted by an attempt to concentrate actual clinical experience so that it may be expressed in such an abstract notation'.

This seems worth quoting at length in order to make clear that Bion is serious about the mathematical form; it is not just window-dressing to impress the uneducated. The 'mere manipulation' is stressed to make clear his vision of the kind of 'exercise in precision' that could assist in training, research, communication. This aspiration is not, certainly, to be confused with the grandiosity of Freud's early albatross, 'Project for a Scientific Psychology' but is rather comparable with the efforts of the young Wittgenstein in his 'Principia Mathematica'. Perhaps we will see later if Bion gives way to contentment with phenomenological description like the later Wittgenstein of the 'Philosophical Investigations'.

With this aid for setting aside our tentative irritation with Bion's method of exposition, we should be able with some calmness to examine the implications of his application of the myth of alpha-function to the three types of emotional linkages, love, hate and knowing, which are the heart of the matter of the 'emotional experiences' to whose perception the alpha-function is applied. Then we can go on to examine what he seems to be meaning by these three emotional linkages. We must remember that Bion has suggested that the digestion of emotional experiences provides the nourishment by truth which keeps the mental apparatus alive and enables it to grow by this process of learning from experience, (p. 42), 'Failure to use the emotional experience produces a comparable disaster in the development of the personality; I include amongst these disasters degrees of psychotic deterioration that could be described as death of the personality'. Clearly he feels that relationships dominated by love and hate have been at the very centre of analytical investigation, particularly by Mrs Klein, and that his attention, with the view of investigation thinking processes, is mainly with K, knowing, and later Un-knowing (minus K). As with love and hate links, K-linkage involves mental pain which may be accepted, modified or evaded and it is naturally the latter two which concern the psycho-analyst who is trying to understand development and its pathology. The truth and the lie emerge as the food and poison of thought and growth of the personality. Historically speaking, then, Bion is going to approach the pathology of thought in a way that transforms the concept of mechanism of defence into mechanisms for modifying the truth so that it is digestible or evading it to form the lie which is the indigestible beta-element or the bizarre object of hallucination or concrete modes of thought where words or other representations of things-in-themselves are treated as the things-themselves, (p. 49), 'Such a manoeuvre is intended not to affirm but to deny reality, not to represent an emotional experience but to misrepresent it to make it appear to be a fulfilment'.

One can see that this approach involves an important amendment to the theory of reality testing which, in Freud's writing, was not given substance, was merely a fact. It is never really touched upon in Mrs Klein's work for she was concerned almost exclusively with the differentiation of the two main areas of reality, internal and external. At the time of her writing, because the phenomena being examined were those related to confusion rather than disorders of thought, her clarification of this geography of mental life seemed to give adequate substance to the problem of reality testing. She went a great distance in demonstrating how different were the laws governing the internal and external worlds. As she was no theoretician of the mind it did not occur to her to relate this to Freud's ideas of primary and secondary process. But truly this addendum to analytical theory did not really fill out a concept of reality testing and nowhere in her work will one find reference to any psychic entity such as a lie. Bion's myth of alpha-function is intended to provide an apparatus which can afford the personality the kind of experience from which comes a 'feeling of confidence' at discerning the truth, analogous to the confirmation of sense data by shared experience with others or confirmation by more than one sense (what Bion calls 'common sense'). This feeling of confidence, he suggests, is made possible by the elaboration of the 'membrane' of the 'contact barrier' between essentially conscious and essentially unconscious representations of the emotional experience being worked upon by alpha-function. The alpha-elements are not the experience of the thing-in-itself but an abstraction and representation of it, while its being thus represented both in conscious and unconscious forms simultaneously gives the personality a 'binocular vision' of the experience from which the 'feeling of confidence' in its reality is derived.

Now such an idea may not seem to say anything substantial until one examines its implication for reality testing. Freud's idea of thought as trial action always carried the implication that testing of the validity of the thought in action would eventually be necessary. At least it would be necessary for correct rather than erroneous ideas. Mrs Klein's introduction of internal world distracted attention from this problem as if it did not matter, as for instance with the operation in psychic reality of omnipotent phantasies. It seemed necessary only to help the patient, for instance, to locate the operation as internal.

Bion seems to imply that it does matter, and not just from the point of view of psychic structure and mental health, but in more alarming ways that make a new sense of the psychoses as 'death of the personality'. Taking physical processes as analogy, one might say that the three theories are comparable in this way: Freud says if you do not have good sexual relations you will develop unpleasant symptoms; Mrs Klein says if you do not receive love you will develop inadequately (mental rickets); Bion says if you do not digest your experiences you will poison and destroy your mind. They are all correct theories at different levels of preoccupation with mental life. From the Freud vertex, reality testing depends on experiences of satisfaction; from the Kleinian, on experiences of security; but from Bion's point of view reality testing depends on 'feelings of confidence' that one is seeing the truth, not of the thing-in-itself, but of one's own emotional experience of it by virtue of binocular vision: simultaneous conscious and unconscious vertices. Therefore the testing in action would not be necessary. Observation and contemplation would not only be sufficient but 'the better part', to borrow a phrase from the story of Mary and Martha. This has, as you can see, the widest implications for the theory of the psycho-analytical method, which Bion will explore later in 'Attention and Interpretation'.

Having described the mythical apparatus, Bion, of course, must also give an equally mythical account of how it could possibly have come into operation, phylo- and onto-genetically. Bion's phylogenetic suggestion, which is probably not a mere analogy, is that the psychic apparatus developed alpha-function by analogy, on the basis of its observations of the function of the alimentary canal, observations which do not, of course, correspond precisely with the observations of modern physiology. From all the sense data bombarding the brain, that neurophysiological apparatus constructs an emotional experience in the mind which alpha-function swallows and sets about digesting to form alpha-elements or dream-thoughts on two levels, perhaps analogous to respiration and deglutition. That seems a tenable myth, in line with Freud's dictum that the ego is in the first instance a body ego that has evolved as a specialized function of the more primitive Id.

But what of onto-genesis? Bion's myth is that the hungry or

otherwise distressed baby has a preconception of a breast which shortly after birth meets a realization that is approximate enough to give rise to a conception of a breast. Thereafter its distress is experienced as an object, a no-breast, which it expels in various ways, mainly by screaming, along with the distressed part of its personality which contains the no-breast as a fear of dying. If the mother is able to receive this by her concern to contain the baby's projective identifications as its means of communication, her function of reverie, implemented by her own alpha-function, will denude the projected part of its distress and be able to return to the infant that part of itself it had projected, along with a present-breast to replace the no-breast. This is the K-link by which the baby introjects a breast as an internal object with whose help alpha-function can become operative in the baby's mind until it is lost by virtue of the sadistic attacks described by Melanie Klein. That would be the basis for an oscillating state of being able and unable to think.

But the study of psychotics has indicated to Bion another possibility that goes beyond Mrs Klein's conception. An operation may take place by means of which the baby establishes an object which assists it to un-think, to mis-understand, to elaborate lies and hallucinations for the purpose of evading rather than modifying frustration and distress. His description is this: (p. 96), '. . . the model I construct is as follows: the infant splits off and projects its feeling of fear into the breast together with envy and hate of the undisturbed breast. Envy precludes a commensal relationship. The breast in K would moderate the fear component in the fear of dying that had been projected into it and the infant in due course would re-introject a now tolerable and consequently growth-stimulating part of its personality. In minus K the breast is felt enviously to remove the good or valuable element in the fear of dying and force the worthless residue back into the infant. The infant who started with a fear he was dying ends up by containing a nameless dread.

'The violence of emotion that is associated with Envy, and can be one of the factors in the personality in which minus K is in evidence, affects the projective process so that far more than the fear of dying is projected. Indeed it is as if virtually the whole personality was evacuated by the infant . . . The seriousness is best conveyed by saying that the will to live, which is necessary before there can be a fear of dying, is a part of the goodness that the envious breast has removed'. He goes on to describe how such an object is experienced as a 'super'-ego that simply asserts its moral superiority, hates development and promotes un-learning and mis-understanding, etc. It operates a function which is the reverse of alpha-function, (p. 98), 'In other words alpha-elements however obtained, are acquired for conversion into beta-elements'.

All this is the mythology which Bion hopes he and other analysts may be able in time to fill with meaning. In order to make it more real, a piece of clinical material to illustrate the theory in action might be helpful. Before ending this chapter a word is necessary concerning a question raised at the beginning of the chapter. Has Bion succeeded in constructing a theory of the mind which will lend itself to a substantial concept of emotions that will distinguish modern psycho-analysis from other psychologies, including Freud's, where the emotions are either primitive anlage, noises in the machine, or bodily manifestations of mental states perceived *as* emotions? Here are his statements about it from Chapter 27, (p. 90), 'Container and contained are susceptible of conjunction and permeation by emotion. Thus conjoined or permeated or both they change in a manner usually described as growth. When disjoined or denuded of emotion they diminish in vitality, that is, approximate to inanimate objects'.

(p. 93) '. . . it is evident that we need to know what emotions are compatible with a commensal relationship and therefore with K'.

'On the replacement of one emotion . . . by another emotion does the capacity for re-formation, and therefore receptivity, of (the container, mother, breast, etc) depend'.

'Learning depends on the capacity for the (growing container) to remain integrated and yet lose rigidity. This is the foundation of the state of mind of the individual who can retain his knowledge and experience and yet be prepared to reconstrue past experience in a manner that enables him to be receptive of a new idea . . . (container and contained) must be held by a constant (emotion) that is capable of replacement . . .'

It seems reasonable to suggest that this is the first cogent statement of a theory of emotions in the history of psycho-analysis. It places emotion at the very centre of mental growth through learning from experience, which Bion rightly distinguishes from learning 'about' things and will greatly elaborate upon in 'Transformations'.

Footnote: A piece of clinical material intended to illustrate the theory in action can be found in the appendix.

Chapter VII   The Elements of Psycho-analysis and Psycho-analytical Objects

In following the evolution of Bion's thought it has gradually become apparent that he has been pursuing a vision of refining and extending the model of the mind, as drawn up explicitly by Freud and modified implicitly by Melanie Klein, so that it might be used as an instrument for investigating disturbances of thought. Such a vision of course includes the possibility of using the psycho-analytical method, so akin to the clinical medical method, for examining pathology for the sake of forming hypotheses about healthy structure and function. Added to this, peculiarly Bionic, one might say, is the interest in formulating matters of the mind in a way that will allow for precision of communication and 'mere manipulation' by 'arbitrary rules' in what he calls variously 'meditative review' and the 'psycho-analytic game', (pp. 99 and 101). This duality of aim makes the present work dual in its essential nature, half scientific, i.e. towards the construction of a scientific deductive system, and half philosophic, i.e. investigating the system as a thing-in-itself. It seems unlikely that this joy in 'mere manipulation' would be a widespread phenomenon among practising analysts and it may not be amiss if its discussion is rather neglected here in our critique of the 'grid', taking it as a method of exposition rather than an instrument meant for use.

Our task in this chapter must be mainly to investigate the grid as the periodic table of psycho-analytical elements and then to trace its implications for the comprehension of what Bion calls the 'molecules' of psycho-analysis, psycho-analytical objects and interpretations. Having already constructed an apparatus, mythical and empty, namely alpha-function, which can operate on the sense impressions of emotional experiences to produce thoughts which can be used for thinking, Bion must now turn his attention to constructing an equally mythic and empty apparatus for manipulating these thoughts in a manner worthy of the name 'thinking' and capable of producing 'truth', the food of the mind. A daunting task!

This he attempts to do by drawing up his periodic table of elements, abstracting from it his molecules of psycho-analytic

324

objects and then investigating the mechanisms, paranoid-schizoid and depressive positions and projective identification (modified and represented as Ps↔D and container-contained ♀♂) by whose operation these molecules interact with one another. Clearly if the digestive system was the model and analogy behind the construction of the apparatus of alpha-function, chemistry is the model and analogy for the grid of elements, the description of psycho-analytic objects and the investigation of their behaviour with one another under the 'causal' influence of Ps↔D and ♀♂. Somehow the digestive system model was in itself infused with life and also lent itself to the phylo-genetic and onto-genetic conception of how the apparatus for alpha-function could have arisen. A chemical model will have neither of these inherent virtues and we must see if Bion is able to breath the life of emotionality and growth into it and to present a cogent description of how such a system might have arisen. We need not, at this point in the history of his ideas, expect him to fill the empty vessels with a great deal more clinical meaning than is absolutely necessary for the purpose of exposition. And surely such clinical reference is thin on the ground in this book, making some chapters fairly incomprehensible on first reading, cf. Ch. 9. It must be left open whether the method of exposition, i.e. using letters and signs of the grid itself, does in any way facilitate the abstractness and emptiness of the various hypothetical apparatuses that Bion is trying to construct or whether it merely imposes an additional and sometimes impossible task of translation, certainly open to error, upon the reader.

Perhaps it would be worthwhile to remember the history of the periodic table which is Bion's model. In the mid-19th century Mendelleyeff and others discovered that by comparing atomic weights, valency and chemical properties, chemical elements could be arranged periodically in a nine-tiered table. Only later was it realized that this was based upon the internal structure of atoms, with their nuclei and circling rings of electrons. The two axes of this table therefore originally had no structural significance and could only be designated by nine columns O-VIII. Therefore the history of its use passed from descriptive classification (weight, valency and properties of combination) to structural delineation (electrons, protons, rings etc).

325

Bion's grid is being structured in exactly the opposite way. He has drawn up a table by designating the meaning of each column in his vertical and horizontal axes for the sake of defining hypothetical elements (say D4, pre-conception-attention) whose realization in clinical phenomenology could then be sought. It is true that the Periodic Table did function somewhat in this way, for the empty spaces in its original description did point the way to the discovery of new elements to fill these voids. So our first problem is to examine the means by which Bion fixed upon the units of the two axes, the horizontal axis (1-6) of use and the vertical axis (A-H) of genesis of thought. In order to do this we must remember that the whole justification for it is Bion's contention that mere description 'of what took place' (i.e. in the consulting room) is neither a 'factual account' nor a 'scientific deductive system' but hangs somewhere in the middle and thus stands as does the 'ideogram' to phonetic alphabet 'words'. The imputation of cumbersomeness may seem irrelevant when we remember a contrary dictum, 'a picture is worth a thousand words'. The grid may be a wild-goose chase, as is strongly suggested in Ch. 19 when Bion tries to adapt the whole apparatus to dealing with 'feeling' rather than 'thinking'. But there is something rather marvellous about it as a method of exposition.

This exposition rests upon the choice of categories, both for the axes themselves (use and genesis) and the components of them, (p. 91), 'The choice of axes may appear arbitrary without further reasons; it stems from the analytic situation itself'. But he is very explicit in his expectations of the elements, their criteria of reality adequacy and capability of articulation to form a scientific deductive system, (p. 3). It therefore becomes extremely confusing when he begins to describe ♀♂ as an element, along with Ps↔D, LHK, R (reason) and I (idea, or psycho-analytic object) when he later calls them mechanisms (♀♂) and Ps↔D) or earlier had called them factors in a function (LHK). This is made even more confusing when he seems to discard ♀♂ as an element in favour of a 'central abstraction' which it must contain or imply, to which the term 'element' should be applied and reaches the conclusion that elements are essentially unobservable.

It is difficult to see how this conforms to the earlier expectation that elements 'must be capable of representing a realization that they were originally used to describe'. Even worse when he tries to explain that 'it will have the same status and quality as the object we aspire to *represent* by the word "line" or a line drawn upon paper, has to the word "line" or a line drawn upon paper' when there is no such object in external reality other than its representation. This breakdown of direct observability seems to explode the chemical analogy from the point of view of scientific method. His recourse to 'common sense' as he had formulated it in 'Learning' does not suffice when he wants to make the further step of defining the 'dimensions' of these elements and he pleads for forbearance (p. 11), 'Implementation of this plan seems, as so often in the case of psycho-analytic investigation, to presuppose what we wish to discover. In writing this I have to start somewhere and this produces difficulties because the start of a discussion tends to impose an appearance of reality on the idea that the matter discussed has a start'. The upshot is for Bion to hook the 'premises' of psycho-analysis firmly to those of philosophy and theology, which seems to make nonsense of the aspiration toward a 'scientific deductive system'.

This capitulation makes it easier to accept the 'dimensions' of sense, myth (or model making) and passion (or LHK with intensity but without violence), as tentative intuitions. It is analogous to an intuition in a 19th-century chemist that elements of chemistry must have structural components in some dynamic relation to one another, with weight, charge, motion, having as yet no means for observing evidences to suggest definitive realities such as electrons, protons, orbits, velocities. But neither the definition of the requirements nor the dimensions of the elements explains the leap to the grid and its arbitrary axes, use (in a passionate two-or-more person relation) and genesis (of thought). Why it is that a cross-indexing of use and genesis should define the qualities of the elements is left quite mysterious. The order in the genetic axis is manifestly logical, as the term 'genetic' implies, but that of the horizontal 'use' axis seems utterly arbitrary. Yet Ch. 8-9 suggests also a necessary logical order. It is also difficult to see an intrinsic difference, for instance, between 'definatory hypothesis' and 'notation' or to recognize that 'attention' and 'action' are terms at the same level of abstraction.

In the vertical (genetic, i.e. logical series in the genesis of thought) axis we meet again in somewhat expanded form the formulations first exposed in the paper on thinking and the book 'Learning'. We must note the differences, however, in order to understand the contribution to his theory that the arrangement in the grid implies. One addendum is the suggestion that beta- and alpha-elements are not only hypothetical but intrinsically unobservable in case they do exist. So it now appears that an alpha-element is not in itself a dream thought, for whose defini- tion Bion returns to Freud's hypothesis of latent content. This raises doubt about the meaning of 'observable' for certainly the manifest content may be observable but not the latent, not even in one's own dream, let alone another person's. It is questionable whether one can say that the patient's dream, rather than his account of his dream, is observable to the analyst.

The second addendum, which opens up the possibility of mobility within the grid, is the modification of the concept 'preconception' as a 'state of mind adapted to receive a re- stricted range of phenomena' (i.e. – part of the innate equip- ment of the mind) to include the idea that 'the conception can however then be *employed as*' (my italics) 'a preconception in that it can express' (or does he mean 'contain') 'an expecta- tion'. He does not help us much with the transition to 'concept' by telling us that it is achieved 'by a process designed to render it free of those elements that would unfit it to be a tool in the elucidation or expression of truth', as if it were a chisel with a burr on its cutting edge.

All in all the components of the two axes of the grid owe virtually nothing to existing psycho-analytic theory but owe their origins to philosophy, their lineage being only slightly indicated by Bion (cf. Kant, Poincaré, Braithwaite, Hume). It is highly original and cannot sustain itself by the respectability of its genesis. It must stand or fall on its own merits. It is not possible to pass on to examine the meaning of the grid itself without a note of exasperated incomprehension. It must be presumed that in using the Greek letter psi (ψ) to represent both horizontal column 2 (denial of the unknown) and also to represent the saturated element in a preconception, Bion means to imply something that he never spells out. It must be supposed that he means that the use involved is accomplished through the use of a preconception as if it were a conception and did not require any mating with a realization to become operative.

One other note. Because of the difficulty of the book it is impossible without consulting Bion personally (which must eventually be done) to be sure about the many apparent printer's errors (it must have been entirely incomprehensible to the poor proofreader). Page 28, for instance: line 4, the figure 5.1 must surely be rather A5. Further down, the statement, 'A state of attention, being receptive to the material the patient is producing, approximates to a preconception and therefore the change from attention to preconception is represented by a move from D4 on the grid to E4'. This should surely read, 'A state of attention, being receptive to the material the patient is producing, functions as a preconception (D4) and will change to a conception (E4)' i.e. when the material arrives. In its original form the word 'pre-conception' should surely read 'change from attention to conception', although even that is unclear.

But passing on to consider the grid itself we soon realize that it is an extraordinarily graphic way of representing the necessary movement of thoughts as they progress through the hypothetical apparatus for thinking that Bion wishes to construct. It is, to go back to the chemical analogy, akin to the chemical flow-sheet which is to be used as the basis for constructing an actual chemical plant that will in fact transform certain raw materials into certain desired products and by-products. In this way it is quite different from a periodic table unless you were a modern-day alchemist who wanted to turn hydrogen into plutonium. Here the brilliance with which Bion is able to use observations on extremes of psycho-pathology for drawing forth implications regarding healthy functioning becomes apparent once more, but the difficulty of following the argument is daunting.

Basically the apparatus consists of concrete equipment, container-contained ($♀♂$) and a dynamic influence (also called a mechanism for some reason) paranoid-schizoid and depressive positions in the sense of Melanie Klein, plus selected fact (equivalent, perhaps, to catalyst) in the sense of Poincaré ($Ps \leftrightarrow D$). The prototype model is the interaction of baby in distress and present breast. When the contained has been enveloped by the container so that alpha-function may ensue, the contained is imagined to be operated upon by Ps↔D in such a way that a process of growth ensues which can be represented on the grid. This movement on the grid is from left to right and from above downward as the contained thought progresses in the sophistication of both its use and its level of abstraction and organization. Ideally, one might say, what starts as beta-element ends as scientific deductive system in action. (G6?) The vision is in a way similar to the view of personality proposed by Roger Money-Kyrle in which the evolution of concepts forms a pyramidal structure based on internal logical necessity ('Cognitive Development' – I. J. Psa – 49: 1968).

All that is imaginative and mythical but fairly clear. We come to difficulty when we try to understand why Bion views progress from left to right in use by virtue of the mechanism container-contained and the dynamic operation of L, H, and K, to differ from movement from above to below in sophistication and level of abstraction by the operation of Ps↔D and why he calls Ps↔D a mechanism infused also with the dynamic of L, H and K. Partly the answer lies in Bion's understanding Melanie Klein's formulations as structural ones, (p. 35), 'The process of change from one category represented in the grid to another may be described as disintegration and reintegration, Ps↔D'. It might be suggested that this mistakes Mrs Klein's description of the consequences of the mechanisms, such as splitting processes, employed in the two positions, for the essences of the positions themselves. But it seems clear that her ultimate use of the term 'position' was essentially an economic one, intended to focus on the central value attitude dominant in the interaction of self and objects.

This is not a criticism of Bion but a reminder that Ps↔D has reference to Mrs Klein's concepts but is not merely a shorthand notation for them. It is possible that in stressing the structural implications, disintegration-integration, at the expense of value attitudes, Bion has posed himself an unnecessary difficulty. This takes the form of his having to distinguish between the 'development of thoughts', A1 to G6 on the grid, and the 'use of thoughts' under the 'exigencies of reality, be it psychic reality or external reality' when 'the primitive mechanisms have to be endowed with capacities for precision demanded by the need for survival'. He has to propose a new function, Reason with a capital R, which seems to drag him back to Freud's picture of the plight of the ego serving three masters, as represented in 'The Ego and the Id'. This brings us to Ch. 9 which is the heart of the book, and a gnarled heart of oak it is.

The central problem is expressed in this way: (p. 37), 'The operation $Ps\leftrightarrow D$ is responsible for revealing the relationship of "thoughts" already created by $\female\male$. But in fact it seems as if $Ps\leftrightarrow D$ is as much the begetter of thoughts as $\female\male$'. To examine it Bion brings in outline a case in which the patient's speech was incomprehensible, equivalent to doodling, but was somehow able to invest the objects of the room, presumably including the analyst, with meaning that had no connection with their forms or functions. Bion says he was using these objects as 'signs', probably equivalent to what Hanna Segal has called 'symbolic equations', rather than symbols. This seems to be the same as psi (ψ), column 2 or the preconception used as if it were already saturated by a realization to form a conception. This would seem to relate to omniscience, confabulation, lying, minus K. The patient was thus mistaking a notational system for symbols and metaphors and trying to think with this inadequate equipment. But Bion sees it as, at least, an attempt to liberate himself from having to manipulate actual objects in order to think. In this way it would seem to have the same relation to thought as play has to phantasy. But Bion thought he could also detect that the patient was attempting to use one particular object to harmonize and give a pattern of meaning to the others, analogous to the function of the selected fact, but of course employed concretely as a beta-element, as a thing-in-itself. One has to stretch the imagination to grasp the gossamer description of the clinical phenomena, but we must take Bion's intuitions of the facts on trust.

What he deduces from this is confrontation with a chicken-and-egg problem: which comes first, $Ps\leftrightarrow D$ or container? This may seem a bit of his 'mere manipulation by arbitrary rules of logic' but the leap that he takes from it is impressive, (p. 39), 'I shall suppose the existence of a mixed state in which the patient is persecuted by feelings of depression and depressed by feelings of persecution. These feelings are indistinguishable from bodily sensations and what might, in the light of later capacity for discrimination, be described as things-in-them-selves. In short beta-elements are objects compounded of things-in-themselves, feelings of depression-persecution and guilt and therefore aspects of personality linked by a sense of catastrophe.' It will be another five years before he can clarify this in the paper on 'Catastrophic Change'. But the immediate use which Bion makes of this sense of catastrophe inherent in the beta element is dazzling. He imagines a primitive situation in which the dispersed beta-elements (which he will soon call an 'un-certainty cloud' suggestive of the theological concept of the 'cloud of unknowing'), seeking a container, are compressed by this search to form an 'abortive prototype' of the contained which is able to use the dispersed state as a 'loose-knit con-tainer'. This process would realize an equally abortive prototype of Ps↔D (taken as fragmentation-integration plus selected fact).

The question must arise: has Bion by this feat of mental and linguistic gymnastics satisfied the second requirement for an hypothesis of a mental apparatus: namely to suggest a possible way in which it could have arisen phylo- and onto-genetically? The poetry is compelling and the description of its implications, of greedy beta-elements full of a sense of catastrophe searching wildly for a saturating realization in the absence of the con-tainer (breast), is hair-raisingly real. But is it convincing compared with Melanie Klein's description of the events pre-cipitating the onset of the depressive position? How does it compare with the description of the formation of concepts of mental spaces outlined in 'Exploration in Autism'? Discussion of these questions should probably wait until we have considered the rest of the book with its investigation of psycho-analytic objects and their dimensions of sense, myth and passion.

Chapter VIII

The Role of Myth in the
           Employment of Thoughts

In the previous chapter an attempt was made to describe and
examine Bion's effort in 'The Elements of Psycho-analysis' to
imagine an apparatus capable of generating thoughts and producing growth in them in the direction of sophistication in both
the level of abstraction and of organization. This he has given
graphic representation by means of the grid, where the possibility
of growth in use and level of abstraction and organization is
represented in a two-axis system, movement within which is
conceived to be implemented by two mechanisms: container-
contained (♀♂) and paranoid-schizoid and depressive positions,
plus selected fact (Ps↔D). He also attempted to give a cogent
description of how such a system could have come into existence
in the species and in the individual, using a quasi-astronomical
model of the 'uncertainty cloud' and the 'loose reticulum'. It was
suggested that by thus emphasizing a structural metaphor and
omitting the economic aspect related to emotional attitude
towards value inherent in Mrs Klein's formulation of 'positions',
he was setting himself an unnecessarily difficult task in regard
to the 'employment' of thoughts in thinking, as contrasted with
the problem of the 'manufacture' and 'growth' of thoughts. It
was suggested that Bion's proposed model might be compared
with Mrs Klein's description of the events which usher in the
depressive position or the examination of the origin of the conception of psychic spaces as outlined in 'Explorations in Autism'
(Meltzer et al). We must now move on to consider the way in
which Bion's apparatus is imagined to function to 'employ'
thoughts and how this is seen to relate to the psycho-analytical
situation and method. It should be emphasized again that in
this discussion the grid is being treated only as a method of
exposition and not as a thing meant for use in 'meditative
review' or 'the psycho-analytic game'.

In order to approach this problem of 'employment' of
thoughts Bion has proposed, intuitively, that the 'elements' of
thought must come together in a tripartite form involving sensa
(row B, alpha-elements), myth (row C) and passion (LHK
with intensity but without violence, but also identified as row G,

scientific deductive system) to form 'psycho-analytical objects' whose contemplation may give rise to other psycho-analytic objects, interpretations. He is going to assume that in the realm of myth the human species has evolved certain trends in pre-conception which, though essentially private to the individual, find certain approximations in the group. The Oedipus myth is one of these, particularly with relation to problems of love and hate in the infant, while the myths of the Tree of Knowledge of Good and Evil and of the Tower of Babel may be taken as examples in the realm of K, knowledge and communication. He says, (p. 45) 'the myth by virtue of its narrative form binds the various components in the story in a manner analogous to the fixation of the elements of a scientific deductive system by their inclusion in the system'. This is seen as essentially a process of nomination or naming (column 3) which leaves the work of filling with meaning still to be done. The myth 'fixes' the elements in their appropriate relation to one another but does not assign their meaning. This must be done by interpreta-tion of the myth, which would, however, be impossible if the myth did not 'fix' the relationships. This 'system' he calls a 'moral system', (p. 46). In so far as the dream can be taken as a 'private' myth its significance for the individual can be investigated by using the 'public' myth, such as the Oedipus myth. But in the individual's 'employment' of thoughts, once his thought has progressed in its 'growth' to take the form of a dream-private-myth that 'fixes' its components in relationship to one another, it may then be used as a preconception to seek a realization in external or internal reality. This process neces-sarily involves mental pain, and in Ch. 11-14 Bion is at his most brilliant in demonstrating, by way of his idea of reversible perspective, one of the many ways in which pain may be so evaded that a static situation results in the growth of the thought. As a consequence no learning can occur.

It is not possible to be absolutely certain that Bion means that mental pain arises at that point in growth of a thought where it becomes fixed in dream-myth, but if this is so it would be his major contribution to a theory of affects, which is so absent in the body of psycho-analytic theory. But of course it does not go very far in investigating the nature of mental pain; it merely locates its point of origin. Yet it is certain that the problem of pain is central to the reasons for Bion calling the myth an integral part of a 'moral system'. While he does not dismiss the view that by resolving conflicts an analysis may be said to diminish suffering, he is quite firm in placing as a more central aim the increase of the patient's 'capacity for suffering'. (pg. 62) This capacity seems bound up with the ability to recognize emotions in their premonitory state 'before they become *painfully* obvious'; the premonition of feelings being in an analogous state vis à vis emotions as preconceptions are to conceptions in the realm of ideas. Anxiety would be closely related to this premonitory state of the emotions, in keeping with Freud's signal theory of anxiety as eventually described in 'Inhibition, Symptom and Anxiety', and gives a new cogency to the old dictum that analysis must be conducted in a state of deprivation if the premonitory states are to be recognizable through the suspension of action and gratification.

If this is Bion's meaning, that emotions in a premonitory state (that is, belonging to a thought that has grown into a dream-myth which is functioning as a preconception searching for a realization) manifest themselves as anxiety, the implication would be that the painfulness of the anxiety is closely bound to the uncertainty of finding a realization which would make the emotion extant rather than premonitory, '*painfully* obvious'. We can therefore assume that Bion is talking of mental pain as being of two sorts, anxiety (by which he must mean both persecutory and depressive, perhaps also confusional and catastrophic) which is related to the premonition of emotion, and other realized emotions which are in their nature painful. This would go some distance to harmonize Freud's 'signal' theory of anxiety with Mrs Klein's classification of mental pains as persecutory and depressive, both being bound to unconscious phantasy. But it also goes further by allowing for this differentiation between painful emotions and mental pain proper, anxiety. There is good reason to believe that the former, painful emotions, are rendered unbearable by their admixture with mental pain and that the efficacy of the psycho-analytical method is at least in part the result of teasing apart these categories of pain.

The next step in this preliminary skirmishing, before an assault on the problem of the employment of thought in thinking, is for Bion to link emotional and ideational 'content' of thoughts. This he does by demonstrating that the grid categories can be just as well used for 'feeling' as 'idea' where 'feeling' is taken to be the premonitory emotion associated with an idea which is bound in the dream-myth, functioning as a preconception. Note that these are the anxieties and not the variants of LH and K as they suffuse the emotional experience whose perception is the object of alpha-function. Having the experiences, having the emotions which are implicit in the experiences, is different from observing and thinking about the experiences. It is this latter with which Bion is concerned. In order for this 'thinking about' to take place, the experiences must become suffused with meaning. Growth of the ideas and emotions, as graphically represented by the grid, is meant to take place in terms of their suffusion with meaning which can grow in complexity, sophistication and level of abstraction, or, if need be, as for instance when new experiences must be distinguished from old ones, shrink to naiveté. This incidentally enables him to place within the grid a host of pathological emotional experiences which are bizarre and can be likened in the realm of emotion to beta-elements in the realm of ideas. Their realization in work with psychotic patients is legion and defies communication by any means other than projective identifications to which few analysts could expect to be receptive.

Where then does this all take Bion in the final assault? The upshot is the conception of psycho-analytical objects, loaded with the meaning of phantasy, emotion and anxiety, which the analyst can hope to reflect by producing his own psycho-analytical object, the interpretation, (p. 102), 'To the analytic observer the material must appear as a number of discrete particles unrelated and incoherent (Ps↔D)'. – 'The coherence that these facts have in the patient's mind is not relevant to the analyst's problem. His problem – I describe it in stages – is to ignore that coherence so that he is confronted by the incoherence and experiences incomprehension of what is presented to him'. – 'This state must endure – until a new coherence emerges; at this point he has reached →D, the stage analogous to nomination or "binding" –. From this point his own processes can be represented by ♀♂ – the development of meaning'. This development of meaning is seen to be aided by the mythology of psycho-analytical theory which the analyst utilizes to give coherence, point and precision to the private myths thrown up by his intuition of the transference situation.

These psycho-analytical objects, the 'molecules' of psycho-analysis, are seen to be compounded of elements from three rows of the grid, B, C and G, that is the sensa, or alpha-elements which have been derived from the perception of the emotional experience, the myth or dream thought in which its elements are bound, and the passion or scientific deductive system into which it would grow if allowed. Is the citadel taken? Has Bion done anything more than 'presuppose what he wished to discover'? He ends defining psycho-analytic objects in terms of the grid categories which were themselves arbitrary, one might insist.

Let us assume that the citadel is not taken, that Bion has not succeeded in finding a method for teasing out the elements that are compounded in thought and therefore in the meeting of minds which is supposed to take place in psycho-analysis. The grid does not really seem a useful instrument for 'meditative review'; the axes of use and growth do not seem to define elements of discrete use-growth quality in any way analogous to the periodic table in chemistry; the tripartite 'molecules' do not immediately suggest clinical realizations; the essential role he asigns to 'naming' for processes of thought is immediately refuted by the non-literary arts and crafts, games and non-verbal modes of communication. Where does the question of 'perspective' fit into the system, if he is to claim that reversible perspective can be used to interfere with it? Let us take the stand that the book is a failure, a hodge-podge of inadequately worked out intuitions compounded from philosophy, mathematics and clinical experience and harnessed to a grandiose vision of precision, perhaps worse, of scientific respectability. Let us subject it to a merciless rejection because of its clotted language, repetitiveness, vague allusiveness, typographical errors and linguistic idiosyncracy. Let us do all that and see what remains and whether we want to bother with the next book written by this fellow.

To begin, one must remember that from 'Learning' onward Bion has set himself a mammoth task and we must watch with patience and suspended judgment as he pursues his way. Thus

'Elements' should be assessed as a battle preceded by skirmishing and not as a war. Has some territory been wrested from the 'formless infinite' of the mysterious realm of mental functions? Has reading this book been an unforgettable experience that has opened vistas of thought that one could never have formulated for oneself? Framed thus, and allowing all the reservations mentioned above, there can be no question about the answer. But what are these vistas? Bion has framed for us a hypothetical apparatus that is capable of generating thoughts that can be used for thinking, which he now proposes to study. This process he divided into two stages, the growth of the elements of thought and the employment of these elements as objects of thought. Let us consider them separately and then try to unite them in a critical way.

The whole realm of thoughts and thinking, as against emotional responses, phantasy and conflict, is a new area to psycho-analytical investigation, opened up by Bion and explored thus far almost single-handed. The ideas Bion brings from mathematics and philosophy defy scholastic classification and are his own personal integration of concepts taken from various sources and passed through the filter of psycho-analytical experience. Many may be aware of concepts such as level of abstraction, notation, publication, etc but it is a feat of imagination to divide thoughts on the basis of co-determination by growth in abstract level and organization linked to use. It gives a certain structural substance to the idea of a 'thought' as a mental product which gives cogency to the view that thoughts are initially empty and must be filled with meaning. Thus the whole view of preconception and 'pre-' conception mating with realization to form conception, with each level of growth in a thought functioning as the preconception for its next elevation in level of abstraction and sophistication of organization, brings alive the realm of thought in the way that Freud, and Abraham's stages in the development of the libido, brought the idea of psycho-sexual maturation to life. One need neither believe it nor grasp it fully to recognize that it is a rather glorious vision, deserving of comparison with the periodic table even if the comparison is inexact. That the concept 'container' means essentially 'container of meaning' makes a link to Mrs Klein's concept of spaces in a way that enriches the concreteness which was perhaps her greatest contribution to our model of the mind, the concreteness of psychic reality. Not only are internal objects concrete in their existence as structures of the mind but this concreteness is necessary in order for them to be able to function as containers of meaning. This concreteness of structure must be well-caulked, guarded by continent sphincters, if they are to perform their functions in the mind and provide the basis through identification for the self to become an adequate container of objects, states of mind, emotion. The link to Mrs Bick's work on skin-container function and of the group which explored the evolution of concepts of spaces in autistic children is unmistakeable.

Thus Bion's idea of the way in which paranoid-schizoid and depressive positions function as mechanisms within the container-contained structure to allow the contained thoughts to grow in complexity and accrue meaning in this process takes Mrs Klein's concept out of its Freudian framework. The 'positions' change from being massive developmental moves and became components of moment-to-moment function. It may still be contended that by dealing with Ps↔D as mechanism rather than as economic principle, by making it thus fairly indistinguishable from container-contained, by depriving it of its reference to value attitudes, Bion has greatly weakened his argument. It is equivalent to earlier days in chemistry when the catalysts were chosen on a purely chance basis since nothing was known of their mode of impingement on the chemical reaction proper. Ps↔D plus selected fact is a bit like selenium in a Keldohl flask: it is there because it works. But this omission of the economic aspect of Mrs Klein's concepts is in keeping with the mathematized effort at rigour which characterizes this book, for it will be noticed that the grid has no place for 'aesthetic', either in use or growth. Perhaps it should come after 'algebraic calculus' as the ultimate level of growth in abstraction and sophistication. His own concept of 'attacks on linking' and the value attitudes involved should have prevented him from equating Ps↔D with disintegration-integration.

When we move on to his handling of the problem of employment of thoughts, we must first acknowledge that this distinction between growth and employment seems confusing when juxtaposed to growth and use. Perhaps he has not made clear enough that he means by 'use' the immediate context in which the thought has its genesis, while by 'employment' he means something very special, namely the capacity of the mind to understand itself, and thereby the possibility to understand other minds. He formulates this possibility in terms of 'psycho-analytical objects': the molecules of psycho-analytical study, the understandings that can become available when the observable elements of thought are brought together. The requisite categories of elements, rows B, C and G (also called sensa, myth and passion) which must combine to form this molecule of understanding is intuited by Bion and nowhere justified or explained. For this reason the chapter on 'Transference' is relatively empty, the chapters on pain are fascinating but lack integration with the rest of the book, the exploration of the Oedipal, Babel and Eden myths is tangential. How Bion equates 'passion' with 'scientific deductive system' is a mystery. One must conclude that he means something like: in order for the thought to grow to a level where it can take its place in a scientific deductive system it must have been apprehended and worked upon in the course of its development in the container by Ps↔D operating with LHK, intensely but without violence. That could lead to a new approach to problems of creativity. Certainly the idea that in psycho-analysis we are studying 'objects' causes a linguistic muddle of the type that Bion has been explicitly at great pains to avoid, yet often violates unnecessarily, as for instance in his various uses of the word 'element'. But perhaps he does somehow mean that his 'psycho-analytical objects' are the very stuff of which the 'objects' of 'object relations' are made. At any rate, by giving such a detailed analysis and synthesis of thought he has offered a new firmness for the much abused and thus unbearably vague term 'understand' when applied to states of mind, one's own and those of others.

All in all one has to say that 'The Elements of Psycho-analysis' is a glorious failure, glorious in its vision and scope of thought and a failure in its organization and hobby-horsishness.

Chapter IX   Psycho-analytical Observation and the Theory of Transformations

It was suggested in the chapters dealing with the 'Elements' that Bion might be viewed from a rather military model as mustering forces, making sallies and skirmishes and periodically trying to take the citadel of the mind by storm. Perhaps this is too sanguinary a model to account for the experience of the reader who finds himself in a near constant state of exasperation eased by moments of delight and illumination. Perhaps we should imagine a present-day Leonardo designing his flying machines and incidentally producing marvellous drawings and paintings and entertaining fireworks shows and mechanical toys. Perhaps our exasperation will be less if we put to one side the desire to see him fly (or crash?) and enjoy the art and fireworks. To do that requires no critical guidance. 'Transformations' has some masterpieces of clinical description, notably the two-fold description of Patient B (p. 19), and sparkles throughout with little fireworks of observation and thought about the psycho-analytical situation and the world it inhabits.

But our task in this book is to take Bion's main purpose seriously and to struggle with our resentment, suspicions that he is mad, feelings of humiliation at his citing authors whose work is hardly known to us as if it were as current as the news on TV, and above all exasperation with the mathematizing. He says explicitly that he rejects the dictum that a system cannot be considered scientific until it can be expressed in mathematical terms. It was not so difficult to forgive the plethora of confusing and sometimes seemingly contradictory signs in the 'Elements' because behind it lay a model of the periodic table and the hope of a new order in chaos. In the present work no such hope sustains us in the face of the proliferation of mathematics-like notations, pseudo-equations, followed by arrows, dots, lines, arrows over (or should it be under?) words and not just Greek letters but Greek words. How are we to bear such an assault on our mentality? Is Bion Patient B in disguise? One could cite a hundred sentences that are at least as equivocal as the patient's 'girl who left about her knickers'.

Before we consign the book to the fire and regret the 25s net that it cost in 1965, let us consider another vertex, as he insists on calling point-of-view. What is this modern-day psycho-analytical Leonardo up to? What is Bion, the phenomenon, *about*? Let us say that in 'Learning' he was trying to build a flying machine out of bits of apparatus called alpha-function on the model of the baby's illusion that it could fly to the breast and that he succeeded in getting a few feet off the ground for a few seconds. That few feet and few seconds was thrilling enough to suggest that he has succeeded in developing what might some day be the air-foil of learning theory. In the 'Elements' he tried to make an astrological table for predicting the evolu-tion of the world of thought and succeeded at least in demon-strating that the cosmos of thought was composed of discrete bodies in ordered relation to one another, even if hopelessly complex for our feeble minds to grasp in its entirety or ever use for prediction. In 'Transformations' he could be said to be working out the navigational instruments for steering his little flying machine amongst the stars once a suitable propulsive force could be devised. Let us see how far he succeeds from the vertex of this model. See how quickly one begins to talk Bionese, if not completely without tears.

What then does this model mean in less fanciful terms and how does it help us to understand his method of work and exposition? This would-be circumnavigator of the cosmos of thought seems to set about things in a rather child-like way which may in fact be the method that mathematicians use. It is suggested in his 'psycho-analytic game' with the grid and his hope of 'mere manipulation of arbitrary symbols'. It is a game but a serious one and seems to go like this. First you must make a psycho-analytical observation. This is essential, and much of Ch. 3 (cf. pp. 29 and 47) is devoted to a detailed description of the requirements for so doing (one of his fireworks which must not, however, detain us at the moment). Next you collect your tools for calculation and apply them to the data of your observation. Finally you try to recognize how inadequate these tools are and set about modifying them to apply once again to the observation. The book conveys the impression that this series of events takes place at least three times, once through Chs. 1-5, for the second time in Chs. 6-9 and a third time in Chs. 10-12.

342

In that sense the book can be read not so much as an exposition of Bion's ultimate thought but as a record of his thinking and a document of his method of thought. For this reason it often gives the impression of being repetitive, inconsistent and wildly veering with changes in the intellectual wind. With this model in mind the plan of these three chapters devoted to 'Transformations' will veer accordingly.

The first episode, Chs. 1-5, is built around three observations, patients A, B and C, representing instances of what Bion calls 'rigid motion' transformation (equivalent to Freud's original description of the transference), 'projective transformation' (related to Melanie Klein's concept of early transference based on part-objects, internal objects, splitting and projective identification) and a parasitic transference in which 'the patient draws on the love, benevolence and indulgence of the host' with the aim of destroying these same qualities. The equipment Bion uses to examine these observations is drawn mainly from 'Learning' and 'Elements' in addition to such established theories of the analytic method as counter-transference. His business, as he stresses again and again, is not with psycho-analytical theories of the personality but with the theory of psycho-analytical observation of the personality. He is planning to develop what he hopefully calls 'the Theory of Transformations' as if it already existed sprung fully armed from his thigh. But we must not be misled, its structure is skeletal, consisting of three moves, O, T-alpha and T-beta (the 'facts', the experience of them and the transformation of them which gives them a possibility of growth and accretion of meaning). The 'growth' involved is 'growth of mental formulation', A to H on the grid, increase in complexity, sophistication and level of abstraction. This growth increases the *generality* of the mental formulation but thereby increases the *specificity* of the uses to which it can be put (horizontal axis). Behind this skeleton of equipment there lies a model, or rather two models. One is the model of the landscape painter transforming a scene of poppies in a field into pigment on canvas meant for public viewing. The second is the model of a lake reflecting trees disturbed by wind and a viewer seeing only the water. It is the same as Plato's image of the cave but with the image disturbed, meaning disturbed by emotion, L, H and K.

Two things strike one immediately. First of all we hear nothing of psycho-analytical objects composed of sensa, myth and passion in this book. So the question must arise: is the Theory of Transformations a new attempt to formulate the objects of psycho-analytical observation and interpretation? The answer is almost certainly affirmative, though Bion makes no such reference. Second, we must wonder if Bion is tackling with his theory the same one essentially assaulted by Freud in the Traumdeutung as the problem of the dream work by which the latent dream-thought was converted into the manifest content of the dream image. Again the answer is almost certainly affirmative although again Bion makes no such link. Perhaps it is implied in his use of the idea of 'work' involved in 'growth' (p. 42). If so it would imply a great modification of Freud's idea which saw the work as employed to hide the truth from the dream censor rather than to give form to nascent thought. This latter would be Bion's view, despite his reservations about 'form' which seems so implicit in the very term 'trans-formation'. (p. 12) Where he is in agreement with Freud is in relating thought and dream to a place midway between impulse and action, which he construes as essentially the capability to deal with problems of relations to objects in their absence. This view of dream and thought seems somehow to beg the question of Melanie Klein's view of the concreteness of internal objects which Bion appears to espouse. It seems at variance with his earlier work on the 'psychotic part of the personality' and the concept of bizarre objects.

In order to get to the heart of this first attempt at formulating the 'Theory of Transformations' it is necessary to quote at some length (p. 37) from Ch. 4: 'It is sometimes assumed that the motive for scientific work is an abstract love of the truth. The argument I have followed implies that the grounds for limiting the *values* that may be substituted for Ta-beta (analyst's transformation) to true statements lies in the nature of values *not* so limited and their relationship to other components of the T (transformation) theory. If truth is not essential to all values of Ta-beta, Ta-beta must be regarded as expressed in and by manipulation of the emotions of patient or public' (what he has already called propaganda) 'and not in or by the interpretation; truth is essential for any value of Ta-beta in art or science.

344

How is truth to be a criterion for a value proposed to Ta-beta? To what has it to be true and how shall we decide whether it is or not? Almost any answer appears to make truth contingent on some circumstance or idea that is contingent itself. Falling back on analytic *experience* for a clue, I am reminded that healthy mental growth seems to depend on truth as the living organism depends on food. If it is lacking or deficient the personality deteriorates. I cannot support this conviction by evidence regarded as scientific. It may be that the formulation belongs to the domain of *Aesthetic*. In practice the problem arises with schizoid personalities in whom the super-ego appears to be developmentally prior to the ego and to deny development and existence itself to the ego. The usurpation by the super-ego of the position that should be occupied by the ego involves imperfect development of the reality principle, exaltation of a "moral" outlook and lack of respect for the truth. The result is starvation of the psyche and stunted growth. I shall regard this statement as an *axiom* that resolves more difficulties than it creates'.

It will be recalled that in the previous chapter it was suggested that in restricting Ps↔D to the status of mechanism (disintegration-integration) rather than taking paranoid-schizoid and depressive positions in the ultimate sense of Mrs Klein's formulation as economic principles related to value attitude, Bion was creating more difficulties than he was resolving, to paraphrase him. It was also suggested that this paralleled his omission of a category of 'aesthetic' in the vertical 'growth' axis of the grid. He appears now to be correcting both of these deficiencies, although it may appear that he is using the term 'value' only in a mathematical sense. But it leads on to a new exploration of the role of L, H and K in processes of thought and thus in analytic observation and interpretation. It can be seen that he has fairly promptly discovered that his skeletal navigational equipment is going to be inadequate for the cosmos he wishes to explore because that cosmos does not in fact correspond to his more astrological than astronomical table. But it also does not correspond, Bion recognizes, to Freud's model of the mind or of the psycho-analytical method. Where Freud was content to see his task as 'finite', namely in conducting transactions between realms of conscious and unconscious, Bion

345

now realizes that he is traversing an infinite cosmos of meaning and only limiting himself to a 'finite universe of discourse' for the purpose of investigation and exposition. This is a major alteration in model of the method, one which is implicit in Melanie Klein's work with its forward, developmental orientation, as against Freud's essentially backward, reconstructive and psycho-pathological orientation. Hindsight always carries the deceptive implication that predictions *could* have been made if only the factors in the field had been adequately known. A forward view that sees the infinite possibilities despairs of such predictive power. Accordingly much of Ch. 5 is devoted by Bion to attacking the concept of causality in the realm of mental functions, a problem which Freud had skirted around by positing 'overdetermination' in place of determinism.

The upshot of this coming to terms with the infinite possibilities in mental function is that Bion must fall back on a more general position that the analyst's equipment is his personality in some state of partial analysis plus his training and experience in the use of the psycho-analytic method. This would seem to make nonsense of the idea of naive participation in the O of the treatment situation unless one realizes that by 'naïve' he means not being empty, but rather being open. In terms of the grid this means, (p. 50), 'Therefore the analyst's state of mind (i.e. in free-floating attention) should not be limited to categories E4 and F4 (conception plus attention and inquiry), say, but rather to the area of categories C to F by 1, 3, 4, 5, (myth, preconception, conception, concept plus definatory hypothesis, notation, attention and inquiry)'. He thus must admit, in describing a clinical situation, (p. 52), 'When I thought I grasped his meaning it was often by virtue of an aesthetic rather than a scientific experience'. He is moving away from the preoccupation with science as explanatory and towards an aesthetic conception of psycho-analytic thought (or Ta-beta) as the observation of phenomena and their meaningful organization to form the analyst's *opinion* of what is going on in the consulting room, and by extension, in the past and present lives of the two members present, analyst and patient. Only the tyrannical 'super'-ego (which probably means a tyrannical part of the self in projective identification with the superego) is interested to establish the cause of things in order to assign blame and prescribe punishment, (p. 59, note 1), 'The theory of causation is only valid in the domain of morality and only morality can *cause* anything. Meaning has no influence outside the psyche and causes nothing'. Or further on, (p. 64, note 2), 'The group is dominated by morality – I include of course the negative sense that shows as rebellion against morality – and this contributes to the atmosphere of hostility to individual thought on which Freud remarked'.

One might think that at this point the whole project is in ruins, that the possibility of precision has been destroyed by the prospect of the infinite possibilities of meaning, by the analyst being reduced to having a mere opinion of what is going on in the patient's mind and of mental events anyhow having no causal chain arrangement but being rather field and pattern problems, available only to aesthetic intuitions. The attempt to establish a Theory of Transformations to describe the methods of observation and communication in the consulting room seems to have had the same abortive result as the conceptual experiment with psycho-analytical objects. But Bion seems to do one of his brilliant turn-abouts and fetches back the idea of 'binocular vision' as the basis of reality testing and gives it a new meaning. Where in previous work ('Elements') he had ascribed reality testing to the operation on the one hand of 'common sense' (that is the correlation of the senses at the level of the emotional experience being observed and worked upon by alpha-function) and to the differentiation of conscious from unconscious effected by the 'membrane' of the 'contact-barrier' thrown up by alpha-function, he now proposes a new meaning, an addendum, to the idea of binocular vision. Perhaps it can be effected by transformations (alpha-function?) of the emotional experience from different points of view (vertices) which can be correlated. This seems to promise a possibility of understanding in greater detail the impact of the different emotional linkages, L. H and K that are operative in the transformation, in the creation of vessels of thought that can grow and accrete meaning, a new significance to the operation of 'love of the truth' to set against the intolerance to frustration, hatred of reality, attacks on linking, parasitism, etc. But it does seem to make some nonsense of his division between L and K and rather to suggest that they are really one, in the Keatsean sense,

'Beauty is truth, truth beauty. That is all ye know on earth and all ye need to know', (p. 70), 'But the problem can also be regarded as concerned with the appropriateness of the grid as an instrument to be used for investigating L or H links. Considering the horizontal axis, there is no difficulty in retaining the headings found useful for K because an L relationship clearly cannot be regarded as excluding K either in logic or in reality'.

So the second experiment in describing the analytic situation has collapsed by the end of Ch. 5 but already a new orientation has been achieved and the new equipment is at hand for the third onslaught.

Chapter X   Analytic Truth and the Operation
of Multiple Vertices

In the previous chapter it was suggested that 'Transformations'
could be read as a series of experiments in thought aimed at
describing the method of psycho-analytical observation as serial
transformations of observable 'facts' into thoughts capable of
'growth' and accretion of meaning, and further that this series
of experiments can be visualized as conducted in a particular
way. The method seems akin to that of the mathematician who
invents arbitrary signs and rules for their manipulation and
sees how far they carry him before new signs and rules need to
be invented. The first such experiment, in the 'Elements' employed signs called psycho-analytical objects composed of three
grid categories from the 'growth' axis, sensa (A), myth (C) and
passion (row G, mysteriously). It seemed never to get off the
ground (if we may return to the model of Leonardo's flying
machine intended to navigate the cosmos of the mind). The
second experiment (Chs. 1-5 of 'Transformations') employed
simple navigational instruments called transformations but
soon discovered that they were somehow produced by love of
the truth and an aesthetic sense which was a function of the
analyst's total personality plus training and experience, and anyhow resulted in nothing grander than his 'opinion' of what was
happening in the consulting room.

So experiment three was initiated by remodelling the concept of 'binocular vision' originally outlined in 'Learning' as a
function of the correlation of the conscious and unconscious,
delineated by the elaboration of the 'contact barrier' composed
of the 'membrane' of alpha-elements. It was now to be
remodelled in a way that might give some substance to the
'empty' differentiation of conscious-unconscious by filling them
with differing points-of-view, (now to be called 'vertices' in
order to eliminate the bias in favour of visual criteria suggested
by 'viewpoint'). Chapter 6 introduces the new experiment. By
remodelling the problem of psycho-analytical communication
through employing 'love of the truth' (K link), the question of
the present and absent object comes to the fore. Pain and
tension which favours hatred of the truth (minus K link)

becomes the stimulus as well as the deterrent of thought, seen now as essentially a technique for solving problems about objects in their absence. Bion illustrates the way in which the mind may employ different sensual vertices, say sight, smell and hearing, by analogy with the way in which the mathematician may deal with the relation of point, line and circle by pre-Cartesian, Cartesian and algebraic means. He is incidentally interested in suggesting that such mathematical problems and their solutions have psychic reality, but this rather adds confusion to the exposition and need not detain us here.

The prototype problem Bion utilizes is the disappearance of the breast, leaving only a point where it used to be, in a field where it may have disappeared either outside or inside the mind (circle). He suggests that a precondition for the solution of this problem, i.e. to be able to think about the breast in its absence or when it has been replaced by the presence of a no-breast (point), is the capacity to bear the pain of the possibility that this observed phenomenon is meaningless. This might be felt as intolerable because the breast, as the container of all meaning, might be felt as destroyed if meaninglessness were acknowledged as a possibility, (p. 81), 'Since the first requisite for the discovery of the meaning of any conjunction depends on the ability to admit that the phenomena may have no meaning, an inability to admit that they may have no meaning stifles the possibility of curiosity at the outset'. This prototype can be applied just as well to problems of time and problems of space as to substantive objects, and thus would have application to psycho-pathological manifestations such as megalo-mania and depersonalization as well as hallucination.

So this third experiment in describing psycho-analytical observation, thought and communication in terms of the means by which observation is transformed into thought which can grow in complexity, sophistication and level of abstraction, and in doing so accrete meaning, has been narrowed down to experiences of absent objects and tolerance to the pain of acknowledging their continued existence, this being contingent on the ability to be curious about the meaning of the phenomenon by acknowledging that it might be without meaning. The ability to think depends on reality testing through 'binocular vision', where the two 'views' are different vertices in the sense of different fields or orderings of the world, say different sense modalities, or other 'positions'. These other positions seem to include models or myths or metaphors, which also include the senses, as in an alimentary or respiratory model of relationship to the world. Vertices of 'sense' and 'system' may also be extended by vertices of 'position', perhaps in the meaning of value attitudes as in Mrs Klein's use of the term. Bion even speaks of the vertex of the 'reproductory system', but does not succeed in making clear if this is the same as 'from the point-of-view of sex' as he had used this in the 'Elements'.

It is curious, considering the idea of multiple vertices, that Bion perseveres in considering verbalization as essential for thought to 'grow' in sophistication beyond the realm of dream and myth (row C), as if he could conceive no notational system other than language. Perhaps he means 'language' and 'verbal' in a very broad sense, but it seems strongly suggested that the problems of external communication ('publication') become confused with thought as internal communication. This may be seen in Bion's discussion of the need for 'rules' of transformation. Perhaps some of the difficulty lies in his employment of the artist's activity as the model for transformations, a difficulty not inherent in the model of the reflection of trees in the water disturbed by wind, which makes a link both with Plato's image of the cave and Wittgenstein's concept of 'seeing as'.

Although there can be no doubt of Bion's commitment to meaning as an inner-world phenomenon which borrows forms from the external world to construct its dream-narratives, he is less unequivocal about the concreteness of this inner world, (p. 103), 'If there is a no-thing, the thing must exist. By analogy, if Falstaff is a no-thing Falstaff also exists: if it can be said that Falstaff, Shakespeare's character who had no real existence, has more "reality" than people who existed in fact, it is because an actual Falstaff exists: the invariant under psycho-analysis is the ratio of no-thing to thing'. The operative phrase seems to be 'if it can be said' which seems to confuse the problem of the limits of language with that of the limits of thought. From the viewpoint of psycho-analytical concepts as tools, this confuses the problem of what can be thought *about* with what exists in psychic reality: objects of imagination confused with internal objects. This seems a surprising bind for Bion to get into when he had already specified that the problems of meaning deal with an infinite, not a finite universe: that is, that *anything* can be thought, as mathematics marvellously illustrates; ordinal numbers, imaginary numbers, the square root of minus 2, etc.

So it seems suggested that at this point Bion's third experiment is beginning to crumble because of his confusing the absent object or no-thing with an internal object or no-thing. Correspondingly the construction which he puts upon 'non-existent' objects and the paradox of the patient who is identified with such an object, is approached by way of the stripping of meaning rather than the construction of the bizarre object. Thus one can begin to see how the search for evolution of thought by way of the grid is leading him further and further from the concreteness of psychic reality expressed in his earliest formulation of bizarre objects as formed by agglomeration of minutely fragmented objects. Under the grid the formation of a delusional system could be 'nowhere' and in 'no time' but it could not be 'a world in which he could live', as Freud said of Schreber's system, (p. 106), 'The domain of thought may be conceived of as a space occupied by no-things; the space occupied by a particular no-thing is marked by a sign such as the words "chair" or "cat" . . .'. By this restriction he imposes upon himself another restriction: (p. 107), '. . . by thought I mean, in this context, that which enables problems to be solved in the absence of the object'. A tautology. He continues, 'Indeed unless the object is absent there is no problem'. But this dictum is then begged, 'The problem is associated with the sense that the realization only approximates to the pre-conception . . .'. This implies that the only problems in life are those of dis-satisfaction. But he has already spoken of the developmental difficulties that can arise through a too-understanding object, corresponding to Melanie Klein's view that an optimal level of anxiety was needed for development to be forwarded.

The blind alley into which he has got himself through his adamant refusal 'to be deterred from discussing a point merely because it is inconceivable', results in an interesting evocation of the biological concept of 'tropism' into the realm of the mind by postulating a consciousness attached to beta-elements as 'an awareness of a lack of existence that demands an existence, a thought in search of a meaning'. This is after all like a pre-conception which he has already assumed by definition to be unobservable. This is Bion at his most recalcitrant, unable to read his own notes but still claiming to be able to use them for contrasting with one another, (p. 109). But he is always amusing when he realizes he is in trouble: 'The argument is, I think, circular: I am relying on the adequacy of the circle's diameter', (p. 111) This could hardly mean anything but that the spurious origins of the argument will have been lost sight of by the time its conclusions are reached.

What does finally emerge quite clearly from this investigation of the denudation of meaning, minus K, retrograde movement in the grid, return to beta-elements by alpha-process working backwards (to mention the various forms in which the problem has been stated at various places in these three books) is a new formulation in terms of vertices, which are now called 'positions', because the image is of points on a circle with arrows pointing in or out. A footnote acknowledges that this formulation of the vertex or position of minus K stands in relation to Melanie Klein's concept of the paranoid-schizoid positions as 'two views of a reversible perspective'. This point is then further illustrated by clinical reference to claustrophobia and agoraphobia to show how the 'unsophisticated' and 'intuitive' psycho-analytical formulation can be reconciled with a 'sophisticated' and 'pre-cise geometric' formulation. This is meant to serve both as an illustration of binocular vision from differing vertices and as an example of the direction in which Bion feels formulation of psychological problems needs to move in order to create a notation that will serve equally well for all the fields that deal with the activities of the mind such as the arts, and presumably social sciences, history, philosophy, etc. None of it is convincing but Bion never means to be, only thought provoking.

What thought, then, has this middle section, this so-called third experiment in formulating the transactions of psycho-analysis, and thus of observation and thought, provoked? Bion, on the background of the formulations in 'Learning' and 'Elements' has investigated observation and thought on the basis of the relationship between the representation of present and absent objects in the mind; using the breast again as proto-type object, but widening his scope to consider also time and space as objects, existence and non-existence as dimensions, meaningful and meaningless as possibilities, and the geometry of point and line as his method of inquiry and exposition. In this widened theatre love of the truth and hatred of the truth (linked to intolerance of mental pain, envy and destructiveness), have been represented to operate, with reference to the grid, in opposite directions with respect to growth and accretion of meaning. The upshot has been a rapprochement with the Kleinian theories of positions as value systems and also with the concept of psychic reality as related to the concrete conception of mental spaces. But Bion has run into difficulty over the question of the existence of absent objects, the no-things that can be represented by point and line with reference to the spaces that can be represented by inside and outside the circle. His geometrical system of representations, will not make certain distinctions, such as between imagined objects of thought and internal objects which exist inside and can be expelled from the mental space. It will also not make an adequate distinction between the objects and spaces of psychic reality and the unreal objects (bizarre objects) that have their non-existence in the no-where of the delusional system. He has further had to beg the question of the nature of the absence of absent objects.

But the experiment is far from a total loss. On the gain side we can say with confidence that the concept of vertices has broadened the flexibility of the idea of positions. It gives a new scope for developing the conception of the 'world' in which a person is living at a particular moment, and opens the way to a new view of splitting processes. Bion has given us in this section a method for conceptualizing the nature of the different parts of the self, not only in terms of psychic tendencies (Melanie Klein) but in terms of the different worlds that each may inhabit, where 'world' is the object of 'vertex'. He has laid the basis for the systematic consideration of dimensionality, and the work in this direction embodied in 'Explorations in Autism' can be viewed as one of its fruits. While he seems to dream of a notation, at once precise and sophisticated, his real contribution seems always to go in the opposite direction, of opening the door to new regions of phenomena which pose even greater problems for our feeble notation, built as it is, necessarily, on the primarily visual and deceptively narrative and pseudo-causal language of the dream. But he has helped us here by slaying the dragon of causality and opening the cosmos of the mind in its infinitude of possibility for the generating of meaning.

Chapter XI

"Learning About" as a Resistance
to "Becoming"

In the two previous chapters it was suggested that 'Transformations' could be read as a series of experiments in mathematical modes of thought, beginning with the last part of 'Elements' and continuing into 'Attention and Interpretation', aimed at evolving a language of precision for describing the methods of observation, thought and communication employed in the psycho-analytical method. The stimulus for this effort, starting with 'Learning', had been the recognition of the role played by disorders of thought in severe mental disturbance, (schizophrenia in particular), related also to phenomena described earlier as peculiar to Basic Assumption Groups. What began as an attempt to avoid the 'penumbra of existing meaning' in ordinary words for the sake of positing an 'empty' hypothetical apparatus of thought: alpha-function, in 'Learning', expanded into a 'periodic table' of the 'elements' of thought, the grid, from which Bion first attempted a description of 'psycho-analytical òbjects', tripartite 'molecules' compounded of sensa, myth and passion.

This first attempt seemed not to lead anywhere and a new attempt, an illustration of the 'psycho-analytic game', has been undertaken in 'Transformations' using the grid to trace the 'growth' of ideas. The second attempt, in the form of a 'Theory of Transformations' failed also but brought forward certain important realizations, such as the central role of aesthetic intuition, its relation to love of the truth, the slaying of the concept of causality in favour of exploration of an infinite universe of meaningful discourse, finally the humbling of the analyst to the position of merely offering 'opinion'. But a third attempt utilized a broadened idea of 'binocular vision' to erect a concept of multiplicity of vertices, again using a mathematizing format but more for analogic illustration than as an experimental method. The attempt to solve the problem seems to come to grief over the failure to distinguish between the internal world of L and K and the delusional world of H and minus K, but it does establish a basis for differential value systems, with special reference to thought and feeling about absent objects.

The fourth attempt to formulate a precise notation for psycho-analytical observation, thought and communication starts, therefore, on a fairly firm ground of K and minus K in dubious battle: the duel of angels, thought and feeling versus anti-thought and anti-feeling. The exposition in these last three chapters becomes gradually less mathematical, finally frankly 'Dodgsonian', and more theological in format. The initial model of the marbles on the tray as an analogue for the patient's statements-on-the-grid, as it were, brings forward again the inconsistency in the structure of the grid. Is minus K to be represented by column 2, or by retrograde movement (anti-growth) on the grid or by a mirror image, an anti-grid? Bion seems to compromise in his elucidation of 'transformation in hallucinosis', (p. 131), '(v) Transformation, in rigid motion or in projection, must be seen to have hallucinosis as one of its media'. The brilliant investigation of the 'milkman cometh' material seems to suggest that hallucinosis belongs to the realm of delusion formation and that its phenomenology would better be encompassed by an anti-grid. This would differentiate such a process from retrograde movement on the grid as the realm of minus K and justify (p. 129) 'the assumption underlying loyalty to the K link (which) is that the personality of analyst and analysand can survive the loss of its protective coating of lies, subterfuge, evasion and *hallucination* and may even be fortified and enriched by the loss'. The suggestion of an anti-grid would remove 'hallucination' from this list and have implications for what was earlier (and will again be later) called 'catastrophic change' and is soon to be called 'Transformation in O'.

For reasons that become clearer in 'Attention', Bion seem keen to establish the category of the mystic who claims to be able to make contact with the 'ultimate reality' of Platonic forms, or Godhead or Kantian thing-in-itself. This seems unfortunate at this point and rather confuses the issue of the discussion, particularly as this ultimate reality is outside the operation of good and evil, of K and minus K, of reality versus delusion. It gives a mystical fogginess to the exposition of mysterious processes of growth and seems unnecessary since in 'Learning' Bion had already made a sufficient distinction between 'learning from experience' which changes the learner and 'learning about' which only adds to his stock of information. One can see that it is necessary for the investigation of megalomania, and for the way in which the patient's megalomania taxes the analyst's capacity to distinguish between love for the truth and megalomania in himself. But the whole discussion of hallucinosis, megalomania, 'hyperbole' in the expression of emotion and the distinction between 'acts' and 'acting out' detracts from the investigation of resistance as an analytic phenomenon because it does not allow for a differentiation of the motive for resistance. Bion is finally driven to acknowledge this distinction, resistance to mental pain and resistance rising out of the nature of the individual; but the opportunity for clarity is already lost. Nonetheless, Chapter 10 is a splendid elucidation of the problem of the megalomanic and deluded character and the special difficulties of the analyst in coping with him, (p. 144), 'The impression such patients give of suffering from a character disorder derives from the sense that their well-being and vitality spring from the same characteristics that give trouble. The sense that loss of the bad parts of his personality is inseparable from loss of that part in which all his mental health resides, contributes to the acuity of the patient's fears'.

Accordingly Chapters 11 and 12 can be read as Bion's last flirtation with mathematical formulation, (p. 156), 'Transformation in K has, contrary to the common view, been less adequately expressed by mathematical formulation than by religious formulations'. From this point on, having consigned his own mathematics to the 'Dodgsonian' or 'Alice in Wonderland' category with wry humour, his thought will move onto the more religious plane, in keeping with the theory of internal, objects, (p. 147), 'The gap between reality and the personality or, as I prefer to call it, the inaccessibility of O, is an aspect of life with which analysts are familiar under the guise of resistance. Resistance is only manifest when the threat is contact with what is believed to be real. There is no resistance to anything because it is believed to be false. Resistance operates because it is feared that the reality of the object is imminent'. Thus the question concerning the psycho-analytic process, and particularly the part in it played by interpretation, can be resolved by Bion into the following formulation, (p. 148), 'Is it possible through psycho-analytic interpretation to effect a transition from knowing the phenomena of the real self to being the real self'. This is his way of stating the problem of the integration of split-off parts as one of the dimensions of growth of the personality. It also brings him up against the problem of whether good and evil are necessary categories of the personality's vertices, a problem suggested, after all, by Melanie Klein's intuition that splitting-and-idealization was the first move in personality development. In Bion's language such a move would not constitute a realization of a preconception but rather the use of a conception *as* a preconception (cycle 2).

Essentially Bion seems to fall back on the fear of the unknown, the intolerance of uncertainty, its connection with impotence, awe, dependence, responsibility in the face of ignorance. These he finds are the ultimate factors militating against perseverance in the search for the truth. It is not clear whether he considers the use of number for the sake of 'binding' constant conjunctions and a preliminary step in 'winning from the void and formless infinite' as a step in K or in minus K in this 'Alice' world, but one is reminded of the constant conjunction of numerology with mystical systems for explaining the universe. Clearly he has little use for quantitative statements in the realm of interpretation. The crux of the matter of interpretation seems to find the following expression: (p. 153), 'The interpretation should be such that the transition from *knowing about reality* to *becoming real* is furthered. This transition depends on matching the analysand's statement with an interpretation which is such that the circular argument remains circular but has an adequate diameter'. This takes us back to what seemed a bit of Puckish intransigence in an earlier chapter and is now to be made absolutely central. What does Bion mean? The statement which follows is either arrant nonsense or mystically profound. Let us assume the former, since it makes it possible to examine the situation, while the cloud of new terminology of orbits, complementarity, etc can only stop the conversation. Let us assume that Bion is shamelessly trying to maintain that a circular argument can go somewhere other than up its own tail, and is prepared to shoot off his numerological fireworks to blind us to this obscurantism. Why should he do this?

If we follow the Bionic logic we would have to say that he is illustrating minus K, column 2, creation of beta-screens, etc in the service of hiding from himself and the reader that he is in trouble. His further recourse to identification with Newton as mathematical genius and theological zany (or 'gaga' in Keynes's terms) does not reassure. The fact seems to be that he is in trouble and Bion in trouble, like Freud in trouble, is often at his most dazzlingly wordy and erudite. The trouble seems to centre on Bion's preoccupation with the function of interpretation and the question of their 'acceptance' by the patient, whether in the service of K or minus K, whether in K or in O, (p. 164), 'Any interpretation may be accepted in K but rejected in O; acceptance in O means that acceptance of an interpretation enabling a patient to "know" that part of himself to which attention has been drawn is felt to involve "being" or "becoming" that person'. The price to be paid may, Bion thinks, be excessive when felt as involving madness, murder, megalomania, etc. Again a brilliant clinical formulation is brought for exemplification but the case is too special to substantiate the general conclusions Bion is trying to reach. In this way he seems to get quite far away from the experience of the transference as the therapeutic process and to return to earlier formulations of Freud regarding transference resistances, development of insight and working through. Consequently he tends to present a picture of the analyst as wielding powerful intellectual equipment for making instantaneous decisions based on precise judgments at a very high level of sophistication and abstraction. Bion of course knows very well that such a picture is ludicrous when confronted with the mediocrity of practising analysts, (p. 167), 'Epistemologically a statement may be regarded as evolved when any dimension can have a grid category assigned to it. For purpose of interpretation the statement is insufficiently evolved until its column 2 dimension is apparent. When the column 2 dimension has evolved, the statement can be said to be ripe for interpretation; its development as material for interpretation has reached maturity'. This sounds distressingly like many of the old dicta for *timing* of interpretation but in fact probably says nothing very much more than that the defensive function of the patient's material needs to be recognized before any proper interpretation, i.e. a meta-psychological statement regarding the transference, can possibly be made. It seems reasonable to suggest that the whole section about circular arguing and the need for the correct diameter to the circle is a bit of the old Dodgsonian leg-pull, behind which is a really serious observation and suggestion: (p. 168) '– the conditions (i.e. for interpretation) are complete when the analyst feels aware of resistance in himself – not counter-transference – but resistance to the response he anticipates from the analysand if he gives the interpretation'. In other words if it does not take courage to say, it probably is not the truth of what you think of the patient's material. The courage required relates to the potential explosiveness of the truth, which may certainly, as Bion asserts again and again, be the food of the mind but also threatens the person, really analyst and patient alike, with the catastrophic change of becoming a different person. This thesis is rather beautifully illustrated in the hypothetical 'sun will rise tomorrow' example, where it can be seen that courage is required to expose the hostility and paranoia that lie behind idealizations.

So the book ends on a rather wry note which implies a some-what sad farewell to a dream of precise formulation, psycho-analytic games, rules for the practice of psycho-analysis, (p. 171), 'The transition from sensibility to awareness, of a kind suit-able to be the foundation of action, cannot take place unless the process of change, T-alpha, is mathematical though perhaps in a form that has not been recognized as such'. This seems really to mean, stripped of its wiliness: if you want to act rather than think, use quantitative modes of thought but do not let yourself know you are doing it. One cannot disrespect the quality of thought and erudition that Bion has mustered for his flirtation with precision, but the whole structure, from 'Learning' through 'Transformations' could be dismissed as 'gaga' were it not for the constantly fruitful penetration of the psycho-analytical method which nestles somehow amidst the mathe-matizing, or more correctly runs like a seam of ore through the granite of wilful manipulation of arbitrary signs and rules. What remains, when the scaffolding is removed, that some people find a work of genius in these three books, taken together as the prelude to 'Attention and Interpretation'?

It could be cogently suggested that by the end of 'Trans-formations' the art of psycho-analysis and the science of psycho-analysis have been welded together and placed on a foundation no longer isolated from the other fields that deal with human mentality – psychology, sociology, history, philosophy, theology, the fine arts, anthropology, palaeontology. This foundation is method, and Bion has done what Freud, with his 'pure gold' scorned to do and Melanie Klein was not equipped to do. All these books, despite their clinical stimulation by phenomena met in the consulting room in the therapy of schizophrenia, thought disorders, etc., are really examinations of the psycho-analytical method. It has been said that the poet is always writing about poetry and the painter is always investigating painting. Bion can be said to be making a systematic attempt to discover what psycho-analysis is *about*, not from the point of view of its objects of study but rather from the experience of the analyst. He is therefore, as he reminds us, not evolving psycho-analytic theories (these he assures us are well cared for by the scientific committee of the psycho-analytical societies) but theories about psycho-analysis as a thing-in-itself.

In order to justify such a sweeping statement, it is necessary to attempt a summary of the structure of thought which does in fact emerge when the mathematical scaffolding is removed, as it has in fact been somewhat stripped in the foregoing chapters. This is needed also as a baseline in order to appreciate the magnitude of the undertaking and achievement in 'Attention'. Perhaps it could be reasonably stated as follows:

The realm of the mind is a world of infinite possibilities of meaning from whose formlessness a coherent internal world must be constructed by thought operating on the perception of emotional experiences. An apparatus, mysteriously modelled on the mother's capacity for reverie, is developed in infancy for the purpose of deriving from these experiences thoughts which may be used for thinking. But at the same time a rival organization for creating lies which can only be used for creating delusions and bizarre objects, or else for evacuation, is developed, the former nourishing the mind for growth, the latter poisoning it. Psycho-analysis is a method for studying the interaction of these two organizations through the medium of the transference and counter-transference, which can reveal the methods by which the mental pain involved in facing the truth is either modified or evaded, mainly through attacks on the linking which the growth of thought creates. This growth, which proceeds in sophistication, complexity and level of abstraction by being put to different uses, depends on the operation, either internally or with an external object, by which the disordered *and painful* thought finds a container that can modify it by means of a shift in value system, or vertex, or view-of-the-world. These painful thoughts are in essence concerned with the meaning of the absence of objects of love and dependence, for without them the self is overwhelmed with despair and nameless dread. But the problem of distinguishing between the evasion of pain and its modification requires reality testing, which in essence is the differentiation between truth and lies, understanding and mis-understanding. This is done by correlating the understanding derived from more than one vertex as well as by using the new thought as a preconception whose realization may be evaluated for its degree of approximation to expectation. In assisting the patient to improve his mental functions and grow in his mental structure the analyst is reduced to offering his opinion, often based more on intuitive aesthetic judgments than precise intellectual evaluation. This latter can, however, be supplemented in tranquil recollection.

Chapter XII   The Bondage of Memory and
                     Desire

An approach to 'Attention and Interpretation' is probably only
possible for someone already 'hardened' to Bion's extraordinary
demands upon the reader, for he goes his way in this book not
only in the expectation that no one 'but a practising psycho-
analyst can understand this book although I have done my best
to make it simple' but that the reader will have not merely
read but mastered the previous books, the grid and the other
quasi-mathematical paraphernalia. It is a book in which one
of the two terms in the title hardly ever appears in the text.
And yet *attention* is the underlying theme of the work.

In so far as this book represents Bion's most organized attempt
to present a theory of psycho-analytical practice, it tends to read
a bit like a handbook for pilgrims to a strange world. Until they
actually arrive and begin to have the experiences and encounter
the objects described, it is all meaningless. The practising
psycho-analyst who, Bion hopes, will be his reader may have
practised analysis for many years without ever entering the
world of Bion's description. This is not merely because he may
not have treated schizophrenics, say, but rather that his 'vertex'
has been so different. He may be sophisticated enough to have
realized that the medical model was too crude for application
to this method and consequently have taken to referring to his
'analysands' rather than his 'patients'. Readings in linguistic
philosophy and philosophy of mind may have made him aware
of the great difficulties inherent in the use of language for
communication. His personal analysis may have humbled him
to a state of tentativeness about his capacities to observe and
understand himself and others. His study of the psycho-
analytical literature may have warned him of the confusion and
inadequacy of theoretical formulation in the field. Study of
history may have enabled him to see or suspect that psycho-
analysis had its historic roots more in philosophy and theology
than in 19th-century science. But it is unlikely that any of this
will have prepared him for the massive onslaught against his
system of intellectual security that Bion's book represents.

In the earlier works the battering mainly took the form of

feeling crushed by a sense of inferior intelligence as this massive equipment of language, signs and symbols was set into the field. Clearly one's intellectual house had been built of twigs at best and the Bion wolf was at the door. But actually it seemed all right; alpha-process did not hurt, the grid turned out to be quite harmless, container and contained seemed almost familiar. One even began to feel a bit of a wolf that could huff and puff at other people's twiggy conceptions. So if one could bear the exasperation and persevere despite the bruising to one's vanity the outcome was quite pleasant. No, one had not taken to playing psycho-analytical games with the grid in the evening instead of watching television nor had one's comprehension and interpretation of one's patients' material altered noticeably. The inner feeling of being different could not be substantiated from observation of feelings or behaviour, yet one knew that there was no choice; one was either with him, Bionic, or against him, minus Bionic. His thought had to be reckoned with.

But towards the end of 'Transformations' the shift in vertex and language from the mathematical to the religious began to take place. Here in 'Attention' a new and more difficult demand is being made upon the reader. He is being asked to throw away the work of two centuries, no, five centuries, of liberating the human mind from the bondage of religion and mysticism. The Renaissance, the Reformation, the Age of Reason, the triumphs of the Scientific Method – all this we are being asked to jettison. Our carefully trained memories, our better-than-Christian desire to help our suffering fellows, our disciplined capacity for understanding – all this is bondage to the realm of the sensuous. We will never be able to enjoy hallucinations and thereby understand the patient who enjoys transformations in hallucinosis if we cling to the paltry sensuous world. By artificially blinding ourselves we can become able to pierce the light with a beam of darkness and un-see the un-real world of no-things.

That is meant to be Cycle 1, an illustration of the resistance to Bion's demands upon us by means of mockery. Cycle 2 could be said to be the rubbery technique, rolling-with-the-punch. 'But Bion isn't really saying anything different from what Freud said. It doesn't involve doing anything different from

365

what I always do. I never keep notes any longer because I realize that my unconscious recollection and ordering of the patient's material is so much more profound than my conscious efforts. I long ago abandoned any desire to cure my patients because I saw clearly that the psycho-analytical method only reorganized the patient's defenses and strengthened his hold on reality. Likewise the corrective emotional experience, which is the essence of the method, depends more on the realities of the analyst's personality than on his intellectual understanding, as Freud thought. I notice as does Bion that I fall asleep occasionally and wake with a rather painful sensation, but this is due to deep contact with my patient's unconscious. In the final reckoning those patients who are able to develop faith in the truth and goodness of the analytical method and their particular analyst thrive and those who cannot leave. So I am basically in agreement with Wilfred but find his way of writing a bit tiresome'.

Cycle 3, the heretic hunter of the Scientific Establishment: 'Under the guise of scientific rigour and linguistic precision Bion is clearly trying to wreck an edifice of theory and technique which has been built by devoted workers over the better part of a century. In Bion's early work, with which I feel in deep sympathy, he was setting about making a rapprochement between mathematical modes of thought and the psycho-analytical theory of the personality as a teachable discipline that could strengthen the student against being swept into action by the counter-transference evoked by very disturbed patients. This was extremely useful potentially, had he succeeded, because it is well recognized that the training analysis of our very carefully selected candidates does not give them a comparable experience on the couch while, on the other hand, it is also recognized that more and more our consulting rooms are filled with borderline patients as the liberalizing of sexual morality, brought about by psycho-analysis, has greatly diminished the prevalence of the neuroses for whose treatment the method was designed. It was disturbing in the earlier works to see references to 'the infinite', Meister Eckhart and the 'religious vertex' but he now seems to have abandoned himself quite completely to an idealization of confusion. He is, after all, rather old now and his so-called novel, 'A Memoir of the Future' is quite absurd and I do not mean in the Kierkegaardian sense, though it has a resemblance to that madman's ravings'.

Having thus set aside these three bits of ourselves, the mocker, the rubberman and the future president of the society, we can set about trying to understand what Bion means and how it is an outgrowth of the earlier work, not an abandonment of it, even though the vertex and the paraphernalia is rather changed. What really are the demands being made upon us? Let us do some reviewing. Freud's discovery of the role of the unconscious in the formation of certain mental aberrations produced the topographic model of the mind in which the original dream-like world of hallucinatory wish-fulfilment under the sway of the Pleasure Principle was gradually relegated to sleep and the unconscious, while consciousness apprehended and acquiesced in a world of reality. Traumatic and unassimiliated experiences of the infantile past continued to exert a pressure in dream-life and symptom formation. This was transformed in the 1920s into the structural model of the mind in which an ego, evolved from the id under the impact of reality learned to use anxiety as a signal in its service to three masters; the demands of the id; the impact of reality; and an internalization of parental authority, the super-ego. Conflict was aggravated by the operation in the id of contrary instincts of life and death. This model was changed by Melanie Klein to include a geography of phantasy in which the self occupied two worlds, internal and external, with which it carried on a continual commerce in meaning through processes of introjection and projection, gradually integrating itself and its objects from an earlier state, characterized by splitting and persecution, by the agency of good experiences and a depressive orientation.

Under Freud's model of the mind, both early and late, the psycho-analytical method was essentially a reconstructive one, whereby early experiences could be understood and the pain accepted and 'worked through' so that symptoms and character distortions could be given up. Under Melanie Klein's model psycho-analysis was essentially a method dependent on the evocation of the transference within which the infantile relationships to internal objects could be worked through from a state of splitting and persecution to one of integration and depressive orientation by means of insights contained in the analyst's interpretations. Under both of these models the great tool was observation of the transference, as resistance in Freud's model, as psychic reality in Klein's. In both the counter-transference was the great hindrance and limitation. In both models emotional relationships and mental pain were the focus of attention.

Bion has been constructing an amplified model of the mind and an amplified model of the method of analysis. In Freud's model growth was taken for granted. In Melanie Klein's model the configuration, if not the achievement, of growth was taken for granted. In Bion's model growth is determined in its possibility and form only by virtue of a set of inherent preconceptions which require emotional experiences sufficiently congruent to serve as realizations in order that a system of conceptions may become gradually organized into concepts and a deductive system for experiencing the world. This is accomplished by alpha-function operating on the emotional experience and creating dream-thoughts which can be used for thinking so that, by the operation of container and contained, under the sway of movement back and forth between persecutory and depressive values (Ps↔D), these dream thoughts may grow in complexity, sophistication and abstractness into a scientific deductive system under the dominance of love of the truth and aesthetic intuition. The mythic dream-thought version of this scientific deductive system is represented by Melanie Klein's conception of the concreteness of psychic reality.

The amplified model of the psycho-analytical method that grows out of this amplified model of the mind has been under investigation in parallel with the elaboration of the model through 'Elements' and 'Transformations' with very little success, unless one strips off the scaffolding which was still needed to sustain its credibility. This scaffolding, quasi-mathematical logic and language, is now being sloughed and what comes under scrutiny first is the requirements of the analyst's state of mind in his consulting room so that he may function in a procedure that could be viewed as consonant with, possibly even conducive to, growth in both analysand and analyst. This state is said to be characterized by the eschewing of memory, desire and understanding. Bion is at great pains to explain what he means, but does so by introducing a new sign,

F, which gathers such vague and confusing qualities that the outcome is rather despair-provoking. The reader cannot fail to sympathize at one point, (p. 48), 'The disciplined increase of F by suppression of K, or subordination of transformations in K to Transformations in O, is therefore felt as a very serious attack on the ego until F has become established'. Why 'F'? Is it row F, 'concept'? He calls it an 'element'. It seems on the other hand to be F as in Freud to designate the attitude expressed by Freud in his letter to Lou Salomé where he spoke of 'artificially blinding myself'. Or is it F as in 'Frightful Fiend' of the Coleridge poem? Or is it F as in 'Act of Faith'? (p. 41), 'The "act of faith" (F) depends on disciplined denial of memory and desire. A bad memory is not enough: what is ordinarily called forgetting is as bad as remembering. It is necessary to inhibit dwelling on memories and desires'.

Probably the most useful understanding is to take F as a compound of all of these, faith, fiend, Freud's blinding, and row F (concept) as a vertex which can produce the beam of darkness, the state of Keatsian negative capability, which can serve as a tool to investigate the utterly non-sensual world of psychic reality. This is Dante following Virgil. It is the feat that Orpheus and Lot's wife did not manage. But how does it differ from 'free-floating attention'? Or is it merely a more detailed description, or prescription for the achievement of, that vague but cherished state of mind? How does Bion's idea of faith harmonize with his idea that the foundations of curiosity lay in the capacity to admit the possibility of meaninglessness?

The idea of free-floating attention seems to be a simple one, conceived as simple to accomplish, on the model of free-floating in water, which does not require an act of faith in the buoyancy of the human body but merely a realization of it for a moment. The child may be required to exercise an act of faith in letting go of daddy or trying to swim without his water-wings, but that is based on experience of daddy's good will already in hand. Bion's act-of-faith would correspond more to floating free in shark-infested waters. It assumes that everyone has a fiend following him, is on the verge of hallucinosis, megalomania, delusions, catastrophic anxiety. There seems every reason to believe this, judging from the impact of drugs, isolation, group pressure, fever, etc. The question must arise, is it really possible

369

to do such a thing in the cosy familiarity of one's own consulting room, living in a fairly democratic country, with a nice spouse, money in the bank, no evidence of cancer, and a patient who has been paying his bill and coming regularly for years? Probably the answer is that it is not possible to achieve this state by practising the discipline that Bion advocates because the 'suspension' of these functions is not possible by an act of the will. But it may be something that does, or might, happen in time with experience of practising the method of psycho-analysis. The act-of-faith would not be an act but a gradual transformation of the person into a psycho-analyst, if one takes this term to mean someone who believes that psycho-analysis exists, that it is a thing-in-itself. In any event Bion seems to suggest that this belief is contingent on the realization of the fiend in one's own mind, that hallucinosis, megalomania, delusion exist and are merely held at bay by some means. Melanie Klein would say they are held at bay by living in the sphere of good objects. Orwell would say the same, or conversely, by not living in the sphere of Big Brother. Evidence in the book suggests that for Bion the sharks that infest his waters are lawyers and judges hearing accusations against him of malpractice when he cannot defend himself, for he has forgotten his patient's name, doesn't even know if he is married and cannot deny that he fell asleep on various occasions in the consulting room. A Kafkaesque world!

Suppose then that we accept that what Bion recommends may in fact happen in time to the practising psycho-analyst, how is it to be distinguished from deterioration? (p. 47, foot-note), 'There are real dangers associated with the appearance (that the state of suspended memory and desire has to that of the severely regressed patient); this is why the procedure here adumbrated is advocated only for the psycho-analyst whose own analysis has been carried at least far enough for the recognition of paranoid-schizoid and depressive positions'. But he must surely mean 'far enough for him to have had a glimpse of the frightful fiend in himself'. This would mean that he has at least come to distinguish that his most catastrophic anxieties relate not to death but to madness, to being devoured into insanity by a shark in himself.

What justification can Bion give for such an aspiration,

370

whether it is to be achieved by his discipline or by the evolution of the person practising psycho-analysis? Is it necessary or is it only desirable in relation to a research interest in psychosis? Bion has several answers to this, (p. 44), 'I am concerned with developing a mode of thought which is such that a correct clinical observation can be made, for if *that* is achieved there is always hope of the evolution of the appropriate theory'. In other words *any* correct clinical observation is impaired by the operation of memory and desire. Second, he seems to believe that the unimpeded evolution of the transference requires this state in the analyst: (p. 42) 'If the analyst has not deliberately divested himself of memory and desire the patient can "feel" this and is dominated by the "feeling" that he is possessed by and contained in the analyst's state of mind, namely, the state represented by the term "desire".' Third, he believes that the problem of envy in the transference is very much aggravated by the analyst's exercise of memory and desire, (p. 48), 'If the psycho-analytic method is narrowly conceived of as consisting in the accumulation of knowledge (possessiveness), in harmony with the reality principle, and divorced from the processes of maturation and growth (either because growth is not recognised or because it is recognized but felt to be unattainable and beyond control of the individual), it becomes a potent stimulus for envy'. And finally that such reliance on memory and desire plays in with the patient's resistances: (p. 51), 'When the psycho-analyst anticipates some crisis, and especially if he has, or thinks he has, good grounds for anxiety, his tendency is to resort to memory and understanding to satisfy his desire for security. . . . This is understood by the psychotic patient, who does not resort to resistances but relies on being able to evoke the resistance-proliferating elements in his analyst; in other words, to stimulate the analyst's desires (notably for a successful outcome of the analysis), his memories and his understanding, thereby intending that his analyst's state of mind will not be open to the experience of which he might otherwise be a witness'.

Before we leave this critique of Bion's views on the eschewing of memory and desire by the analyst, we must note the weaknesses in the foundations of the concept, for they will be dealt with to some extent later in the book. First of all, Bion has not yet distinguished between psychic reality and the unreal world of delusions and hallucinations. Second, he has only made a very weak attempt to explain why growth is so feared, which leaves one to assume that it is the possibility of regression and madness, not growth, which stirs the unbearable anxiety. His weak attempt is this: (p. 53), 'Of all the hateful possibilities, growth and maturation are feared and detested most frequently. This hostility to the process of maturation becomes most marked when maturation seems to involve the subordination of the pleasure principle . . . the change from pleasure principle to reality principle does mean abandonment of control over the proportion of pain to pleasure'. He will need to bring a more powerful concept to bear in order to harmonize the position of love for the truth as the driving force of development with this detestation of growth. But these weaknesses do not detract at this point from the overall harmony between this concept of the eschewing of memory and desire and Bion's model of the mind. The essential feature is his emphasis on the emotional experience and how the discovery of the truth about its nature is the food of the mind's growth. Everything that interferes with the rich 'perception' of the emotional experience weakens the capability of alpha-function to produce dream-thoughts suitable for thinking. Attention to, longing for, interest in, dwelling on, clinging to, ruminating over – all the many modes of pre-occupation with past and future detract from the intensity of the experience of the moment and its perception. As this is the *sine qua non*, it is also the point at which resistance to change, in life and in analysis, directs its attack. Attention to the moment is requisite to its observation and for Bion the richness of thought is limited by the richness of observation. Hence his suspicion of number, so diametrically opposed to his valuing mathematical modes of thought.

Chapter XIII   The Psycho-analytic Couple and the Group

The rounding out of Bion's views in 'Attention and Interpretation' does not clearly declare itself until he begins to examine the relationship of the individual to the group. He means, in regard to the special problem of psycho-analysis, but perhaps to human relationships in general, the juxtaposition of the relations of individuals to one another *as* individuals to their involvements in group functions and mentality. The circling back to the work in 'Experiences in Groups' shows again the internal integrity of Bion's life work and its progressive tightening and complexity, a fact which is superficially belied by the shifts in paraphernalia of exposition in the various major works. In the present book, where the language has shifted to the religious vocabulary, it is clear that the linguistic paraphernalia is the inevitable equipment of the religious vertex on the world. In 'Elements' and 'Transformations' Bion was inclined to hedge this with claims that the mathematical mode of expression was analogic rather than intrinsic. But in retrospect it is clear that he had a period of romance with a mathematical dream of a precise and quantifiable world of essential internal harmony threatened mainly by the failure of alpha-function, of containers to contain and of selected facts to be discovered to implement Ps↔D. It was not the case that he had abandoned the death instinct, the role of envy, innate destructiveness, etc. in his thought, but that the mathematical dream had no place in it for aught but confusion as the enemy of growth. In consequence the anti-growth elements in the mind could be relegated to a single 'use', column 2.

The failure of the mathematical vertex to contain the violence of emotionality of mental life and the impending explosion of that container of formulation when swollen with this fermenting stuff led to its abandonment in favour of the religious vertex. Thus the ultimate reality is no longer 'O' but 'God' and the striving to 'become O' is now the striving for direct contact with and fusion with God, while the person who claims to accomplish this is to be called the 'mystic'. The mutual need that exists between the mystic and the group that he belongs to, either in the constructive or destructive sense, is to be taken as the model for understanding the workings of psycho-analysis as a 'messianic idea', presumably one amongst many existing in the world but to be best investigated on the model of the most successful messianic idea of all time, the Christian one. While this seems to put psycho-analysis on a grand scale, and to place Bion in a self-aggrandizing position as the new Messiah, this would be a gross misunderstanding of his method of exposition. He is trying to investigate the workings of the psycho-analytical method using the tools he has devised, the grid, container-contained, Ps↔D and vertices. Words like 'messianic', 'god', 'establishment', 'explode', etc., carry what he would call the penumbra of bigness, importance. To understand him one must put this aside and think of little messiahs, little gods, little explosions as well. The question of size in cosmic terms is irrelevant. Quantity has really dropped away from his work. Everything is quality now, so it does not matter if it is psycho-analytical micro-biology or psycho-analytical astronomy we think we are dealing with, the qualities are the same. It is the language of the religious vertex as a tool of investigation, a new model, not the trumpeting of the prophet. The problem in a sense is the same as used to be spoken of about aircraft and submarines, that they needed to be invented by geniuses so that they could be operated by idiots.

Taking the religious vertex Bion shows us a view of psycho-analysis that is of this sort, that great ideas exist in the world, that they are discovered by thinkers and transmitted for use to non-thinkers, for which purpose they must find a 'language', not necessarily verbal, that can both contain the idea without being exploded by its pressure of meaning nor be so rigid as to compress the idea and thus reduce its meaningfulness. He wishes to treat 'psycho-analysis' as a thing-in-itself which existed in the world prior to its discovery by the mystic genius of Freud (big or little does not matter) who gave it form in his writing and practice and teaching. From this arose, by virtue of this new thing being uncontainable by the medical establishment, a new messianic establishment, eventually the Int. Psa. Assoc. whose function was both evangelical and conservative. Upon this model of psycho-analytical history the individual practitioner becomes the idiot employing the equipment devised by the genius, but must belong to an established society of idiots who think they are geniuses because that society entitles them to participate in the genius of a Freud, or Klein or Bion. Without this form of participation they would not be able to function in their consulting rooms to carry for their patients a messianic-genius significance which is essential to the work. Of course this places them in danger of thinking themselves geniuses or messiahs, but this is the industrial hazard of the job (talking from the religious vertex, remember, for the sake of investigation and description). However, this establishment which confers the sense of participation upon its members to enable them to function with sincerity and conviction as psycho-analytical priests administering the psycho-analytical sacraments (religious vertex, not to be taken literally), also imposes upon them the conservatism of the group, faithfulness to the old new-ideas and resistance to new new-ideas, unless they can be proven to be implicit but previously unnoticed in the gospels containing the old new-ideas. These notions have their origin in Bion's earlier work on groups in which there seemed implicit a tendency for the three basic assumption groups to have a certain evolutionary sequence or cycling to the effect: the pairing group eventually produces the messianic leader and becomes the dependent group which is embattled as the fight-flight group upon the leader's death and must seek a new pair to gather its hope into.

This then is the social-psychological setting of the practising psycho-analyst, viewed from the religious vertex, within which Bion wishes to investigate the operation of the individual, or rather the couple, analyst-analysand. His focus is on the requirements for making observations, for upon the accuracy and detail of this observation 'of the emotional experience' the richness of all subsequent mental processes and thus of growth depends. He has spent the first third of the book describing and limiting his dictum, which, voiced appropriately to the religious vertex, would read, 'Abandon your memory and your desire and your understanding and follow me' rather than 'Thou shalt not remember, thou shalt not desire, thou shalt not understand'. That is, New rather than Old Testament, exhortation rather than prohibition, as different from one another as, 'Those who are not for me are against me' is from, 'Those who are not against me are for me'. Bion quotes the latter. The inquisitor would have to quote the former. Bion presents himself as the mini-mystic of the psycho-analytical group who claims that 'he comes not to destroy but to fulfill' the prior messianic messages of Freud and Melanie Klein. He is a new prophet of the 'mutative interpretation'. Taken in this way one can see that a 'process' view of psycho-analysis would serve as a comfort to the idiots that they need not really be geniuses in order to be sufficiently so apprehended by their patients that their interpretations, accurate or otherwise, precise or vague, may induce the 'catastrophic change' that is necessary for growth of the mind. From the religious vertex we practising idiots may reasonably be content to perform the rituals and sell our religious medals to induce in our patients the emergence of Faith that 'their redeemer liveth'; that, in Melanie Klein's poetry, good internal objects exist: the acknowledgement of psychic reality.

But of course Bion is not himself content nor is he willing to encourage others to be content with being idiotic practitioners of psycho-analysis. He has discovered a way to creative work and is encouraging others to do the same, for them to practise what he thinks he has practised to achieve the 'beam of darkness' which can illuminate the non-sensuous world of psychic reality. He has found a formulation to express the tolerance of anxiety which is necessary to its accomplishment, found it in Keats's letter to his brothers in which he described the capacity to tolerate uncertainty, the 'negative capability' which he saw underlying the work of Shakespeare, whom he revered above all other writers.

But these exhortations to discipline do not really capture the essence of what Bion is describing, for he has already made it clear that to attain these ends it is necessary to withstand the 'frightful fiend' in oneself. This fiend he is able now to investigate in a richer way than beta-element or column 2 was able to suggest, than minus L or minus K could describe. He is now able to describe in full mystic richness the function of the liar in oneself. The glorious parable on page 100 captures the social context of political lying and makes the necessary rapprochement between his own theories, designated as row F, G or H, and those of Melanie Klein, designated as row C, myth or dream-thought. 'By contrast the feeble processes by which the scientists again and again attempted to support their hypotheses

376

made it easy for the liars to show the hollowness of the pre-
tensions of the upstarts and thus to delay, if not to prevent, the
spread of doctrines whose effect could only have been to induce
a sense of helplessness and unimportance in the liars and their
beneficiaries'. This presentation of Melanie Klein's picture of
the inner world makes it clear that the concreteness of psychic
reality has the same texture as the concreteness of politics, that
life and death of the mind are as much in the balance in the one
as life and death of the culture 'and its beneficiaries' are in the
other. Thus 'value' is at last brought into focus and prominence
in Bion's work, but with the admission that, (p. 101) 'If value
is to be the criterion' (for action based on decision) 'difficulty
arises because there is no *absolute* value: the individual does not
necessarily believe it is better to create than to destroy; a
suicidal patient may seem to embrace the opposite view'. One
could add to that the pervert, the psychopath, the schizophrenic. They all behave as if they believed that it were better
to destroy than create. This is the frightful fiend, the liar, the
operator of H and minus K.

Still talking from the religious vertex and row C (Kleinian
formulation) the struggle for development involves the taking
of nourishing truth and avoiding poisonous lies; these nourishing truths are produced by good internal god-like objects while
the poisonous lies are excreted by foul-fiendish devils in the
self, or the two may become fused and con-fused to form the
'super'-ego. The decisions upon which the choice rests at any
moment focuses on the choice between the risk of catastrophic
change being induced by the messianic idea versus the preservation of a sense of power and importance by means of lies. This
formulation will require, in terms of the grid format for the
tabulation of thought processes, a negative grid, not merely
column 2. Every category of the 'elements' of thought can be
turned into a lie by the 'thinker'. Bion sees the manufacture of
lies as an employment of positive ingenuity, while the achievement of truth is more passive, requiring submission to the
operation of container and contained, the mechanism of Ps$\leftrightarrow$D
under the vertex of L, K and, if possible F, where the value is
placed on creating rather than destroying.

By thus distinguishing, from the religious vertex, between
Paradise and **Pandemonium** (after Milton) Bion has finally

made the necessary step of distinguishing between psychic reality and the world of lies, the delusional system. What has not yet been accomplished, but only hinted at or left unscathed by ineffectual sallies, is the source of the hatred of growth, other than the minus K of the 'frightful fiend', the minus L that is manifest in intolerance to pain and frustration. Bion has frequently hinted that this is related to what he calls 'catastrophic change' but is yet to illuminate. It is rather irritating to find that the only reference to it in the index says 'see Chapter 10' which does not in fact mention it. The brief mention of pre- and post-catastrophic states in 'Transformation' was little help. The paper given to the British Psa. Soc. in 1966 and published in their Bulletin is very little different from chapter 12. Since it is central to the whole question of affects and mental pain, and thus is the mainspring of Bion's elaborated model of the mind, it will be used as the basis for summary in the final chapter. What remains to be discussed in this one is a question: did the introduction of the differentiation between parasitic, symbiotic and commensal modes of relationship between container and contained add to or at least enrich the model? And did the eventual formulation of 'patience' and 'security' as dimensions of the analyst's experience add anything to the investigation of the psycho-analytical method?

The attempt in Chapter 12 to transform the model of container-contained into one so flexible that it can serve to describe politics, the analytic situation and the structure of the personality hinges on the differentiation of thought and action in practice. Action can be the stable and customary actions which form the matrix of the container, say in the actions of the establishment in politics, of the habitual and stable actions of the patient or analyst in analysis. This container of actions must be flexible enough not to crush yet strong enough not to be destroyed by the new or messianic thought. The dogmatic must contain the messianic; the method must make thought possible in both analysand and analyst. But, he points out, the actions unavoidable even in communication always favour the preservation of the sense of power against the necessary experience of helplessness, negative capability. The use of parasitic, symbiotic, commensal do not appear, being based on biological models devoid of meaningfulness, to add to Bion's capacity to investigate the state of tension and conflict between the container and the messianic idea. He is driven back to Melanie Klein's descriptions of paranoid-schizoid and depressive positions, giving them a new operational slant under the designations 'patience' and 'security'. But he can go no further than Keats's negative criteria for 'patience' that it should be in uncertainty 'without irritably reaching after fact and reason' while 'security' is the state enjoyed once the new pattern has 'evolved', (p. 124), 'I consider the experience of oscillation between "patience" and "security" to be an indication that valuable work is being achieved'. The loaded words are 'valuable' in Ruskin's sense of 'life-giving' and 'achieved' in Keats's sense of 'Man of Achievement'. He finally falls back on the frightful fiend, envy, (p. 128), 'If the envy were to assume an aspect of whole object it could be seen as envy of the personality capable of maturation and of the object stimulating maturation'. This is congruent with his view that attacks are essentially attacks on linking, a view in advance of Mrs Klein's formulation on envy. Envy, in Bion's view and in Bion's terms, would not be aroused either by container or contained but only by their successful (symbiotic) conjunction.

Chapter XIV   Review: Catastrophic Change and
the Mechanisms of Defence

In order to bring to an end this study of the development of
Bion's model of the mind, it is necessary to attempt to clarify
the concept which is probably most central and least mentioned
of all his ideas. Except for the paper titled 'Catastrophic Change'
which he read to the British Psycho-analytical Society in 1966,
and which incidentally, in its body never mentions the concept
of the title, this phrase appears nowhere in the books. And yet
all the books are about it, just as 'Attention and Interpretation'
is certainly about attention, although it is never mentioned in
the text. The paper 'Catastrophic Change' was a prelude to
'Attention' and is virtually identical to Chapter 12. In so far as
its focus is upon the relationship of container and contained, in
the individual and in his relationship to the group, the dread
of change and the tendency for change to manifest itself as
catastrophe is brought out more clearly than in the later book
chapter entitled 'Container and Contained Transformed'. Bion's
model of container and contained must be juxtaposed to his
idea that the truth does not require a thinker to exist, but rather
that the thinker needs to find the truth as an idea which he can
make grow in his mind. Among the ideas which exist in the
world awaiting thinkers are certain ones which, from the
religious-historical vertex, he chooses to call 'messianic' ideas.
The relationship of container to contained in the individual,
in so far as ideas institute a conflict between thought and the
impulse to action, is not so observable in the ordinary course of
events, but becomes dramatically manifest when an idea of
messianic significance enters. In order to describe these processes
of catastrophic change induced by the messianic idea Bion
employs the congruent relationship of the individual mystic to
his group. The group, as container, must find some means of
expanding to hold this new phenomenon in order, on the one
hand, not to crush or squeeze or denude the messianic idea, or
similarly to destroy the mystic or 'sink him without a trace,
loaded with honours'. But it also must avoid being fragmented
or exploded by the mystic or the messianic idea. These relations
of container to contained, whether of experiences in the indivi-

dual, the individual in a group, the meaning in a word, the significance in a symbol, or the passion in a relationship – in whatever dimension of container and contained, the relationship can be categorized as parasitic, symbiotic or commensal. His application of these biological ideas to the realm of the mind is this: (Scientific Bulletin of the Brit. Psa. Soc., No. 5, 1966, p. 21)

> '*Commensal* – the thought O and the thinker exist quite independently of each other. There is no reaction, or, as we should ordinarily say identifying ourselves with the thinker, the truth has not been discovered even though it "exists".
>
> *Symbiotic* – the thought and the thinker correspond and modify each other through the correspondence. The thought proliferates and the thinker develops.
>
> *Parasitic* – Thought and thinker correspond but the correspondence is category' (i.e. column) '2, meaning that the formulation is known to be false but is retained as a barrier against a truth which is feared as annihilating to the container or vice versa'.

A 'critical situation' is said to develop when the commensal approaches the symbiotic, as a 'discovery' threatens. The 'critical situation' calls up the image of atomic reactors.

This then is the prototype of anxiety in the Bionic model of the mind, and it can be seen that this catastrophic anxiety lurks behind all lesser anxieties. It is what would be 'signalled' by Freud's final conceptualization, 'signal anxiety'. It would underlie the mental pains of the paranoid-schizoid and depressive positions of Mrs Klein's model; it would correspond to Mrs Bick's 'dead end' and 'endless falling' and 'liquefaction'; to Bion's own formulation in 'Learning' of 'nameless dread'; or my own delineation of 'terror' of dead objects. It is perhaps the 'moment of truth' of the bullfight with its many levels of symbolic reference, good and evil, male and female, life and death, Christian and Pagan, human and animal. It is clear that Bion sees the 'absolute truth, O', as not containable, requiring some degree of falsification to be held within the individual mind. Only the mystic claims to hold or behold it, but even he cannot communicate (publish) it without some degree of falsification. It is the degree and the motive for falsification that makes the difference between the truth that can be contained and allowed to grow in the mind and the lie which destroys the truth and replaces it with 'morality'.

Having now described the crucial aspect of Bion's ideas as they lend themselves to employment in the psycho-analytical consulting room, it should be possible to review the history of the evolution of the model of the mind which underlies our practice, as it has progressed in the line of the 'Kleinian Development' from Freud through Klein to Bion. It is of course too big a task for this context but the method of approach and an outline of the general scheme should be possible. It is proposed, therefore, to review the salient features of the model of the mind implicit or explicit in the writings, particularly the clinical ones, of all three and to see what these different models imply with respect to the concept: mechanisms of defence; assuming that all the areas of psycho-pathology which reveal themselves through the transference in analysis are based upon defence against anxiety. It may not be true, and perhaps one of the advances implicit in Bion's work is an approach to other areas of pathology, but it can be said with certainty that psycho-analysts unanimously assume that they are studying 'defence neuro-psychoses', to use Freud's earliest term.

Freud's eventual model of the mind, as defined in papers such as 'The Ego and the Id', 'Beyond the Pleasure Principle', 'The Problem of Anxiety', and 'Splitting of the Ego in the Service of Defense' probably goes something like this: an undifferentiated mass of psychic energy, both creative and destructive, finds its manifestation in the mental representations of the Id, which the Ego, having evolved from the Id and having developed a capacity, consciousness, for the perception of psychic qualities, seeks to put into action in the world in order to reduce tension to a minimum. But to the complexities inherent in the conflict of Life and Death instincts there is added the task of serving or evading the demands of the real world and of an internal institution, the super-ego derived from childhood relation to parents and variously modified by later experiences with figures of dependence, authority and admiration. In this plight, 'serving three masters' the Ego resorts to various devices: interposing thought between impulse and action; actions to modify external reality: hallucinatory wish fulfilment and the mechanisms of defence. These latter serve to modify the signal anxiety engendered by conflict in the Ego aroused by the incompatible demands of its various 'masters'. The development of the Ego, its psycho-sexual development, consists of a series of stages, partly determined by the maturation of the physical organism and partly by increasing and varied demands of the environment, whereby the leading erogenous zone of contact, the nature of the object and the aim of relationship progress from primary narcissism to genitality.

Under this model psycho-analytic practice tends to confine itself to areas of disturbance beyond the narcissistic stages, where ambivalence to part– and whole-objects in the outside world are aggravated by harshness of the demands and threats emanating from the super-ego. Its method is to study the free associations, to relieve resistances by investigation of the transference, and to interpret dreams in order that a reconstruction of the development of the disturbance may be achieved and worked through with the patient, thus relieving the repressions, abating the perversions and enabling psycho-sexual development to proceed. Mechanisms of defence, which correspond in many ways to the 'dream work' that transforms the unacceptable latent content into a manifest content acceptable to the dream censor (?super-ego), are relinquished by the patient once they are made conscious, if by so-doing the economic interplay of pleasure and reality principles is facilitated rather than aggravated. The list of mechanisms of defence, headed by repression, projection, introjection, denial, negation, isolation of affects and splitting of the ego, is open to new members as they are described. But mechanisms are named for their manifestations; the actual mechanism, probably at base chemical or neuro-physiological, is not observable but can only be construed with uncertainty.

Freud's model of the mind is an explanatory model of a mechanical causal system aimed at explaining deviations in normal development and functioning as a basis for therapy. It is not a system of psychology for describing the life of the mind, although it rests upon observations of phenomena and not in any way upon neuro-physiological or neuro-anatomical facts.

Melanie Klein's explicit model of the mind is completely

Freudian, but the model implicit in her clinical descriptions is quite different. It is not an explanatory model of a causal system but a description of the geography of phantasy life in which a theatre for the generating of meaning is found to exist 'inside' the mind whereby the forms of the external world can be imbued with meaning and emotional significance. It is a model that emphasizes development which is seen to commence shortly after birth through the baby's experiences with the mother, or first with her breast. By means of splitting the self and object into good and bad, and by phantasies of introjection and projective identification, implemented by a sense of omnipotence, the baby constructs from its gratifying and frustrating experiences an internal world of objects and parts of the self in which its unconscious phantasies and dreams manipulate the meaning and emotional significance of its experiences. These then serve as its model for construing its experiences, and consequently regulating its behaviour, with objects in the outside world. Since it assumes that external objects also have an internal world as concrete as its experience of its own, its 'world', which at first is the body of its mother, is the object of its epistemophilic instinct in respect of both its exterior and interior qualities. The Life and Death instincts of the Id manifest themselves in the emotional impulses which arise from gratifying and frustrating events, namely love and hate, much complicated by envy in the two-body relation, later augmented by jealousy in the three-body or Oedipal situations. Bad objects, bad parts of the self and objects damaged by its omnipotent attacks in the internal and external world engender persecutory anxieties which it variously defends against by splitting processes, projective identification, denial of psychic reality and dependence upon good or idealized objects, all implemented in unconscious phantasy and action with varying degrees of omnipotence. When love and dependence upon good objects grows to a certain point, solicitude for its own safety and comfort tends to give way to concern for the welfare of its loved objects and a new system of values or economic principle: the depressive position, is ushered in. In so far as it can maintain a depressive orientation, development through the reintegration of splitting of self and objects takes place, omnipotence is gradually relinquished and schizoid mechanisms are abandoned in favour of trust and dependence upon internal objects and those figures in the outside world who carry the transference from these internal ones. Progress from part-object to whole-object relationships strengthens the internal situation and identification with internal objects enables the ego to grow in strength, while reintegration of its splitting amplifies the complexity of the mental functions it can manage. An adult part of the personality, developed through its introjective identifications, assumes more control of its relations to the outside world while its infantile relationships are more and more confined to internal objects, thus lessening the tendency to transference.

Under this model psycho-analytical therapy is mainly aimed at making possible a re-experiencing of the essence of the developmental process through the transference, its evolution being facilitated by interpretation. It is essentially a corrective developmental experience in which reintegration of split-off parts of self and objects is facilitated by achievement of the depressive position. But the goodness of this experience may even modify the virulence of the death instinct as it is represented in attitudes of envy and their interference with the development of gratitude and thus of love. As a model for use in scientific investigation it is quite powerful in the investigation of object relations and narcissistic organizations. The mechanisms of defence completely lose their mechanistic quality and neurophysiological foundation, become infinite in variety since they are unconscious phantasies implemented with omnipotence. For the sake of description they are gathered under the headings of schizoid mechanisms (splitting and projective identification), manic mechanisms (denial of psychic reality) and obsessional mechanisms (omnipotent control and separation of objects).

The world described by Melanie Klein's model of the mind is a world of emotional relationships, full of meaning, value and significance as categories of experience but has no direct means of describing man as a thinking creature in a world of other individual thinking creatures. It can describe intimate relationships but not the world of casual and contractual ones.

If Freud's world is one of creatures seeking surcease from the constant bombardment of stimuli from inside and out, a world of higher animals; and Melanie Klein's world in one of holy babes in holy families plagued by the devils of split-off death

385

instinct; Bion's world is one of the questing mind seeking the absolute truth with inadequate equipment. Like Freud he sees the mind in isolation, but struggling to free itself from the protomental level of basic assumption group-life, and yet needing the group for survival and perpetuation of its discoveries of the truth. Like Melanie Klein he sees the mind as developing in the context of the infant-mother relationship but for him it is a relationship whose essence is understanding rather than gratification, failure of such understanding rather than frustration. The growth of the mind is not, as in Freud, the natural realization of innate processes, all going well; nor, like Melanie Klein's is it a process of complicated unfolding given sufficient nurturing and protection; it is rather seen by Bion as the growth of the capacity for thinking about emotional experiences which enable the individual to learn by becoming a different person with different capabilities from the person of the past. The life of the individual is in the moment of his being himself having experiences and thinking about them, the past and the future being hindrances in so far as he is living in them rather than in the present. Nothing described by Freud or Melanie Klein is thus replaced by Bion's model, but would be relegated to row F (scientific deductive system about man as intelligent animal) and row C (the mind's mythology about itself and its origins) respectively. Neither would be seen as incorrect or irrelevant, but variously incomplete and inadequate for certain clinical (and philosophical) tasks.

Bion's model of the mind as a thinking and learning apparatus is concerned with understanding the emotional experiences that impinge upon it as it watches them in its head with its capacity for selective attention through its organ of consciousness for the perception of psychic qualities, like Plato's cave dwellers. It has an apparatus for converting these emotional experiences into thoughts that can be used for thinking, that is for manipulation with a view to increasing their level of abstraction and sophistication. This apparatus (alpha-function) it had introjected as a breast during infancy; a breast that was able to receive the baby's projective identifications of parts of itself in chaotic distress of bombardment by emotional experiences, accompanied by the fear that it was dying; and could furthermore divest these parts of their distress, order their chaos and return them to the baby in a state equivalent to having phantasies or dreams. This form of communication by projective identification continues to be available in later relationships but, in order to communicate anything other than a state of mind, more abstract means, employing sign and symbols are required, and in order to form them from the row C elements (unconscious phantasy) a similar system of containment and interaction of the container with its contents of thoughts is evolved through identification with this introjected breast. If this containment is possible: that is, if the mind can hold a new idea without compressing its meaning and without being disrupted by it; if it can bear the stirrings of catastrophic anxiety engendered, it can bring to bear a movement from a paranoid-schizoid value set to a depressive orientation to the new idea which, with the help of a selected fact to organize the new with older ideas, enables growth of the idea to take place. By this means, if truth is loved, it can grow and be digested and nourish the mind by learning from experience. But if the truth is hated or if the anxiety is evaded or if the apparatus is defective, lies, the poison of the mind, may eventuate instead. These lies are probably of three sorts: emotional experiences not changed into thoughts (beta elements), thoughts degraded by the apparatus for growth of thought (alpha-function) working in reverse, or possibly by an identical negative apparatus operated by a 'frightful fiend' part of the personality. By this last means experiences may be turned into lies that can be used for constructing a world of unreality, the delusional system and hallucinosis.

Operating with this model of the mind, the psycho-analyst would conceive of his task as one dedicated to sharing with the patient the emotional experience of the moment, seeking, as the mother with the baby, to receive in reverie the projective identifications, etc. But he would also aim to facilitate the growth of new ideas by offering his opinion at levels of abstraction and sophistication above the level of myth or dream thought. His capacity to function in this way would be limited by his ability to free himself from concern with the past and future of the relationship and his tolerance of the catastrophic anxiety he would need to share with the patient.

In the Bionic model mechanisms of defence are various forms of lies, embracing those described by Melanie Klein but also lies at a more sophisticated and abstract level. In addition various forms of failure of the apparatus could be studied which are not merely mechanisms of defence against anxiety but disorders of the capacity to think, of attacks upon the capacity for thought, and of attempts to live in a world of anti-thought. In so far as group life, with its roots in protomental phenomena at a level in which emotion and bodily experiences and events are indistinguishable, stands in conflict with the individual's capacity to learn from experience, Bion's model of the mind opens up to observation and study an area of conflict previously not noted or attended to but relegated to the category of acting out. Seen as a model superimposed upon those of Freud and Melanie Klein, Bion's model would seem to open a vast area of phenomena to the psycho-analyst which he has not previously had the conceptual tools to observe and consider. This vast area could reasonably be called the area of mindlessness in mental life, one of which: autism, my colleagues and I have begun to explore. Bion's concepts proved useful for deepening understanding of the element of mindlessness in obsessional phenomena, in fetishism and in two-dimensional areas of object relations. Mrs Bick, in parallel with Bion, can be seen to have been studying phenomena of failure of primary containment and its effects upon the personality when 'second skin' manoeuvres are employed to augment the defective containment.

Perhaps it would not be too optimistic to say that Bion's work has broadened the scope of psycho-analysis in the same exponential proportions that Mrs Klein's work can be seen in retrospect to have done. These elevations of Freud's work to the third power, so to speak, have enabled psycho-analysis to grow from a narrow therapy of the neuroses and perversions, marred by overweaning ambitions to explain everything, to a scientific method which may prove to be adequate to investigate and describe everything and explain nothing.

Appendix   A note on Bion's Concept
"Reversal of Alpha-function"*

DONALD MELTZER, M.D. (OXFORD)

When a new theory is proposed in psycho-analysis it can be said to undertake two functions: one is to organize the clinical phenomena that have already been observed in a more aesthetic (beautiful?) way; the other is to provide a tool of observation that will open to view previously invisible phenomena of the consulting room. Wilfred Bion, beginning with his papers on schizophrenia, sought to amplify the model of the mind which we employ in psycho-analysis so that processes of thinking and disturbances in this capacity could be investigated. The first systematic presentation of this effort, 'Learning from Experience' (Heinemann, London, 1962) formulated an 'empty' concept of alpha-function by means of which the 'sense impressions of emotional experiences' were converted into elements to be used in various ways: as building-blocks for dream thoughts; which in turn could be used for thinking; to be available for storage as memory; and by their continuity to form a 'contact barrier' that might separate conscious from unconscious mental processes.

The 'emptiness' of this model was stressed over and over by Bion, along with the caution against over-hasty attempts to fill it with clinical meaning. He himself has been almost single-handedly exploring its possible meaning in the series of books which followed, namely 'Elements of Psycho-analysis'†, 'Transformations'‡ and 'Attention and Interpretation'§. It is with a certain trepidation that this paper is offered as a tentative exploration of his fascinating idea that alpha-function can perhaps operate in reverse, cannibalizing the already formed alpha-elements to produce either the beta-screen or perhaps

* First published in the 'Festschrift for W. R. Bion', Ed. J. Grotstein, New York, J. Aronson, 1978.
† Heinemann, London, 1963.
‡ Heinemann, London, 1965.
§ Tavistock, London, 1968.

389

bizarre objects. It is probably best to quote rather than to paraphrase. He writes (p. 25, 'Learning from Experience'), in evaluating the analyst's and patient's separate contributions to the situation in which the beta-screen is being formed:

'The analysand contributes changes which are associated with the replacement of alpha-function by what may be described as a reversal of direction of the function'.

And here he adds a note:

'The reversal of direction is compatible with the treatment of thoughts by evacuation; that is to say, that if the personality lacks the apparatus that would enable it to "think" thoughts but is capable of attempting to rid the psyche of thoughts in much the same way as it rids itself of accretions of stimuli, then reversal of alpha-function may be the method employed'.

He continues,

'Instead of sense impressions being changed into alpha elements for use in dream thoughts and unconscious waking thinking, the development of the contact-barrier is replaced by its destruction. This is effected by the reversal of alpha-function so that the contact barrier and the dream thoughts and unconscious waking thinking, which are the texture of the contact-barrier, are turned into alpha-elements, divested of all characteristics that separate them from beta-elements and are then projected, thus forming the beta-screen'.

Further,

'Reversal of alpha-function means the dispersal of the contact-barrier and is quite compatible with the establishment of objects with the characteristics I once ascribed to bizarre objects'.

He further points out that there is an important difference in his conception of the beta-element and the bizarre object; the latter is 'beta-element plus ego and superego traces'.

Before we can embark upon the clinical material through which meaning may be poured into the 'empty' vessel of thought, it is necessary to remind the reader of an historical item. Bion has amplified Melanie Klein's concept of sadistic and omnipotent attacks upon internal objects and the structure of the self to include also attacks on individual functions of the ego and upon 'linking' in general as the basic operation in thought, its prototype being the link between infant and breast. To test the usefulness of Bion's formulations it is necessary to demonstrate that they make possible an integration of observations not possible by previous formulations. The particular question that will arise in connection with the material to follow is this: does the formulation of alpha-function and its possible reversal extend the range of psycho-analytic observation and thought beyond that made possible by Mrs Klein's formulations regarding sadistic attacks, splitting processes and projective identification with internal objects?

Clinical Material – a 35-year old man.

The session begins perhaps two minutes late: no comment. He has had a horrible dream, which it takes him some considerable time to tell against strong resistance, in the form of a 'what's the use' attitude. The background of the dream collects before the dream is actually presented, including some material of previous sessions which had dealt with his feelings of ingratitude to his mother's friends whom the two of them had visited in Germany in the summer. He had never sent a thank-you note but yesterday had received an invitation for Christmas. He hates ingratitude in himself or others and yesterday's material had centred on a fellow of the college (his initials D.M.) whose furniture the patient had helped to move; D.M. has never thanked the patient nor invited him to dinner. Today's material then veers off into a description of his sensitivity to his surroundings and how he will lose his room in college next year and have to find one in another which he hates. It is connected with the Institute in the U.S.A. where he spent two miserable years and he also feels at loggerheads with X who tried to bully him into accepting the 'great honour' of being a fellow at his college.

In the dream there is a huge L-shaped room like one at the American institute but also, by virtue of the grey lino, like his present room, as it was before he had bullied and cajoled the authorities into carpeting and decorating. He had also exchanged all the horrible furniture for a rather nice settee and

391

chairs. Yes, he realizes that this excessive dependence on external comfort implies a defect in his internal sense of security. In the dream *someone was talking about an old woman who had been dreadfully deformed by an accident. Then she seemed to be there on the floor, alive but so deformed she was hardly recognizable as a human. One extraordinary and somehow particularly horrible feature was that originally she had had extremely long fingernails, extending not only outward but also up her fingers, and under the skin of the arm. These seemed to have been struck and driven up her arm so that their ends stuck out near her elbows. The point seemed to be that she was suing for compensation but this was refused on the ground that she was so completely deformed that one could get no idea at all of what had been her original state. This applied particularly to the fingernails, for, although they did not protrude from her fingers but only from her elbows, the intervening nails did not show through the skin. The impression of horror did not seem to be accompanied by any emotion other than aversion.*

I suggest to him that the background of the dream indicates that the problem is one of guilt and reparation, neither of which can be set in motion unless the mutilated object can be recognized and connected with its former undamaged and perhaps young and beautiful state, i.e. his mother as a young woman in his childhood as compared with the old woman, equated with her friends in Germany, who kept being generous to him despite his ingratitude, thus becoming old and empty. In order to get rid of this tormenting sense of guilt it is necessary to so attack the old mother that her disfigurement defies connection with the original object, thus becoming 'some old woman' rather than 'mummy'. But is there not a mathematical technique that he mentioned yesterday, called 'transpositional equations', connected with analytical geometry, whereby, if the distortion of the grid of reference can be demonstrated, two objects which seem grossly different can be shown to be basically identical but projected on to different grid systems like distortions in a picture on a piece of rubber? He agrees; his work deals with the mathematics which makes such crude analogies unnecessary. (I am thinking of the pictures of fish and skulls in D'Arcy Thompson's 'Growth of Form' and he confirms this reference). The long fingernails therefore represent the lines of the grid and if they can be made visible and the grid rectified to its basic axes, the image of the beautiful young mother can be rediscovered in the dehumanized old woman. The motto of the defence would be, 'If you damage mummy and the sight of it causes you guilt and remorse, smash her beyond all recognition until you feel only horror and revulsion'.

Discussion

We were approaching the first holiday break of this man's analysis, which had been arranged at an interview just prior to the previous summer holiday when he was expecting his mother to come all the way from Australia to visit him and take him to see some aristocratic friends of hers in Germany. The patient had not seen his mother for some years and was disturbed, not only at finding her looking much older than his image of her, but also at finding his prior devotion much cooled. He is the eldest of her children and the only 'successful' one, having been rather arrogantly independent since early childhood.

From the Kleinian point of view it is a rather ordinary dream that illustrates the thesis that retreat from depressive anxiety referrable to damaged internal objects follows a route whereby the depressive pain is felt as persecutory depression and opens the way to further attacks on the damaged object as a persecutor. The parallel material of his associations suggests that the room in college which he had made cosy by 'bullying and cajoling' the authorities to carpet, hiding the old lino which reminded him of the 'two miserable years' in the United States, was to be taken away: that is, that the analysis was threatening to return him to a state of misery (the analyst being from the U.S.) as revenge for his not feeling 'honoured' at being accepted for analysis (as with X's invitation). The analyst, like the fellow with the same initials (D.M.), is to contain the split-off attribute of ingratitude.

But what could a Kleinian formulation make of these finger-nails which, instead of growing out, had been driven in the reverse direction until they stuck out at the old woman's elbow? What could it make of the refusal of compensation on the grounds that the old woman was so horribly deformed that no idea could be established of her previous state? Perhaps we can assume that the imponderable nature of the deformed old woman is exactly the quality that makes her a bizarre object in Bion's sense rather than a mutilated object in Mrs Klein's. In the courtroom of the dream no one seemed to doubt that she had been a human, that there had been an accident, that her fingernails had been driven up her arm. But somehow the *frame of reference of thought* had been destroyed, a frame having a particular connection with the patient's overriding professional preoccupations. One might say that his work has to do with getting to the truth about problems of analytical geometry through formulae which would be far more precise than the 'crude analogies' of grid-distortion.

Not only could Kleinian formulations before Bion have made no headway with such a problem; they would not have been able even to state the problem itself: namely the attack on thinking. They could approach only the attack on feeling, where, of course, they go quite some distance. In contrast a Freudian formulation would probably focus attention on the castration anxiety, which is most certainly an element in the dream (are the woman's nipples the remnants of her penis, smashed up and driven inward and upward until they stick out of the breasts?).

Bionic Recapitulation

The patient is facing the first holiday break of his analysis and feels that his jealousy of the other analytical children is going to drive him to attack his internal analytical mother with a view to lessening the devotion and its consequent separation pain. But the return to analysis would hold him to a state of mind of misery about these attacks, hating himself for ingratitude, perhaps even reducing him to having to beg, rather than bully, the daddy-authorities to redecorate the mummy and make her cosy once more. That would be unbearably humiliating to such an independent baby. Although he has spent years developing a mode of thought for seeing the truth with precision in such situations, he is prepared to destroy that mental capacity (alpha-function of a particular sort) by making it run in reverse (instead of growing outward to form the lines of a grid of reference, the fingernails are driven backwards to disappear under the skin, appearing only at the elbows). The consequence is a beta-element 'plus ego and superego traces' (the distorted old woman, having only traces of the mother and of his discarded ego-capacity for thinking with transpositional equations). She is now a bizarre object, uncontainable in thought, suitable only for evacuation.

Implications

Let us take the 'crude analogy' of a geometric grid on a piece of rubber as a model of a piece of mental equipment, a particular bit of alpha-function apparatus. Place on it a picture of an old woman and pull the ribber in various ways until the picture of a beautiful young woman appears. Take this as a model of alpha-function operating on 'the sense impressions of an emotional experience'. Such a bit of apparatus may be essential for the creation of an image that makes it possible to connect the old woman who visits the patient from Australia with the young beautiful mother who insisted on having other children against his sage advice.

Postscript

The analysis progressed very well through the next term bringing forward memory after memory of the catastrophic reactions to the births of his next siblings, reactions which progressively relegated his father to a position of negligible importance in his life and consolidated his status as mother's little husband and advisor. As the second holiday break approached he became rather restive, left early to go to Australia to visit his family on the grounds that his next sibling (who had the same Christian name as the analyst) needed his help and advice. While there he did a group-therapy 'experience' during which he developed a manic state, thought he was the Messiah, and returned late to break off the analysis, full of 'gratitude' that the analysis had laid the background for his total cure in the group. He was, however, willing to see the analyst once a week to help him, that is, the analyst, understand how this transformation had come about. Over the next two months he gradually slipped into a state of depression after breaking off completely in a rage at the analyst's 'stupidity'. He finally returned to analysis in time to make a more satisfactory preparation for the long summer break. It was of interest that he could not bring himself to pay his fees until the last day, by which time the four months of work came to almost the precise amount he had paid for the five-day group 'therapy'.

Dr Bion wrote me a kind and interesting note when I sent him the paper:

> 'aesthetic (beautiful) way' – Now I would use as a model: the diamond cutter's method of cutting a stone so that a ray of light entering the stone is reflected back *by the same path* in such a way that the light is augmented – the same 'free association' is reflected back by the same path, but with augmented 'brilliance'. So the patient is able to see his 'reflection', only more clearly than he can see his personality as expressed by himself alone (i.e. without an analyst).

INDEX

Psychoanalysis of Children, 175, 188, 204
knowing (K), 313, 316, 318, 322, 326, 334, 357, 359, 360, 377
    K link, *see* link(s)
    minus K link, 349
    transformation in K, 358, 369
    Un-knowing (minus K), 318, 321, 331, 353, 357, 360, 376, 377, 378
    see also love: L H K
knowledge:
    child's thirst for, 52, 68
    Freud's theory of, 68
    love subsumed under, 65
    pursuit of, Freud's, 26
    thirst for, 160, 303, 312
        Bion's work on, 161
        and curiosity, 64, 66 (*see also* curiosity)
        motives underlying, 161
        and psychic reality, 209
        as sublimation, 160–161
Kraepelin, E., 7
Krafft-Ebbing, R., 9

language:
    Bion's feeling for, 286
    Bion's usage of, 274, 288
    difficulties in use of, 364
    as instrument or deterrent, 275
    patient's uses of, 291, 299
    use of, 57, 58
    latency period, establishment of, 171, 176
    technique in analysis of, 147
latency, 129, 137
    and impairment of curiosity, 66
law of talion, 181
learning, 322–323
    'about', 358
    from experience, 311, 316, 318, 322–323, 357, 387, 388
    as function of relationship to breast, 303
    and object relations, 313
    problem of, 303

a skill, 311
un-learning, 322
Leonardo da Vinci, 62–72, 104, 105
    death of father, 70
    Freud on, 160
    and homosexuality, 65, 70, 113
    and identification with mother, 70, 71, 84, 120
    and Michaelangelo, 65
    obsessionality of, 70
    repression of affects, 69–70
    his theory of love, 69
    and young boys, 84
    see also Freud: *Works*
liar, 376–377
libido:
    damming-up of, 52, 84, 87
    detachment of, 77
    development of, 43, 83
    developmental phases of, 153
    distribution of, 77
    homosexual, 75
    manipulation of, 106
    narcissistic, 204
    object-, 84, 92
    regression of, 44, 75
    stages of organization, 125
    stickiness of, 108, 137
    theory, 40, 76, 78, 84, 91, 106, 108, 112, 113, 114, 122, 141, 145, 167, 175, 204
    withdrawal of, 124
lie (untruth), 318, 319, 321, 331, 363, 377, 382, 387
    manufacture of, 377
    organization for creating, 362
    three sorts of, 387
Liebault, 15
life:
    before conception, child's interest in, 50
    hatred of, 304, 308
    instinct, 167
    unified/as entity/continuity of, 82, 95, 104
linguistic philosophy, 109
linguistics, 291